Polly Pinder's
Party Cakes

Polly Pinder's
Party Cakes

SEARCH PRESS

First published in Great Britain 1993

Search Press Limited
Wellwood, North Farm Road,
Tunbridge Wells, Kent TN2 3DR

Based on the following books published by Search Press;
copyright © respectively 1984 and 1985 Search Press Ltd.

Decorating Cakes for Children's Parties by Polly Pinder
Decorating Cakes for Special Occasions by Polly Pinder

ISBN 0 85532 769 3 (pb)

Printed in Spain by A.G. Elkar, S. Coop. 48012 Bilbao

Contents

Introduction

Ever since I began work on my first cake book, designing cakes has become a marvellous obsession. Luckily the possibilities seem limitless, as do effective and amusing subjects; for I hope to also bring a touch of humour to the cake-decorating scene in general.

My previous experience of cake decorating was nil; and I still, whenever I gaze in wonder at the intricate designs of the traditionally iced cake, consider myself a novice. I have learned a great deal, however, and now my knowledge has been extended still further – not least by the delight of discovering that I can actually pipe a 'real' flower (page 121) and create a piece of lattice work (page 126). I hope that this will encourage those who consider cake decorating to be beyond their present skill – all that is required for success is planning, time, and patience.

Patience is certainly needed when one is trying to make pieces of cake fit properly into the design and on to each other, or when, for instance, balancing the arch above the door of the house-warming cake. In addition, I hope that some of the techniques I have adopted will work as a springboard for the readers who are trying out new ideas.

It has been pointed out that I give no directions for 'cutting' the cakes. I realize, of course, that this is a particularly important part of most celebratory parties, but I can only suggest that a cake be dismantled, as far as possible, and then cut in the way which seems most obvious to the cutter; I feel one should not be too precise about it – some of the designs are so complex (compared to the conventional square or round decorated cakes) that it is too much to expect to end up with a perfectly neat little square for each person. My feeling is that the time and patience involved in completing the cake are fully rewarded by the reaction of onlookers – the moment of presentation and the shouts of acclamation and recognition that ring out (it really does happen, particularly if a little alcohol has previously been consumed!). That will fill the decorator with enough pride to last at least until the next cake! The fact that one can eat the cake, in whatever shape, is a bonus.

General Notes

The cakes

If you make these cakes from the traditional fruit mixture, they can be made weeks, or even months, in advance. Although many people prefer to use their own favourite recipe for this type of cake, I have drawn up a chart on page 10 with ingredients and quantities for the particular size and shape required. As children generally prefer sponge cake to fruit cake, I have given the sponge-cake recipe in the instructions for each of the children's cakes, but you can also make any of the adults' cakes from sponge cake if you prefer: there is a separate chart on page 10 giving similar details.

As well as the normal cake tins, food cans are also used to give more variety to the shapes of the cakes. These should be washed, left to dry in a cool oven, and then well greased. To make releasing the cakes easier, I cut out the bases and replace them with baking foil, then stand the cakes on a baking sheet. They should be just over half

filled with mixture and set on a lower shelf than the larger cakes. When the cakes are baked, leave them until they are cold, remove the foil, run a sharp knife around the cakes, and carefully push them out.

Method for baking rich fruit cake

Line the cake tin with a double thickness of greased (melted lard or oil) greaseproof paper and tie a double thickness of brown paper round the outside.

Pre-heat the oven to 300°F (150°C), Gas Mark 2.

Most of the dried fruit bought now is pre-washed, but it may be as well to sort through for any pieces of stalk or grit.

Quarter the cherries and, if necessary, chop the mixed peel. Wash them both in warm water and dry thoroughly.

Put the currants, raisins, sultanas, cherries, mixed peel, grated lemon rind, and almonds in a basin. Mix thoroughly. Sieve the flour, cinnamon, and spice into another basin. Mix thoroughly. Cream the butter in another basin, then add the sugar. Cream until light and fluffy. Beat in the black treacle. Add the eggs, one at a time. Beat well and add a tablespoon (tbsp) of flour mixture after each egg. Carefully fold in the remaining flour, then fold in the fruit. Stir in most of the brandy (keep 1–2 tablespoons to be added after baking).

Transfer the mixture to the tin. Using a wet spoon, spread it evenly, making a slight hollow in the centre.

Place the tin on folded newspaper in the centre of the oven. For the larger cakes, reduce heat to 275°F (140°C), Gas Mark 1, after two-thirds of the baking time.

To test whether baking is complete, insert a skewer into the centre of the cake: it should come out clean.

When the cake is completely cold, wrap it in greaseproof paper and place it in an airtight tin – if the cake is too large for a tin, wrap it securely in tin foil.

After one week remove the cake from its wrapping, pierce the top, at intervals, with a skewer, and carefully pour in the remaining brandy. Rewrap and keep for four to five more weeks. I would not recommend freezing the cakes.

Sponge-cake mixture

This can be used as an alternative to the rich fruit mixture. A chart with ingredients and quantities for the size and shape of the cake required is given on page 10.

This is the method for baking: beat the butter and sugar until pale and fluffy (substitute margarine for butter if desired). Gradually add alternate equal quantities of flour, ground rice, and beaten egg and milk. The mixture should have a soft dropping consistency; a little more milk may be needed. The cakes are baked in the centre of the oven at 350°F (180°C), Gas Mark 4, and are ready when a firm light-golden crust has formed and the cake has come slightly away from the sides of the tin. Allow to cool in the tin before removing, then leave overnight on a wire tray.

The plain sponge mixture can be varied in several ways: by adding glacé cherries, chopped walnuts, raisins, chopped bananas or honey (as a rough guide, if the recipe requires 220g (8oz) of butter, add the same quantity of fruit or nuts); by replacing one tablespoon of flour and one of ground rice by two tablespoons of cocoa powder; or by adding essences – orange, lemon, raspberry, etc. The larger cakes can be split and filled with butter-cream and/or jam. (If a cake has to be cut into different shapes, it is better to add a flavouring rather than fruit or nuts). You should eat a sponge cake within a week or it will become dry and start to shrink.

Marzipan

To make 450g (1lb) of marzipan, mix in a basin 110g (4oz) of caster sugar, 110g (4oz) of icing sugar, and 220g (8oz) of ground almonds. Make a well in the centre and add 1 teaspoon (tsp) of lemon juice, ½ teaspoon of orange-flower water, and a few drops of almond essence (a teaspoon of rum can be added if the cake is to be kept for months rather than weeks). Mix thoroughly, then add sufficient beaten egg to make a manageable paste. Turn on to a dusted (50/50 mixture of icing sugar and cornflour) surface and knead gently until smooth. Wrap securely in cling film until required.

When you are ready to decorate it, the cake should be brushed with warm sieved apricot jam, then covered with the marzipan. The cake must then be left to dry for 48 hours.

Apricot jam

This is used to coat the cakes before applying marzipan (apricot has the least intrusive flavour). It should be gently heated with a little water and then sieved to remove skin and hard pieces, just prior to brushing a thin film on to the cakes.

Icing

Fondant

This is an icing which has liquid glucose added to make it pliable and easy to model. To make 450g (1lb) drop the white of an egg into a basin and slowly mix in 450g (1lb) of sieved icing sugar and two tablespoons of warmed liquid glucose. The quantities of icing sugar and egg white are not absolutely critical; more or less of one or the other may be needed to achieve the correct consistency, which should be easy and firm to work with – if it feels floppy, add some more sieved icing sugar; if it becomes stiff and difficult to handle, add a little more egg white. Some recipes require a quarter of an egg white. As this is difficult to measure, make a rough guess, being generous rather than careful.

Egg white is also needed to secure pieces of fondant to vertical parts of the cake. This should be applied sparingly with a pastry brush or small paintbrush – if too much is used, the fondant will slip off or begin to weep at the seams.

Fondant which is not needed immediately should be wrapped in cling film and kept in an airtight container at room temperature, not in the refrigerator.

Ready-made commercial fondant can be bought in 220g (8oz) blocks from cake-decorating specialists and some supermarkets. It is very convenient if you are short of time.

Flavour and colour are added to the fondant at the kneading stage, when all the icing sugar and glucose have been mixed in. If pale fondant is required, add the colour, drop by drop, from a metal skewer. When a large piece of fondant needs to have a very deep colour, make a well in the centre, carefully pour in the colour, then give a liberal shake with the dredger (containing 50 per cent icing sugar and 50 per cent cornflour) and knead thoroughly.

Gum tragacanth (powdered gum) is sometimes used as a hardening agent. Use 1–2 teaspoonsful per 220g (8oz) of icing sugar. It is very useful if the fondant is to remain flat, but problems start when you mould and shape round cakes, for it dries rapidly and fine cracks can appear on the surface. The secret is to work quickly. The gum can be bought from most chemists. It is rather expensive but is worth having if you intend to do more than one fondant cake.

Royal icing and piped writing

To make 220g (8oz) of royal icing, drop one egg white into a very clean basin (with no trace of grease) and slowly mix in 220g (8oz) of sieved icing sugar. This can be done by hand or in the mixer, using a beater rather than a whisk, on the slowest speed.

Again, the quantities are not critical: you may need more or less of one or the other to obtain the correct consistency. Some recipes need only one-eighth of an egg white. As with the fondant, make a rough guess, erring on the side of generosity. The correct consistency can really only be judged after a little practice with the icing bag – it should be neither too runny to lose its shape nor too stiff to flow easily from the bag.

As with the fondant, add colour, drop by drop, from a metal skewer. To obtain a shaded effect on piped work, drop a generous teaspoonful each of two coloured icings, side by side, into the bag.

If you have not done piped writing before, it may be as well to practise on the table-top first.

To pipe directly on to the iced cake, first write the word on greaseproof paper, then attach the paper, with two dabs of royal icing, to the cake. Stick a sewing needle, at intervals, through the pencil lines. Remove the paper. Use the needle marks as guides and the original drawn letters as a reference.

To centre a word on the cake, using a tape measure or ruler, find the centre of the cake and mark with a pin. Find the centre of the word by measuring, mark with a pencil, then lay the pencil mark over the pin mark.

Royal icing can be stored in an airtight container and kept in the refrigerator for as long as three weeks, after which it will have to be gently beaten again before being used.

Icing bags and nozzles

I prefer to make my own disposable bags. They are more convenient and easier to use than the commercial tubes and bags, which one has to be continually washing when using different coloured icings.

Buy a packet of flat sheets of greaseproof paper (rather than a roll). Cut a strip off the sheet to make a square. See the illustration: fold the square into a triangle; fold point **A** to point **C**; then point **B** to point **D**; then point **C** to point **E**. Snip a small piece from point **X**. Open the bag and drop the nozzle in, making sure that half of it comes out at the bottom. Drop in a couple of teaspoons of royal icing, fold the flap over, fold the two corners **Y** and **Z** inwards, then pipe away! As the icing is used, fold the top of the bag over again.

Ateco icing nozzles have been used for most of the pipe work on the cakes in this book, but if they are not available in your area you can use the equivalent in another make – where possible I have drawn the nozzles and the shape produced by each.

You can buy a small nozzle brush – which is extremely useful when washing the nozzles – from cake-decorating specialists or kitchen equipment shops.

Spacers

Spacers are used to ensure an even piece of flat fondant or marzipan. They are placed at each side so that the rolling pin rolls over them and the fondant or marzipan at the same time.

Spacers can be bought from cake-decorating specialists, but it is cheaper to buy a packet of flat lolly sticks (LS) and make your own. These are usually about 2mm (¹⁄₁₀in) thick. Make four spacers (use adhesive tape to join the lolly sticks together) 4 LS long, the first pair 1 LS thick and the second pair 2 LS thick – see the drawing. Sometimes a piece of fondant needs to be 3 or 4 LS thick. As these pieces are usually quite small, the spacers do not have to be long – simply tape the required number together. Again, see the illustration.

Colouring

The basic colours can be bought from most supermarkets. For unusual shades you will probably have to go to a cake-decorating specialist. The only *edible* gold and silver I have found comes in powdered form.

Steel rule

This can be bought from cake-decorating specialists and some kitchen equipment shops. It is used to ensure a perfectly flat surface when covering a cake with royal icing – I use it as a straight-edge for cutting fondant and marzipan.

Hints

A flexible tape measure, rather than a ruler, is handy for measuring the cake, marzipan, and fondant pieces.

When measuring a cake which has to be cut into a complex shape, use coloured-headed pins as markers, just pushing them half into the cake.

A turntable is extremely useful when decorating the cakes. I find the home-made version (placing the cake board on a plate and then on top of an inverted plate) not really adequate – but it could suffice.

Making an icing bag

Rich fruit cake

	130mm (5in) square cake and 150mm (6in) round cake	150mm (6in) square cake and 180mm (7in) round cake	180mm (7in) square cake and 200mm (8in) round cake	200mm (8in) square cake and 230m (9in) round cake	230mm (9in) square cake and 250mm (10in) round cake	250mm (10in) square cake and 280mm (11in) round cake	280mm (11in) square cake and 300mm (12in) round cake	300mm (12in) square cake and 330mm (13in) round cake
Currants	110g (4oz)	170g (6oz)	280g (10oz)	360g (13oz)	500g (18oz)	670g (24oz)	900g (32oz)	1.4kg (48oz)
Raisins	80g (3oz)	140g (5oz)	200g (7oz)	280g (10oz)	360g (13oz)	530g (19oz)	620g (22oz)	1.1kg (36oz)
Sultanas	60g (2oz)	80g (3oz)	110g (4oz)	200g (7oz)	200g (7oz)	360g (13oz)	390g (14oz)	500g (18oz)
Chopped mixed peel	30g (1oz)	60g (2oz)	60g (2oz)	80g (3oz)	110g (4oz)	140g (5oz)	200g (7oz)	250g (9oz)
Glacé cherries	40g (1½oz)	70g (2½oz)	80g (3oz)	110g (4oz)	140g (5oz)	220g (8oz)	280g (10oz)	350g (12oz)
Chopped blanched almonds	30g (1oz)	60g (2oz)	60g (2oz)	80g (3oz)	110g (4oz)	140g (5oz)	200g (7oz)	250g (9oz)
Grated rind	½ lemon	½ lemon	¾ lemon	1 lemon	1 lemon	1 lemon	1½ lemons	2 lemons
Plain flour	100g (3½oz)	170g (6oz)	210g (7½oz)	340g (12oz)	390g (14oz)	590g (21oz)	670g (24oz)	825g (29oz)
Ground cinnamon	½ tsp	½ tsp	¾ tsp	1 tsp	1½ tsp	2 tsp	2½ tsp	2¾ tsp
Ground mixed spice	¼ tsp	¼ tsp	½ tsp	¾ tsp	1 tsp	1¼ tsp	1½ tsp	1¾ tsp
Butter	80g (3oz)	140g (5oz)	170g (6oz)	280g (10oz)	340g (12oz)	500g (18oz)	590g (21oz)	800g (28oz)
Soft brown sugar	80g (3oz)	140g (5oz)	170g (6oz)	280g (10oz)	340g (12oz)	500g (18oz)	590g (21oz)	800g (28oz)
Medium eggs	1½	2½	3	5	6	9	11	14
Black treacle	1 tsp	1 tsp	1 tbsp	1 tbsp	1 tbsp	2 tbsp	2 tbsp	2 tbsp
Approximate cooking time	2 hours	2½ hours	2¾ hours	3¼ hours	3¾ hours	4¼ hours	5¼ hours	6-6½ hours
Brandy	3 tbsp	4 tbsp	5 tbsp	5 tbsp	6 tbsp	7 tbsp	7 tbsp	9 tbsp

Sponge cake

Butter	110g (4oz)	170g (6oz)	220g (8oz)	280g (10oz)	340g (12oz)	390g (14oz)	450g (16oz)	500g (18oz)
Caster sugar	110g (4oz)	170g (6oz)	220g (8oz)	280g (10oz)	340g (12oz)	390g (14oz)	450g (16oz)	500g (18oz)
Medium eggs	2	3	4	5	6	7	8	9
Self-raising flour	110g (4oz)	170g (6oz)	220g (8oz)	280g (10oz)	340g (12oz)	390g (14oz)	450g (16oz)	500g (18oz)
Ground rice	60g (2oz)	80g (3oz)	110g (4oz)	140g (5oz)	170g (6oz)	200g (7oz)	220g (8oz)	250g (9oz)
Grated lemon rind (optional)	½ lemon	1 lemon	1½ lemon	2 lemons	2½ lemons	3 lemons	3½ lemons	4 lemons
Lemon juice or milk	2 tsp	1 tbsp	4 tsp	2 tbsp	6 tsp	3 tbsp	8 tsp	4 tbsp
Approximate cooking time	1 hour	1¼ hours	1 hour 20 mins	1 hour 20 mins	1 hour 30 mins	1 hour 30 mins	1 hour 40 mins	1 hour 40 mins

N.B. Cooking time is approximate. The cake is ready when a firm light-golden crust has formed and the cake has come slightly away from the sides of the tin.

Children's Party Cakes

Drum

The cake itself can be decorated in a day, but the drumsticks must be left to harden for at least 24 hours. As the sponge does not need to be trimmed to a particular shape, dried fruit or nuts can be added to the mixture. Alternatively, each of the two cakes can be split in half and filled with jam and/or butter-cream.

Please read the General Notes on pages 6 to 9 before decorating the cake. Also read through the step-by-step instructions and check the ingredient and equipment lists.

Ingredients for cake

220g (8oz) butter
170g (6oz) caster sugar
280g (10oz) self-raising flour
170g (6oz) ground rice
140ml (5fl oz) milk beaten with 3 large eggs
Make from this recipe: 2 x 150mm (6in) round cakes

Ingredients for fondant and royal icing

790g (1¾lb) icing sugar, plus 110g (4oz)
1¾ egg whites, plus ½
just under 4 tbsp liquid glucose
flavouring (optional)
Also: warm sieved apricot jam; 50/50 mixture of cornflour and icing sugar in a dusting dredger; red, green, yellow, and brown food colouring.

Equipment

Mixing bowls; sieve; spoons; rolling pin; steel rule; sharp-pointed knife; lolly sticks (LS) as spacers; pastry brush; greaseproof paper for icing bags; *Ateco* (or equivalent) icing nozzles 1, 2, and 3; 230mm (9in) round silver cake board.

1. Having left the cakes overnight, slice the tops flat and sandwich the cakes together with jam and/or butter-cream. Brush with jam. Make the 790g (1¾lb) of fondant. Roll a piece for the top to 2 LS thick (cut round the cake tin). Carefully apply fondant.

2. Measure circumference and depth of cake. Roll fondant to 2 LS thick and cut a piece to fit. Lay cake on fondant and roll along. Carefully transfer cake to centre of silver board. Measure circumference again. (Keep back 110g (4oz) of the fondant.)

3. Cut remainder in two. Colour half red, half green. Roll to 1 LS thick; cut eight strips in each colour 65mm (2½in) long, 30mm (1¼in) deep. (Work four in each colour for base of drum first, then roll out and repeat for top of drum.) Brush backs with egg white and carefully apply.

4. Roll two drumsticks, one red, one green, 150mm (6in) long. Shape as shown. Leave to dry on a dusted surface for 24 hours. Take remaining white fondant, colour it orange (mix red and yellow) and roll to 4 LS thick. Cut a strip 10mm (³/₈in) wide to go around top of drum. Brush egg white around drum edge; attach strip.

5. Add brown to orange trimmings. Roll to 1 LS thick. Cut sixteen strips 10mm (³/₈in) wide – cut eight pieces 30mm (1¼in) long and eight pieces 50mm (2in) long. Brush backs with egg white and position over joins of red and green fondant with the shorter strips at bottom, longer strips at top.

6. Make the 110g (4oz) of royal icing. With *No. 3 nozzle* and yellow icing, pipe a line of continuous dots to and from the brown strips as shown. Go around the cake, then start again with a second line next to the first. Pipe a large dot at the top of each strip, as shown.

7. With *No. 2 nozzle* and orange icing, pipe a line of continuous dots inside orange strip on top of drum; three lines on red and green panels, as shown; and a line on base of bottom panels. Pipe a line across each brown strip and a circle on panels, as shown.

8. With *No. 1 nozzle* pipe a tassel on each large yellow dot. Pipe top part first, then the strands – each ending with a dot – then the tie, as shown.

Xylophone

This cake can also be decorated in a day, but as with the previous one, the hammer and bars should be left to dry for at least 24 hours. The cake can have added fruit or nuts, or can be sliced lengthways and filled with jam and/or butter-cream.

There should really be eight bars on the xylophone (an observant child will no doubt point this out). Unfortunately the loaf cake is not long enough to accommodate eight and thinner ones would, I think, look rather mean. If comments are made, perhaps you can formulate an imaginative retort!

Please read the General Notes on pages 6 to 9 before starting to decorate the cake. It is a good idea also to read through the step-by-step instructions and check the ingredient and equipment list.

Ingredients for cake

170g (6oz) butter
110g (4oz) caster sugar
220g (8oz) self-raising flour
110g (4oz) ground rice

110ml (4fl oz) milk beaten with 2 large eggs
Make from this recipe: 1 x 900g (2lb) loaf cake

Ingredients for fondant and royal icing

450g (1lb) icing sugar, plus 110g (4oz)
1 egg white, plus ½
2 tbsp liquid glucose
Also: warm sieved apricot jam; 50/50 mixture of corn-flour and icing sugar in a dusting dredger; red, blue, yellow, mauve, and brown food colouring; twelve edible silver balls.

Equipment

Mixing bowls; sieve; spoons; rolling pin; steel rule; sharp-pointed knife; lolly sticks (LS) as spacers; pastry brush; greaseproof paper for icing bag; *Ateco* (or equivalent) icing nozzle No. 3; 230mm (9in) square silver cake board.

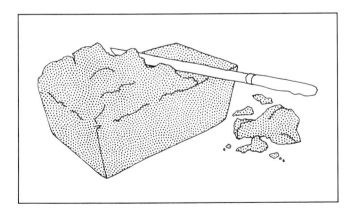

1. Having left the cake overnight, slice the top flat. If desired, slice in half and fill with jam and/or butter-cream. Make the 450g (1lb) of fondant.

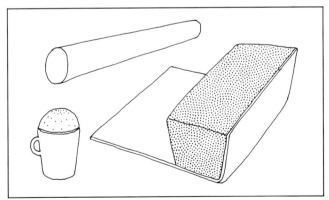

2. Take 340g (12oz) of the fondant and colour it greeny-blue. Measure across cake, then brush it with warm jam. Roll fondant to 2 LS thick and lay one side of cake on top. Carefully roll cake over, covering the three sides. Transfer cake to centre of silver board.

3. Measure short sides of cake. Roll fondant to 2 LS thick and cut to fit. Carefully apply. Trim if necessary. Make a circle 25mm (1in) diameter and about 10mm (³⁄₈in) deep. Push a hole in centre as shown.

4. Take pieces of remaining white fondant. Colour red, orange, yellow, mauve, pink, and green. Roll each piece to 2 LS thick and cut to 75 x 25mm (3 x 1in). Carefully put to one side on a dusted surface.

5. Mix all coloured and white trimmings together. Roll fondant to 4 LS thick. Cut into six pieces 50mm (6in) long, 10mm (³⁄₈in) wide. Brush backs with egg white and attach to cake as shown.

6. Add brown to remaining fondant. Roll a handle 140mm (5¹⁄₂in) long, tapering slightly at one end. Leave to dry on a dusted surface for at least 24 hours.

7. Make the 110g (4oz) of royal icing. Colour slightly paler than fondant on cake. Pipe double lines of continuous dots on seams of fondant, then a single line round base and lines down front and back, as shown.

8. Make a slight indent with paintbrush handle at each end of bars. Dab on a little egg white, then drop on a silver ball. Brush tops of bar supports with egg white, then carefully position the bars on top. Attach handle to hammer-head, securing with egg white.

There was an old woman . . .

. . . who lived in a shoe, although it might be more accurate to say, 'There was an old woman who lived in a hiking boot'! I thought it might be better to have round cakes rather than the loaf cakes normally used for this subject – the finished shoe is not quite as I had intended, but the flat surfaces make it easier to decorate.

The food colouring used for the little children is 'Flesh'. This is not available from supermarkets but can be bought from cake-decorating specialists. If you have difficulty obtaining it, use pink with a drop of brown added.

The cake will take two days to decorate. All three components can be split and filled with butter-cream.

Please read the General Notes on pages 6 to 9 before starting to decorate the cake. Also read through the step-by-step instructions and check the ingredient and equipment list.

Ingredients for cake

280g (10oz) butter
220g (8oz) caster sugar
360g (13oz) self-raising flour
200g (7oz) ground rice
220ml (8fl oz) milk beaten with 4 large eggs
filling (optional)
Make from this recipe: 1 x 150mm (6in) round cake; 2 x 115mm (4½in) round cakes

Ingredients for fondant and royal icing

790g (1¾lb) icing sugar, plus 110g (4oz)
1¾ egg whites, plus ½
almost 4 tbsp liquid glucose
flavouring (optional)
Also: warmed sieved apricot jam; 50/50 mixture of cornflour and icing sugar in a dusting dredger; yellow, brown, blue, orange, black, and flesh food colouring.

Equipment

Mixing bowls; spoons; sieve; rolling pin; steel rule; sharp-pointed knife; lolly sticks (LS) as spacers; pastry brush; greaseproof paper for icing bag; *Ateco* (or equivalent) icing nozzles 1, 2, and 65; 300mm (12in) round silver cake board.

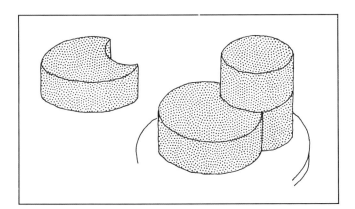

1. Having left the cakes overnight, slice the tops flat. Cut a curved piece out of the large cake, as shown, so that the small cake will fit flush. Sandwich the cakes together with butter-cream and/or jam. Position in centre of silver board.

2. Make 790g (1¾lb) of fondant. Keep back 140g (5oz) and colour the remainder pale brown. Roll to 2 LS thick. Cut circles to fit tops of cakes (cut around baking tins). Brush sponge with warm jam and apply fondant.

3. Measure around tall cake and cut fondant to fit. Apply as before. Measure around large cake and cut fondant to fit. Apply as before, then trim surplus if necessary.

4. Colour the remaining fondant with more brown. Roll to 3 LS thick and cut a strip to go around base of shoe 10mm (³/₈in) wide (this can be cut in three or four sections). Mark tread with blunt edge of a knife.

5. Model remaining brown to form a tongue, as shown. Brush top and bottom (at back) with egg white and attach to shoe. Let it fall across the join of the cakes, i.e. do not push it into corner. Leave to dry overnight.

6. Break off some white fondant and colour it pale orange. Roll to 1 LS thick. Cut one round window and seven square of different sizes. Brush backs with egg white and apply to shoe walls.

7. Break off more white fondant and colour it pale blue. Model a square chimney. Score a deep line around top, and two lines down each side. Roll a small piece and attach to top. Attach chimney to shoe with egg white. Push candle-holder in whilst fondant is still soft.

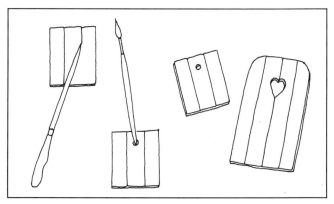

8. Roll blue fondant to 1 LS thick. Cut a door and shutters to fit the windows. Score vertical lines with knife, as shown. Brush backs with egg white and apply to shoe. Make small holes in shutters and cut a little heart in the centre of the door. '

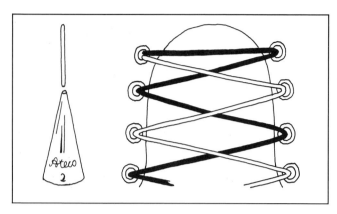

9. Make up the 110g (4oz) of royal icing. Colour some dark brown (add black to brown colouring). With *No. 2 nozzle*, pipe circles down each side of the tongue, then pipe laces, criss-cross, from and to each hole. Pipe cross-stitch around tops of shoe. Pipe a line of stitching above and below sole of shoe.

10. Colour some icing bright orange. With *No. 2 nozzle*, pipe around each window. With *No. 1 nozzle*, pipe leading on windows, then pipe around each window again.

11. With *No. 2 nozzle*, pipe blue around door and shutters. Pipe hinges and knobs, and decoration on chimney. Pipe round heart on door.

12. With *No. 2 nozzle*, pipe green stems up the sides of the shoe. Using a different green and *No. 65 nozzle*, pipe leaves on stems.

13. Colour the remaining white fondant flesh (or pink with a drop of brown added). Model little children as shown. Fix together with egg white whilst fondant is still fairly soft. Attach to shoe and silver board with egg white.

14. Using *No. 1 nozzle*, pipe yellow crinkly hair on children. Put candle in candle-holder.

Mary, Mary, quite contrary

This is a pretty cake which will charm any little girl.

When buying the silver food-colouring for the bells be sure to buy the edible sort (it comes in powdered form).

The basin I use as a base for Mary's dress is slightly smaller than the smallest toughened-glass mixing bowl. It holds just under 560ml (1pt) of water and has a diameter of 125mm (5in).

The cake can be decorated in two days.

Please read the General Notes on pages 6 to 9 before starting to decorate the cake. Also read through the step-by-step instructions and check the ingredient and equipment lists.

Ingredients for cake

450g (16oz) butter
340g (12oz) caster sugar
560g (20oz) self-raising flour
200g (7oz) ground rice
220ml (8fl oz) milk beaten with 6 large eggs
filling (optional)
Make from this recipe: 1 x 180mm (7in) round cake; 1 pudding-basin cake

Ingredients for fondant and royal icing

670g (1½lb) icing sugar, plus 170g (6oz)
1½ egg whites, plus ¾
3 tbsp liquid glucose
flavouring (optional)
Also: warm sieved apricot jam; 50/50 mixture of corn-flour and icing sugar in a dusting dredger; green, pink, flesh, blue, yellow, and silver food colouring; edible silver balls.

Equipment

Mixing bowls; sieve; spoons; rolling pin; steel rule; sharp-pointed knife; lolly sticks (LS) as spacers; pastry brush; small paintbrush; greaseproof paper for icing bags; *Ateco* (or equivalent) icing nozzles 1, 2, 15, 66, and 82; 255mm (10in) round silver cake board.

1. Leave the cakes overnight. Slice the tops until the surfaces are completely flat. Turn the round cake upside down and position it in the centre of the silver board.

2. Make the fondant. Keep back 220g (8oz) and colour the remainder pale green. Measure across round cake. Roll fondant to 2 LS and cut a circle to cover cake. Brush cake with warm jam. With help of rolling pin, apply fondant.

3. Break off a piece of white fondant. Roll to 1 LS thick. Measure depth of pudding cake. Cut a piece to fit – about 110mm (4¼in) at widest part, as shown. Brush area to be covered with jam and apply fondant.

4. Brush top of pudding cake with jam. Take a piece of green fondant weighing about 80g (3oz). Model top of dress and body in two separate pieces, as shown.

5. Take a piece of white fondant. Colour it bright pink. Roll to 1 LS thick and cut a strip 25mm (1in) deep to fit bottom edge of panel. Apply with egg white, smoothing top edge of pink fondant into the white. Cut a white strip, same depth, to go over the pink. Cut a fancy edge with a cocktail cutter.

6. Continue adding a little more pink to strips. Work five fancy strips in all, then finish with a white one, deeper than the others, for the top of the dress. Take some white fondant and add flesh colouring. Model a head and neck and attach to body with egg white. Leave both cakes to dry overnight.

7. Position Mary on cake, towards the back. Add a little blue to some white fondant. Roll to 1 LS thick. Make gathered part of dress in two pieces as shown. Brush beneath waistline with egg white. Attach one rectangle of fondant, gathering into waist. Repeat with other piece – gathers will be smooth if fondant is soft.

8. Take a little more white fondant and colour it flesh. Model two arms and attach them to body with egg white. Bend arms around slightly to support flowers. With a little green or blue fondant, model two small rectangles for sleeves. Attach around tops of arms with egg white.

9. Take another small piece of fondant (any colour) and make it into a roll. Lay across arm, securing with egg white. Model a little hat from a circle of remaining pink fondant. Attach to head with egg white.

10. With *No. 2 nozzle*, pipe white decoration around edge of bonnet. Pipe edging on layers of pink dress and a line of dots at bottom edge. With *No. 1 nozzle* and blue icing, pipe zigzag line around edge of blue dress and on sleeve edges. Pipe tiny dots underneath pink layers and on white icing of bonnet, as shown.

11. Using fondant trimmings, model little bells with a flat side to go against side of cake. Attach a silver ball underneath each, securing with egg white. Leave to dry for twenty minutes, then attach to sides of cake with a dab of icing. Paint with silver colouring.

12. Take a ball of white fondant and mix in silver to make grey. Roll into lengths about 80mm (3in) long, tapering at both ends. Curl around as shown. Leave to dry for twenty minutes, then attach to sides of cake with a dab of icing.

13. With *No. 1 nozzle*, pipe pale-yellow hair. Paint little blue eyes and red lips on the face. With *No. 82 nozzle*, pipe thick green stems for bells and shells. With darker green and *No. 2 nozzle*, pipe finer stems on sides of cake and over fondant in Mary's arms.

14. With dark green icing and *No. 66 nozzle*, pipe leaves coming up from base of cake. With very pale yellowy-green and *No. 15 nozzle*, pipe clusters of flowers at tops of finer stems and on stems in Mary's arms.

Train

I thought a tender or truck full of jolly pink pigs would be a change from the usual sweets or chocolates. It would be fun to have the pigs in different flavours, say strawberry, banana, lemon, and orange – the flavouring should not make any difference to the colour.

As it is impossible to buy a cake board to fit the train, I had to join two 200mm (8in) boards together. Tape the boards on top and underneath, using a clear adhesive tape.

The cake can be decorated in a day, but two days would be better. Please read the General Notes on pages 6 to 9 before you start. Also read through the step-by-step instructions and check the ingredient and equipment lists.

Ingredients for cake

280g (10oz) butter
220 (8oz) caster sugar
360g (13oz) self-raising flour
200g (7oz) ground rice
220ml (8fl oz) milk beaten with 4 large eggs

Make from this recipe: 1 x 200mm (8in) square cake; 2 x 140g (5oz) food-can cakes

Ingredients for fondant and royal icing

1.34kg (3lb) icing sugar, plus 110g (4oz)
3 egg whites, plus ½
6 tbsp liquid glucose
flavouring (optional)
Also: warm sieved apricot jam; 50/50 mixture of cornflour and icing sugar in a dusting dredger; yellow, blue, and red food colouring; edible silver balls.

Equipment

Mixing bowls; sieve; spoons; rolling pin; steel rule; sharp-pointed knife; lolly sticks (LS) as spacers; pastry brush; paintbrush; greaseproof paper for icing bags; *Ateco* (or equivalent) icing nozzle No. 2; 60mm (2¼in) round cutter; 2 x 200mm (8in) square silver cake boards; clear tape.

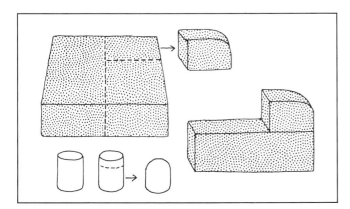

1. Having left the cakes overnight, slice the tops flat. Cut square cake in half. Cut a 60mm (2½in) piece from one half, rounding off one of top edges, as shown. Cut one of little cakes to 50mm (2in) high, and round off top. Attach cabin to engine with jam and/or butter-cream.

2. Make the 1.34kg (3lb) of fondant (in two batches for ease). Position engine at slight angle on board. Colour 560g (1¼lb) of fondant pale yellow. Measure dimensions, then brush with jam. Roll fondant to 2 LS thick, cut each piece to size, and apply: sides, front, top of body, and front of cabin.

3. Cut top of cabin and back in one piece. Make a hook, as shown, and attach to back with egg white. Roll trimmings to 2 LS thick and cut four circles with cutter. Leave on a dusted surface. Colour 450g (1lb) of fondant pale blue. Position tender on board. Cover as before: back, front, sides, then top.

4. Roll fondant to 2 LS thick and cut five more wheels. Roll a small piece, place around hook, and attach to front of tender with egg white. Measure circumference of chimney, then brush with jam. Cut fondant (2 LS thick) and apply. Position on engine using jam to secure.

5. Brush top of chimney with jam and apply one of blue wheels. Brush top and sides of dome. Cover top with newly cut yellow wheel, and cover sides as for chimney.

6. Add blue trimmings to about 80g (3oz) of white fondant. Roll to 4 LS thick and cut strips 10mm (³⁄₈in) wide to go round top of carriage. Attach with egg white. Add a little red to remaining white fondant. Model pigs' heads, as shown. Attach ears and noses with egg white. Mark smile with blunt edge of knife.

7. Position each head in carriage while still soft. Attach silver balls with dabs of egg white. Put a little fondant underneath two heads at front to give impression of bodies. Slice off back of seventh head and attach to cabin window.

8. Make the 110g (4oz) of royal icing. Colour half blue, half yellow. Pipe continuous dots along all fondant seams and around base of cakes. Pipe lines on cabin top and on wheels, as shown. After thirty minutes, attach wheels to engine and carriage, using egg white to secure.

Winnie-the-Pooh

Winnie-the-Pooh is one of the best-loved characters in children's literature. Here he is indulging once more in his favourite pastime, eating honey.

The cake can be completed in two days. To give a more realistic appearance the chintz design on the chair and tablecloth is painted rather than piped. Pooh himself is modelled from fondant, but almond paste (marzipan) may be used instead – deduct 220g (8oz) of icing sugar and half an egg white from the fondant ingredients and replace with 220g (8oz) of almond paste.

As it is difficult to make a really smooth cut when dried fruit is added to a cake, I suggest you use only a filling for this one.

Please read the General Notes on pages 6 to 9 before starting to decorate the cake. Also read through the step-by-step instructions and check the ingredient and equipment lists.

Ingredients for cake

170g (6oz) butter
110g (4oz) caster sugar
220g (8oz) self-raising flour
110g (4oz) ground rice
110ml (4fl oz) milk beaten with 2 large eggs
filling (butter-cream)
Make from this recipe: 2 x 130mm (5in) square cakes

Ingredients for fondant and royal icing

900g (2lb) icing sugar, plus 60g (2oz)
2 egg whites, plus ¼
4 tbsp liquid glucose
flavouring (optional)
Also: warm sieved apricot jam; 50/50 mixture of corn-flour and icing sugar in a dusting dredger; yellow, brown, pink, green, blue, and black food colouring; two edible silver balls for Pooh's eyes.

Equipment

Mixing bowls; spoons; sieve; rolling pin; steel rule; sharp-pointed knife; lolly sticks (LS) as spacers; pastry brush; small paintbrush; greaseproof paper for icing bag; *Ateco* (or equivalent) icing nozzle No. 2; 250mm (10in) square silver cake board.

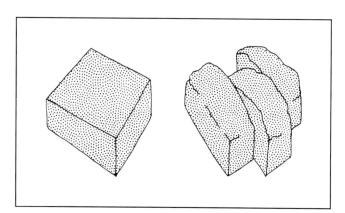

1. Having left the cakes overnight, trim one to form a neat square. Cut middle section out of other cake (leaving a slightly rounded top, which forms back support of chair).

2. The two remaining pieces will form arm rests. Cut a piece from the end of each. Trim these ends into half-circles and join with butter-cream to form the little round table.

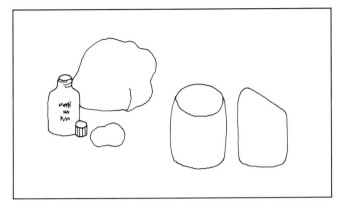

3. Make 220g (8oz) of fondant (or use equivalent amount of marzipan). Keep back a small ball for honey, and colour the remainder brown. Make Pooh's body from a roll, rounding off edges at top and bottom. Form top surface to slope forward slightly. Stand body on a piece of dusted greaseproof paper.

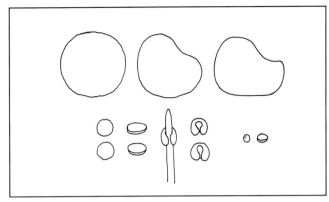

4. Model the head, as shown, from a round ball. Model ears from two small balls – flatten them slightly, then curve round a knitting needle. Make a small ball for the nose and flatten slightly.

5. Make holes for eyes, then press in two silver balls, securing with egg white. Attach ears and nose, securing with egg white. Score mouth as shown, with blunt edge of a knife. Attach head to body, using egg white to secure.

6. Model legs and arms from a roll 15mm (⁵⁄₈in) in diameter and 160mm (6¼in) long. Flatten the paws slightly, then form the feet. Score paw marks using blunt edge of a knife. Bend one arm round slightly. Leave everything to dry overnight.

7. Add a little black and some pink to remaining brown fondant. Model the honey jar. With black colouring, paint Pooh's eyes and nose, dots round his mouth, and rims round top and bottom of jar, then write **Honey** on jar. Mix brown (pink with a drop of black) and paint inside ears, mouth, and paw marks.

8. Colour white ball of fondant with yellow and a little brown – for honey. Put some on top of jar, running down sides. Attach legs to body using egg white. Position jar on legs. Attach arms. Smear blobs of honey on paws and chest.

9. Make 670g (1½lb) of fondant. Colour pale yellow. Put chair base on silver board. Roll fondant to 1 LS thick and cut pieces to fit inside arms, inside back and seat of chair. Brush sponge with jam and apply pieces. Attach arms to chair with a film of jam.

10. Roll fondant to 2 LS thick. First cut and apply front of chair, then arm and back tops, then the sides, and finally the back.

11. Roll fondant to 2 LS thick and cut a circle slightly larger than the table top. Brush sponge with jam and apply fondant, curving over edges of sponge. Roll fondant to 1 LS thick and cut circle about 150mm (6in) in diameter. Place over table, pressing gently in to form folds. Neatly trim edge if necessary.

12. Add pink to remaining yellow fondant. Roll to 1 LS thick and cut four strips 200mm (8in) long and 25mm (1in) wide. Gather each strip carefully to each side of chair. Attach with egg white. Trim top of frill straight, then press gently into chair side.

13. Paint chintz design on chair and tablecloth using green, blue, and pink colouring. (Follow a reference from a magazine, or copy the simple interpretation above.)

14. Make a square brown cake with fondant trimmings. Apply honey-coloured fondant on top, with some down the sides. Paint black currants on cake. Attach cake to top of table using egg white.

15. Push candle into cake. Make up the 60g (2oz) of royal icing. Colour pink. With *No. 2 nozzle*, pipe dots along all chair seams, along top edge of frill and round bottom edge of tablecloth. Place table beside chair on silver board. Carefully position Pooh in the chair.

Superman

The idea for this cake was given to me by Joseph, my eldest son. I had intended skyscrapers with Superman heroically diving down to save some helpless victim. An ingenious way of suspending him in mid-flight was eluding me, so Joseph's idea was very welcome.

When I was making this cake Superman's arm fell off because I did not allow him enough time to dry, so I concealed the break with his cape! Twenty-four hours should be sufficient, but he must be handled with great care.

Please read the General Notes on pages 6 to 9 before starting to decorate the cake. It is also a good idea to read through the step-by-step instructions and check the ingredient and equipment lists.

Ingredients for cake

280g (10oz) butter
220g (8oz) caster sugar
360g (13oz) self-raising flour
200g (7oz) ground rice

220ml (8fl oz) milk beaten with 4 large eggs
Make from this recipe: 1 x 200mm (8in) square cake

Ingredients for fondant and royal icing

790g (1¾lb) icing sugar, plus 110g (4oz)
1¾ egg whites, plus ½
just under 4 tbsp liquid glucose
flavouring (optional)
Also: warm sieved apricot jam; 50/50 mixture of corn-flour and icing sugar in a dusting dredger; red, blue, yellow, flesh, and black food colouring.

Equipment

Mixing bowls; sieve; spoons; rolling pin; steel rule; sharp-pointed knife; lolly sticks (LS) as spacers; pastry brush; greaseproof paper for icing bags and tracing; card; pencil; sewing needle; *Ateco* (or equivalent) icing nozzles 1, 2, and 3; 250mm (10in) square silver cake board.

1. Having left the cake overnight, slice the top flat. Make the 790g (1¾lb) of fondant. Colour 340g (12oz) blue and 110g (4oz) red, and put the red to one side, wrapped. Measure sides of cake, then brush with jam. Roll fondant to 2 LS thick and cut to size.

2. Carefully apply each side, rounding off top edge with hands. Roll trimmings to 1 LS thick and cut a circle roughly 90mm (3½in) diameter. Brush area on top of cake with a thin film of jam and apply fondant in centre towards back, as shown. Cover the cake with a clean tea towel.

3. Make a card template from the shape given above, then trace the symbol on to greaseproof paper. Colour 45g (1½oz) of fondant yellow, roll to 1 LS thick, and cut around template six times. Place tracing over each shape and prick through pencil lines with needle.

4. Make the 110g (4oz) of royal icing. Colour about 4 tsp red. With *No. 2 nozzle*, pipe lines over needle marks. When all six are complete, add more egg white to icing to make it runny. With *No. 1 nozzle*, fill in areas inside lines. Leave symbols to dry for 24 hours on a dusted surface.

5. Take the remaining blue fondant and model Superman's body and arms, as shown – the body is about 65mm (2½in) high and the arms 80mm (3¼in) long. Lay them flat on a dusted surface and attach the arms with egg white.

6. Colour a piece of fondant flesh and model a head and neck, in one piece, and hands. Mark nostrils and mouth. Model hands from fat oblongs, bent over to form fists. Mark fingers with blunt edge of knife.

7. Attach head to body, and hands to arms. Flatten a small piece of yellow fondant and cut a symbol. Brush back with egg white and attach to chest.

8. With *No. 2 nozzle* and red icing, pipe a line around symbol and **S** inside (this is rather too small to fill in, so use the nozzle like a pencil and fill the letter in as you pipe). Pipe around the mouth. Mix a little blue icing and pipe a line around arm joints and neck. Leave to dry on a dusted surface.

9. Colour the remaining fondant yellow. Roll to 2 LS thick. Measure top of cake, then brush with jam, apart from blue circle. Apply fondant. Carefully cut a hole for Superman.

10. Smear inside hole with royal icing. Slide Superman on to a fish-slice and carefully position him in hole. Roll yellow fondant to 2 LS thick and cut wedge shapes. Brush around hole with egg white and attach wedges – Superman has just burst through the cake. Mark cracks on cake with blunt edge of knife.

11. Roll red fondant to 1 LS thick and roughly to shape as shown. Quickly brush back of Superman with egg white and carefully attach cape, with a flourish.

12. With *No. 2 nozzle* and black icing, pipe hair and curl on forehead, the eyes, and the brows. With same nozzle, pipe red dots on edge of cape.

13. Roll the remaining red fondant to 1 LS thick. Cut a strip about 150mm (6in) long and 12mm (½in) wide. With *No. 2 nozzle* and yellow icing, pipe **HAPPY BIRTH-DAY** (or appropriate message). Cut strip and centre the two pieces on cake, using icing to secure.

14. Attach symbols, again using icing to secure – one on each side of cake and two at side of writing. Using *No. 3 nozzle* and red icing, pipe continuous dots along seams of fondant on cake. Push required number of candle-holders into back of cake.

Humpty Dumpty

Humpty Dumpty, famous for his fall from the wall, can be decorated in two days. The piping is very simple: just straight lines (although these may have to be practised on the kitchen table if you have not piped before). The two pudding basins used for making Humpty are 125mm (5in) in diameter and hold just under 560ml (1pt) of water. Dried fruit can be added to the ingredients as none of the cakes needs to be cut into pieces. Butter-cream or jam is used to sandwich the pudding cakes together.

The stone wall can be made to look more realistic by leaving the fondant to dry for about twenty minutes before applying it to the sponge – the surface will develop fine cracks.

Please read the General Notes on pages 6 to 9 before starting to decorate the cake. Also, read through the step-by-step instructions and check the ingredient and equipment lists.

Ingredients for cake

220g (8oz) butter
170g (6oz) caster sugar
280g (10oz) self-raising flour
170g (6oz) ground rice
140ml (3fl oz) milk beaten with 3 large eggs
filling
dried fruit or flavouring (optional)
Make from this recipe: 2 pudding cakes; 1 x 900g (2lb) loaf cake

Ingredients for fondant and royal icing

900g (2lb) icing sugar, plus 60g (2oz)
2 egg whites, plus ¼
2 tbsp liquid glucose
flavouring (optional)
Also: warm sieved apricot jam; 50/50 mixture of corn-flour and icing sugar in a dusting dredger; blue, red, yellow, black, and green food colouring.

Equipment

Mixing bowls; spoons; sieve; rolling pin; steel rule; sharp-pointed knife; lolly sticks (LS) as spacers; pastry brush; small paintbrush; greaseproof paper for icing bag; *Ateco* (or equivalent) icing nozzle No. 2; 250mm (10in) square silver cake board.

1. Having left the cakes overnight, slice the tops from the two pudding cakes, so that the surfaces are flat. Slice the top and one of the long sides from the loaf cake. Stand loaf cake on its side, in the centre of the silver board.

2. Make 450g (1lb) of fondant. Colour half of it cream (drop of blue and red with a little yellow), and the other half pale blue. Measure pudding cake over round surface. Roll cream fondant to 2 LS thick, then cut a circle to fit. Brush sponge with jam and carefully apply fondant, smoothing the surface with your hands.

3. Repeat with the other cake and blue fondant. If edges need trimming, stand cake on upturned basin and carefully slice away excess – keep trimmings for arms and legs.

4. Make another 450g (1lb) of fondant. Break off 340g (12oz) and add black colouring – mix only partially to give streaky effect. Roll to 2 LS thick. Measure front and sides of wall, and cut one piece of fondant to fit. Leave to dry for twenty minutes.

5. Brush cake with jam and apply fondant. Measure back and top. Roll fondant to 2 LS thick and cut fondant to fit. Apply as before. Score horizontal lines all round wall, then vertical lines to form stones. Leave everything to dry overnight.

6. Using a dry paintbrush, lightly paint a corner of each stone in the wall. Sandwich the two pudding cakes together with butter-cream and/or jam. Stand Humpty on dusted greaseproof paper.

7. Colour remaining white fondant red and roll to 2 LS thick. Measure circumference of Humpty and cut a belt to fit, 20mm (³/₄in) wide. Brush back of belt with egg white and carefully attach around his middle.

8. Roll fondant to 2 LS thick. Cut a circle and model into shape of a cap. Attach to head with egg white. (If you have one, a tiny dish can be used as a mould for the cap; I use one belonging to a tea-strainer.)

9. Roll fondant to 1 LS thick. Cut three buttons and pierce holes with skewer or similar. Brush backs with egg white and attach below belt. Add more red and a little blue to remaining fondant and model a bow tie. Attach front of belt with egg white.

10. Break off some of the remaining blue fondant and model a nose. Roll some of cream fondant to 1 LS thick, cut out eyes, then add smaller circles in blue. Roll a strip of cream fondant for mouth. Attach all the pieces to the face using egg white.

11. With blue colouring, paint in eyes and a line along the mouth. Position Humpty on wall, using egg white to secure. Roll cream fondant to form two legs and flatten the feet slightly. Attach them to body and wall with egg white.

12. Roll blue fondant to form two arms. Attach to body and edge of wall with egg white. Mark fingers with blunt edge of knife. Break off some of remaining grey fondant, add red, and mould around top of arms to make sleeves.

13. Break off more of remaining grey fondant and form into little rocks. Stick them to board with egg white. Poke candles into larger rocks. Make up the 60g (2oz) of royal icing. Pipe pink icing down Humpty's sleeves and a line of pink on each shoe.

14. Pipe red lines on belt and lines going to centre of hat, ending with a blob in the middle. Pipe a line on each side of buttons. Pipe a double strap on each shoe and a tiny button on the pink icing. Pipe green grass along bottom edge of wall, in crevices, and around some of the stones on the board.

40

Sleeping Beauty's Castle

This cake will take about four days to decorate, so patience is required – but the result is well worth while. I recommend it for a very, very special occasion.

The marbling effect on the tiles is obtained by only partially mixing the colour (or colours) into the fondant.

If any fondant remains after each session, cover it with greaseproof paper, keep in an airtight container, then add it to the next batch or use for making small items (a little egg white may need to be added if it has become hard). The conical shapes on which the roof tiles are stuck are not visible, so these can be made from leftovers.

To vary the greens in the piped foliage, add a little more yellow or blue, or even a spot of red, to an existing green.

Please read the General Notes on pages 6 to 9 before starting to decorate the cake. Read also through the step-by-step instructions and check the ingredient and equipment lists.

Ingredients for cake

450g (16oz) butter
340g (12oz) caster sugar
560g (20oz) self-raising flour
340g (12oz) ground rice
280ml (10fl oz) milk beaten with 6 large eggs
flavouring, filling or dried fruit
Make from this recipe: 1 x 200mm (8in) round cake; 1 x 115mm (4½in) round cake; 1 x 400g (14oz) food-can cake; 4 x 140g (5oz) food-can cakes

Ingredients for fondant and royal icing

1.57kg (3½lb) icing sugar, plus 110g (4oz)
3½ egg whites, plus ½
7 tbsp liquid glucose
flavouring (optional)
Also: warm sieved apricot jam; 50/50 mixture of corn-flour and icing sugar in a dusting dredger; red, blue, yellow, green, brown, and black food colouring.

Equipment

Mixing bowls; sieve; spoons, rolling pin; steel rule; sharp-pointed knife; lolly sticks (LS); pastry brush; greaseproof paper for icing bags; fine paintbrush; *Ateco* (or equivalent) icing nozzles 1 and 15; 350mm (14in) square silver cake board.

1. Having left the cakes overnight, slice the tops until they are perfectly flat. Make 670g (1½lb) fondant. Colour with drops of red and blue. Roll to 2 LS thick and cut a circle for the large cake, then cut from this a circle for the small cake. Coat tops with jam, then cover.

2. Measure round the cakes. Roll fondant to 2 LS thick, then cut to fit. Score horizontal lines using steel rule. Coat cake sides with jam, then cover. Score vertical lines to form bricks. Make 670g (1½lb) fondant and colour as before.

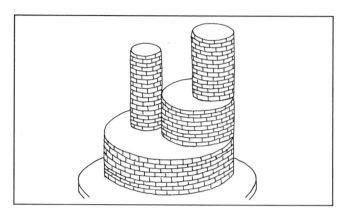

3. Put one of the small cakes on top of another, securing with jam. Cut four circles to fit tops of cakes (2 LS thick), then cover as before. Measure circumference and depth of cakes, cut fondant to fit, and score horizontal lines. Apply fondant and score vertical lines as before. Leave overnight.

4. Position large cake towards the back of the silver board. Position other three cakes as indicated. Make up the royal icing and store in airtight container. Add a little egg white (if necessary) and red colour to remaining fondant. Knead.

5. Cut steps (**A** and **B**) for front and side doors. Position with dabs of royal icing. Cut main steps (**D**), then cut a double step (**C**) a little wider. Position as shown. Cut four steps (**E**) and position.

6. Add a little blue to fondant. Roll to 4 LS thick, then cut about forty squares. Roll fondant again to 2 LS thick and cut another forty squares. Position round tops of two main cakes, using dabs of icing to secure. Press required number of candles into fondant whilst still soft, then remove.

7. Add drops of black to remaining fondant. Roll to 1 LS thick. Cut ten little windows as shown. Brush the backs with egg white and attach where indicated – four go to the back.

8. Add brown to rest of fondant. Roll to 2 LS thick. Cut four doors and score as shown. Brush backs with egg white and attach where indicated.

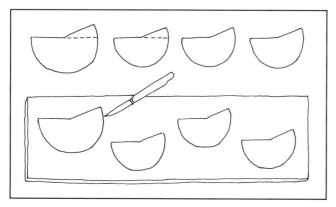

9. Cut from a piece of thin card one circle 190mm (7½in) in diameter and three circles 145mm (5¾in) in diameter. Cut out wedges as shown. Fold cones around and check that they fit the cakes; they should overhang a little. Using cards as templates, cut one large and three small roofs.

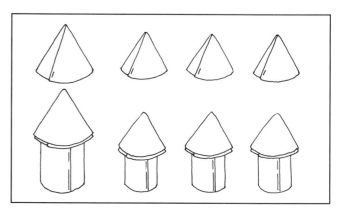

10. Fold templates into cones and secure with staples. Dust outside of cones liberally with cornflour. Place fondant carefully around each cone. Secure edges with egg white. Stand each cone on a can. Leave overnight. Position the two small cakes 20mm (¾in) from front of castle and secure with icing.

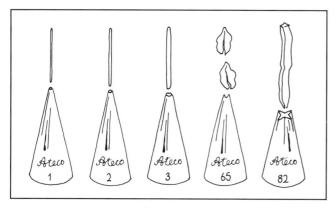

11. Make eight icing bags. With *No. 1 nozzle* and two shades of green, pipe grass at intervals around base and top of cakes, on steps, and in crevices. *No. 2*: pipe grey down centre and around each window. *No. 82*: pipe five brown tree trunks, at back, at each side, by steps, and on small castle. Continue branches with *No. 3*.

12. With *No. 3 nozzle*, put two greens in an icing bag and pipe four vine stems – at back, at side, at front, and on small castle. *No. 65*: pipe dark-green leaves on trees; light-green on vines. *No. 1*: pipe white flowers (four dots) on trees. *No. 1*: pipe black handles and hinges on doors. Leave to dry overnight.

13. Make 220g (½lb) marbled fondant. Roll to 1 LS thick and cut roof tiles. Starting at bottom edge, stick tiles to fondant cones using egg white. Make four blue balls, flatten slightly, score round edges, then secure to top of roofs with icing. Leave to dry on cans overnight.

14. Smear icing round top edges of each of the four castle parts. Carefully press the roofs into position. Smear a little icing on the under-sides of the two small towers and position as indicated. Finally, secure the candles in their holes with a little dab of icing.

Racing track

When this cake was made, I was unable to obtain the correct-sized silver board: I taped four 200mm (8in) boards together and the fondant roads were laid to cover up the joins (but they do give the cake a little more interest).

The cars on the track are based on 'Formula Fords', the lowest of the Formula cars in which most racers begin their careers (they are also the easiest to model).

The cake can be decorated in two days. Please read the General Notes on pages 6 to 9 before starting. It is also a good idea to read through the step-by-step instructions and check the ingredient and equipment lists.

Ingredients for cake

340g (12oz) butter
250g (9oz) caster sugar
420g (15oz) self-raising flour
250g (9oz) ground rice
250ml (9fl oz) milk beaten with 5 large eggs
butter-cream for filling

Make from this recipe: 1 x 180mm (7in) round cake; 1 x 900g (2lb) loaf cake

Ingredients for fondant and royal icing

1.12kg (2½lb) icing sugar, plus 170g (6oz)
2½ egg whites, plus ¾
5 tbsp liquid glucose
flavouring (optional)
Also: warm sieved apricot jam; 50/50 mixture of corn-flour and icing sugar in a dusting dredger; green, black, silver, yellow, red, and blue food colouring.

Equipment

Mixing bowls; sieve; spoons; rolling pin; steel rule; sharp-pointed knife; lolly sticks (LS) as spacers; pastry brush; paintbrush; greaseproof paper for icing bags; 55mm (2¼in) round cutter; 15mm (⅝in) round cutter; *Ateco* (or equivalent) icing nozzles 1, 3, and 9; 400mm (16in) square silver cake board.

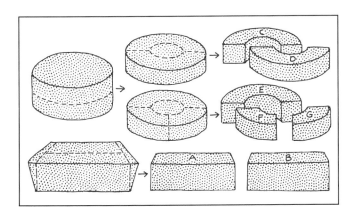

1. Having left the cakes overnight, slice the tops flat. Slice the round cake in half. Cut away sloping sides from loaf cake, then cut in half lengthways. Press large cutter in centre of both round cakes, then cut each cake in half, and one half in half again, as shown.

2. Position pieces on board, as shown. Cut remaining half of loaf cake to fit spaces, then cut a sloping piece to go inside track. Go round track with knife, levelling surfaces and neatening joins. Stick all pieces together with butter-cream. Make the 1.12kg (2½lb) of fondant. Colour 1kg (2¼lb) green.

3. Brush inside walls of track with warm jam. Measure depth of wall and then roll fondant to 2 LS thick. Cut into manageable pieces and apply. Repeat with outside walls. Cut roads to fit where indicated, 2 LS thick and 25mm (1in) wide. Attach to board with egg white.

4. Add black to green trimmings to make grey. Brush top of track with jam. Apply as before, cutting fondant roughly to shape, then trimming after application. Add more black to some of trimmings for tunnels. Roll to 1 LS thick and cut three circles with large cutter. Cut in half and apply where indicated.

5. Make the 170g (6oz) of royal icing. With *No. 3 nozzle* and green icing, pipe continuous dots along track edges, then around base and tunnels. Pipe black continuous dots along edges of roads on board. With *No. 1 nozzle* and white icing, pipe markings on track, as shown (pipe a line across fondant joins).

6. Add blue to some grey trimmings and model two cars as shown, 5 LS thick and about 50mm (2in) long, 12mm (1⁄2in) wide. Add black to remaining trimmings. Roll to 3 LS thick and cut thirty-two wheels with small cutter. Make indent in each centre with *No. 9 nozzle*, then paint silver. Leave on dusted surface.

7. Using remaining white fondant, model six more cars in different colours (break a little piece from each colour and make six helmets, as shown). Leave to dry for an hour.

8. Attach wheels and helmets to cars, using egg white. With *No. 1 nozzle* and white icing, pipe goggles on helmets. Using different-coloured icing, pipe lines on helmets, then numbers and lines on cars. Leave for thirty minutes, then attach to track with egg white.

Rocket on the moon

Decorating this cake will take two to three days. Because of the weight of the rocket it is as well to add a little gum tragacanth (see page 8) to the fondant covering the main cake to act as a hardener. (If you do not use it, then make the cake as near as possible to the party day so that the rocket will not sink into the cake and spoil the shape.)

The candles used in the photograph are 'Magic Candles', which relight themselves after being blown out. They are great fun, but if you use them it is best to remove them with the holders (bottom ones first) and douse them under the tap – otherwise you may have to throw a bucket of water over the cake!

Please read the General Notes on pages 6 to 9 before starting to decorate the cake. Also read through the step-by-step instructions and check the ingredient and equipment lists.

Ingredients for cake

280g (10oz) butter
220g (8oz) caster sugar
360g (13oz) self-raising flour
200g (7oz) ground rice
220ml (8fl oz) milk beaten with 4 large eggs

flavouring, filling, or dried fruit
Make from this recipe: 1 x 200mm (8in) round cake; 1 x 420g (15oz) food-can cake

Ingredients for fondant and royal icing

900g (2lb) icing sugar, plus 110g (4oz)
2 egg whites, plus ½
4 tbsp liquid glucose
gum tragacanth (if desired)
flavouring (optional)
Also: warm sieved apricot jam; 50/50 mixture of cornflour and icing sugar in a dusting dredger; blue and green food colouring; edible silver balls for decoration.

Equipment

Mixing bowls; sieve; spoons; rolling pin; steel rule; sharp-pointed knife; lolly sticks (LS) as spacers; pastry brush; greaseproof paper for icing bags; *Ateco* (or equivalent) icing nozzles 1, 2, 15, and 22; 255mm (10in) round silver cake board.

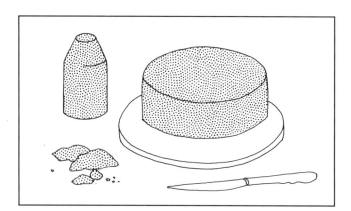

1. Having left the cakes overnight, trim the rocket as indicated, sloping at one end and with a flat top. Slice the top of the round cake until it is flat, then position it upside down in centre of silver board.

2. Make the fondant, adding flavour if desired. Cut in two and cover one half. (Knead 2 tsp gum tragacanth into remaining half). Roll out to 2 LS thick, then cut circle to cover top and sides of cake. Brush cake with jam, carefully apply fondant, then trim round bottom edge.

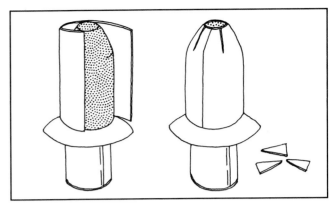

3. Place rocket on an upturned tea plate, then put the plate on a small jar or tin so that it can swivel round. Colour the remaining half of fondant pale blue. Measure height and circumference of rocket.

4. Roll fondant to 2 LS thick and cut to size. Brush sponge with jam. Carefully wrap fondant around sponge. Cut out four Vs at top to fit nozzle.

5. Take a little of the blue fondant, add some more blue, and model a nose-cone for the rocket. Place it on waxed paper. Leave everything to dry overnight.

6. Measure circumference of rocket again, roll fondant to 1 LS thick, and cut three strips 20mm (³⁄₄in) wide. Brush backs with egg white, then position as indicated.

7. Make up the 110g (4oz) of royal icing and keep in an airtight container. Spread a film of jam on top of the rocket, add dabs of royal icing, and press on the nose-cone of the rocket.

8. Roll blue fondant to 1 LS thick. Cut ten strips 10mm (³⁄₈in) wide and attach where indicated on rocket. Cut nine strips to fit on nose-cone. Position strips with egg white but avoid seam of fondant at back of rocket. Cut out and attach five round, white windows (1 LS thick).

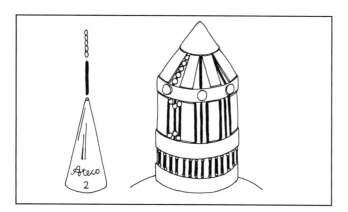

9. Using *No. 2 nozzle*, pipe blue lines where indicated. Add silver balls as soon as each line has been piped. Pipe little dots at top and bottom of each line near base of rocket. Leave to dry overnight.

10. Carefully transfer rocket to cake (rocket seam underneath). Secure with lines of royal icing and position rough lumps of white fondant (moon rocks) to support – these are secured with dabs of icing.

11. Add more blue to blue fondant and model eight small rockets 14mm (1/2in) in diameter and 55mm (2 1/4in) long. Roll fondant to 2 LS thick and cut a circle to fit base of rocket. Coat sponge with jam and apply fondant.

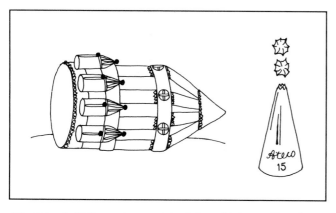

12. Attach little rockets with dabs of icing. Pipe lines where indicated (*No. 2*) and position silver balls. Using *No. 15* small star nozzle, pipe stars around base seam, on strip seams and at base of nose-cone.

13. Position more moon rocks on surface. Model two craters, as shown, and position in front of rocket using egg white to secure.

14. Add green to remaining white fondant: model two heads with big ears and two arms. Place inside the craters. Stick a pair of antennae on each head with dabs of icing. Mark mouths with a knife.

15. Using *No. 1 nozzle*, pipe green eyes, noses, and crinkly hair on to moon-men, then a dot on each antenna. With *No. 15 nozzle*, pipe pale-blue stars on moon surface. Using *No. 22 nozzle*, pipe larger stars round base of moon.

Novelty Birthday Cakes
for Adults

Fast-food addict

Apart from those who have suddenly become weight-conscious, most people are happy to have chips with everything. This cake would be ideal for those who will eat nothing but chips and the usual accompanying greasy food. A couple of sausages could also be added – there are instructions for making grilled sausages on page 82.

The cake can be decorated in a day. To add more fun, each item of food could have a different flavour – peppermint chips, vanilla egg, strawberry beans, banana beefburger!

The base is made from a 200mm (8in) round cake. Ingredients and quantities for this are given on page 10 and the method of baking on pages 6 to 7. Instructions for making royal icing and fondant are on pages 7 to 8. If you are making your own fondant, it will be easier to make the 790g (1¾lb) in two batches, keeping it securely wrapped in cling film and in an airtight container until required.

Please read the General Notes on pages 6 to 9 before starting to decorate the cake. Also read through the step-by-step instructions and check the ingredient and equipment lists.

Ingredients for fondant and royal icing

790g (1¾lb) icing sugar, plus 30g (1oz)
1¾ egg whites, plus ⅛
almost 4 tbsp liquid glucose
flavouring (optional)
Also: warm sieved apricot jam; 50/50 mixture of corn-flour and icing sugar in a dusting dredger; yellow, blue, green, brown, and orange food colouring.

Equipment

Mixing bowls; spoons; sieve; rolling pin; steel rule; sharp-pointed knife; lolly sticks (LS) as spacers; pastry brush; small paintbrush; crinkled chip cutter; greaseproof paper for icing bag; *Ateco* (or equivalent) icing nozzle No. 3; 250mm (10in) round silver cake board.

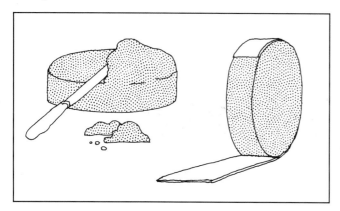

1. Having left the cake overnight, slice the top flat. Turn the cake over and place in centre of silver board. Make the fondant. Measure circumference and depth of cake. Roll fondant to 2 LS thick and cut a piece to go round cake. Brush cake sides with warmed jam. Roll cake on to fondant.

2. Brush top of cake with jam. Roll fondant to 2 LS thick. Cut circle to fit (cut round the cake tin). With help of rolling pin, apply fondant.

3. When fondant is dry, paint repeating flower design around sides. Make up the royal icing. Pipe a line of continuous dots around top fondant seam.

4. Take 170g (6oz) of fondant. Add brown colouring and a little black. Add more brown and partially mix. Start to shape the beefburger, pinching top to give an uneven surface. Make three grill grooves with paintbrush handle and paint some black in the grooves. Leave to dry, then bend a little to make surface cracks.

5. Take 80g (3oz) of fondant. Colour orange with a little brown. Form into baked beans. Flatten some pieces to make bean sauce. Position beefburger on cake, then put dribbling sauce and beans around, using egg white to secure.

6. Take 140g (5oz) of fondant. Colour it with a little yellow and partially mix in a little brown. Roll to 4 LS thick and cut into chips with crinkled cutter. Arrange around back of beefburger, securing with egg white.

7. Take about 60g (2oz) of fondant. Form white of egg from a ball, flatten it, and smooth it. Form yellow yolk from a ball, flatten slightly, and round off.

8. Position egg white in remaining space of cake, then secure yolk with egg white. Brush beefburger, chips, and egg yolk with egg white to give nice greasy finish.

Lazy gardener

There are those for whom weeding, mowing lawns, sowing seeds, planting bulbs, and trimming hedges are a labour of love – and there are those into whose hearts these tasks strike terror. This gardener has finally given in to his nagging family and made an effort to explore unknown terrain – only to put up a hammock and experience the pleasure of sleep in the open air.

The base is made from a 200mm (8in) round cake. Ingredients and quantities for this are given on page 10 and method of baking on pages 6 to 7. Instructions for making royal icing, marzipan, and fondant are given on pages 7 to 8. If you are making your own fondant, keep it securely wrapped in cling film and in an airtight container until required.

The cake can be decorated in a day (after the covering of marzipan has been left to dry for 48 hours), but in order to allow the pieces of foreground to dry properly, it is best to leave them for one night and assemble everything the following day.

Please read the General Notes on pages 6 to 9 before starting to decorate. Also read through the step-by-step instructions and check the ingredient and equipment lists.

Ingredients for fondant and royal icing

560g (1¼lb) icing sugar, plus 280g (10oz)
1¼ egg whites, plus 1¼
2½ tbsp liquid glucose
flavouring (optional)
Also: 450g (1lb) marzipan; warm sieved apricot jam; 50/50 mixture of cornflour and icing sugar in a dusting dredger; yellow, green, blue, red, brown, and black food colouring.

Equipment

Mixing bowls; spoons; sieve; rolling pin; steel rule; sharp-pointed knife; lolly sticks (LS) to use as spacers; pastry brush; small paintbrush; greaseproof paper; *Ateco* (or equivalent) icing nozzles 1, 2, 3, 13, 65, and 66; 250mm (10in) round silver cake board.

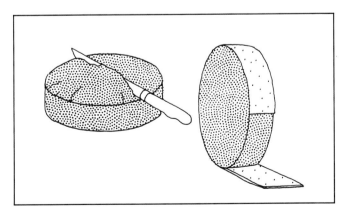

1. Cut the top of the cake flat, then turn it over. Measure the depth and circumference and brush with jam. Roll marzipan to 2 LS thick. Cut a piece to fit round the cake, then roll the cake along, as shown.

2. Brush the top with jam. Roll marzipan to 2 LS thick, lay the cake on top, then carefully cut round. Leave the cake to dry for 48 hours.

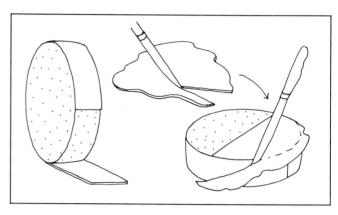

3. Take a little white fondant, add yellow, and model the hammock – indent the centre with a finger and pinch the edges thin to give the appearance of fabric. Model two brown legs with feet and bend them at the knee. Attach legs inside hammock with egg white. Paint black shoes. Leave to dry on a dusted surface.

4. Colour 340g (³/₄lb) of fondant green. Cover cake sides exactly as for marzipan, but using egg white instead of jam. Brush half the cake top with egg white. Roll green trimming (2 LS thick) to a rough semicircle shape, then cut a straight side with a knife. Lay fondant on cake and trim edges.

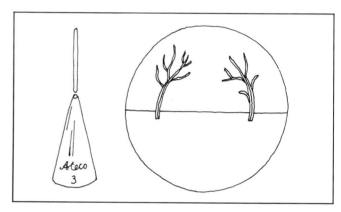

5. Take 170g (6oz) of fondant. Partially mix in blue colouring. Roll (2 LS thick) to a rough semicircle shape and, as before, cut a straight side with a knife. Lay fondant on cake and trim edges.

6. With *No. 3 nozzle* and dark-brown icing, pipe bending tree trunks with several branches, as shown, about 50mm (2in) in from each side and the trunks extending about 15mm (¹/₂in) over the green fondant.

7. Position the hammock between the trees at a slight angle. Secure with icing. With *No. 2 nozzle* and yellow icing, pipe ropes from hammock to each tree trunk, as shown.

8. With *No. 65 nozzle* and two shades of green in the icing bag, pipe leaves on trees. With *No. 1* and darkish green, pipe blades of grass, some clumped together, getting larger towards the foreground. Work to within 30mm (1¹/₂in) of the cake edge. Using same nozzle and white icing, pipe little flowers (getting larger as before) on the grass.

58

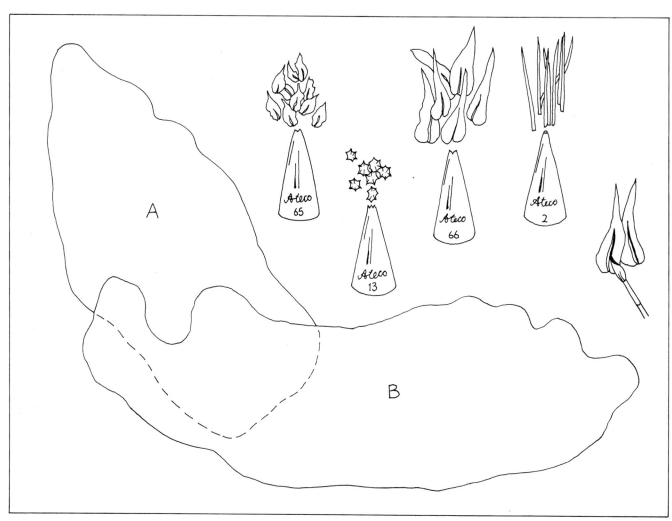

9. Roll green fondant trimmings to 1 LS thick. Cut out the shapes as shown above. Cut two each of **A** and **B**. Put the shapes on a dusted surface. With *No. 65 nozzle* and dark-green icing, cover the **A** pieces with leaves. Using *No. 13 nozzle* and pink and mauve icing, pipe flowers of varying sizes between the leaves.

10. With *No. 66* and *No. 2 nozzles*, pipe grass and long leaves on shape **B**. (Vary the greens by adding more or less blue, yellow, or red.) When the leaves are dry, paint lines of darker green at each side of the leaf vein. Leave the pieces to dry overnight.

11. Mix green and blue fondant trimmings and roll to 2 LS thick. Cut out two supports for the two **A** shapes. Attach these with egg white to the cake, then attach the shapes. Roll fondant to 6 LS thick. Cut a support for shape **B** and attach as before.

12. With dark-green icing and *No. 66 nozzle*, pipe folding ribbons over the seams under the shapes – pipe two under **B** and one each under the **A**s.

Computer maniac

Computers appear to have become an integral part of our lives: children are instructed in them at school, and classes are available which teach the use of computers in household accounts, or enable mothers to keep pace with technology until returning to work.

There are those who feel threatened by computers and those who are indifferent. There are also those who are obsessed by computers – this cake is for them.

The computer is made from one 180mm (7in) square cake and one 230mm (9in) square cake. Ingredients and quantities for these are given on page 10 and the method for baking on pages 6 to 7. Instructions for making royal icing, marzipan, and fondant are on pages 7 to 8. If you make your own fondant you may find it easier to make the 1.34kg (3lb) in two or three batches, keeping each piece securely wrapped in cling film and in an airtight container until required.

The cake can be decorated in one to two days, after the covering of marzipan has been left to dry for 48 hours. The design on the screen – a birthday cake firing and being fired at – can easily be changed to something more appropriate or personal. Just follow the basic instructions using your own drawings or lettering.

Please read the General Notes on pages 6 to 9 before starting to decorate. Also read through the step-by-step instructions and check the ingredient and equipment lists.

Ingredients for fondant and royal icing

1.34kg (3lb) icing sugar, plus 110g (4oz)
3 egg whites, plus ½
6 tbsp liquid glucose
flavouring (optional)
Also: 1.12kg (2½lb) marzipan; warm sieved apricot jam; 50/50 mixture of cornflour and icing sugar in a dusting dredger; yellow, brown, black, green, blue, and red food colouring.

Equipment

Mixing bowls; spoons; sieve; rolling pin; steel rule; sharp-pointed knife; lolly sticks (LS) as spacers; pastry brush; greaseproof paper; *Ateco* (or equivalent) icing nozzles 1 and 2; tracing paper; waxed paper; stiff white card; adhesive tape; 280mm (11in) square silver cake board.

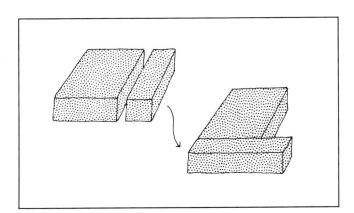

1. Slice the tops of both cakes flat. Cut a 50mm (2in) slab from the smaller cake and attach it to one of the narrow sides using jam and a sliver of marzipan. Trim excess cake to give a 230 x 130mm (9 x 5in) oblong.

2. Roll marzipan to 2 LS thick and brush narrow ends of narrow cake with jam. Stand cake on marzipan and cut round it, as shown. Brush top and front with jam. Roll marzipan to 2 LS thick. Lay cake on as before, covering top and front with one piece.

3. Cover three sides and top of square cake, as with narrow cake. Roll marzipan to 1 LS thick and cover under-side of cake (which will be the back when it stands up). Leave both cakes to dry (square cake standing on uncovered side) for 48 hours.

4. Colour 1.12kg (2½lb) of fondant yellow with a little brown. Knead well. Cover both cakes exactly as for marzipan, but using egg white to secure instead of jam.

5. Add 220g (8oz) of fondant to trimmings, then mix in brown. Roll to 4 LS thick. Cut strips 13mm (½in) wide. Cut strips into forty-nine cubes. Smooth the top edges of each with fingers. Cut one strip 120mm (4¾in), two strips 30mm (1¼in) and two 25mm (1in) long. Roll fondant to 6 LS thick and cut two strips 40mm (1½in) and one 30mm (1¼in).

6. Roll fondant to 1 LS thick, cut a narrow strip, and attach to keyboard with egg white. Leave all other pieces on lightly dusted surface. Roll fondant to 1 LS thick. Cut ten pieces 10mm (³⁄₈in) wide for front and top of square cake. Attach with egg white. Apply to side and top first, then front, then top corners.

7. Make the royal icing. Take two or three teaspoonsful and colour with yellow and a little brown. With *No. 1 nozzle*, pipe letters, numbers, and symbols on pieces, as shown in photograph. Neatly secure each piece in position with a dab of icing.

8. Break off half remaining brown fondant and add a little black. Roll to 1 LS thick and cut a piece 140 x 165mm (5½ x 6½in). Round off the corners. Lay square cake on its back. Brush a thin film of egg white on area to be covered, then carefully apply piece.

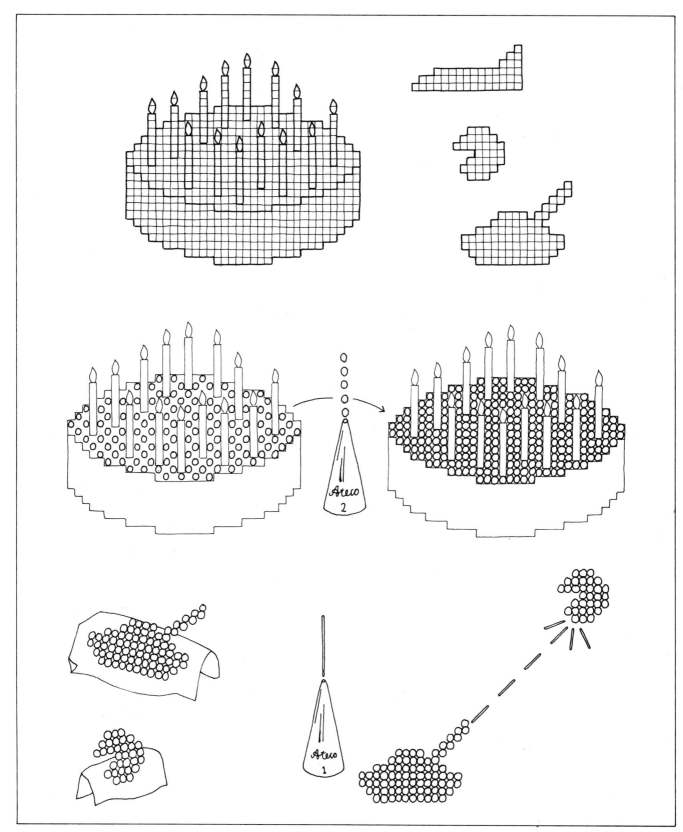

9. Trace the above drawings on to stiff white card. Tape waxed paper over the drawings; then, using fairly stiff icing and *No. 2 nozzle*, pipe a dot in each square (the dots must touch but not run into each other) – pipe the area with alternate dots, leave for thirty minutes, then fill in the remaining dots, as shown.

10. Pipe white icing for birthday cake top and candle flames and pale grey for cake front. Pipe blue candles, red tanks, yellow pac-men, and green planes. Dry overnight. Carefully remove waxed paper and attach pieces to screen with dark icing. With *No. 1 nozzle*, pipe white fire marks. Attach cake to keyboard with blobs of icing.

Career woman

Although it has been socially acceptable for women to go out to work since the war, only now are careers for them expanding into previously male-dominated areas. More are taking high managerial posts and positions of authority, and this cake, without being too specific, is for them.

The chair and desk are made from one 200mm (8in) round cake and one 130mm (5in) square cake. Ingredients and quantities for these are given on page 10 and method for baking on pages 6 to 7. Instructions for making royal icing, marzipan, and fondant are on pages 7 to 8. If you make your own fondant, it will be easier to make the 1.23kg (2¾lb) in three batches, keeping each piece securely wrapped in cling film and in an airtight container.

The cake will take one or two days to decorate, after the covering of marzipan has been left to dry for 48 hours.

Please read the General Notes on pages 6 to 9 before starting. Also read through the step-by-step instructions and check the ingredient and equipment lists.

Ingredients for fondant and royal icing

1.23kg (2¾lb) icing sugar, plus 110g (4oz)
2¾ egg whites, plus ½
5½ tbsp liquid glucose
flavouring (optional)
Also: 1kg (2¼lb) marzipan; warm sieved apricot jam; 50/50 mixture of cornflour and icing sugar in a dusting dredger; red, yellow, blue, brown, black, and gold food colouring.

Equipment

Mixing bowls; spoons; sieve; rolling pin; steel rule; sharp-pointed knife; lolly sticks (LS) as spacers; pastry brush; small paintbrush; greaseproof paper; *Ateco* (or equivalent) icing nozzles 1, 2, 3, and 65; 300mm (12in) round silver cake board.

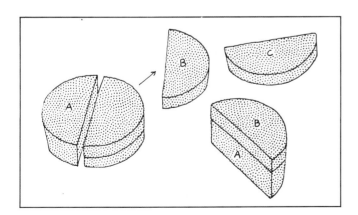

1. Slice the top of the cakes flat. Cut the round cake in half (**A**), then slice one of the halves in half (**B** and **C**). Attach **B** to **A** using jam on each surface and a sliver of marzipan in between.

2. Cut 40mm (1½in) from each side of **C**. Cut 25mm (1in) from the square cake and slice it in half (**G** and **H**). Attach **C** to **F** using jam and marzipan as before.

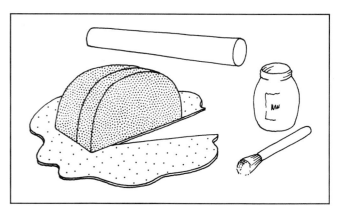

3. Put **G** and **H** against **C** and trim the ends to follow the curve, as shown. Put **D** and **E** against **G** and **F**, then cut the ends to fit flush with the chair front. Attach **D** to **G** and **E** to **H** using jam and marzipan as before.

4. Brush back of desk with jam. Roll marzipan to 2 LS thick and apply as shown. Measure desk front, brush with jam, cut marzipan to fit, then apply. Brush top with jam and apply marzipan as for back.

 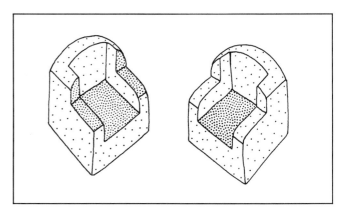

5. Roll marzipan to 1 LS thick and apply to inside of chair arms. Attach arms to chair with jam and a sliver of marzipan. Cover rest of chair (with marzipan 2 LS thick) in the following order: inside back, back, and sides.

6. Continue with the front and arm fronts (in one piece), top and arm tops (in one piece), arm (in two pieces), and finally the seat. Leave the chair and desk to dry for 48 hours.

7. Follow instructions for applying marzipan, and cover desk (apart from top) and chair with fondant coloured with drops of yellow, red, and blue. Apply with egg white instead of jam. After applying front of desk and inside back of chair, mark squares with blunt edge of knife.

8. Add brown and black to trimmings; partially mix to give wood-grain effect. Roll to 2 LS thick and lay on table-top (after brushing marzipan with a thin film of egg white). Trim the edges neatly.

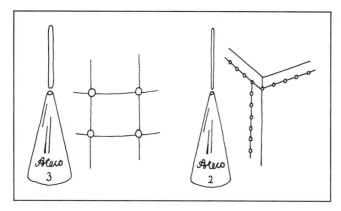

9. Make the royal icing. Colour some same colour as fondant. With *No. 3 nozzle*, pipe buttons on upholstery. With *No. 2 nozzle*, pipe nail heads on fondant seams of chair. When dry, paint gold. Position both cakes on silver board, as shown.

10. Colour 110g (4oz) of the fondant trimmings with black. Model body pieces as shown and secure in chair with egg white. Model white cuffs, collar, and shirt front and attach with egg white. Colour about 45g (1½oz) of fondant with flesh.

11. Model a knee and leg, as shown. Squeeze the knee between desk and chair with the leg next to it. Model head and hands, then attach. Model a little pink bow tie, as shown, then attach. With *No. 2 nozzle* and appropriate-coloured icing, pipe hair. Paint eyes and lips, then lace trim down front of shirt.

12. Mix the colours and model five telephones. Use just under 30g (1oz) for each. Cut the dials (white fondant) about 15mm (⅝in) in diameter and smaller circles (same colour as phones) for the centre of the dials. Attach receivers, dials, and centres with egg white. Paint finger holes as shown.

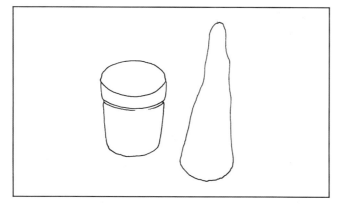

13. Colour a small piece of fondant with red and a little brown. Model a plant pot about 25mm (1in) high. Mark a groove at top with blunt edge of knife. Model a green support, as shown, about 40mm (1½in) high, and attach to pot. Secure pot to corner of desk with a dab of icing.

14. With *No. 1 nozzle* and dark-green icing, pipe squiggly stems over support, down side of pot, and on desk. With *No. 65 nozzle* and two shades of green in icing bag, pipe variegated leaves. Secure telephones to desk with icing. With *No. 2 nozzle* and black icing, pipe curling leads from the handset to the back of each telephone.

Compulsive knitter

Hand-knitting was extremely popular in the late 1920s, with designers like Elsa Schiaparelli producing knitwear to complement the lively, sporty fashion scene of the time: but, even through the 1950s (sloppy joes, Aran and mohair) and the streamlined 1960s, clicking needles became synonymous with grannies and expectant mothers. In recent years, dyes and yarns have been developed and used in such exciting, imaginative ways that the art of hand-knitting has been given a new dimension. This cake, then, is for someone who knits compulsively, anywhere and any time.

The base is made from a 180mm (7in) round cake. Ingredients and quantities for this are given on page 10 and the method for baking on pages 6 to 7. Instructions for making royal icing, marzipan, and fondant are given on pages 7 to 8.

The cake can be decorated in a day (after the covering of marzipan has been left to dry for 48 hours), but piping the balls of wool and the knitting around the sides of the cake is time-consuming, so you may find it easier to break off and finish the following day.

Please read the General Notes on pages 6 to 9 before starting to decorate the cake. Also read through the step-by-step instructions and check the ingredient and equipment lists.

Ingredients for fondant and royal icing

560g (1¼lb) icing sugar, plus 280g (10oz)
1¼ egg whites, plus 1¼
2½ tbsp liquid glucose
flavouring (optional)
Also: 450g (1lb) marzipan; warm sieved apricot jam; 50/50 mixture of cornflour and icing sugar in a dusting dredger; orange, green, red, yellow, blue, and gold food colouring.

Equipment

Mixing bowls; spoons; sieve; rolling pin; steel rule; sharp-pointed knife; lolly sticks (LS) as spacers; pastry brush; small paintbrush; greaseproof paper; *Ateco* (or equivalent) icing nozzles 1 and 3; waxed paper; adhesive tape; stiff card; 230mm (9in) round silver cake board.

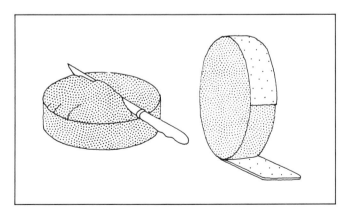

1. Slice the top of the cake flat, then turn it over. Roll marzipan to 2 LS thick and cut a strip to the same depth and circumference as the cake. Brush cake sides with jam, then roll it along the strip, as shown.

2. Brush the top of the cake with jam. Roll marzipan to 2 LS thick and place cake on top. Neatly cut round it. Leave the cake to dry for 48 hours.

3. Meanwhile, make the royal icing. Draw several lines, 60mm (2½in) long, on the stiff card. Tape waxed paper over the card. Using *No. 3 nozzle*, pipe the lines, dragging the nozzle at the end so as to finish with a point. Pipe a dot at the beginning of each line, as shown. Leave to dry.

4. Take about 45g (1½oz) of fondant and model a support for the knitting, as shown. Take 75g (2½oz) of fondant, divide into five, and colour with red, blue, green, yellow, and orange. Make two balls from each colour, then cut each ball in half. Leave on a dusted surface.

5. Cover the cake with white fondant, exactly as for marzipan but using egg white instead of jam. Position the cake on the silver board. While the needles are still attached to the waxed paper, paint them with gold.

6. Secure the support to the cake with a dab of icing. Roll fondant to 1 LS thick and cut out the knitting shape, as shown – it will drape from the support to the edge of the cake.

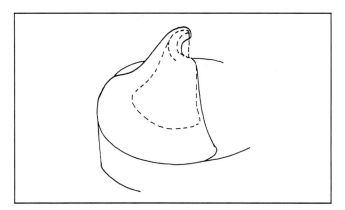

7. Fix the shape to the support with egg white – attach it about one-quarter of the way down the back of the support, then over the top and out towards the edges of the cake. Smooth the edge so that it blends into the cake fondant.

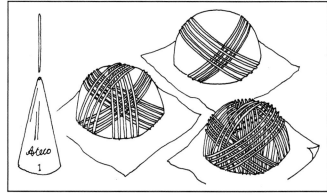

8. Put each half-ball on to a little square of waxed paper. Colour two to three tsp of icing with blue. Using *No. 1 nozzle*, pipe lines of wool over four of the half-balls, as shown. Leave to dry for about twenty minutes.

70

9. Starting at the top of the support, pipe six rows of knitting as shown. When the band is complete, pipe a loopy line down each side to neaten the edge.

10. Choose the best pair of knitting needles. Carefully remove tape from waxed paper and card, then peel waxed paper from back of needles. Neatly secure on the first row of knitting with tiny lines of icing. Carefully pipe stitches over the needles. Join blue half-balls together with blob of icing.

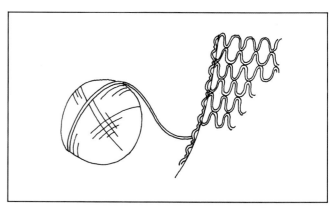

11. Stand the two balls on waxed paper. Pipe lines all the way around to cover up the join – hold nozzle just above the back of the ball, allow icing to fall, then move nozzle around to the front, tucking the line of icing underneath. Quickly push hanging line at the back underneath, using fingernail or knife point.

12. Leave the balls to dry for twenty minutes, then carefully position them on the cake (as shown in photograph) with a neat blob of icing. Pipe a strand of wool coming from each, the one in the foreground going behind the piece of knitting and up to the needles.

13. Repeat stages 7 to 9, using red icing. Position the balls as shown in the photograph, then pipe a strand of wool coming from each.

14. Continue until all the balls and knitting around the sides of the cake are complete. Pipe a continuous row of dots, in red, around the bottom edge of the cake, then pipe a row of loops over it.

Diet freak

This is for those (and I am one) who are excessively weight-conscious – the life-long dieter. We seldom achieve our elusive 'ideal weight', and if we do, we immediately relax, indulge again, and are back to square one. We are the ones who sigh, 'Blessed are those who eat fat and remain thin.'

The cake could be presented as a birthday cake, or given at the end of a successful (or failed) diet.

The base is a 200mm (8in) square cake. Ingredients and quantities for this are given on page 10 and the method for baking is on pages 6 to 7. Instructions for making royal icing, marzipan, and fondant are given on pages 7 to 8. If you are making your own fondant, it will be easier to make the 900g (2lb) in two batches, keeping it securely wrapped in cling film and in an airtight container until required.

Gum tragacanth, which can be bought from most chemists, is used as a hardening agent for the plate. The cake is very simple to decorate (the striped effect may take a little time, but it is not difficult) and can be completed in one to two days, after the plate and covering of marzipan have been left to dry for 48 hours.

Please read the General Notes on pages 6 to 9 before starting to decorate. Also, read the step-by-step instructions, and check the ingredient and equipment lists.

Ingredients for fondant and royal icing

900g (2lb) icing sugar, plus 60g (2oz)
2 egg whites, plus ¼
4 tbsp liquid glucose
1 tsp gum tragacanth
flavouring (optional)
Also: 670g (1½lb) marzipan; warm sieved apricot jam; 50/50 mixture of cornflour and icing sugar in a dusting dredger; blue, yellow, bright green, and silver food colouring.

Equipment

Mixing bowls; spoons; sieve; rolling pin; steel rule; sharp-pointed knife; lolly sticks (LS) as spacers; pastry brush; small paintbrush; greaseproof paper; *Ateco* (or equivalent) icing nozzles 1, 2, and 3; 250mm (10in) square silver cake board; waxed paper; 180mm (7in) round plate.

1. Cut a 180mm (7in) circle of waxed paper. Make 30mm (1¼in) cuts around the edge and position it on the plate. Dust liberally.

2. Mix the teaspoon of gum tragacanth with a little water. Take 170g (6oz) of fondant, add the liquid gum, and dust liberally while kneading. Add drops of blue colouring. Knead well, then roll to 2 LS thick.

3. Cut a 180mm (7in) circle – cut round a baking tin if possible. Carefully lift and position on the plate. Smooth the fondant with fingers. Leave to dry.

4. Cut the top of the cake flat, then turn it over. Brush the sides with jam. Roll marzipan to 2 LS thick. Lay each side of the cake on the marzipan and cut to fit. Repeat this process for the top. Leave the cake and plate to dry for 48 hours.

5. Take 670g (1½lb) of fondant and colour half yellow. Dust a sheet of waxed paper. Roll thin pieces of fondant, approximately 240mm (9½in) long. Push them gently together, yellow and white alternately, using a little egg white if they do not adhere. Continue until a 240mm (9½in) square is complete.

6. Roll the square to 2 LS thick. Measure the cake depth, then cut a piece to fit each side. Apply with egg white. Trim edges. Draw cake size, with a strong black line, on a piece of waxed paper. Turn it over and dust. Repeat stage 5, taking the strips diagonally across.

7. When the square is complete, roll to 2 LS thick. Carefully (but confidently) flip the square over on to another sheet of waxed paper. Lightly brush the cake top with egg white.

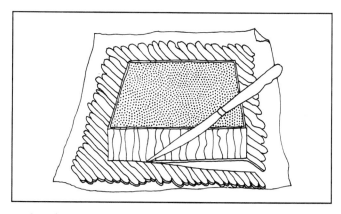

8. Carefully lay the cake on the fondant, then trim the edges. Lift the cake, position it on the silver board and smooth the fondant surface with your hands.

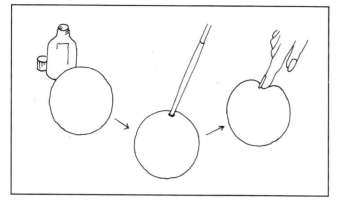

9. Take some of the fondant trimmings, add red, and roll into a very smooth ball. Indent the top centre with paintbrush handle and then with index finger. Place carefully on a dusted surface and leave to dry.

10. Colour a small piece of fondant dark green – add a little red to yellow and blue. Roll the stalk as shown and bend it slightly. Press remaining fondant until fairly thin, then cut calyx. Gently ease calyx into tomato. Push paintbrush handle down centre and position the stalk in the hole.

11. Make the 60g (2oz) of royal icing. Trace the above drawings on to greaseproof paper. Attach each drawing to the cake with a tiny dab of icing. Using a sewing needle, prick through the pencil lines into the fondant.

12. With *No. 2 nozzle*, pipe white icing over the needle marks. Leave to dry for an hour, then add drops of water to some of the icing. Using a small spoon, carefully fill in the outlines. Leave to dry for two to three hours; longer if possible.

13. Carefully slide fondant plate from waxed paper and plate. With *No. 1 nozzle*, pipe squiggles on plate, as shown. Add a drop of blue to remaining icing, and with *No. 3 nozzle*, pipe continuous dots round plate edge.

14. Paint knife and fork with silver. Secure plate on cake with a dab of icing. Carefully transfer tomato to plate, taking care not to squash it, or the surface will crack. Secure with a dab of icing.

Cakes for Special Occasions

Midsummer

There are many themes which would happily cover this subject – characters from Shakespeare's *A Midsummer Night's Dream*; or some crazy scene depicting Midsummer madness, Druids, and Stonehenge; but as midnight barbecues are a good way of celebrating I thought a charcoal grill would make an interesting design for a cake. Having sweet replicas of the real thing may cause slight confusion, particularly at the party's end when the alcohol has been flowing freely, but so much the better. You might even flavour the culinary fakes – banana kebabs, almond sausages, strawberry drumsticks.

The grill is made from a 230mm (9in) square cake. Ingredients and quantities for this are given on page 10 and the method for baking on pages 6 to 7. Instructions for making royal icing, marzipan, and fondant are given on pages 7 to 8. If you are making your own fondant, you may find it easier to make the 1.12kg (2½lb) in two batches, keeping each piece securely wrapped in cling film and in an airtight container until required.

The cake can be decorated in a day, after the covering of marzipan has been left to dry for 48 hours. It always helps when copying food in fondant to have some form of reference, either a good colour photograph from a magazine or cookery book, or the real thing.

Please read the General Notes on pages 6 to 9 before starting to decorate. Also read through the step-by-step instructions and check the ingredient and equipment lists.

Ingredients for fondant and royal icing

1.12kg (2½lb) icing sugar, plus 110g (4oz)
2½ egg whites, plus ½
5 tbsp liquid glucose
flavouring (optional)
Also: 560g (1¼lb) marzipan; warm sieved apricot jam; 50/50 mixture of cornflour and icing sugar in a dusting dredger; black, red, orange, yellow, blue, green, and silver food colouring.

Equipment

Mixing bowls; spoons; sieve; rolling pin; steel rule; sharp-pointed knife; lolly sticks (LS) as spacers; pastry brush; small paintbrush; greaseproof paper; *Ateco* (or equivalent) icing nozzles 3 and 4; stiff white card; waxed paper; adhesive tape; 300mm (12in) square silver cake board.

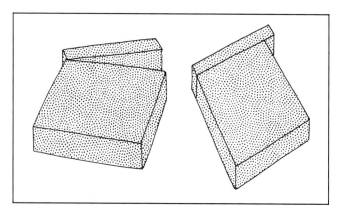

1. Slice the top of the cake flat, then turn the cake over. Cut a 25mm (1in) piece from one side and attach to the other, as shown, with jam and a sliver of marzipan. Trim off the excess.

2. Roll marzipan to 2 LS thick. Measure the sides of the cake, brush with jam, cut marzipan to fit, then apply. Measure top, brush with jam, cut marzipan to fit, then apply. Leave to dry for 48 hours.

3. Take 450g (1lb) of fondant. Break off two lumps. Partially mix red and orange into one. Add black to the other to make dark grey, then partially mix in more black to give streaky effect. Colour the remaining fondant grey.

4. Flatten the grey fondant to an oblong half the size of the cake. Dot with pieces of red and dark grey, as shown, then roll everything to 2 LS thick. Brush the cake top with a thin film of egg white, apply fondant, and neatly trim the edges.

5. Mix 220g (8oz) of fondant in with the trimmings and add a little red. Cover cake sides exactly as for marzipan, but using egg white instead of jam. Make the royal icing.

6. Using a ruler and sharp knife, mark the grid on the charcoal surface. Mark the lines at 13mm (½in) intervals. With No. 4 nozzle and black icing, pipe along the scored lines.

7. Roll fondant trimmings to 2 LS thick. Cut strips 10mm (³/₈in) wide to fit around edge of cake. Secure them in position with egg white. Roll pieces of white fondant, 1 LS thick, to fit each corner – pieces should be about 20mm (⁷/₈in) wide. Attach with egg white and trim inside corners.

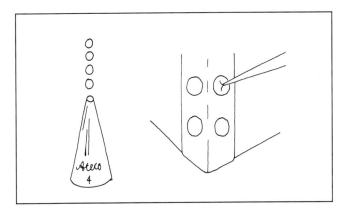

8. With No. 4 nozzle and white icing, pipe screw heads on the corner pieces. (As each head is piped, gently push the point of the icing back into the blob with the end of a wet knife – this gives a perfectly round and smooth surface.)

9. Take about 150g (5oz) of fondant, add yellow, brown, and blue, a little at a time, until meat colour is reached. Form a roll and cut into thirteen rough pieces. Make the texture by using a sawing motion with knife when cutting off the smooth surface. Paint brown on the meat to accentuate grain.

10. Add red to trimmings. Flatten and cut into five pieces, as shown. Bend slightly. Add green to some white fondant and make four pieces of green pepper, as you did with the red.

11. Push meat and peppers together, securing with egg white. Pierce both ends of each row with a skewer. Leave on a dusted surface overnight.

12. Draw the skewer pieces on to stiff card, then tape waxed paper over the drawings. With *No. 3 nozzle* and white icing, pipe the lines 40mm (1½in) long, trailing to make a point at the end. Pipe the lines with loops on the end, as shown. Leave to dry overnight.

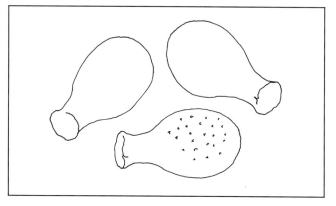

13. Take about 150g (5oz) of fondant. Colour with a little yellow and brown to make a creamy fawn. Divide into three, and model the drumsticks, as shown. Make the textured skin by rolling a nutmeg grater over the surface.

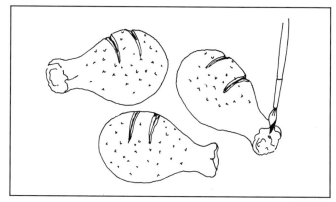

14. Make the grill marks with the paintbrush handle. Paint the joint area roughly with brown. Mix yellow with a little brown and paint areas of the drumsticks. Paint brown in the grill marks, and uneven spots of brown all over the surface. Leave to dry.

15. Add a little brown and red to the remaining white fondant. Divide into three and roll smooth sausages. Bend them slightly. Make grill marks with paintbrush handle.

16. Mix red and a little brown and brush areas of the sausages. Paint grill marks with brown. Leave to dry for thirty minutes, then split one of the sausages and pull apart carefully. Leave to dry overnight.

17. Paint the corners of the barbecue pan silver. Paint the skewer pieces while they are still on the waxed paper. When dry, carefully peel off the waxed paper. Pipe icing into the holes in the pieces of meat, then carefully push in the skewers.

18. Paint the grill (not entirely, to give the appearance of being charred) with silver. Position the food. Leave loose, or secure with neat blobs of icing.

Twenty-first birthday

Although eighteen is now usually considered the age of majority, twenty-one will, I believe, always be an important birthday. The figures on the cake depict four stages: the one-year-old potty training; the over-energetic, ever dirty seven-year-old; the 'try anything and everything' fourteen-year-old – if this bears no resemblance at all to your own child, you could remove the (illegal) beer and cigarette, but keep the spots; and the grown-up, confident, very sensible twenty-one-year-old.

This cake is obviously for a boy, but the figures can easily be changed. Directions are given in stage 19.

The structure is made from a 300mm (12in) square cake. Ingredients and quantities for this are given on page 10 and the method for baking on pages 6 to 7. Instructions for making royal icing, marzipan, and fondant are on pages 7 to 8. If you are making your own fondant, you will find it easier to make the 2kg (4½lb) in four batches, keeping each piece securely wrapped in cling film and in an airtight container until required.

The cake will take one to two days to decorate, after the covering of marzipan has been left for dry for 48 hours.

Please read the General Notes on pages 6 to 9 before starting to decorate. Also read through the step-by-step instructions and check the ingredient and equipment lists.

Ingredients for fondant and royal icing

2kg (4½lb) icing sugar, plus 170g (6oz)
4½ egg whites, plus ¾
9 tbsp liquid glucose
flavouring (optional)
Also: 1.34kg (3lb) marzipan; warm sieved apricot jam; 50/50 mixture of icing sugar and cornflour in a dusting dredger; yellow, red, flesh, blue, black, brown, and gold food colouring.

Equipment

Mixing bowls; spoons; sieve; rolling pin; steel rule; sharp-pointed knife; lolly sticks (LS) as spacers; pastry brush; small paintbrush; greaseproof paper; *Ateco* (or equivalent) icing nozzles 1, 2, and 4; 50mm (2in) round cutter; coloured-headed sewing pins; 21 candles and candle-holders; sewing needle; 300mm (12in) square silver cake board.

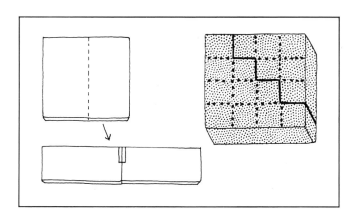

1. Cut the cake board in half using a serrated bread knife or saw. Put the two pieces together and stick a piece of tape over the join, underneath and halfway across the top. Slice the top of the cake flat, then mark with the pins into sixteen 75mm (3in) squares. Cut carefully.

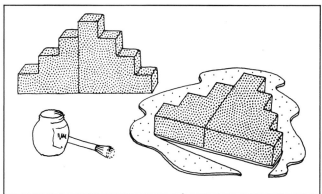

2. Join the cake together with jam and a slice of marzipan 1 LS thick. Brush back of cake with jam. Roll marzipan to 1 LS thick, lay cake on top, and cut around the shape. Carefully lift and repeat with front, then each step, using marzipan at 2 LS thick. Leave to dry for 48 hours.

The ages depicted here are, I feel, fairly typical and certainly add humour to the theme of the cake; but if the slouching fourteen-year-old seems to be going too far for your own child you can remove the cigarette and beer (not least on legal grounds!) – but keep the spots!

84

3. Brush the back of the cake with a thin film of egg white. Roll 670g (1½lb) of white fondant (upon a generously dusted surface) to 1 LS thick and roughly to the shape of the cake. Lay cake on fondant and cut round.

4. Take 110g (4oz) of white fondant trimmings, add a little yellow, and roll to 2 LS thick. Cover the outer squares, securing with egg white. Add remaining white trimmings to yellow trimmings and add more yellow colouring. Roll to 2 LS thick and cover next two panels as shown.

5. Add 220g (8oz) of fondant to trimmings and more yellow colouring. Cover the next two panels. Add 170g (6oz) fondant to trimmings, add yellow and drops of red to make bright orange, then cover centre panel.

6. Take 450g (1lb) of white fondant. Measure each step in turn, roll fondant to 2 LS thick, cut to fit, then apply. Start at the bottom of each side, covering top step last. Roll 110g (4oz) of white fondant to 1 LS thick and cut four 50mm (2in) circles. Leave them to dry on a dusted surface.

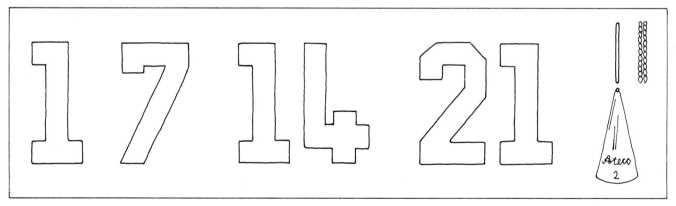

7. Make the royal icing. Draw four 50mm (2in) circles on greaseproof paper, then trace 21, 14, 7, and 1 in each. Attach paper circles, with two dabs of icing, to fondant circles, then prick through the pencil lines with the needle. With *No. 2 nozzle* and orange icing, follow the needle marks.

8. Add drops of water to some orange icing and, using a skewer or small spoon, fill in the numbers. Leave to dry for two hours. With *No. 2 nozzle* and orange icing, pipe lines of continuous dots on panel seams, then pipe lines of white continuous dots inside the orange ones.

9. Secure the circles to the appropriate panels with egg white. Pipe orange continuous dots around each circle, then two more around **21**. With *No. 1 nozzle* and orange icing, pipe squiggly lines all over the centre panel. When dry, paint these and the lines around **21** gold.

10. Carefully lift the cake and secure it to the silver cake board with smears of icing. With *No. 4 nozzle* and white icing, pipe a line of continuous dots along the front and back of the bottom edge. Take 110g (4oz) of fondant. Colour 90g (3oz) with flesh and the remainder blue.

11. Model a handle and potty, as shown. Attach the handle with egg white and support with two lolly sticks until dry. Secure the potty to the lowest step with a blob of icing. Model the pieces, legs first, and attach with egg white; then the body and arms, as shown. Model the head.

12. Flatten two little white balls, and attach as shown. Paint the eyes, then attach the head to the body. Mark fingers, toes, and mouth with a knife, and a navel with the paintbrush handle. With about 45g (1½oz) of flesh fondant, model legs, hands, and head for next figure. Attach and paint eyes.

13. Mark a mouth. Model brown short trousers and attach to legs. Model and attach brown shoes. Model green body, bend slightly, then attach to trousers and step. Model arms, attach, then secure hands. Paint freckles across nose, and dirt (watered-down black) on cheeks and chin. Attach head to body and side of step.

14. Roll a tiny piece of white fondant to cigarette shape and leave it to dry. Colour about 60g (2oz) of fondant brown. Model and attach legs for fourteen-year-old. Model black shoes and attach, supporting until secure. Colour about 90g (3oz) of fondant blue. Model and attach body, slouching, and arms.

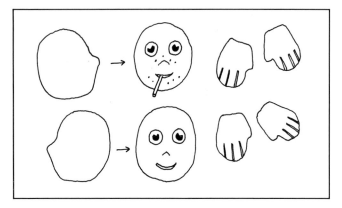

15. Colour about 60g (2oz) of fondant flesh. Model two heads and four hands. Mark fingers and mouths with knife. Attach and paint eyes. Push cigarette carefully into the corner of the mouth, then paint red spots on chin and nose. Attach this head to the blue body.

16. Colour about 60g (2oz) of fondant black. Model and attach legs, as shown. Model and attach dark-brown shoes, supporting the left-hand one until secure. Model and attach glass of beer.

17. With about 75g (2½oz) of white fondant, model and attach body, collar, and arms. Attach head and hands. Model and attach a black bow tie.

18. With *No. 1 nozzle* and appropriately coloured icing, pipe the hair: a little for baby; slightly dishevelled for seven-year-old; long and unkempt for fourteen-year-old; and fairly neat for 'birthday boy'. Pipe a moustache if appropriate. Insert candle-holders and candles – eight on the first two steps and five on the third.

19. Figures for a girl: the baby remains the same. Model a little skirt, as shown, for next figure. Colour fondant for body and sleeves pale green. I would suggest keeping the cigarette for the fourteen-year-old (children usually try it at about this age), and the spots, but change the large beer glass to a smaller one and pipe longer hair. Model a skirt and legs, as shown. You could paint red lips and green eye-shadow to indicate first experiments with make-up. For the last figure, model dress, then legs, then arms in one piece, then neck. Pipe straps and lace on bodice, then the necklace and bracelet. Paint these and shoes gold.

Office party

Christmas is usually the time for office parties, but there may be other reasons (or excuses) for revelry – the retirement of a staff member, centenary celebrations of the company, etc. As soon as my publisher saw this cake, she said, 'It suggests a debauch!' Which is true, but then some office parties tend to go that way! The success of the cake depends on how realistic the objects are, so it helps to have the real thing in front of you while modelling. If you want to leave the objects on the tray loose, rather than securing them with icing, they can be given away as mementos at the end of the party.

The tray is made from two 200mm (8in) square cakes. Ingredients and quantities for these are given on page 10 and the method for baking is on pages 6 to 7. Instructions for making royal icing, marzipan, and fondant are on pages 7 to 8. If you are making your own fondant, it will be easier to make the 1.45kg (3¼lb) in two or three batches, keeping it securely wrapped in cling film and in an airtight container until required.

The cake can be decorated in two days, after the covering of marzipan has been left to dry for 48 hours. Please read the General Notes on pages 6 to 9 before starting to decorate. Also read through the step-by-step instructions and check the ingredient and equipment lists.

Ingredients for fondant and royal icing

1.45kg (3¼lb) icing sugar, plus 60g (2oz)
3¼ egg whites, plus ¼
6½ tbsp liquid glucose
flavouring (optional)
Also: 1kg (2¼lb) marzipan; warm sieved apricot jam; 50/50 mixture of cornflour and icing sugar in a dusting dredger; red, green, yellow, black, gold, and silver food colouring.

Equipment

Mixing bowls; spoons; sieve; rolling pin; steel rule; sharp-pointed knife; lolly sticks (LS) as spacers; pastry brush; small paintbrush; greaseproof paper; *Ateco* (or equivalent) icing nozzle No. 3; two 250mm (10in) square silver cake boards; adhesive tape; tin foil; waxed paper. To use as reference: bottle cork, ring pull, and bottle cap.

1. Cut one of the cake boards down to 100mm (4in) and then join it to the other with tape – the board will cut quite easily with a serrated bread knife. Cover the joined board neatly with tin foil.

2. Slice the tops of the cakes flat and cut one in half. Attach one of the halves, with jam and marzipan, to the whole cake. Cut the remaining half into four strips as shown.

3. Cut the strips so that they fit on three sides of the cake. Remove them and trim, so that they are not quite as deep as the cake. Cut a slope from the main cake as shown, then trim the ends of the two longest strips to fit.

4. Measure front, top, and back of cake, then brush with jam. Roll marzipan to 2 LS thick, cut to fit, and apply with the help of the rolling pin. Trim edges. Attach longest strips of cake with jam, then cover insides and tops, as shown.

5. Cover three sides of the back strip of cake and position, securing with jam. Cut pieces of marzipan for both ends of the long strips of cake. Apply as before.

6. Carefully turn the cake on its side and cover, as shown. Repeat with the other side. Leave the marzipan to dry for 48 hours.

7. Meanwhile, take a little fondant, colour it green, and roll to 1 LS thick. Cut an oblong 45mm (1¾in) deep and 90mm (3½in) wide. Cut the corners off. Leave to dry on a dusted surface.

8. Colour 1kg (2¼lb) of fondant red. Cover the cake exactly as with marzipan in stages 4, 5, and 6, but using egg white instead of jam. Stand the cake on waxed paper when covering the last side. Position the cake on the silver cake board.

9. Make the 60g (2oz) of royal icing and colour it red. Pipe a line of continuous dots along the outer edge seams of fondant. Pipe **IN TRAY** and two screw heads on the green plaque.

10. To make the corks, colour about 280g (10oz) of fondant with yellow, red, and a little black – refer to a real cork. Model ten straight, four capped, and two champagne, as shown. Leave to dry for three hours.

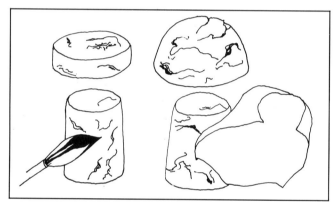

11. Pierce the tops of four straight corks with the pointed knife to resemble hole made by corkscrew. Mark irregular straight lines on tops of remaining straight corks, as shown.

12. Using black and a little red colouring, fill in the surface cracks on the champagne and capped corks, brush over the surface with colour, then wipe away excess with a slightly damp cloth. Leave the pieces to dry for an hour, then assemble with egg white.

13. Paint straight corks lightly with black and a mixture of red, yellow, and black. The result should not be as detailed as other corks. Fill in the irregular lines on the tops. Leave to dry, then paint numbers (with the mixed colour) on the sides of four corks, as shown.

14. Generously dust and knead some white fondant. Flatten a small piece with fingers, dust the working surface, lay the ring pull on the fondant and carefully cut round. Curl flap up slightly. Continue until seven have been made. Leave to dry.

15. Flatten two circles of fondant with fingers, as shown, and attach to champagne corks with egg white. Roll remaining fondant into balls, roughly the size shown. Flatten into circles 6mm (just less than ¼in) thick, then mark edges with round edge of a dinner knife.

16. To make the cigarettes, colour some fondant with yellow, red, and a little black – use a real cigarette for reference if possible. Make a perfectly smooth roll 25mm (1in) long. Cut both ends straight. Make five in all.

17. Make five white rolls, exactly the same, but different lengths. Carefully stick white and brown rolls together with egg white. Leave to dry for about ten minutes. Using fingernails, pinch ends of cigarettes to make rough surface.

18. Paint a strong black line between rough and smooth surfaces, as shown. Using watered black, paint areas of the rough surfaces, leaving some white. Mix red, yellow, and a little black, add water, then paint brown area coming away from the black line.

19. Paint three lines of fake lettering on white part of cigarette as shown. Paint the bottle tops gold. Paint the ring pulls, screw heads on plaque, and tops of champagne corks all silver.

20. (Additional ring pulls and bottle tops can be made with red fondant trimmings; the colour will not show through the gold and silver.) Attach plaque to front of tray with dabs of icing. Position pieces in tray, leave loose, or secure with dabs of red icing.

Retirement

Retirement used to be synonymous with quiet contentment: slippers, feet up, pottering in the garden, knitting by the fire, reading, and other gentle pursuits. Now, health (and funds) permitting, it usually denotes the onset of a life full of activity and new challenges. As water sports have become so popular, I have used this theme to suggest freedom and adventure.

The sea is made from a 200mm (8in) round cake. The ingredients and quantities for this are given on page 10 and the method for baking on pages 6 to 7. Instructions for making royal icing, marzipan, and fondant are given on pages 7 to 8. If you make your own fondant, you may find it easier to make the 670g (1½lb) in two batches, keeping each securely wrapped in cling film and in an airtight container until required.

The cake design is simple. It can be decorated in a day, after the covering of marzipan and the sail have been left to dry for 48 hours. The wave effect around the cake is made by laying three colours (blue, white, and mauve) together and pushing one colour into the other at intervals with the fingers. The fondant is then rolled out flat.

Please read the General Notes on pages 6 to 9 before starting to decorate. Also read through the step-by-step instructions and check the ingredient and equipment lists.

Ingredients for fondant and royal icing

670g (1½lb) icing sugar, plus 60g (2oz)
1½ egg whites, plus ¼
3 tbsp liquid glucose
flavouring (optional)
Also: 450g (1lb) marzipan; warm sieved apricot jam; 50/50 mixture of cornflour and icing sugar in a dusting dredger; blue, mauve, flesh, and gold food colouring.

Equipment

Mixing bowls; spoons; sieve; rolling pin; steel rule; sharp-pointed knife; lolly sticks (LS) as spacers; pastry brush; small paintbrush; greaseproof paper; *Ateco* (or equivalent) icing nozzles 1, 2, and 4; waxed paper; 250mm (10in) round silver cake board.

1. Slice the top of the cake flat and turn the cake over. Measure depth and circumference. Roll marzipan to 2 LS thick, then cut a strip to fit round the sides. Brush sides with jam and roll the cake along the strip, as shown.

2. Brush the cake top with jam. Roll marzipan to 2 LS thick, lay the cake on it, then cut round, as shown. Leave to dry for 48 hours. Meanwhile, mix the royal icing and make the sail.

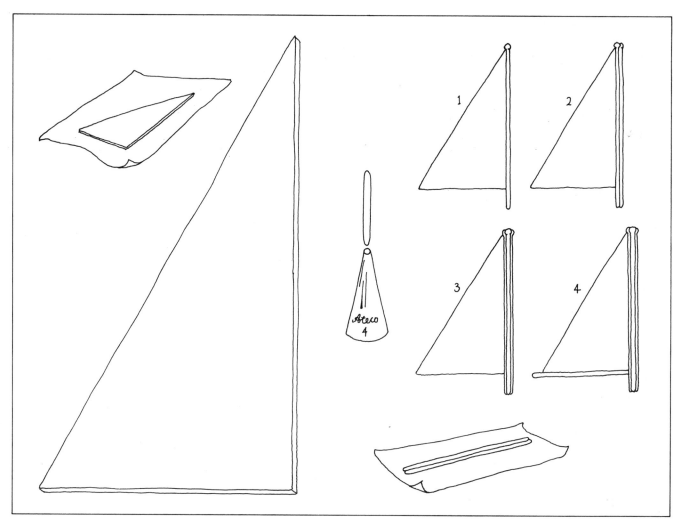

3. Take 60g (2oz) of fondant and roll to 1 LS thick. Cut the sail: horizontal side 75mm (3in) and vertical side 125mm (5in). Lay it carefully on a piece of waxed paper.

4. With *No. 4 nozzle*, pipe lines as shown in the diagram – three lines on vertical side, ending in three blobs at the top and one line along the base. On another piece of waxed paper, pipe a double line 135mm (5¼in) long. Leave sail, and support it to dry on a flat surface.

5. Take 450g (1lb) of fondant. Colour 170g (6oz) blue and 170g (6oz) mauve, and leave the remainder white. Take just over half of each piece, roll lightly together as described on previous page, then roll to 2 LS thick and cut a piece to fit around cake. Secure with a thin film of egg white.

6. Lightly mix trimmings with remaining colours. Roll to 2 LS thick. Brush a thin film of egg white on cake top, lay fondant on, and neatly trim the edges. Secure cake to silver board with a smear of icing.

7. Add 90g (3oz) of fondant to trimmings from sail. Make a roll roughly 150mm (6in) long, then form it into a boat shape, as shown. Push finger into end to make a hollow about 50mm (2in) long. Position boat on cake, securing with egg white.

8. Tip the front of the cake board up and slide a tin or jar underneath. With *No. 2 nozzle* and white icing, pipe two parallel lines along side of boat. Repeat with other side and back. Pipe two lines across front of boat and a line round indented area.

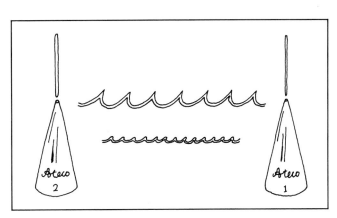

9. With the same nozzle, pipe two wavy lines around top of cake. With *No. 1 nozzle*, follow the top wavy line. Pipe squiggles, as shown on the photograph, along the sides of the boat to suggest foam.

10. Roll some blue trimmings to 1 LS thick. Cut a strip, slightly curved, 20mm (³⁄₄in) deep and 150mm (6in) long. With *No. 2 nozzle*, pipe **HAPPY RETIREMENT** or an appropriate message. Pipe little waves above the lettering. With *No. 1 nozzle*, pipe a chain round the edge of the fondant. Paint the sail-supports gold.

11. Using a skewer or knitting needle, carefully make a slanting hole at the front of the boat, then one in the centre 75mm (3in) from the front. Carefully push sail in centre hole, allowing it to rest on boat side. Push double line in to rest on sail. With *No. 2 nozzle*, pipe two circles around base of poles.

12. Pipe three blobs at top of double line. Pipe three lines at both sides of centre circles and two lines from end of the sail to back of boat. When dry, paint all lines gold. Model the figure pieces as shown, then assemble in boat with egg white. Paint eyes. Pipe necktie with *No. 2 nozzle*.

Cornucopia –
Harvest Festival/Thanksgiving

The Cornucopia, or Horn of Plenty, was originally part of Greek mythology – Amelthea, one of the daughters of the Cretan king, once fed the infant Zeus with goat's milk. In gratitude Zeus gave her the goat's horn and promised that whoever possessed it would have everything in abundance that he or she desired. We have adopted the symbol and use it to represent the rich collection of produce gathered at harvest time.

The base and horn are made from a 200mm (8in) square cake and a 180mm (7in) round cake. Ingredients and quantities for these are given on page 10 and the method of baking on pages 6 to 7. Instructions for making royal icing, marzipan, and fondant are on pages 7 to 8. If you are making your own fondant, you may find it easier to make the 1.12kg (2½lb) in two batches, keeping each piece securely wrapped in cling film and in an airtight container until required.

The cake will take one to two days to decorate, after the covering of marzipan has been left to dry for 48 hours. It always helps when copying food in fondant to have some form of reference, either a good colour photograph from a magazine or cookery book, or the real thing.

Please read the General Notes on pages 6 to 9 before starting to decorate. Also read through the step-by-step instructions and check the ingredient and equipment lists.

Ingredients for fondant and royal icing

1.12kg (2½lb) icing sugar, plus 110g (4oz)
2½ egg whites, plus ½
5 tbsp liquid glucose
flavouring (optional)
Also: 800g (1¾lb) marzipan; warm sieved apricot jam; 50/50 mixture of cornflour and icing sugar in a dusting dredger; yellow, black, red, green, brown, and blue food colouring.

Equipment

Mixing bowls; spoons; sieve; rolling pin; steel rule; sharp-pointed knife; lolly sticks (LS) as spacers; pastry brush; small paintbrush; greaseproof paper; *Ateco* (or equivalent) icing nozzles 2 and 4; stiff card; adhesive tape; waxed paper; smooth metal skewer or knitting needle; nutmeg grater; 280mm (11in) square silver cake board.

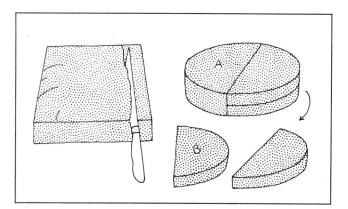

1. Slice the top of the cakes flat. Turn the square one over and cut the round one in half. Slice one of the halves in half, as shown (only one of these will be required).

2. Brush the top of **A** and the under-side of **B** with jam. Stick them together with a sliver of marzipan in between.

3. Trace the above shape on to card and use it as a guide. Position it 75mm (3in) along from the corner of the semicircular cake, as shown, and cut carefully around. Trim a little bit of cake from the square corners of the top and under-side, so that the edges are rounded.

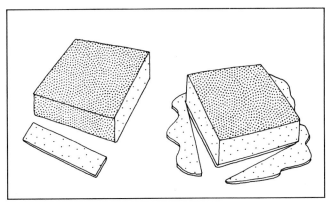

4. Measure the sides of the square cake. Brush with jam, then roll marzipan to 2 LS thick. Cut to size, then apply. Roll marzipan to 2 LS thick, brush cake top with jam, lay it on the marzipan and cut round the edges as shown.

5. Roll marzipan to 2 LS thick. Brush top of horn with jam and cut marzipan to fit. Measure the front and back of horn, brush with jam, and apply marzipan, smoothing over the joins with your hands. Cover the ends as with top of square cake. Leave both cakes to dry for 48 hours.

6. Meanwhile, make the fruits. The six apples, six tomatoes, and two bunches of grapes are made from just under 220g (8oz) of fondant. Use about 22g (³/₄oz) for each apple and colour two of them pale green and four a darker green. Roll to a smooth ball, indent centre with thumb, then pierce with skewer as shown.

7. When the dark apples are dry, paint areas of streaky red. Colour 30g (1oz) of fondant red, roll the tomatoes, then indent and pierce the centres. Colour 30g (1oz) of fondant dark brown. Roll a thin piece and cut into stalks. Leave until dry, then brush ends with egg white and push into apples.

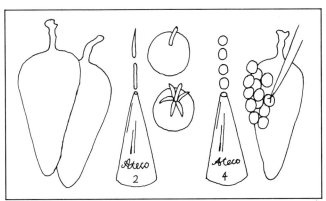

8. Model the remaining brown into two bunches of grapes, with stalks, as shown. With *No. 2 nozzle*, pipe green stalks in tomato holes, then leaves. Lay grape bunches on waxed paper. With *No. 4* and purple (red and blue mixed) icing, pipe the grapes. As each grape is piped, push point of icing back into blob with a wet knife.

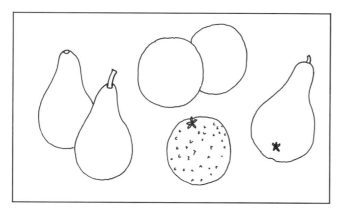

9. Model three pears yellowy-green, and pierce tops as before. Roll stalks and attach when dry. With just over 60g (2oz) of fondant, model three oranges. Roll each one over nutmeg grater. With *No. 2 nozzle*, pipe brown calyx on each orange and on under-side of one pear.

10. Colour 30g (1oz) of fondant bright orange and model seven carrots. Mark horizontal lines across each with a sharp knife. Lay them on waxed paper and, with *No. 2 nozzle* and green icing, pipe stalks 20mm (³⁄₄in) long, ending with rough foliage. Push nozzle down, then up, to form little peaks.

11. Colour a little fondant green and make bumpy rolls for beans, pointed at one end and flat at the top. With *No. 2 nozzle*, pipe stems. Colour 15g (¹⁄₂oz) of fondant yellow. Roll four corn-cob shapes. Place on waxed paper and, with *No. 2 nozzle* and fairly stiff yellow icing, pipe lines of corn.

12. Colour 670g (1½lb) of fondant pale yellow. Cover the square cake exactly as for marzipan (stage 4), but using egg white instead of jam. Add 220g (8oz) to trimmings, then partially mix in a little black to give a streaky appearance. Cover the top, front, back, and narrow end of horn exactly as for marzipan.

13. Add more black to a piece of fondant and cover large end of horn. Form the remaining fondant into rolls and attach to horn with egg white. Mark grooves with a knife handle.

14. Trace the drawing above on to greaseproof paper. Prick through pencil lines with a sewing needle on to the cake sides – five on each side at 20mm (¾in) intervals. With *No. 2 nozzle* and pale-yellow icing, pipe the corn. Pipe continuous dots along top and bottom edges and down each corner of cake.

15. Position the horn on the cake, securing it with neat blobs of icing. Carefully position the fruit and vegetables, again securing with dabs of icing.

Christening

This cake was originally made to commemorate the birth of Prince Harry. I have not included the Union Jack backdrop in the instructions, so your cot will simply stand in the centre of the base cake. You can replace the crown on the cushion with a gold or silver rattle. The crown on the side of the cot can be replaced by a small plaque with the child's name. If the child is a girl, pink colouring can be used instead of blue. Do make sure that the gold or silver is the edible type of food colouring, unless you wish to keep the rattle, cushion, and plaque as mementos.

The cot is made from a 200mm (8in) square cake and the base from a 250mm (10in) square. Ingredients and quantities for these are given on page 10 and the method for baking on pages 6 to 7. Instructions for making royal icing, marzipan, and fondant are given on pages 7 to 8. If you are making your own fondant, you may find it easier to make the 1.57kg (3½lb) in two or three batches, keeping it securely wrapped in cling film and in an airtight container.

The cake will take two or three days to decorate, after the covering of marzipan has been left to dry for 48 hours.

Please read the General Notes on pages 6 to 9 before starting to decorate. Also read the step-by-step instructions and check the ingredient and equipment lists.

Ingredients for fondant and royal icing

1.57kg (3½lb) icing sugar, plus 220g (8oz)
3½ egg whites, plus 1
7 tbsp liquid glucose
flavouring (optional)
Also: 1.12kg (2½lb) marzipan; warm sieved apricot jam; 50/50 mixture of cornflour and icing sugar in a dusting dredger; food colouring – royal and turquoise blues or rose and salmon pinks, flesh, brown, and gold or silver; edible silver balls.

Equipment

Mixing bowls; spoons; sieve; rolling pin; steel rule; sharp-pointed knife; lolly sticks (LS) as spacers; pastry brush; small paintbrush; 'spade' cocktail cutter; greaseproof paper; *Ateco* (or equivalent) icing nozzles 1, 2, 3, and 13; 360mm (14in) square silver cake board.

1. Cut the smaller cake in half, then sandwich together with jam and marzipan. Shape the bottom half as shown, cutting a slope in about 10mm (⅜in), then out again. Measure 10mm (⅜in) in from each edge on the top and scoop out an oblong about 20mm (¾in) deep.

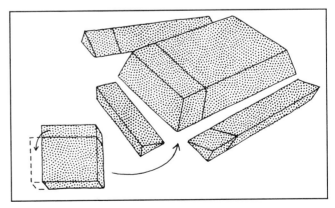

2. Cut a 50mm (2in) strip from the larger cake. Attach the strip, using jam and marzipan, to one of the short sides and trim to make an oblong 200 x 300mm (8 x 12in). Measure 10mm (⅜in) in from each of the four top edges and cut slopes, as shown.

3. Measure the cot sides, then brush with the warm sieved jam. Roll marzipan to 2 LS thick and cut to fit, each side in two pieces, as shown. Line the inside and top with marzipan 1 LS thick.

4. Brush the sides of the base cake with jam. Roll the marzipan to 2 LS thick, cut to fit, then apply. Repeat for top of cake. Leave base and top to dry for 48 hours.

5. Meanwhile, make a support for the cot hood – cut a strip of card 75mm (3in) wide and 140mm (5½in) long. Cut another one 75mm (3in) wide and 240mm (9in) long. Bend the longest card so that it fits across the width of the cot, then staple or tape the bent card to the straight piece, as shown.

6. Take 670g (1½lb) of fondant and colour pale turquoise/ rose pink. Roll a piece for the cot hood to 2 LS thick. (Wrap the remainder in cling film and place in an airtight container.)

7. Lay the card hood on its back, on the fondant, and cut round – this will be the hood back. Leave to dry on a dusted surface. Cut fondant to fit over the card, dust card liberally, then carefully lay fondant on top. Leave the hood to dry with the marzipanned cakes.

8. Cover the cot with the turquoise/rose fondant, as with marzipan (stage 4), but using egg white to secure instead of jam. Do not cover flat bottom of inside cot.

9. Add a drop of flesh to a little white fondant and model baby's head, as shown. Paint eyes and lips. Use watered-down pink for rosy cheeks. Make a little white shawl, as shown, and position around head. Model the pale-royal-blue/salmon pillow and position in the cot. Place baby's head on pillow, securing with egg white.

10. Model body shape, as shown, then position in cot. Model royal-blue/deep-rose cushion and white rattle, as shown. Pierce a hole in rattle ball with paintbrush handle and push rattle handle in, with a dab of egg white, when dry.

11. Roll some pale-royal-blue/salmon fondant to 1 LS thick and cut a blanket. Using point of *No. 1 nozzle*, make the pattern, as shown, then lay blanket over baby. Roll a piece of white fondant to 1 LS thick, curl one edge over paintbrush handle, then position as shown.

12. Colour some fondant brown and model little teddy bear, in pieces, as shown. Mark mouth with blunt edge of knife, and the eyes with paintbrush handle. Stick head to body with egg white, then position in corner of cot. Position legs and arms, securing with egg white.

13. Using blue/pink fondant trimmings, roll to 1 LS thick and cut into strips. Cut out shapes, as shown, with 'spade' cocktail cutter. Attach to bottom edge of cot with egg white. Using same fondant 1 LS thick, cut plaque for baby's name.

14. Cover base cake with white fondant, exactly as for marzipan (stage 5), but using a thin film of egg white to secure side pieces instead of jam. Position on silver board.

15. While hood is still on card support, attach frills. Roll white fondant to 1 LS thick. Cut into strips 20mm (³⁄₄in) wide and roughly same length as hood. Nip along each strip with thumb and forefinger to make the fondant thinner. Paint a line of egg white along hood, as shown. Make gathers while attaching strip.

16. Pull gathers out with paintbrush handle, as shown. Work up to hood top, then repeat with other side and back. Stick narrow strips of soft fondant on to cot edge, then very carefully remove card support and position hood. Make frill to go round cot (in pieces). Attach as before, trimming away excess fondant at top edge.

17. With *No. 13 nozzle* and blue/pink icing, pipe around edge and inside of hood, then continue around top of cot frill. Pipe three lines on top of hood, dropping silver balls on to middle line whilst icing is still wet. Pipe down corner seams of cot.

18. With *No. 1 nozzle* and white icing, pipe braid and tassels on cushion, tassels over cot frill, name of child on plaque, and decoration, as shown, on plaque and rattle. When the icing has dried, paint with gold or silver. Also paint rattle handle.

19. With *No. 2 nozzle* and alternate pale- and dark-blue/pink icing, pipe lines of continuous dots down sides of base cake, at 10mm (³⁄₈in) intervals. With *No. 3 nozzle*, pipe dark blue/pink around bottom, and white around top edge.

20. Position cot, at an angle, on the base cake and then cushion with rattle at the side. Attach plaque to the side of the cot with a dab of icing.

Teenage party

This cake is for those parents who are brave enough to arrange a teenage party and extend a warm welcome to the friends of their teenage offspring.

The house is made from three 150mm (6in) square cakes. Ingredients are given on page 10 and the method for baking on pages 6 to 7. Instructions for making royal icing, marzipan, and fondant are on pages 7 to 8. If you make your own fondant, it will be easier to make the 1.12kg (2½lb) in two batches, keeping each securely wrapped in cling film in an airtight container until required.

The cake will take one to two days to decorate, after the marzipan has been left to dry for 48 hours.

Please read the General Notes on pages 6 to 9 before starting to decorate. Also read through the step-by-step instructions and check the ingredient and equipment lists.

Ingredients for fondant and royal icing

1.12kg (2½lb) icing sugar, plus 110g (4oz)
2½ egg whites, plus ½
5 tbsp liquid glucose
flavouring (optional)
Also: 1.12kg (2½lb) marzipan; warm sieved apricot jam; 50/50 mixture of cornflour and icing sugar in a dusting dredger; bright red, brown, yellow, blue, and flesh food colouring.

Equipment

Mixing bowls; spoons; sieve; rolling pin; steel rule; sharp-pointed knife; lolly sticks (LS) as spacers; pastry brush; small paintbrush; greaseproof paper; *Ateco* (or equivalent) icing nozzles 1, 2, 13, and 65; 200mm (10in) square silver cake board.

1. Slice the tops of the cakes flat. Brush the top of one and the under-side of another with jam, then sandwich them together with a piece of marzipan 1 LS thick. Divide the roof (third cake) into six sections, marking with coloured-headed pins, as shown.

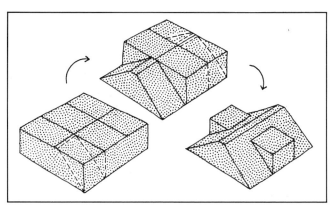

2. Leaving a narrow ridge on top of the roof, cut the four sloping sides, as shown. Continue the slope down a little way on the two centre pieces, then slice flat for the top of the dormer window, as shown. (If bits of the cake have broken off, try to stick them back on or fill the holes with marzipan.)

3. Keep one of the cut-away slopes and cut into a wedge – this will help to support the roof. Roll the marzipan to 2 LS thick, brush sides of house with jam, lay it on the marzipan, then cut to fit. Continue until all sides and top are covered.

4. Apply marzipan to all roof surfaces, including under-side. Cover the wedge with marzipan 1 LS thick. Leave everything to dry for 48 hours. Take 900g (2lb) of fondant, break off about 75g (2½oz), colour it yellow, then cover and put to one side. Colour remaining fondant brick (bright red and brown).

5. Cover the house as with marzipan (stage 3), but using egg white instead of jam. Mark each wall with bricks directly after application – I used a long sharp knife for the horizontal lines and an artist's palette knife for the vertical lines. Position the house on the silver board.

6. Cover the under-side of the roof, then gable ends, then the sides of the dormer windows, marking bricks as before. Cover wedge with fondant 1 LS thick. Roll the yellow fondant to 1 LS thick; cut windows of varying sizes, and a door shape. Attach with egg white.

7. Add brown to remaining yellow fondant, roll to 2 LS thick, and cut a door. Leave to dry on a dusted surface. Model a chimney with remaining brick fondant. Mark bricks and paint brown circle on top. Leave to dry. Take about 110g (4oz) of fondant and colour blue.

8. Roll to 1 LS thick and cut two pieces to fit roofs of dormer windows. Indent lines with blunt edge of knife, then attach roofs with egg white. Cut strips 20mm (¾in) wide, mark lines, and, starting from bottom, attach to roof, each strip overlapping half of the previous one. Complete both sides of roof, stopping at top ridge.

9. Attach chimney with egg white. Roll a piece of blue fondant for roof ridge and attach. Make the 110g (4oz) of royal icing. Roll some blue fondant to 1 LS thick, cut to fit two sides of the silver board. With *No. 1 nozzle* and yellow icing, pipe **IF YOU MUST RAISE THE ROOF – DO IT QUIETLY!!!**

10. With *No. 2 nozzle* and brown icing, pipe windows, door, and two lines on fondant seam round top of house. Pipe two climbers up the walls. Position door with a line of icing. With *No. 65 nozzle* and green icing, pipe small leaves on climbers and tall leaves up walls. With *No. 13 nozzle*, pipe pink flowers on climbers.

11. Brush under-side and top-side of the wedge with egg white, then position the roof. Colour some fondant flesh and some brown. Make sixty small balls and attach to the windows with egg white. Add the top half of a body to some – these should slope in at the bottom to show that the person is hanging out of the window.

12. Model six little bodies raising the roof. Five can lean against the roof support to hide it, and put one at the corner, as shown in the photograph. Model one more and position it just peeping round the door. Secure all with egg white.

13. With *No. 1 nozzle* and dark-brown, light-brown, and yellow icing, pipe hair on heads. Paint smiling lips and eyes. Carefully attach writing to silver board, using egg white and a line of icing to secure.

111

Christmas Eve

This is one of my favourite cakes. Having manoeuvred his way down the chimney and safely delivered the seasonal gifts, Father Christmas now finds himself stuck – the mince pies and sherry must have added a few inches to his waistline.

This is made from two 180mm (7in) square cakes. Ingredients for these are given on page 10 and method for baking on pages 6 to 7. Instructions for making royal icing and fondant are on pages 7 to 8. If you make your own fondant, it will be easier to make the 1.34kg (3lb) in three batches, keeping each securely wrapped in cling film in an airtight container until required.

The cake can be decorated in a day, but you may find it easier to do it in two days. Please read the General Notes on pages 6 to 9 before starting. Also read through the step-by-step instructions and check the ingredient and equipment lists.

Ingredients for fondant and royal icing

1.34kg (3lb) icing sugar, plus 30g (1oz)
3 egg whites, plus 1/8
6 tbsp liquid glucose
flavouring (optional)
Also: warm sieved apricot jam; 50/50 mixture of corn-flour and icing sugar in a dusting dredger; black, red, brown, green, yellow, and blue food colouring.

Equipment

Mixing bowls; sieve; spoons; rolling pin; steel rule; sharp-pointed knife; lolly sticks (LS) as spacers; pastry brush; 15mm (5/8in) round cutter; greaseproof paper for icing bags; *Ateco* (or equivalent) icing nozzle No. 1; small paintbrush; 250mm (10in) square silver cake board.

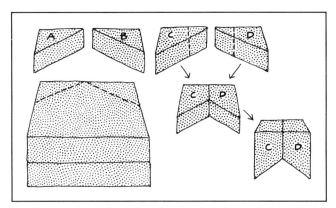

1. Having left the cakes overnight, slice the tops flat. Put one cake on top of the other, measure 90mm (3½in) up each side, and cut to top middle point, as shown. Take two of the remaining pieces and cut off 40mm (1½in), as shown (the larger pieces join to make the chimney).

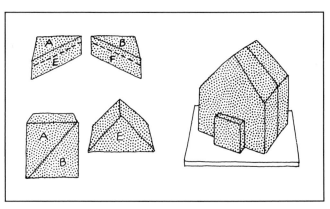

2. Slice a third from the two remaining pieces. The two shallow pieces will join to make porch (trim to make a 75mm (3in) square). One of the deep pieces will be porch roof. Sandwich main house and porch together with butter-cream. Position, at an angle, on silver cake board.

3. Make 900g (2lb) of fondant and colour grey. Measure house-back, then brush with jam. Roll fondant to 2 LS thick, cut to size, and carefully apply. Mark stones with blunt edge of knife. Repeat process of covering for both sides of porch, porch (in one piece), and gable end, marking stones after each application.

4. Cover base of porch roof with fondant 1 LS thick. Brush back and base with jam and position on top of porch. Roll fondant to 2 LS thick, cut to fit front porch roof, apply, and mark stones.

5. Measure dimensions of roofs then brush with jam. Roll fondant to 1 LS thick, cut to size, then carefully apply. Join chimney pieces together with jam and a layer of fondant. Leave to dry (overnight if possible).

6. Make the 30g (1oz) of royal icing. Measure sides of chimney, then brush with jam. Roll fondant to 2 LS thick, cut to fit, then apply. Stand chimney upside down and mark stones. Brush inside sponge with jam, then dab icing along inside join. Carefully position on roof.

7. Make 450g (1lb) of fondant. Brush top of chimney with jam. Take 110g (4oz) of fondant, flatten with hands, and apply to chimney, pushing it gently down sides. Colour some fondant pale yellow, roll to 1 LS thick, and cut three oblong windows roughly 45mm (1¾in) long and 30mm (1¼in) deep; and two round windows.

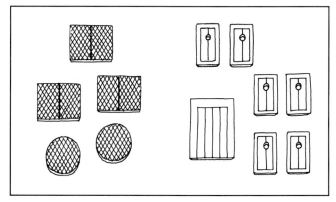

8. Paint brown leading on windows. Brush backs with egg white. Attach round windows to each side of porch and others to each wall of house. Roll some green fondant to 1 LS thick, cut a door and shutters for oblong windows, and mark grooves whilst still soft. Brush backs with egg white, then apply.

9. Make brown fondant, roll to 2 LS thick, and cut sills for windows (half circles for round ones) and surround for door. Brush with egg white and apply. Take white fondant, brush tops of windows with egg white, and attach snow.

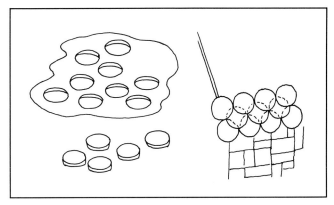

10. Take grey trimmings. Cut in two, and add green to half and blue with a little yellow to the other half. Roll to 1 LS thick and cut tiles about 15mm ($^5/_8$in) in diameter. Starting at bottom edge, apply with egg white to both roofs, stopping 20mm ($^3/_4$in) from top ridge.

11. Using soft white fondant, cover roof ridges and around base of house, as shown. Colour about 170g (6oz) of fondant red and some flesh, for hands and head. Model hands and head as shown. Stick hands to chimney and mark fingers with blunt edge of knife.

12. Model body and arms as shown. Position, with head, securing with dabs of egg white. Model a hood – a flat triangle – and attach to head. Roll some white fondant and attach around hood and sleeve edges.

13. Make a little pink nose and attach to face. Press two small white balls flat and attach to face, for eyes. Repeat with red fondant for mouth. Paint eyes with blue colouring, as shown.

14. With *No. 1 nozzle* and white icing, pipe beard and eyebrows. Pipe icicles hanging from some of roof tiles – press nozzle gently into tile, let some icing come, then pull sharply. With brown icing, pipe handles on door, windows, and shutters, then hinges on shutters.

Christmas

It is generally believed that the first Christmas tree was erected in the eighth century by Saint Boniface, a Christian missionary in Germany. He set up a fir tree to replace the oak, which was sacred to the pagan god Thor, and then decorated it with offerings to the child Jesus. The German reformer Martin Luther is thought to have started the custom of lighting the tree with candles. Queen Victoria's husband, Albert of Saxe-Coburg, introduced the tree to England, and German immigrants took the idea to America.

The tree is made from six round cakes: four 130mm (5in), one 150mm (6in), and one 180mm (7in). Ingredients for these are given on page 10 and method for baking on pages 6 to 7. Instructions for making royal icing, marzipan, and fondant are given on pages 7 to 8. If you make your own fondant, it will be easier to make the 1.23kg (2¾lb) in three batches, keeping it securely wrapped in cling film and in an airtight container.

The tree can be completed in a day, but the covering of marzipan must be allowed to dry for 48 hours. During this time the decorations can be made.

The candle-holders must be pliable plastic, so that they can be cut and bent without snapping. If these are unavailable, rigid plastic ones can be used, but they will have to be stuck into the tree at an angle.

Please read the General Notes on pages 6 to 9 before starting to decorate. Also read through the step-by-step instructions and check the ingredient and equipment lists.

Ingredients for fondant and royal icing

1.23kg (2¾lb) icing sugar, plus 280g (10oz)
2¾ egg whites, plus 1¼
5½ tbsp liquid glucose
flavouring (optional)
Also: 1kg (2¼lb) marzipan; warm sieved apricot jam; 50/50 mixture of cornflour and icing sugar in a dusting dredger; green, red, and gold food colouring; edible lustre powder.

Equipment

Mixing bowls; spoons; sieve; rolling pin; steel rule; sharp-pointed knife; lolly sticks (LS) as spacers; pastry brush; small paintbrush; greaseproof paper; *Ateco* (or equivalent) icing nozzles 1, 2, and 3; fifteen pliable plastic candles; oil-based gold paint (for candle-holders); fifteen red candles; 230mm (9in) round silver cake board; tracing paper; stiff white card; waxed paper; adhesive tape.

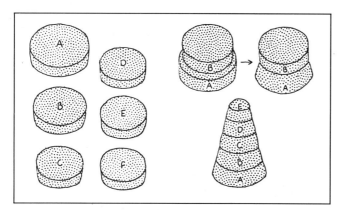

1. Slice the tops of the cakes flat. Brush top of **A** and under-side of **B** with jam. Lay a sliver of marzipan on **A** and put **B** on top. Trim sides of **A**, sloping in to the bottom of **B**, as shown. Brush top of **B** and under-side of **C**; repeat as with **A** and **B**. Trim **D** and **E** to make the conical shape shown.

2. Apply marzipan in strips as shown – measure circumference of bottom of cake and roll marzipan to 2 LS thick. Brush area of cake with jam and apply strips. Continue until sides are covered. Roll marzipan to 1 LS thick. Brush bottom of tree with jam, then stand cake on marzipan and cut round it.

3. Brush top with jam, lay on a piece of marzipan 1 LS thick, and trim edges. Measure sides of **F**, and brush with jam. Roll marzipan to 2 LS thick, cut to size, then roll cake along it. Leave both cakes to dry (the tree on a generously dusted surface) for 48 hours.

4. Meanwhile, make the decorations. Trace the snow-flakes below on to tracing paper, then on to pieces of stiff card. Tape pieces of waxed paper over the drawings. Using *No. 2 nozzle* first, for the solid lines, and *No. 1 nozzle* for the broken lines, pipe three snowflakes.

5. Carefully remove tape and slide waxed paper on to another flat surface. Put some fresh waxed paper on to the card and repeat piping. Make fifteen snowflakes in all. Trace fairy's wings on to tracing paper, then on to stiff card. Cover with waxed paper as before and, using *Nos. 1 and 2 nozzles* (*No. 1* for broken lines), pipe the wings.

(Pipe two sets of wings, then choose the better set). Repeat tracing-and-piping method, using *No. 2 nozzle* for wand (pipe two) and stars (pipe twenty). Leave all to dry for 24 hours, then paint half the stars, the wand, and edges of wings with gold. Use paintbrush to dust remaining stars with lustre powder.

6. Colour 900g (2lb) of fondant green. Apply to tree exactly as for marzipan, but using egg white instead of jam. Colour 200g (7oz) of fondant red and cover base, as for marzipan. Once applied, mark vertical lines with blunt edge of knife.

7. Make round baubles with remaining red fondant and dust with lustre powder. Cut a nick at the top of each candle-holder stem. Bend stem backwards, then paint with oil-based gold.

8. Attach base to tree with egg white, then base to the cake board with a blob of icing. With *No. 3 nozzle*, pipe pine needles on tree. Work five rows, starting at bottom and working up. Take the nozzle down, dragging to make a point at the bottom as shown.

9. Model a support from green fondant trimmings, about 60mm (2¼in) high. Attach to centre top of tree with icing. Roll white fondant to 1 LS thick and cut a 130mm (5in) circle; lay it over support, attaching with egg white. Cut another circle, about 60mm (2¼in), and attach over large one.

10. Model body, neck, and head, as shown, then attach. Push wand into waist, then model arms and attach. With *No. 2 nozzle*, pipe loops around edges of dress and neck, then pipe eyes and hair. Pipe a line of icing down the back and attach wings. Dust fairy with lustre powder and paint piping gold. Melt bottom of candles and push into holders. Carefully push holders into sides of tree and secure the lip of each holder at the back with a neat blob of green icing. Carefully peel waxed paper from back of snowflakes and stars. Pipe a blob of green icing where a snowflake is to be positioned, then very carefully lift snowflake and secure to tree. Repeat for remaining snowflakes and stars. Attach baubles in the same way, holding each one for a little while until it feels secure.

House-warming

When people have a house-warming party, they usually give it with a great sense of pride – they have moved into a property and decorated it in their own very special way. It has always amazed me how quickly, after moving, people feel happy to allow detailed inspection. We have lived in our present house for thirteen years and the experience has been not unlike painting the Forth Bridge, but we never manage to get back to the other end! Children, of course, always manage to find the piece of loose wallpaper and cannot resist pulling; they draw little things on perfectly secure wallpaper; they hide in wardrobes and loosen hinges; they crack windows and chip paint. Perhaps we will have a house-warming when they have all left home.

The door, surround, and step are made from a 300mm (12in) square cake. Ingredients and quantities for this are given on page 10 and the method for baking on pages 6 to 7. Instructions for making royal icing, marzipan, and fondant are on pages 7 to 8. If you make your own fondant it will be easier to make the 1.68kg (3¾lb) in several batches, keeping each piece securely wrapped in cling film and in an airtight container.

The cake will take one to two days to decorate, after the covering of marzipan has been left to dry for 48 hours.

Please read the General Notes on pages 6 to 9 before starting to decorate. Also read through the step-by-step instructions and check the ingredient and equipment lists.

Ingredients for fondant and royal icing

1.68kg (3¾lb) icing sugar, plus 170g (6oz)
3¾ egg whites, plus ¾
7½ tbsp liquid glucose
flavouring (optional)
Also: 1.57kg (3½lb) marzipan; warm sieved apricot jam; 50/50 mixture of cornflour and icing sugar in a dusting dredger; black, yellow, red, brown, green, and gold food colouring.

Equipment

Mixing bowls; spoons; sieve; rolling pin; steel rule; sharp-pointed knife; lolly sticks (LS) as spacers; pastry brush; *Ateco* (or equivalent) icing nozzles 1, 2, 3, 4, 66, and 96; 330mm (13in) square silver cake board.

1. Slice the top of the cake flat. Cut a 25mm (1in) piece from one side (this will be the bottom step), then cut 25mm (1in) from the end, as shown. Cut off a 100mm (4in) slab (top step), then cut a door from remaining cake 100 x 200mm (4 x 8in). Cut a 40mm (1½in) slope from the door, as shown, 7mm (¼in) from bottom.

2. Roll marzipan to 2 LS thick. Brush sides of steps with jam. Cut marzipan to fit, then apply. Cover the steps (front and top of each with one piece), using the rolling pin to help with largest piece. Roll marzipan to 1 LS thick. Cover back of top step, back of door, back of surround, and top and side of door.

3. Roll marzipan to 2 LS thick. Cover sides, top and front of porch, then front of door. Leave everything to dry for 48 hours. Colour 780g (1¾lb) of fondant grey. Cover steps, back of porch, and back of door exactly as with marzipan, but using egg white instead of jam.

4. Add 60g (2oz) of fondant to trimmings, then mix in yellow. Roll to 1 LS thick. Cover top and right-hand side of inside porch, then side of door. Secure large step (with blob of icing) 150mm (6in) from front of board with small step in front. Colour 560g (1¼lb) of fondant brick (red and black).

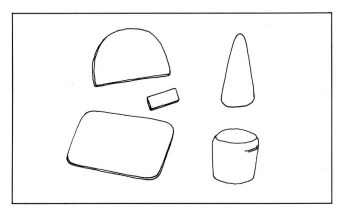

5. Roll fondant to 2 LS thick. Cut and apply pieces for sides, top, and front (in two pieces) of porch, marking bricks with knife after each application. Colour 170g (6oz) of fondant the same colour as your own front door. Roll to 2 LS thick, cut to size, and apply. Colour 60g (2oz) of fondant yellow. Roll to 1 LS thick.

6. Cut semicircle to fit above door. Add brown to trimmings, cut doormat 70 x 100mm (2¾ x 4in) and round off corners. Cut letterbox 10 x 30mm (³/₈ x 1¼in). Leave to dry on a dusted surface. Model a plant pot with brick trimmings. Add green to remaining trimmings and model a shrub.

7. With *No. 1 nozzle* and red icing, pipe **WELCOME** on doormat. Fill lettering in with dots, then pipe dark-brown dots on remaining surface. With *No. 4 nozzle* and dark-brown icing, pipe trellis on right-hand side of wall. Attach semicircle with egg white, then pipe around and mark windows. Pipe around door and down sides of opening. Pipe green ivy stems up left-hand side of wall. Pipe four oblongs on door (similar colour to door), then knocker and knob. With *No. 2 nozzle* and darker green, pipe flower stems over trellis, needles on shrub, and handle on letterbox. With lighter green, pipe stems on steps. With *No. 66 nozzle* and dark- and light-green icing in the bag, pipe the ivy leaves. With *No. 96 nozzle* and white and pink icing in the bag, pipe flowers on trellis. With *No. 2 nozzle*, pipe yellow flower centres, and flowers on steps. Position letterbox, doormat, and plant pot with egg white. Carefully position porch (secure with icing) and slide door underneath. Cover top of door with fondant 1 LS thick. Paint letterbox, knocker, and door-knob with gold.

Wedding anniversaries

This ornate fan spanning twenty-five years is in the traditional mode. The idea can be used for any anniversary, after the tenth, by altering the colour scheme and the width and number of fan pieces. It would probably be too difficult to fit any more than fifty pieces on the cake. I have drawn up a list of traditional anniversaries which is given on page 126.

Making the fan pieces is not difficult, but time and patience are needed. Once set, however, the pieces are extremely fragile. It is best to slide them gently from one surface to another where possible; or very carefully pick them up in the middle with thumb and forefinger. If they do break, unless they are completely shattered, a little blob of runny icing on the break will be enough to secure them. In the instructions I have suggested making more than the required number, just in case.

The base is made from one 300mm (12in) square cake and one 130mm (5in) square cake. Ingredients for these are given on page 10 and the method of baking, along with instructions for royal icing, marzipan, and fondant, is given on pages 6 to 8. If you make your own fondant, it will be easier to make the 1.34kg (3lb) in three batches, keeping each piece securely wrapped in cling film and in an airtight container until required.

Please read the General Notes on pages 6 to 9 before starting to decorate the cake. Also read through the step-by-step instructions and check the ingredient and equipment lists.

Ingredients for fondant and royal icing

1.34kg (3lb) icing sugar, plus 450g (1lb)
3 egg whites, plus 2
6 tbsp liquid glucose
flavouring (optional)
Also: 1.12kg (2½lb) marzipan; warm sieved apricot jam; 50/50 mixture of icing sugar and cornflour in a dusting dredger; blue, black, flesh, and silver food colouring; edible silver balls.

Equipment

Mixing bowls; spoons; sieve; rolling pin; steel rule; sharp-pointed knife; lolly sticks (LS) as spacers; pastry brush; small paintbrush; greaseproof paper; *Ateco* (or equivalent) icing nozzles 1, 2, 3, and 4; stiff white card; adhesive tape; tracing paper; HB graphite pencil; skewer; waxed paper; coloured-headed sewing pins; twenty-five candles and holders; oil-based silver paint; 400mm (16in) square silver cake board.

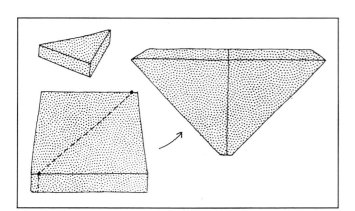

1. Slice the tops of the cakes flat. Cut the small cake across diagonally (only one half is used). Cut the large cake diagonally, as shown, 12mm (½in) from the two opposite corners. Stick the two pieces together with jam and a strip of marzipan.

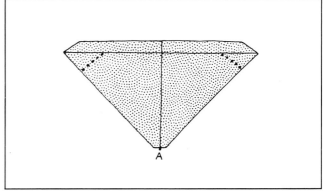

2. From the centre bottom, **A**, measure a 330mm (13in) curve coming in from the edges. Mark the curve with the sewing pins, then carefully cut the corners off.

123

3. Trim the cut-off corners so they fit at the top of the fan, then stick them with jam and marzipan. Continue to measure, mark, and trim the 330mm (13in) curve. Fill the top gap with pieces from the last trim.

4. Carefully position the cake on the board. Measure the cake sides, then brush with jam. Roll marzipan to 2 LS thick, cut to fit, then apply. Brush cake top. Apply marzipan 2 (LS) thick with help of rolling pin. Neatly trim edges. Cover small cake. Leave both to dry for 48 hours. Meanwhile, follow stage 5 on page 125.

6. Using the HB graphite (not lead) pencil, trace the above numbers on to a strip of tracing paper. Carefully arrange the twenty-five fan pieces in pairs on the table. Turn the paper over and very carefully trace each number on to a heart. (You may be able to draw the numbers freehand, instead of tracing).

7. With *No. 2 nozzle*, pipe the numbers. Pipe dots around each heart. Then leave to dry.

    Trace **CONGRATULATIONS** on to one of the solid fan pieces. With *No. 2 nozzle*, pipe over the pencilled letters. When dry, carefully paint the numbers, little hearts, and lettering silver. Leave to dry.

8. Take 1.12kg (2½lb) of fondant. Cover sides of large cake sides with white fondant at 2 LS thick, exactly as for marzipan, but using egg white instead of jam. Roll a piece of fondant to 2 LS thick and cut a 100mm (4in) arc to fit base of fan, as shown.

9. Colour remaining fondant blue. Roll to 2 LS thick and to roughly the shape of the fan. Brush a thin film of egg white on marzipan and apply fondant with the help of the rolling pin. Trim edges. Add 90g (3oz) of white fondant to blue trimmings and cover the small cake.

5. Trace the above two fan pieces on to three pieces of stiff white card, and then tape waxed paper over the drawings. Pipe the outer line and large heart with *No. 3 nozzle*; the ten horizontal lines and one vertical line with *No. 2 nozzle*; and the remainder with *No. 1 nozzle*. Using a skewer, fill in the areas shown with watered icing. Leave the six pieces to dry for about three hours, then carefully remove the tape and leave the pieces on a flat surface (still on the waxed paper) to dry overnight. Repeat until twenty-eight pieces have been piped. Pipe two more pieces, filling in the areas shown. When the first pieces are dry, peel off the waxed paper. Leave under-side to dry.

The basic shape of this silver (twenty-fifth) wedding anniversary cake can be used for other anniversaries. The filigree fan piece will have to be redrawn, making it slightly narrower for more years and wider for fewer years. Here is a list of traditional anniversary names: ten – tin; eleven – steel; twelve – silk; thirteen – lace; fourteen – ivory; fifteen – crystal; twenty – china; twenty-five – silver; thirty – pearl; thirty-five – coral; forty – ruby; forty-five – sapphire; fifty – golden; sixty – diamond.

126

10. Make a cone, as shown, about 70mm (2¾in) high, from remaining blue trimmings. Attach to small cake with egg white. Colour 45g (1½oz) pale blue (keep some for arms), attach little collar, then roll to 1 LS thick and gather and attach skirt. Colour 30g (1oz) grey, then model and attach shoes and trousers.

11. Model the body and attach shirt-front and collar, as shown. Attach body to legs. Colour a little fondant flesh, model the heads, paint eyes, then attach. Model and attach arms and hands. Support joined hands until position is secure. With *No. 1 nozzle* and white icing, pipe hair, and decorations on dress.

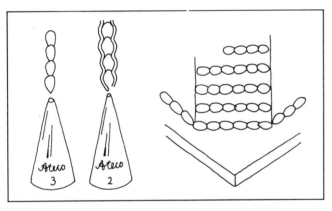

12. With *No. 3 nozzle* and blue icing, pipe continuous dots around top of small cake. With *No. 2 nozzle* and white icing, follow top and bottom of blue line. Paint part of dress decorations and hair silver. With *No. 3 nozzle* and white icing, pipe continuous dots around base of fan and around fondant seam at the top, then eight lines at point of fan, as shown.

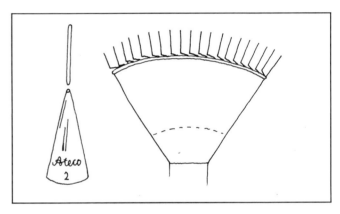

13. Very carefully arrange fan pieces on cake. With *No. 2 nozzle* and white icing, secure the pieces at the bottom with neat lines and, at the top, gently push the nozzle underneath each heart and pipe as large a blob as possible. Mark a circle 40mm (1½in) from both sides.

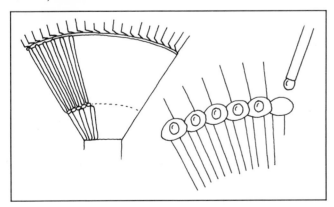

14. With *No. 3 nozzle* and blue icing, pipe lines to the circle, then pipe the circle with a line of continuous dots. With *No. 4 nozzle*, pipe large dots to cover the lines, securing the fan pieces. Place a silver ball on each dot (use a straw to suck the ball, then release as it touches icing). Pipe nine lines to the fan point.

15. With *No. 2 nozzle* and blue icing, follow top and bottom of continuous dots around base of cake. Position small cake and, with *No. 3 nozzle*, pipe continuous dots around base. Paint four candle-holders silver, then push into cake. Secure all candles in holders, then push into fan at an angle, as shown.

SECOND EDITION

Jonathan Wilson

ESSENTIALS of
BUSINESS
RESEARCH

A Guide to Doing Your Research Project

Los Angeles | London | New Delhi
Singapore | Washington DC

Los Angeles | London | New Delhi
Singapore | Washington DC

SAGE Publications Ltd
1 Oliver's Yard
55 City Road
London EC1Y 1SP

SAGE Publications Inc.
2455 Teller Road
Thousand Oaks, California 91320

SAGE Publications India Pvt Ltd
B 1/I 1 Mohan Cooperative Industrial Area
Mathura Road
New Delhi 110 044

SAGE Publications Asia-Pacific Pte Ltd
3 Church Street
#10-04 Samsung Hub
Singapore 049483

Editor: Jai Seaman
Assistant editor: Lily Mehrbod
Production editor: Ian Antcliff
Copyeditor: Richard Hutchinson
Indexer: Avril Ehrlich
Marketing manager: Alison Borg
Cover design: Francis Kenney
Typeset by: C&M Digitals (P) Ltd, Chennai, India
Printed and bound in Great Britain by Ashford
Colour Press Ltd

Library of Congress Control Number: 2013939977

British Library Cataloguing in Publication data

A catalogue record for this book is available from
the British Library

ISBN 978-1-4462-5732-6
ISBN 978-1-4462-5733-3 (pbk)

Essentials of
BUSINESS
RESEARCH

Contents

List of Figures

List of Tables

Companion Website

Author: Jonathan Wilson

Pub Date: January 2014

Pages: 392

Learn more about this book

Book Home

Welcome to the companion website for the second edition of *Essentials of Business Research* by Jonathan Wilson.

About the Book

Concise, authoritative and jargon-free, the new edition of Jonathan Wilson's best-selling introduction to business research is the perfect guide to completing a successful research project.

Written specifically for business students it highlights each stage of the research process, guiding the reader through actionable steps and explicitly setting out how best to meet a supervisor's expectations.

Easy to navigate and full of practical advice it supports core themes such as choosing a topic and writing a proposal with easy to follow tips and detailed screenshots and diagrams.
Key student features include:

- 'You're the Supervisor' sections - helps students to meet learning objectives

- 'Common questions and answers' - real-world advice on how to tackle common challenges

- Examples from many different types of businesses across cultures

- Detailed guidance on software packages such as SPSS and NVivo

- Student case studies

- Annotated further reading sections

- Chapter objectives and summaries

A must-have title for all business and management students this is the ideal companion for achieving success in your research project.

Instructor Resources

This site is password protected 🔒

Please read the information to your right. To access the site, click on the sign in button on the right hand side below.

The section of the companion website contains resources which are available free of charge to lecturers who adopt the second edition of *Essentials of Business Research*.

The following material is available for lecturers:

- PowerPoint Slides

First-time Users

Many of the materials on the instructor site, are only available to Faculty and Administrative Staff at Higher Education Institutions who have been approved to request Review Copies by SAGE.

To create an account, please click here. In order to be approved, you must provide your institution and the course that you are or will be teaching. Once you have created an account and you have been validated as a faculty member, you will be able to access the instructor site.

Please note: Validation usually takes approximately 24-48 hours to be completed.

If you have any questions, please contact SAGE Customer Service at +44 (0) 20 7 324 8500 from 8:30 am to 5:00 pm.

Returning Users

If you already have an account with SAGE, log in using the email address and password created when registering with SAGE.

Sign In ▶

This book is dedicated to my students at Anglia Ruskin University who remind me why I decided to become a lecturer in the first place. I would also like to dedicate this book to my family, especially my beautiful daughter Jemma and mother Jean. It is only due to their love and support that I was able to write this book.

Jonathan Wilson

Preface to the second edition

Since the publication of the first edition in 2010, the feedback I have received from both lecturers and students suggests that *Essentials of Business Research: A Guide to Doing Your Research Project* has delivered on what it set out to achieve. That is, to offer a concise, student-focused guide to business research. In most cases, the feedback has been overwhelmingly positive – it is always nice to receive a positive response from readers, especially students! However, when writing the second edition I was particularly interested in some of the recommendations as to areas of improvement. I am grateful for these suggestions and have tried to incorporate many of them in the new edition.

Like the first edition, this book is intended for both undergraduate and postgraduate students undertaking a research methods module and/or business research project. It is also an ideal text for research project supervisors and those teaching research methods. In relation to the latter, the book is set out with this in mind. Each chapter is organized in a clear, thematic way, therefore making it straightforward for students to follow.

Why the need for a second edition? Has writing a research project really changed that much in the last three years? Well, in many cases, no it hasn't. The research project continues to be a feature of many university degree programmes. Moreover, it remains a significant piece of work that is often the culmination of three or four years of study. However, certainly from my own experience of teaching research methods and supervising students, it is apparent that there are particular elements of the research process that are often difficult for students to grasp. One of these elements is research methodology. As with the first edition, this book provides a detailed overview of research methodology. Yet, in an attempt to make the whole issue of methodological approach more explicit, I have introduced the *Honeycomb of Research Methodology* in Chapter 1. The main aim behind this framework is to illustrate the key concepts of research in a honeycomb diagram, so as to show you in simple terms how they fit into your research methodology.

In this edition, I have striven to introduce new material and pedagogical features which improve the book and reflect changes in the subject area. For example, in the relatively short period of time since the first publication there are certain things that have changed. Undoubtedly, students are increasingly moving away from more traditional data collection tools to online data collection. The ease of use and accessibility means that there is a growing trend towards web-based data collection tools such as Survey Monkey, so Chapter 6 has been expanded to include a section looking at online data collection. A new pedagogical feature in each chapter is 'Research in Action'. This examines a particular aspect of an actual academic piece of research or research practice, depending on the topic covered within the chapter. More general updates include new case studies and learning material to aid business students with their research project. Once again, I have introduced *student case studies* as many students are interested in the challenges faced by their peers.

A popular feature in the first edition and included in this revised book is 'You're the supervisor'. This requires the reader to take on the role of the research supervisor by answering typical student questions. The importance of the supervisor is stressed throughout, as they typically play an important role in the research process. At the end of each chapter there is also a *case study, common questions and answers, references* and *further reading*. A useful *glossary* section is provided at the end of the book. These are all intended to help test and further your knowledge of the subject. It is worth noting that I have avoided making major changes and have endeavoured to maintain the conciseness and student focus that was so well received in the first edition. A summary of the key features include:

- 'You're the Supervisor' sections – helps students to meet their learning outcomes;
- 'Common questions and answers' – provides students with an invaluable point of reference for some of the challenges they are likely to face while undertaking their research project;
- Research in Action;
- a full student glossary;
- student case studies;
- annotated further reading sections and summary and references at the end of each chapter.

This edition also includes a revised companion website containing extensive material for lecturers and students, including:

- chapter-by-chapter links to academic journal articles demonstrating each method's application;
- chapter-by-chapter links to YouTube resources to provide further context;
- chapter-by-chapter PowerPoint slides to help lecturers and students;
- copies of completed student research projects;
- author video and audio podcasts.

The 11-chapter structure of the first edition remains the same: Chapter 1 sets out by introducing business research, in particular the differences between academic and organizational research. In Chapter 2 we concentrate on how to develop a research topic. Chapter 3 focuses on how to conduct a literature review, while Chapter 4 deals with the importance of addressing ethical issues. Chapter 5 looks at establishing a research design, Chapters 6 to 7 describe data collection – primary and secondary, respectively. In Chapter 8 we focus on sampling techniques. I also give advice on how to overcome sampling problems. Chapters 9 and 10 examine data analysis, the former being quantitative analysis, while the latter qualitative analysis. Finally, Chapter 11 deals with the important task of writing up. It provides a detailed look at the typical structure, content and presentation of your research project. Finally, I would like to express my gratitude to lecturers, students and reviewers who provided invaluable feedback on the first book; I hope that readers will provide a similar level of feedback on this revised second edition.

Jonathan Wilson, Cambridge

Acknowledgements

I am grateful for the support I have received from my colleagues, friends and family during the writing of this book. I am particularly indebted to Jai Seaman of Sage Publications for her commitment and guidance throughout the publication process. I would also like to acknowledge the invaluable feedback from my students at Anglia Ruskin University. I have taken on board many of their comments in this revised second edition.

Above all, I would like to extend my sincere gratitude to my former PhD supervisor Dr Ross Brennan, now at the University of Hertfordshire, who has been instrumental throughout my academic career.

I am grateful to the following for permission to reproduce copyright material:

Table 1.3 from Saunders, M., Lewis, P. and Thornhill, A. (2007) *Research Methods for Business Students* (4th edn), reprinted by permission of Prentice Hall, Harlow, Essex;

Figure 1.4 reprinted by permission of The Market Research Society;

Table 1.5 and an extract from 'ARU presentation and submission of major projects and dissertations for taught higher degrees', 5th edn, September 2007, reprinted by permission of Anglia Ruskin University;

Pages 30–31 'ICT: Is it still a turn on?' Clapperton, G., *The Guardian*, reprinted by permission of Guardian News & Media;

Pages 39–40 'Difficulty issues', from Jankowicz, A.D. (2005) *Business Research Projects*, Copyright©2005 Cengage Learning. Reproduced with permission from Cengage Learning

Page 105 'Professional standards, ethics and disciplinary procedures in accordance with Royal Charter bye-laws', reprinted by permission of the Chartered Institute of Marketing;

Table 3.5 from Raimondo, M. (2000) 'The measurement of trust in marketing studies: A review of models and methodologies', Proceedings of the 16th Annual IMP Conference, Bath, September, reprinted with kind permission from the author;

Page 308 'Structure of an argument', from Levin, P. (2005) *Excellent Dissertations*, reprinted by permission of McGraw-Hill;

Page 308 'Structure when testing a theory', from Levin, P. (2005) *Excellent Dissertations*, reprinted by permission of McGraw-Hill;

Figure 7.2 from Blumberg, B., Cooper, D.R. and Schindler, P.S. (2008) *Business Research Methods* (2nd edn), reprinted by permission of McGraw-Hill, Maidenhead;

Table 8.1 from Malhotra, N.K. and Birks, D.F. (2006) *Marketing Research: An Applied Approach* (2nd edn), reprinted by permission of Prentice Hall, Harlow, Essex;

Figure 11.5 from Saunders, M.N.K. and Davis, S.M. (1998) 'The use of assessment criteria to ensure consistency of marking', *Quality Assurance in Education*, 6 (3): 162–71; reprinted by permission of Emerald Publishing Ltd.

Every effort has been made to trace copyright holders. However, if any have been inadvertently overlooked, the publishers will be pleased to make the necessary arrangement at the earliest opportunity.

1

An Introduction to Business Research

┌─ Learning Objectives ───┐

After reading this chapter, you should be able to:

- know what research and business research are, and why they are important in both business and academia;
- understand the key concepts of research;
- be aware of the relationship between the key concepts of research as illustrated in the 'Honeycomb of Research Methodology';
- understand the rationale for using multi-strategy research;
- appreciate how business research is linked to the organization;
- be aware of the research skills required to undertake research;
- know the stages in the research process;
- understand the differences between academic and organizational research; and
- know the role played by research project supervisors and the kind of support they provide.

└───┘

Introduction

Research is one of those words that you are likely to come across on an almost daily basis. You may have read in the newspaper that the latest market research study links passive smoking to an increased likelihood of lung cancer. Or perhaps a news headline makes reference to a groundbreaking piece of medical research into a possible cure for HIV/AIDS. To be sure, illustrations of various types of research are regularly publicized in the media. However, the information provided often only relates to research findings. What exactly is research? What distinguishes business research from other types of research? This chapter aims to answer these questions and sets out to provide a clear introduction to business research.

This chapter starts by clearly defining and explaining research, and more importantly business research. In order to emphasize the message that an understanding of research, methodology and methods is an essential requirement to your project, we spend a reasonable amount of time looking at these particular terms. Following this, readers are first introduced to *The Honeycomb of Research Methodology*. This is a new feature of the second edition. One of the aims of the honeycomb is to show the six main elements that combine to make up the centre segment – research methodology. We begin by examining the first three of these elements, also referred to as the 'key concepts of research', and consider the relationship between all three concepts. The other elements of the honeycomb are addressed later in the book. Next, we look at how business research is linked to the organization and explore the necessary research skills required to be an effective researcher. This is followed by an overview of the likely steps that you will go through when conducting your research. Although the majority of this book is aimed at business students, the next part of this introductory chapter provides an insight into the differences between academic and organizational research. Mature students and those of you who have worked within a business setting may already be familiar with the nature of organizational research. However, it is important to understand the differences that exist, not least because it will impact on your approach towards your research project.

The last section looks at the role of the project supervisor. The importance of your project supervisor cannot be underestimated. Unfortunately, many students fail to use their supervisor to good effect. Therefore, I have included a section, 'The role of the supervisor', in Chapter 1 in order to illustrate the importance of the supervisor from the outset. Finally, the chapter concludes with a case study, 'You're the supervisor', and common questions and answers. These pedagogical features are a common theme within each chapter. They are designed to aid you during the research process by including actual student case examples, common student questions that I have come across in the context of project supervision, and finally what I call 'role reversal', where you are required to answer questions from the project supervisor's perspective.

The Meaning of Research

Although the title of this book makes reference to 'business research', I think it is worth having a review of what is actually meant by the term 'research'. The majority of students usually take some kind of research skills module as part of their study programme. For that reason, some of you may have an understanding of what is meant by research.

While research is important in both business and academia, there is no consensus in the literature on how it should be defined. The main reason for this is that different people can interpret research differently. However, from the many definitions there appears to be conformity that:

- research is a process of enquiry and investigation;
- it is systematic and methodical; and
- research increases knowledge.

Let us look at each of the above points in turn. First, a 'process of enquiry and investigation' suggests that research is all about having a predetermined set of questions, and then aiming to answer these questions through the gathering of information, and later analysis. Second, 'systematic and methodical' imply that your research must be well organized and go through a series of stages. Finally, 'research increases knowledge' is relatively self-explanatory. Your own knowledge about your chosen subject will certainly improve as a result of your research, but so too, hopefully, will that of your audience, and this may also include your project supervisor!

Research can be defined as a 'step-by-step process that involves the collecting, recording, analyzing and interpreting of information'. As researchers, we are interested in improving our knowledge and understanding of our chosen topic. To do this effectively, researchers must have a clear set of research questions. The importance of research questions cannot be stressed highly enough. The research questions are the main focus of any project, and can probably best be described as *'the glue that holds the project together'*.

Generally speaking, research is all about generating answers to questions – to advance knowledge. The nature of these questions depends on the topic of research. For example, a marketer might carry out research to investigate consumer perceptions about a certain brand. Or a medical researcher might want to explore the association between recovery times and different medical treatments. Although the research questions are tailored towards a particular topic, essentially the process that researchers go through usually involves a similar series of stages, and I shall address these later on in this chapter.

In addition to research, it is likely that you have come across *methods* and *methodology*. It is necessary to distinguish the difference between the two terms as students often use them interchangeably, although there is a distinct difference. *Methodology* can be defined as 'the approach and strategy used to conduct research'. In general, methodology is concerned with the overall approach to the research process. This includes everything from your theoretical application to the collection and analysis of your data. On the other hand, *methods* refer to the different ways by which data can be collected and analyzed.

Business Research

The purpose of business research is to gather information in order to aid business-related decision-making. *Business research* is defined as 'the systematic and objective process of collecting, recording, analyzing and interpreting data for aid in solving managerial problems'. These managerial problems can be linked to any business function, e.g. human resources, finance, marketing or research and development. Your research project can also be interpreted as business research in the sense that it will be related to business and management. In some cases, this may encompass more than one particular business discipline. For instance, a study might focus on the level of marketing knowledge among finance managers (marketing and finance). Some examples of areas of business and possible research issues are shown in Table 1.1.

TABLE 1.1 Examples of business research

Business aspect	Research issues
Consumer behaviour	Buying habits, brand preference, consumer attitudes
Human resources	Employee attitudes, staff retention, material incentives
Promotion	Media research, public relations studies, product recall through advertising
Product	Test markets, concept studies, performance studies
Finance	Forecasting, budgeting, efficiency of accounting software

Why Research is Important

We have already established that research is all about providing answers to questions and developing knowledge. These questions in themselves are significant, hence the need to conduct research. You are likely to have conducted your own research to address questions that are important to you. For example, if the international students among you wish to return home for Christmas, it is unlikely that you would buy a ticket from the first airline that you see advertised. Instead, you would probably do some research to find out if there exists a cheaper alternative carrier. This may involve exploring various airline websites, or asking friends and family. Quite simply, research is the key to decision-making. Without sufficient information, decision-making is likely to be more difficult.

Importance of research in business

In business, research is important in identifying opportunities and threats. Often, a company's success or failure is dependent on the actions undertaken as a result of conducting research. Although carrying out business research does not guarantee success, it is likely to increase the possibility that a new product, service, brand identity or even an event is successful. In some cases, the level of research conducted can be questionable, especially if public opinion is markedly different to that of an organization's viewpoint, as illustrated in the following case example.

─RESEARCH IN ACTION─

The London Olympics 2012 logo

The logo of the London 2012 Olympic Games was unveiled to the world in June 2007. At a cost of £400,000, it was hailed as 'dynamic' and 'vibrant' by organizers, while its 'graffiti style' was designed to appeal to the younger generation and work across a variety of media platforms.

Designed by leading brand consultants Wolff Olins, the logo took the best part of a year to produce and bears a resemblance to the year 2012. However, shortly after its launch, the design came up against widespread disapproval, with one Jewish person even ringing the BBC to complain that it was reminiscent of the infamous Nazi SS symbol.

Design guru Stephen Bayley condemned it as 'a puerile mess, an artistic flop and a commercial scandal'. An online petition to get the logo scrapped received thousands of signatures, while research conducted by Ipsos MORI, one of the UK's leading research companies, found a similarly negative response. For example, when questioned 'Do you approve or disapprove of the logo?' only 16% of respondents commented that they approved of the logo.

Although the London Organising Committee of the Olympic and Paralympic Games (LOCOG) stressed that the logo was paid for by private money, Mr Bayley voiced his astonishment that the emblem – available in blue, pink, green and orange – had cost £400,000. 'That's outrageous,' he said. 'There are 5,000 talented designers who could have done the job for £10,000.' (Carlin, 2007; Ipsos MORI, 2007)

In the case of the London Olympics 2012 logo, it can be questioned as to whether LOCOG carried out sufficient research prior to choosing the new logo. Later media coverage suggests that many people eventually warmed to the design, thus il lustrating that business research may only provide a snapshot of people's opinion, and that attitudes can change over time.

Why studying research methods is important

The London Olympics 2012 logo example highlights why research is important in a commercial setting. However, as mentioned in the introduction, it is also an important part of your course. Your research project is probably the culmination of three to four years of hard study. Yet, for those students who participate in a research skills module as part of their study programme, in some cases the module is perceived as not being essential, or even relevant. There are perhaps two reasons for this. First, it is often embedded within a course and sits alongside modules that are relevant to your chosen subject. For example, if you are studying a finance degree, you will probably take modules in auditing, management accounting, corporate finance, etc. Yet a first glance at your study timetable may raise the question 'What is this module?', or perhaps 'I'm here to study for a degree in finance, not research skills!' A common problem facing us poor lecturers is to try to get across the message that research skills *is* relevant to your course, provides a wide range of transferable skills and, above all, serves to provide the necessary skills in order to successfully complete your research project. Second, when taking a research skills module, students usually have a wide range of questions from the outset. In general, if these questions are addressed early, it can certainly help to alleviate some of the apprehension regarding the subject. Examples of some of the more common questions students tend to ask towards the beginning of learning research skills is shown in Table 1.2.

What are the long-term benefits of studying research skills?

As mentioned, in the short term, the primary importance of studying research skills is so that you are aware of what is required in order to satisfactorily complete your

TABLE 1.2 Your research questions answered

Question	Answer
What is research?	Research can be defined as a 'step-by-step process that involves the collecting, recording, analyzing and interpreting of information'.
Why do I need to learn about business research?	An essential part of most business-related study programmes is the research project. Learning about business research helps you to successfully complete your project as well as provide transferable skills that can be used in a wide variety of business and management positions.
How do I conduct research?	This book fully explains everything you need to know about how to conduct research. By the end of the book you should be in a position to answer this question!
Where do I conduct research?	This might seem obvious. However, international students may decide to conduct research in their own country, particularly if focusing on cross-cultural research, while those students who work part-time may conduct some aspects of their research in the workplace.
When do I conduct research?	In general, undertaking your research project commences towards the end of your final year of study. However, check with your university or college.

research project. However, the skills learned through studying research skills can also have long-term benefits, such as helping you to become a better reader of the research of others. This is an important skill for anyone going into business. For instance, at some point in your career you will probably be required to read and interpret a business report. This could be on any subject. If you have learned about research skills and research in general, then you are far more likely to be capable of understanding the study, not to mention interpreting the results and drawing your own conclusions.

Having experience of carrying out research is also an important requirement if you wish to continue with your education. Like undergraduate degrees, master's programmes usually require the submission of a major research project. These tend to be based on a larger number of words (typically 20,000–25,000). Yet much of what you learn through studying research skills can still be fully applied.

Key Concepts of Research

Having established the nature of research – in particular business research and why research is important – this next section takes a more theoretical look at research. Under the broad heading of 'key concepts of research', we shall look at research philosophies, research approaches and research strategies. By the end of this section you should understand each of these concepts, how they relate to your research project and the relationship between them.

The Honeycomb of Research Methodology

In order to understand the key concepts of research and how they fit into your methodology, we now consider the *Honeycomb of Research Methodology* (see Figure 1.1). In this honeycomb, the three highlighted elements or key concepts of research are joined with three other elements to make up research methodology. Put another way, in the honeycomb, the six main elements – namely: (1) research philosophy; (2) research approach; (3) research strategy; (4) research design; (5) data collection and (6) data analysis techniques – come together to form research methodology. This structure is characteristic of the main headings you will find in a methodology chapter in a business research project. The purpose of the numbered segments is to help you to see at which stage each element falls within the chapter.

Earlier in the chapter we looked at methodology, noting that there is a distinction between methodology and methods. At this point, it is also worth stressing that there are many different interpretations of 'research methodology'. Once again, my view is that methodology is 'the approach and strategy used to conduct research'. Several authors share a similar view. For example, Somekh and Lewin (2005: 346) defined methodology as both 'the collection of methods or rules by which a particular piece of research is undertaken' and the 'principles, theories and values that underpin a particular approach to research'. By way of example, let us say you wanted to construct your own house. Your methodology would not only include your proposed plan, but also consideration would be made as to the type of materials, timeframe, the approach to building the house, your views on sustainability and quality controls.

The highlighted segments in Figure 1.1 include a list of the main research philosophies, research approaches and research strategies, respectively. We will examine the contents of each list later in this section. However, they are by no means exhaustive. In particular, you will come across a wide range of different types of research philosophies. It is important that you read additional literature on these key concepts as it will give you a more in-depth understanding of how they might feature in your own research.

How does the Honeycomb of Research Methodology compare to other research models? Several research methods textbooks show the fundamentals of research methodology in the form of either a linear-type diagram, or a series of layers. Although these types of examples are ideal for highlighting the elements set out in the honeycomb, they often fail to address three key issues. First, although a research methodology chapter typically follows a set structure, you may not necessarily consider each element in the order that it is structured within the chapter. For example, once your research strategy has emerged from your research approach, your next step might be to decide to conduct interviews (data collection) and then choose to analyze a single case (research design). This is why the Honeycomb of Research Methodology not only shows the typical structure of a research methodology chapter by including numbered segments, but also recognizes the fact that the thought process may not necessarily be linear. This is illustrated by showing the six outer elements combining to make up the centre segment, research methodology, as

Epistemology: Positivism,
Interpretivism, Pragmatism
Ontology: Objectivism, Subjectivism
Axiology: Value-free, Biased

Research philosophy 1

Descriptive statistics
Inferential statistics
Grounded theory
Narrative analysis
Discourse analysis
Visual analysis
Content analysis

Data analysis techniques 6

Research approach 2

Inductive
Deductive

Research Methodology

Data collection 5

Research strategy 3

Quantitative
Qualitative
Combining quantitative and
   qualitative strategies
   (multi-strategy research)

Interviews
Questionnaires
Observation
Secondary data

Research design 4

Action research
Case study
Experimental
Longitudinal
Cross-sectional
Archival analysis
Comparative

FIGURE 1.1   The Honeycomb of Research Methodology (©2013 Jonathan Wilson)

opposed to a series of stages or layers. Second, other research models do not always indicate the link or relationship between each of the elements. And finally, the six elements are not always considered in the context of writing a methodology chapter as part of a business research project.

We will now consider the three key concepts of research. Other elements of the Honeycomb of Research Methodology are explored later in the book. Research design is examined in Chapter 5, while data collection is covered in Chapters 6 and 7. Finally, data analysis techniques are considered in Chapters 9 and 10, along with a summary on the relationship between the six elements.

Research philosophy

In general, your research philosophy is linked to your views on the development of knowledge. In other words, what you think constitutes knowledge will impact the way that you go about your research. Subconsciously, this is something that comes naturally. Nonetheless, an understanding of research philosophy is important because it is fundamental to how you approach your research. Mark Easterby-Smith et al. (2002) suggest there are three reasons why an understanding of philosophical issues is very useful. First, it can help to clarify *research designs*. This entails considering the type of evidence required and how it is to be collected and interpreted. Second, knowledge of philosophy can help the researcher to recognize which designs work best. Finally, knowledge of philosophy can help the researcher identify and adapt research designs according to the constraints of different subject or knowledge structures. In short, an understanding of research philosophy is important as it gets you thinking about your own role as a researcher. Research philosophies are now fully explained in the next section.

Epistemology (what is the nature of knowledge?)

Epistemology refers to the nature of knowledge, which means how we conceive our surroundings. The key question that epistemology asks is 'What is acceptable knowledge?' – 'A particularly central issue in this context is the question of whether or not the social world can and should be studied according to the same principles, procedures and ethos as the natural sciences' (Bryman and Bell, 2007: 16). If you intend adopting an approach similar to that of the natural scientist, then your epistemological approach is likely to be positivist.

Positivism takes an *objective* view when conducting research and is detached from those involved in the study. On the other hand, you may be critical of the positivist approach and prefer to take an active role when carrying out your research. If that is the case, then you are likely to adopt an *interpretivist* view to your research. Unlike positivists, interpretivists often look at one particular subject in-depth. The purpose of their research is therefore not to generalize, but to be actively engaged in their research through high levels of interaction and/or participation.

Positivism and interpretivism are perhaps the two most well-known research philosophies. Each one is different in terms of what constitutes knowledge, although certain aspects can come under the heading of both philosophies. Positivism and interpretivism are essentially related concepts in the sense that as a researcher, whichever approach you choose, you need to produce a convincing set of findings and argue that your findings are valid. Treating the concepts as related is of benefit because it can help to promote mixed methodologies in order to help validate your findings. The next section of this chapter examines the main research paradigms in greater detail.

Positivism   If you assume a *positivist approach* to your study, then it is your belief that you are independent of your research and your research can be truly objective. Independent means that you maintain minimal interaction with your research participants when carrying out your research. Through being detached in this way, the hope is that you can be truly objective. To put it another way, as a researcher your own personal biases have no part in the research effort.

Positivists believe that research needs to be carried out in a scientific nature. It is empirical research that follows a strict set of guidelines and should be carried out by appropriately trained scientists. The carrying out of this research is usually based on a deductive approach, moving from theory to observation. In general, positivists want their findings to have applicability to the whole of a population. Analysis of observations is likely to be quantifiable as opposed to qualitative. Moreover, there is likely to be a high level of reliability to positivist research due to a highly structured approach. Reliability is fully discussed in Chapter 5.

Researchers critical of the positivist approach are likely to argue that interesting insights are liable to be lost if one adopts positivism. For example, *post-positivists* argue that reality can never be fully apprehended, only approximated (Guba, 1990: 22). Post-positivism relies on multiple methods as a way of capturing as much of reality as possible.

Certain studies are unlikely to lend themselves well to a positivist approach. For instance, if you wish to study shopping habits at your local supermarket, as well as establish consumer perceptions governing pricing, you are more likely to adopt an interpretivist view.

Interpretivism   You may not agree with the positivist approach because you believe that the social aspects of business are too complicated to be measured along the same basis as the natural sciences. If so, then you might be inclined to adopt the role of the interpretivist researcher. *Interpretivism* is an epistemology that supports the view that the researcher must enter the social world of what is being examined. If you decide to assume an interpretivist perspective, then you are likely to analyze social actors within their own cultural setting. This may involve observations that are qualitative and subjective in nature.

A key factor for the interpretivist researcher is to understand the social world of the research participants. Thus, interpretivists are often interdependent with their research and their research is truly subjective. Interdependent means that the researcher is likely to interact with research participants. In certain circumstances, researchers may even observe research participants while working alongside them (participant observation). This illustrates the interpretivist's view of research as being both collaborative and participatory. The carrying out of this research is usually based on an inductive approach, moving from observation to theory.

Overall, interpretivists view the world as complex and open to interpretation. It is the interpretation of findings that can lead to problems associated with reliability. In spite of this, it is often not the intention to generalize, but to provide interesting new insights into a particular context.

Researchers critical of interpretivism tend to focus on the issue of measurement and reliability. Because studies tend to be qualitative, they do not normally adopt any precise systems of measurement. Consequently, reliability in the sense of accuracy and repeatability can be called into question. For instance, to what extent has the researcher adopted a thorough approach? If a poor record has been kept in relation to data collection and analysis, then it makes it all the more difficult for future researchers to come along and carry out the same piece of work.

Pragmatism   The philosophical debate is often centred on the differences between positivism and interpretivism. If you are unable to choose, or believe that your research is not aligned with either of these philosophies, then you are perhaps a *pragmatist*. The pragmatic paradigm does not align itself with any one philosophical stance and recognizes the importance of both the physical and social world. Pragmatist researchers focus on the 'what' and the 'how' of the research problem

(Creswell, 2003: 11). Pragmatism is generally viewed as the most popular paradigm for mixed methods social enquiry (Greene, 2007), although mixed methods could be used with any paradigm. Pragmatists place the research problem and research questions at the centre of the research and use the methods they consider to be the most appropriate in generating the most significant insights into their research. For example, if you are interested in researching how small companies in your region are coping with the current economic downturn, you may believe that the 'best way' to tackle this research question is to interview the owners of the companies and administer a questionnaire survey to employees. In short, this example can be described as taking a pragmatic stance. The focus is clearly on the research problem, while employing methods considered the most appropriate in answering the research question.

Ontology (the way we think the world is)

While epistemology is concerned with 'What is acceptable knowledge?', *ontology* is concerned with the nature of reality. In essence, it asks how we perceive the social world, or to put it another way, the way we think the world is. You need to decide whether you consider the world is external to social actors, or the perceptions and actions of social actors create social phenomena. If you consider the latter onto-logical stance, then you will adopt the subjectivist view. Subjectivism is clearly linked to interpretivism in that the researcher examines the motivation and social interactions of respondents. As a researcher you need to understand the subjective beliefs and attitudes motivating respondents to act in a particular way. For example, if you decide to analyze management perceptions towards their business networks, you are likely to record a wide range of feedback based on each person's own expe-rience and perceptions. In effect, what you are doing is analyzing business networks based on everyday interaction that management experience. Business networks are therefore viewed by analyzing the subjective experiences of individual actors, namely, management.

Conversely, you may take an external view of the world, associated with objec-tivism. Objectivism is an ontological stance that implies that social phenomena are based on external realities that are beyond our reach or control. Citing the earlier 'business networks' example, rather than involving social actors directly in the research, objectivism would deal with business networks as being external to social actors. Analysis would then be on treating business networks as tangible objects that are clearly defined and external to the everyday changing interactions involving individual actors.

Axiology (role of values in inquiry)

Axiology is concerned with the nature of value. Although this includes notable ethical issues that we will cover in Chapter 4, axiology is essentially concerned with the role that your own perception plays in the research. Your values play a role throughout the entire research process. Positivists consider the process of research as value free. One reason for this is that they are independent of their research. Or to put it another way, they are 'from the outside looking in'.

Interpretivists consider that they are interdependent with their research, or in many cases 'embedded'. They are unlikely to be value free as they consider their own values. Thus, the interpretivist needs to work hard to ensure the production of a credible set of results. You will have your own values in terms of collecting and interpreting your data, and presenting your findings. In short, values are included in the research process. Sometimes these values are likely to be explicit. For instance, you may decide to choose judgemental sampling, thereby choosing respondents whom you perceive as 'adding value' to your study. Or the values can be implicit, such as interpreting findings in a cross-cultural study based on your own cultural values.

How do I know which philosophy to adopt?

You may already see yourself as a particular type of researcher. For instance, you may consider yourself to be a more 'creative, hands-on' person, and therefore inclined to think that interpretivism is best suited to your way of thinking. Alternatively, if you see yourself as someone who prefers accurately measuring information, and taking a non-participatory role in your research, then you may opt for a positivist stance. In reality, the approach you take largely depends on your proposed research questions, along with your own assumptions as to how you should go about your research.

Research approach

Research methods are often associated with two approaches – *inductive* and *deductive*. Let us look at each of these in turn. First, Kenneth F. Hyde (2000: 83) defined *inductive* as 'a theory-building process, starting with observations of specific instances, and seeking to establish generalisation about the phenomenon under investigation'. In other words, if you decide to follow an *inductive approach* to your study, you will be seeking to make observations about your research, and then perhaps contribute to a new theory. Conversely, a *deductive approach* 'begins with and applies a well-known theory'. For example, if your research project was focused on cross-cultural management and based on a deductive approach, then you may decide to apply Geert Hofstede's (1980) cultural theory. In other words, you are applying theory rather than attempting to generate new theory through an inductive approach.

One of the main distinguishing features between business research in an academic setting and 'real life' is *theory*. Quite simply, your own research project requires theoretical content. However, an important question you will need to answer quite early on is: 'How will theory feature in my study?' This brings us to the important distinction between 'induction' and 'deduction'. A *deductive approach* is concerned with developing a *hypothesis* (or hypotheses) based on existing theory, and then designing a research strategy to test the hypothesis. 'In this type of research, theory, and hypotheses built on it, come first and influence the rest of the research process – this type of research is often associated with the *quantitative* type of research' (Ghauri and Grøhaug, 2005: 15). On the other hand, an inductive approach would collect data and develop theory as a result of your data analysis. This type of research is often associated with the *qualitative* type of research. These two types of research strategy are examined later in this section.

At this point, it is worth stressing that I have discussed the dichotomy between qualitative/quantitative research and inductive/deductive. By dichotomizing these terms my intention is to make them easier to understand. Many researchers now challenge such dichotomization by recognizing that there is no reason why overlap cannot take place. For instance,

> as evaluation fieldwork begins, the evaluation may be open to whatever emerges from the data – a discovery or inductive approach. Then, as the inquiry reveals patterns and major dimensions of interest, the evaluator will begin to focus on verifying and elucidating what appears to be emerging – a more deductive approach to data collection and analysis. (Patton, 1991: 194)

The approach you choose may depend on existing literature, e.g. can you see a gap in the literature that needs to be filled, or possibly your type of research questions, e.g. looking at relationships between variables or theory-building. It is worth remembering that if deciding to follow an inductive approach, you need to demonstrate excellent knowledge of the subject. Figure 1.2 shows how theory fits into each approach. Clearly, theory can be applied from the outset (deductive) or be produced as an outcome (inductive). In addition, Table 1.3 summarizes the major differences between deductive and inductive approaches to research.

FIGURE 1.2 How theory fits into your research

TABLE 1.3   Major differences between deductive and inductive approaches to research

Deduction emphasizes	Induction emphasizes
• Scientific principles	• Gaining an understanding of the meanings humans attach to events
• Moving from theory to data	
• The need to explain causal relationships between variables	• A close understanding of the research context
• The collection of quantitative data	• The collection of qualitative data
• The application of controls to ensure validity of data	• A more flexible structure to permit changes of research emphasis as the research progresses
• The operationalization of concepts to ensure clarity of definition	• A realization that the research is part of the research process
• A highly structured approach	• Less concern with the need to generalize
• Researcher independence of what is being researched	
• The necessity to select samples of sufficient size in order to generalize conclusions	

Source: Saunders et al. (2007)

Once again, Table 1.3 dichotomizes deductive and inductive in order to show you the distinction between the two approaches. This distinction is somewhat ambiguous. For example, an inductive approach could also involve the collection of quantitative data. Similarly, a deductive approach may involve the collection of qualitative data, e.g. through interviews. The table is intended to highlight the traditionally perceived differences between the two approaches. Still, this does not mean that a certain amount of overlap cannot take place. Then why make the distinction? In essence, making the distinction between theory and research by considering deduction and induction can help you to decide how to go about your research. Moreover, it can help you to identify which approach existing researchers are taking in your chosen area of research. For instance, if the majority of researchers appear to be adopting an inductive approach, you may decide to 'add something to the literature' by adopting a deductive approach.

Research strategy

Two terms often used to describe the main research strategies to business research are *qualitative* and *quantitative*. Norman K. Denzin and Yvonna S. Lincoln (2000: 8) described the distinction between *qualitative* and *quantitative* as follows:

> the word 'qualitative' implies an emphasis on the qualities of entities and on processes and meanings that are not experimentally examined or measured (if measured at all) in terms of quantity, amount, intensity or frequency. *Qualitative researchers* stress the socially constructed nature of reality, the intimate relationship between the research and what is studied, and the situational

constraints that shape inquiry. Such researchers emphasize the value-laden nature of inquiry. They seek answers to questions that stress how social experience is created and given meaning. In contrast, *quantitative studies* emphasize the measurement and analysis of causal relationships between variables, not processes. Proponents of such studies claim that their work is undertaken from within a value-free framework.

In all likelihood, these are terms that you may have come across before. In short, the main difference is that quantitative research is usually associated with numerical analysis, while qualitative is not. Nevertheless, comparing the two strategies on the basis of analysis is rather simplistic. A number of other key differences also exist. For example, a quantitative strategy is viewed as objective and involves data collection methods such as questionnaires. Yet a qualitative approach is viewed as subjective and involves data collection methods such as interviews. Increasingly, researchers are using mixed methods that offer the advantage of overcoming single-method studies. The next section in this chapter takes a closer look at qualitative and quantitative research.

Qualitative research

Once again, quantitative research examines data that are numerical, while qualitative inquiry examines data that are narrative. *Qualitative research* shares good company with the most rigorous quantitative research, and it should not be viewed as an easy substitute for a 'statistical' or quantitative study (Creswell, 1998). A qualitative strategy is usually linked with an inductive study. As we have already established in this chapter, an inductive theory means that theory is likely to be an outcome, rather than applied from the outset.

Combining qualitative research and inductive theory are common as they are well suited to providing insights that allow for the generation of theoretical frameworks. For example, you might be interested in studying the impact that Chinese cultural values have on Sino-European joint venture performance. If no theoretical framework exists in this particular area, then one option would be to undertake an inductive approach. In the first instance, this may involve identifying cultural values and establishing how these will be measured. Next, interviews might take place with Chinese and European managers involved in the running of the joint venture. This would then be followed by an analysis of your findings. Lastly, depending on your results, you may then propose a theoretical framework that illustrates the relationship between the cultural values and joint venture performance.

Quantitative research

'A *quantitative approach* to research might draw a large and representative sample from the population of interest, measure the behaviour and characteristics of that sample, and attempt to construct generalizations regarding the population as a whole' (Hyde, 2000: 84). Unlike qualitative research, quantitative research is often associated with a deductive approach. In other words, theory is applied from the outset. Analysis is usually statistical and involves analyzing the results following theoretical application. Rather than generating a theoretical framework as a possible outcome, you would apply an existing theory that would help interpret your findings. Furthermore, because you have probably applied a theory that has been used by several previous researchers, interestingly your results can often be compared with current studies. Using the joint venture example again, let us assume that now that you have analyzed the relationship between cultural values and joint venture performance, you are keen to know how many years managers intend remaining in a joint venture. The nature of this question is objective and will generate numeric or quantitative data.

A comparison of qualitative and quantitative research

One way of describing qualitative and quantitative research is to compare the differences between the two. These differences include:

- the rejection of quantitative, positivist methods by qualitative researchers;
- qualitative researchers believe they can get closer to the actors' perspective through detailed interviewing and observation;
- qualitative researchers are more likely to confront the constraints of everyday life, while quantitative researchers tend to abstract themselves from this world and consequently they seldom study it directly; and
- qualitative researchers tend to believe that rich descriptions are valuable while quantitative researchers are less concerned with such detail (Näslund, 2002: 328).

Qualitative and quantitative methods do not necessarily have to be used exclusively. 'One might use qualitative data to illustrate or clarify quantitatively derived findings, or one could quantify demographic findings, or use some form of quantitative data to partially validate one's qualitative analysis' (Strauss and Corbin, 1990).

Most research projects and researchers, however, place their emphasis on one form or another, partly out of conviction, but also because of training and the nature of the problems studied.

When comparing a qualitative and quantitative study, in a qualitative study, the research question often starts with a *how* or *what* so that initial forays into the topic describe what is going on. This is in contrast to quantitative questions that ask *why* and look for a comparison of groups (e.g. is Group 1 better at something than Group 2?) or a relationship between variables, with the intent of establishing an association, relationship, or cause and effect, e.g. did variable X explain what happened in variable Y? (Creswell, 1998).

Although some students shy away from quantitative research for fear of statistics, it is worth noting that although data collection can be time-consuming and problematic, data analysis is relatively straightforward. This is in contrast to qualitative research where conducting a small number of interviews may seem uncomplicated, yet the analysis, often typing and analyzing interview transcripts, can be extremely time-consuming. To give you some idea, transcribing a one-hour interview is likely to involve in the region of 5,000–6,000 words!

Finally, your research strategy is likely to be a matter of choice. Once again, it is not simply a question of one or the other. In many respects your strategy does not need to follow a qualitative/quantitative divide. Increasingly, students are recognizing that using mixed methods for their data collection can add value to their study. For example, you may wish to administer a questionnaire survey that explores customer satisfaction in your workplace, while you are also interested in conducting follow-up interviews with those individuals who appear to be particularly dissatisfied.

In short, do not be 'pigeon-holed' into one strategy or the other, but consider the merits of adopting an eclectic approach.

Combining qualitative and quantitative research (multi-strategy research)

In the previous section I briefly introduced the term 'mixed methods' and the possibilities available to researchers for combining qualitative and quantitative research. According to Tashakkori and Teddlie (1998: 17–18), mixed method studies are those that 'combine the qualitative and quantitative approaches into the research methodology of a single study or multi-phased study.' However, arguably this is perhaps taking a simplistic view of so-called 'mixed methods', as research can involve different paradigms, more than one researcher and a number of research methods. In brief, mixed methods are complex and should be viewed at a strategic level. This view is shared by Bryman (2001), who argues that a more suitable term for 'mixed methods' is 'multi-strategy'. This is because 'mixing' implies combining qualitative and quantitative methods in some way. Arguably, a more accurate description is that qualitative and quantitative are not combined, but you have multiple levels. Therefore, for the remainder of this book I will use the term 'multi-strategy' as opposed to 'mixed methods'. Multi-strategy research can be viewed as 'pragmatic research' in that the research does not attempt to 'fit' into any one paradigm, but the researcher uses whichever methods he or she considers work best for their particular study.

What is the rationale for using multi-strategy research?   Prior to considering the merits of conducting multi-strategy research, it is important to note the underlying reasons why some scholars are critical of this approach. First, it can be argued that qualitative and quantitative methods rest on different paradigm assumptions and cannot be easily combined. Second, carrying out multi-strategy research is time-consuming and likely to be expensive. Third, a student may not be familiar with both forms of data and lack the required skills to conduct both qualitative and quantitative research. Finally, carrying out multi-strategy research is rarely an essential requirement at most academic institutions.

Proponents of multi-strategy research cite a number of reasons why it should be a serious consideration when conducting research. These include:

- Multi-strategy research helps to answer questions that can only be answered by combining qualitative and quantitative research. For example, 'Why do respondents provide certain answers in a questionnaire survey?' In other words, qualitative data can be used to determine quantitative results.
- Multi-strategy studies are practical and do not restrict the researcher to 'sticking to' well-defined research paradigms. In other words, it adopts a pragmatic approach to research.
- Multi-strategy research can come across as more comprehensive and in-depth than being restricted to purely qualitative or quantitative. For example, if you decided to research the Eurozone crisis, restricting your analysis to numerical data does not address people's overall opinions on key issues associated with the crisis.

How can multi-strategy research be incorporated into my study?   If you are considering using multi-strategy research, a key question is deciding how the combination of qualitative and quantitative research should be incorporated into your study. For example, should qualitative come before quantitative? Should both the qualitative and quantitative phases be conducted at the same time? Creswell (1995) addresses the issue of how and when multi-strategy research should be undertaken by proposing the following four what he refers to as 'mixed method designs':

- Two-phase studies: The researcher first conducts a qualitative phase of a study and then a quantitative phase, or vice versa. The two phases are separate. For example, the first phase might involve carrying out a focus group (qualitative), followed by administering a question-naire survey (quantitative).
- Parallel studies: The researcher conducts the qualitative and quantitative phases at the same time.
- Equivalent status designs: The researcher conducts the study using both the quantitative and the qualitative approaches (about equally) to understand the phenomenon under study.
- Dominant/less dominant studies: The researcher conducts the study 'within a single dominant paradigm with a small component of the overall study drawn from an alternative design'

(Creswell, 1995: 177).

Tashakkori and Teddlie (1998) also propose a fifth design – designs with multilevel use of approaches. The authors describe this design as using different types of methods at different levels of aggregation. For example, data could be analyzed qualitatively at the individual level, quantitatively at the departmental level, qualitatively at the company level and quantitatively at the organizational level.

Writing up and multi-strategy research   Similar to data collection, a key issue for multi-strategy researchers is deciding how to write up multi-strategy findings. In essence, if you decide to undertake multi-strategy research, the presentation of your findings depends on which multi-strategy design you have chosen. For example, if carrying out a two-phase study, then it makes perfect sense to present the findings in the order that each research approach was undertaken.

Multi-strategy research from a business setting   Multi-strategy research is certainly receiving greater acceptance in the academic community. Evidence of this is that there is now even an academic journal in this area – the *Journal of Mixed Methods Research* (JMMR). According to the publishers, the journal's scope includes 'delineating where mixed methods research may be used most effectively, illuminating design and procedure issues, and determining the logistics of conducting mixed methods research'.

What is the relationship between research philosophy, research approach, and research strategy?

Earlier in the chapter, the Honeycomb of Research Methodology illustrated the six main elements that make up research methodology. By now, you should begin to see a relationship between the first three of these elements, the key concepts of research, and recognize how choice of research philosophy is likely to influence both choice of research approach and research strategy (see Table 1.4). The intention of this table is to get you thinking about how your own preferences, values and choice of topic may influence your epistemological stance.

Once again, to illustrate the relationship between the key concepts of research, if your epistemological stance is a positivist one, then you are likely to view knowledge as an object (objective), or in other words it exists independently of the mind. In addition, your research approach is likely to be deductive, whilst adopting a quantitative research strategy. In essence, your choice of research philosophy is likely to determine your research approach and research strategy. For example, if you intended applying existing theories for measuring a company's performance, using financial measures and statistical data, while administering a questionnaire to gather this data, then there is a clear thread here from epistemology (positivist), ontology (objective), to research approach (deductive), followed by research strategy (quantitative). If you are taking an interpretivist stance, then your ontological view is likely to consider knowledge as an idea that is independent of someone's mind (subjective), research approach is likely to be inductive, while undertaking a qualitative research strategy. However, pragmatism does not take one epistemological stance, as pragmatists place the research problem and research questions at the centre of the research. In addition, they use methods they consider to be the most appropriate in generating the most significant insights into their research;

TABLE 1.4 Positivism, interpretivism and pragmatism epistemologies

	Research approach	Ontology	Axiology	Research strategy
Positivism	Deductive	Objective	Value-free	Quantitative
Interpretivism	Inductive	Subjective	Biased	Qualitative
Pragmatism	Deductive/inductive	Objective and subjective	Value-free/biased	Qualitative and/or quantitative

typically, this involves multi-strategy research. The researcher adopts both an objective and subjective point of view. Morgan (2007: 71) refers to the relationship between theory and data in the pragmatic approach as a version of 'abductive reasoning' that moves back and forth between induction and deduction. In other words, in terms of ontology, a multiple view is chosen in order to achieve the research question(s).

Finally, remember that your epistemology does not have to be quite so rigid. Your choice in this respect is down to your decision as an independent researcher. When considering your research problem and research questions, you should ask yourself which is your preferred philosophical stance, how this relates to your research approach, and the research strategy required to help you to address your initial research questions.

How Business Research Links to the Organization

Of course, businesses also have to make important decisions in terms of how they approach research, such as decisions governing qualitative and quantitative strategies. Yet, the extent of their involvement in business research often depends on the size and resources within an organization and whether or not it is carried out in-house or outsourced to a third party. We have established that business research is conducted in order to aid business-related decision-making, usually in response to external market conditions. For example, a car manufacturer might decide to conduct research exploring why a particular model has witnessed a sudden decline in sales. However, we have yet to examine how business research links to the organization in terms of how it is carried out and by whom. Frequently, large companies will employ research agencies to carry out research on their behalf, while small and medium sized enterprises (SMEs) tend to conduct research in-house. Research may be conducted on an *ad hoc* basis or at regular intervals.

Ipsos MORI is one of the UK's leading market research agencies. Clients include Toyota, Nokia, the BBC and Norfolk County Council. Figure 1.3 shows the possible

Step 1: Norfolk County Council (NCC) commission Ipsos MORI to conduct research into people's views on education provision within the county
Step 2: Ipsos MORI collect data on behalf of NCC
Step 3: Ipsos MORI analyze data on behalf of NCC
Step 4: Ipsos MORI report findings to NCC
Step 5: NCC considers the report findings then takes the appropriate action*

*If NCC is unsatisfied with the service provided by Ipsos MORI, or certain aspects of the findings do not meet with their approval, additional research may be required.

FIGURE 1.3   Possible steps taken by a market research agency steps Ipsos MORI may take when conducting research on behalf of the UK local authority, Norfolk County Council.

Unlike Norfolk County Council, unfortunately you do not have the luxury of a market research agency to carry out research on your behalf! Nevertheless, essentially the steps involved are not dissimilar to those required when undertaking your own research project. Clearly, your own project will also include a set of objectives, data collection and findings. These stages will be explored in greater detail when we look at 'research process' later in this chapter.

Research Skills

In order to be able to successfully complete your research project, it is essential that you are familiar with the skills required. This section is devoted to what I would call the 'key skills' that should be a characteristic of every student researcher.

Research practitioners and student researchers share similar skills when conducting research. Still, there are some notable differences. First, let us look at the skills required to be a research practitioner. As illustrated in the above Ipsos MORI example, research practitioners are usually working on behalf of a client or clients, and are paid a flat fee for doing so. The size of the fee depends on a number of factors, such as the amount of work involved, the number of researchers appointed, the timeframe, the geographical coverage and the number of agencies able to carry out the research. Obviously, to justify their fee, research practitioners have to portray a range of qualities – communication and presentation skills, an ability to work to deadlines, effective organizational management and attention to detail. Although these do not all apply to a student researcher, certain qualities, such as organizational management and working to deadlines, are certainly relevant.

The next section discusses essential skills that should help you to achieve a better overall performance when undertaking your research project. Let us look at each of these in turn.

Dedication

Undertaking any form of research is a time-consuming and usually an extremely challenging process. Your research project is no different. It is important that you adopt a dedicated approach from the outset. Starting your project a few short weeks prior to the submission deadline is unlikely to produce a piece of work of sufficient standard. Naturally, taking into account certain considerations in your research is likely to lead to higher levels of dedication. If you choose a topic that you consider interesting, you will find it much easier to motivate yourself towards your study. Similarly, if you choose a topic that you already have some knowledge and experience of, this can increase your level of motivation. On the other hand, remember that if you choose a topic simply on the basis of it being perceived as an easy option, you may find it difficult to motivate yourself to complete your project to a satisfactory conclusion.

Responsibility

Both a practitioner and student researcher need to consider areas of responsibility while doing their research. To give you some idea of the responsibilities required of a practitioner researcher, Figure 1.4 illustrates some of the key professional responsibilities expected of researchers working on behalf of the Market Research Society. MRS is the world's largest association serving all those with professional equity in the provision or use of market, social and opinion research, and in business intelligence, market analysis, customer insight and consultancy (www.mrs.org.uk).

1 Researchers shall ensure that participation in their activities is based on voluntary informed consent.
2 Researchers shall be straightforward and honest in all their professional and business relationships.
3 Researchers shall be transparent as to the subject and purpose of data collection.
4 Researchers shall respect the confidentiality of information collected in their professional activities.
5 Researchers shall respect the rights and well-being of all individuals.
6 Researchers shall ensure that respondents are not harmed or adversely affected by their professional activities.
7 Researchers shall balance the needs of individuals, clients and their professional activities.
8 Researchers shall exercise independent professional judgement in the design, conduct and reporting of their professional activities.
9 Researchers shall ensure that their professional activities are conducted by persons with appropriate training, qualifications and experience.
10 Researchers shall protect the reputation and integrity of the profession.

FIGURE 1.4   The principles of the MRS 'code of conduct': MRS Code of Conduct (2010)

Source: https://www.mrs.org.uk/pdf/code_of_conduct.pdf Accessed 20 September 2013

As a student researcher you have a number of responsibilities to consider. For example, if you decide to conduct in-depth interviews, research participants must be asked whether or not they wish the information provided to remain confidential. Second, you have a responsibility to complete your project in line with your own university or college code of conduct on project submission. A key feature of this is likely to be avoiding plagiarism, i.e. claiming that someone else's work is your own. Lastly, you have a responsibility to yourself to make sure that your final project provides an accurate insight into your findings. Several of the points highlighted above relate to ethical standards.

Language

If English is not your first language, it is worth allowing additional time to conduct your research. Having your grammar checked by a native English speaker can also help. Even if English is your native language, you may still lack confidence when it comes to writing up. Reading articles from peer-reviewed journals can help you to

TABLE 1.5 Research methods – examples of learning outcomes

Learning outcomes (threshold standards)	
On successful completion of this module the student will be expected to be able to:	
Knowledge and understanding	1. Demonstrate a critical understanding of the different approaches to research used in business/management and the social sciences.
	2. Identify and justify decisions regarding their chosen topic, research questions and research methodology.
Intellectual, practical, affective and transferable skills	3. Synthesize and critically evaluate the current theoretical and methodological developments in their chosen field of study, making clear their own contributions to this body of work.
	4. Demonstrate the required skills and abilities needed to successfully plan, organize, undertake and communicate the findings of a piece of small-scale business/management research.

Source: Anglia Ruskin University (2008)

get a feel for the writing style required to complete your project. This is particularly true in relation to the literature review (Chapter 3).

Although you are not writing an English language project, the reader still needs to be able to make sense of what it is that you are trying to say. Avoid simple errors such as 'costumer' (customer or consumer). Essentially, you must show good use of grammar and punctuation in your writing. Many universities and colleges award marks for presentation; this usually includes the level of English. Of course, a sound understanding of Microsoft Word can help greatly when it comes to writing your project. Certainly, electronic tools such as spell-check and a thesaurus are extremely useful. Just remember to set the required English language function!

Finally, anyone can become a solid researcher. This primarily relates to having the required academic ability to fulfil the learning outcomes laid down by your academic institution. Although these tend to vary between institutions, often they are along similar lines. Table 1.5 provides an example of learning outcomes that are likely to be expected of you by your institution.

Academic skills required to complete your project may have been taught to you as part of a research skills module. Still, in some institutions study programmes do not include such a provision. Therefore, a book such as this can help guide you through the research process. In addition, past student projects and peer-reviewed journals can be a useful guide to academic requirements.

During your course you will have studied a wide range of modules. For many students, their chosen topic is often based on a subject they have studied earlier in their degree. If you are studying a BA (Hons) in Finance, for instance, you may have particularly enjoyed corporate finance, and this may then form the basis of the topic for your project. Because you have chosen a subject that you already have knowledge about, you are more likely to be confident about your ability to produce a competent piece of work related to that subject.

Management

This primarily relates to time management and organizational management. Producing a time management plan from the outset will help you to keep on track with your research. A time management plan that you design for yourself will also allow you to build in the flexibility you need to meet other work/life commitments. Organizational management is also something you need to get into the habit of doing at an early stage in your research. From my own experience as a student, I learned how important organizational management is the hard way. Trying to find dozens of references without an organized record is by no means an easy task! I quickly learned the error of my ways and from then on adopted a strict regime of organization.

As you begin to amass a large amount of data, keeping an organized file will help you enormously. This can be done either using a lever arch file or electronically. Whichever method you choose, you will undoubtedly notice the benefits of keeping an organized file of your work. This is especially true during your writing-up stage.

Research Process

Earlier, I noted that a practitioner researcher and student researcher go through similar stages when conducting research. Yet there are some notable differences. First, as a student researcher your research needs to contain a certain amount of theory. Second, often a key support during your research is your project supervisor. The significance of the supervisor is explained later in this chapter. Given the supervisor's importance, it is something that I will make reference to on several occasions throughout the course of this book.

As is similar to research methodology, the majority of textbooks on research skills make reference to the research process by illustrating a series of stages. In reality, your research is unlikely to follow a logical series of steps. For example, you will probably start at the literature review stage in order to generate ideas. Furthermore, you may find that you have a problem with your methodology and, as a result, you need to go back and rethink your objectives. Basically, what I'm saying here is that by all means use the stages model as a guide, but be prepared to revisit stages, or perhaps even start with the literature review. A typical example of the *research process* is as follows:

- *Establish an intention.* Obviously, you need to have a basic purpose prior to carrying out your research. In the case of your project, your focus will be on starting and eventually completing your research within the time period laid down by your college or university.
- *Choosing a research topic.* Before you start, you need a subject. Generally, your choice of topic is likely to be influenced by what interests you, having suitable access to information, or

perhaps career aspirations. The latter can help become a useful selling tool when attending job interviews following your graduation. The nature of the research topic and how to generate ideas and establish research questions are covered in Chapter 2.

- *Conduct a literature review.* A literature review is an essential part of academic research. Basically, it is an acknowledgement of what has already been written on your chosen subject. It helps to identify 'gaps' in the existing literature that may assist you in forming the basis of your study as well as helping to avoid repetition.
- *Research design.* Your research design is a systematic plan of the data collection and analysis phases of your project. This is fully explored in Chapter 5.
- *Address ethics.* Ethics are the principles and values that underpin the way researchers conduct their research. Although I have briefly highlighted ethics during this introductory chapter, this is discussed in detail in Chapter 4.
- *Collect data.* The process of gathering your data from often a wide range of sources. These are likely to include both primary and secondary data. We will examine the main data collection methods in Chapters 6 and 7, followed by sampling techniques in Chapter 8.
- *Analyze data.* The process of analyzing your results to see the extent to which they address your research questions/hypotheses. The tools of analysis depend on whether you have collected quantitative or qualitative data. These are addressed in Chapters 9 and 10 respectively.
- *Write up.* At some point all that information that you have gathered, probably over several months, needs to be written up. This will fall within the structure of your research project guidelines. Perhaps one of the main questions concerning writing up is when to start. This, along with other issues related to writing up and presentation, is tackled in the final section Chapter 11.

Many students have commented to me that their own research was by no means a linear process. The majority of these tended to consult the literature in order to generate ideas; from this, research ideas were then formulated. Other students place little emphasis on consulting the literature. They know exactly what they want to do and are more likely to follow the typical stages in the research process. It may be that they are mature students and have valuable experience and knowledge about a certain industry, or are perhaps a part-time student who has received support from his or her company to conduct research based on their place of work. Either way, this is really personal choice. The same can be said for the writing-up stage. I have known many students who have started writing as soon as they have sufficient information to be able to do so. Others prefer writing up when all of the relevant stages have been successfully completed. Once again, this is personal choice.

Differences Between Academic and Organizational Research

Academics are often preoccupied with research that helps to build or question theory, and helps develop research approaches. Many universities require academics to publish in leading academic journals. In business and management, these are often journals that practitioners are unlikely to read, such as the *Journal of Marketing* and the *Journal of Consumer Research*. The practical application of these studies is not always clear. They may be largely theoretical and focus on the key literature, thereby making them irrelevant to many applied researchers.

When it comes to decision-making:

> Qualitative researchers in particular are geared towards providing information that will help clients make a better decision. They, too, build models or theories but perhaps the latter are less formal and often relatively specific to a narrow piece of transient consumer behaviour. Likewise, they have a viewpoint on reality and epistemology but this is less often articulated. Qualitative applied researchers are driven by mainstream commercial reality – a need to attract and retain clients. (Keegan et al., 2008: 108)

I have mentioned that academics build or question theory. Similarly, theoretical application is of course an important aspect to your own research project. One reason for conducting research is to develop and apply concepts and theories. *Basic* (or *pure*) *research* attempts to expand our knowledge about a particular subject. Academic researchers usually undertake basic or pure research. For example, academic researchers might be interested in how consumers make decisions when buying a range of different products. This might involve analyzing their beliefs and attitudes towards a diverse range of brands. Essentially, basic research tends to be of an exploratory nature. Alternatively, *applied research* is undertaken when a decision must be made in relation to a real-life problem. Examples of the research applied researchers might carry out include:

- how to improve medical care provision within a particular town or city;
- how to combat an increase in violent crime; and
- how to increase the usage of public transport.

Researchers working in the commercial sector are more likely to answer questions to specific problems. For example, an organization considering an electronic payroll system for the company's accounts department may conduct research to find out if employees prefer their existing system or the proposed electronic version. In some cases, studies conducted as a result of basic research may have an influence on applied research. For instance, the example above, 'How to increase the usage of public transport', might be influenced by existing basic research findings into what motivates people to use public transport.

Work-based or professional practice project

For some students, there is perhaps a 'blur' between what can be described as academic and organizational research. The reason for this is that many universities now offer bespoke courses to companies. Employees in these organizations are often at managerial level, study part-time, and the course is funded by their employer. Although there is an 'academic element', the research project is likely to be based on the student's employer, and/or their role in the organization. This type of so called 'work-based' or 'professional practice' project sometimes results in the findings being implemented within the organization. Let us take an example of an online retailer. As part of their work-based project, an employee may intend to find out why shoppers buy online (pure research) and how online sales for their company can be increased (basic research). Once again, from experience, I know that in some instances the empirical findings of such studies have been implemented by a student's employer.

The Role of the Supervisor

A supervisor involved in organizational research usually ensures that his or her team fulfils their research brief. In short, they oversee a particular *research project*. The onus is on the supervisor to make sure that the team carries out a research project within a given timeframe, while meeting a set of predetermined objectives.

On the other hand, an academic supervisor's role is not to manage a student when doing their research, but to play a supportive role. Unlike a supervisor engaged in organizational research, there is no onus on the academic project supervisor to contact the person carrying out the research, in this case the student.

The majority of textbooks on research skills make a rather 'limited' reference to the project supervisor. Although your final research project is probably an individual piece of work, do not be afraid to seek advice and support whenever you feel it is necessary. An obvious point of contact is your project supervisor. Yet, surprisingly, there are some students who perhaps meet up with their supervisor only once or twice during their research. In some cases, no contact is made at all. This is unfortunate. Typically, a supervisor is allocated on the basis of a student's choice of research topic, although there are institutional differences in terms of how supervisors are allocated.

Though I believe no scientific study has been undertaken in this area, often there appears to be a relationship between the number of supervisor–student meetings and the quality of a student's final project. There are perhaps two reasons for this. First, in many institutions the first marker is the project supervisor. Obviously, if you have met your supervisor on several occasions, then you are more likely to understand his or her expectations governing your study. Not only that, their specialist area is likely to be linked to your chosen area of study. Thus, it makes sense to question your supervisor over theories, sources of information and access to data, etc. Second, meeting your supervisor can also help to build your own confidence while doing your research, certainly in relation to overcoming potentially difficult areas.

My experience is that the majority of students are unclear about research methodology yet fail to look for support from their research supervisor. Your supervisor can be a major influence on your project. While much of the responsibility for your success lies with you, the role of the supervisor cannot be ignored. They can be an invaluable source of information regarding literature, idea generation, research methods and writing up. Conducting research can be a lonely business. Quite simply, having a general discussion with someone who is able to relate to your research can be extremely refreshing.

It is vital that you keep your supervisor up to date on your progress throughout your research. They are then able to ensure that you are fully on track with your study and are able to complete it within the timeframe. If you are unclear about any aspect of your research, don't hesitate to ask your supervisor.

In summary, using your supervisor effectively can provide you with a number of advantages:

- Access to an individual who is likely to be a specialist in your chosen topic. Because this is often the case, your supervisor will be able to identify and discuss the strengths and weaknesses of your chosen topic. In addition, they are likely to be very familiar with relevant literature, particularly key authors in your chosen field.
- Whether your supervisor is a specialist in your chosen field or not, they will undoubtedly be familiar with the required structure of your research. Your supervisor will be able to provide you with constructive support and advice governing important chapters such as literature review, methodology and results and analysis.
- Even if you believe that you are familiar with the rules and regulations governing the compiling and submission of your research project, it is still wise to liaise with your supervisor to make sure that you have fulfilled your institution's requirements. For student researchers, particularly international students, rules and regulations governing issues such as plagiarism, word length, extensions, binding and referencing may well be completely alien. Easy marks can often be lost through failure to understand these issues. Sadly, despite the importance stressed to students of adhering to rules and regulations governing the research project, their ability to follow these is often a disappointment.

You can only really capitalize on the above advantages if you carefully organize and plan your supervisor meetings. Fundamentally, this involves three stages: (1) preparation for a meeting with your supervisor; (2) during the meeting with your supervisor; and (3) following a meeting with your supervisor. Each of these stages is addressed below:

- *Preparation.* You must agree a set time with your supervisor and do all you can to stick to the agreed time slot. Failure to arrive on time, or cancelling at the last minute, is unlikely to go down well, especially if it is your first meeting! Also, make sure that you have a predetermined set of questions ready to discuss with your supervisor. Ideally, you should choose a sufficient number of questions to be covered within your allotted meeting time. For example, if you have arranged a 15-minute meeting, obviously arriving at your supervisor's office with a list of 25 questions is far too many! Unfortunately, failure to establish a set of questions prior to meeting their supervisor is all too common among student researchers.
- *During.* Once you meet your supervisor, do not hesitate to work through your predetermined list of questions. It is of primary importance that you fully understand your supervisor's answers to each respective question. If in doubt, do not be afraid to clarify their answer. For example, saying something like 'So, what you're saying is …' or 'Do you mind if I clarify your answer?' Remember that one of the main roles of your supervisor is to guide you through the research process. Therefore, if in doubt, ask.
- Your essential tools during your meeting should be a pencil and notepad. Very few people have the gift of being able to recollect everything that was discussed during a meeting. Hence the need to write things down! Not only should you write down the answers to your supervisor's

Date/time	Comments	Signature
16 Sept. 2008	Discussed literature review. Key authors recommended – Kotler (1998), Hofstede (1980) and Fang (2001). Some problems with structure – begin by defining key constructs, adopting a critical approach.	Dr Ron Taylor

FIGURE 1.5   Extract from a student/supervisor meeting log

questions, but also a plan of action. In other words, clear targets to be achieved prior to the next meeting. Finally, agree a date and time of your next meeting. I have found that some students like to keep a meeting log with their supervisor. In the main, this includes date and time, along with a summary of the key issues discussed during the course of the meeting. Lastly, the supervisor then signs the meeting log as confirmation that the meeting took place (see Figure 1.5).

- *Following.* When you return home, make sure that you read through, and understand, your notes arising from the meeting. The longer you leave them laying in the bottom of your bag, the greater the likelihood that you will forget suggestions made by your supervisor. Preferably, keep your supervisor meeting notes in a well-organized file for future reference.

How often should I see my research supervisor?

Figure 1.6 illustrates a possible approach to incorporating your supervisor meetings when working on your research project. In short, each stage of the research process involves a meeting with your supervisor. For instance, when deciding on your

FIGURE 1.6   Research process, including the role of the research supervisor

research topic, you meet your supervisor in order to discuss your ideas. Following your meeting, you can then decide whether or not to act on your supervisor's advice. This may involve developing your topic or, quite possibly, reconsidering your ideas.

Now, I'm not suggesting that all students need to adopt this approach. In reality, some students have sufficient knowledge and experience to carry out a very good research project, involving minimal contact time with their supervisor. Unfortunately, it is often those students who need to see their supervisor the most who fail to arrange an adequate number of meetings. Remember that in most institutions the onus is on the student, not the supervisor, to make contact. A supervisor's specialist knowledge and experience is probably the best source available to students. To not use it will ultimately lead to an inferior piece of work being submitted.

If you have any issues concerning your research project, in most cases your research supervisor can resolve these. The number of times you meet your supervisor is largely dependent on your knowledge of your chosen topic, research expertise, the extent to which you understand your institution's rules and regulations governing the research project and, finally, whether or not you experience any unforeseen circumstances during your project that prevent you from making progress. This can be anything from a change in personal circumstances to problems with your methodology.

RESEARCH IN ACTION

Multi-strategy research

ICT: Is it still a turn on?

Figures about the small and medium sized enterprise (SME) market fly around with alarming regularity – they're spending this, there are that many of them and so on. *The Guardian* has conducted some of its own research to try to quantify the market and find out where it is placed as regards information and communication technology (ICT).

According to *Guardian* figures, there are 4 million small and medium sized enterprises (SMEs) in the UK, when an SME can have between two and 199 employees. These companies account for 55.6% of employment in the UK and, between them, spent £9.6bn on ICT in 2003, up 21% from 2002. This figure is forecast to grow to £14.4bn by 2006. The larger companies are clearly spending more on technology, with an average of £21,298 going out of companies with 50–199 people, compared to £4,271 from companies with between two and five employees (note, though, that the figures per head work out vastly more expensive for the smaller companies). Unsurprisingly, IT and internet companies spent most in the area, with professional services coming second.

What was more interesting was the qualitative rather than quantitative elements of the survey. Forty-one per cent of SMEs disagreed with the statement 'We only invest in new technology when existing equipment breaks down', and three-fifths of respondents intended to upgrade their equipment in the next year. Presumably, this means more SMEs are noting benefits from staying ahead of the competition in terms of the technology deployed. This ties in neatly with the idea that the buying decisions are heading out of the hands of the specialist IT staff and, indeed, away from the boardroom – over two-thirds of non-directors are involved in authorizing ICT spend.

Internet awareness is high among the SME community. Even among the smallest companies, comprising between two and five people, 72% have a website, rising to 99% when you look at the top end; an average of 26% of those companies accept orders online and broadband is clearly spreading – an average 67% of companies across the SME spectrum have it. Of the companies with broadband, 59% said it had improved their business performance a lot, 23% said it had made a little difference and the rest said it made no difference at all. Fast upload, download and general internet access were the main benefits.

Of the most interest, however, was the perceptions of suppliers and availability of certain products. Thirty-three per cent of non-broadband companies said they wouldn't get it within the next 12 months because it wasn't available, but they took no account of cable modems or fixed wireless alternatives. Twenty-seven per cent thought most ICT suppliers were not interested in servicing their needs, and 31% felt the ICT suppliers didn't appreciate their needs – these are minorities of course, but substantial minorities.

Finally, wireless technology, although much written about, continues to be a minority pursuit. Although there were variants according to company size, only 32% of companies in the SME sector were using any form of wireless technology. Sixteen per cent were using Bluetooth, 21% had Bluetooth of some description and only 8% were mobile through GSM/3G. Forty-nine per cent of those with the technology felt it was delivering benefits. (Clapperton, 2004)

As illustrated in the above article, by undertaking multi-strategy research the researchers were not only able to determine the amount SMEs spent on ICT (quantitative), but also when SMEs are likely to purchase ICT equipment and their perceptions of suppliers (qualitative). Clearly, understanding the relationship between SMEs and ICT is a complex subject. The premise of using multi-strategy research in this case provides a better understanding of this relationship. If the researchers had undertaken mono-method research, such as a purely quantitative-based study, they would have missed the interesting set of qualitative findings generated from the investigation. Moreover, combining both methods generates more of a 'complete picture' of the phenomenon.

Often, students have ambitions of conducting multi-strategy research. If you think that your own project may involve using multi-strategy research, bear in mind that it remains a challenge for three reasons. First, you may find it difficult to complete your research on time. Second, there is likely to be a financial cost incurred. Finally, not all researchers have the necessary skills required to carry out research of this type. In spite of the potential drawbacks, it is worth considering the merits associated with multi-strategy research in the early stages of your research.

Summary and Conclusion

This chapter has introduced the concept of research, in particular business research. It has drawn attention to the key concepts of research – research philosophy, research approach and research strategy. The link between business research and the organization has been discussed, along with the necessary research skills required to be an effective researcher. Here are the key points from this chapter:

- The research questions are the main focus of any project, and can probably best be described as '*the glue that holds the project together*'.
- Research can be defined as a 'step-by-step process that involves the collecting, recording, analyzing and interpreting of information'.
- Methodology is concerned with the overall approach to the research process. This includes everything from your theoretical application to the collection and analysis of your data. On the other hand, methods refer to the different ways in which data can be collected and analyzed.
- The Honeycomb of Research Methodology illustrates the six main elements that make up research methodology, presents the key concepts of research, and provides a framework for structuring your methodology chapter.
- An understanding of epistemology is important because it is fundamental to the way you approach and interpret your research.
- Research epistemologies include: positivism, interpretivism and pragmatism. The latter is typically associated with mixed methods or multi-strategy research.
- Consider whether a multi-strategy approach might be preferable to a mono-method design and think about the implications of doing multi-strategy research.
- Make sure that you make full use of the support and advice of your research supervisor.

CASE STUDY — The Relevance and Importance of Research Methods Classes

David Parker, a final year BA (Hons) student in Business and Management, was now three weeks into his research methods module. The first part of the module had examined research philosophy and introduced the undergraduate research project. Although David had enjoyed earlier modules covering all areas of business, he was finding it difficult to see how studying research methods would benefit his aspirations of becoming an Advertising Director.

Case study questions

1. How would you convince David of the value attached to studying research methods?
2. What are the key skills David requires in order to complete his research project?

YOU'RE THE SUPERVISOR

Angela is currently in the process of starting her undergraduate research project. She has undertaken a short course on research skills as part of her study programme. Angela understands the general concept of multi-strategy research, but is still unclear as to the benefits associated with doing this type of research. She has turned to you, her supervisor, for advice on how she might justify carrying out multi-strategy research.

Supervisor question

- How would you respond to Angela?

1. I find starting my research project quite daunting and do not understand many of the terms associated with research philosophy. How important is it to fully understand the terminology?

Answer: This depends on the institution and the level/type of degree programme you are studying on. However, I would say that it is certainly important to know the basic differences between the main research epistemologies. The reason for this is that you will almost certainly be required to make reference to research philosophy in your methodology chapter. This is in addition to being able to justify your research approach. The marker of your project will be looking to see if you have a firm grasp of your chosen methodology in your research project. It is of course very difficult to demonstrate this if you do not have a solid understanding of the key concepts examined earlier in this chapter.

2. As an international student, I have found that the academic requirements associated with doing a research project in the UK are very different to my home country. Where can I go for advice?

Answer: Most universities offer some type of research methods module or workshop that is designed to support students before or during their research. You can of course seek advice from your research supervisor. Your supervisor will be acquainted with the rules and regulations governing content, structure and submission. Moreover, in some institutions you will find that it is possible to read through past projects. For example, the business faculty at my own institution keeps a selection of past projects. The reference library system in place means that students can read through examples of good practice, thus gaining an invaluable insight into structure and presentation.

3. Do I need to meet with my supervisor and what kind of support can my supervisor give me during my research?

Answer: In response to the first part of this question, the short answer is yes! Although the generic research process is typically the same for all researchers, your supervisor is likely to be an expert in your chosen research topic. This means that they are able to recommend key sources of information that you can turn to when carrying out your research. Your supervisor may also be able to provide valuable feedback on draft chapters of your work. Again, whether your supervisor is able to read through work in progress depends on the institution. At some institutions, supervisors are permitted to read through an entire draft prior to submission, while in others, supervisors may not be allowed to read through students' work. Typically, from my experience, the majority of institutions allow supervisors to read through one chapter or perhaps 20% of a student's work before submission. If your university falls into this category, then I suggest asking your supervisor to read through the chapter that you have the most concerns with.

(Continued)

(Continued)

4. How much time do I have to allocate to each stage in the research process?

Answer: There is no easy answer to this question as it usually depends on a number of factors. Not least, the amount of time that you are able to devote towards your research. Obviously, for part-time students and those with demanding responsibilities, the chances are that the research process will take longer. Other issues can also make finishing within the required timeframe challenging. These include: experiencing difficulties with your research methodology, a change in personal circumstances or possibly even your supervisor moving to another institution. In theory, the latter should not be such an issue. As discussed earlier in the chapter, having an effective time management system in place can certainly help ensure that you meet your deadline. Another consideration is that you may find certain stages take longer than expected because of your choice of research methodology. For example, conducting multi-strategy research will ultimately mean that your data collection and analysis will take longer than if you opted for a mono-method design.

References

Anglia Ruskin University (2008) *Research Methods for Managers, Module Guide.* Cambridge: Anglia Ruskin University.

Bryman, A. (2001) *Social Research Methods.* Oxford: Oxford University Press.

Bryman, A. and Bell, E. (2007) *Business Research Methods* (2nd edn). Oxford: Oxford University Press.

Carlin, B. (2007) 'Olympic chiefs under fire for "puerile" logo', *The Telegraph*, 4 June 2007, http://www.telegraph.co.uk/news/uknews/1553545/Olympic-chiefs-under-fire-for-puerile-logo.html, accessed 25 July 2012.

Clapperton, G. (2004) 'ICT: Is it still a turn on?' *The Guardian*, 30 September 2004.

Creswell, J.W. (1995) *Research Design: Qualitative and Quantitative Approaches.* Thousand Oaks, CA: Sage.

Creswell, J.W. (1998) *Qualitative Inquiry and Research Design: Choosing among Five Traditions.* Thousand Oaks, CA: Sage.

Creswell, J.W. (2003) *Research Design: Qualitative, Quantitative and Mixed Methods Approaches* (2nd edn). Thousand Oaks, CA: Sage.

Denzin, N.K. and Lincoln, Y.S. (2000) *Handbook of Qualitative Research* (2nd edn). Thousand Oaks, CA: Sage.

Easterby-Smith, M.P.V., Thorpe, R. and Lowe, A. (2002) *Management Research: An Introduction* (2nd edn). London: Sage.

Ghauri, P. and Grøhaug, K. (2005) *Research Methods in Business Studies: A Practical Guide.* London: FT/Prentice Hall.

Greene, Jennifer, C. (2007) *Mixed Methods in Social Inquiry.* San Francisco, CA: John Wiley & Sons.

Guba, E.G. (1990) 'The alternative paradigm dialog', in E.G. Guba (ed.), *The Paradigm Dialog.* Newbury Park, CA: Sage, 17–30.

Hofstede, G. (1980) *Culture's Consequences: International Differences in Work-related Values.* Beverly Hills, CA: Sage.

Hyde, K.F. (2000) 'Recognising deductive processes in qualitative research', *Qualitative Market Research: An International Journal*, 3 (2): 82–89.

Ipsos MORI (2007) 'Attitudes towards The London 2012 Olympics Logo', http://www.ipsos-mori.com/researchpublications/researcharchive.aspx?keyword=London+2012+Olympics, accessed 25 July 2012.

Keegan, S., Tinsan, J. and Nancarrow, C. (2008) 'Practitioner perspectives – bridging practitioner–academic divide', *Qualitative Market Research*, 11 (1): 107–112.

Market Research Society (2010) 'Code of Conduct', online source: www.mrs.org.uk/pdf/code_of_conduct.pdf, accessed 20 September 2013.

Morgan, D.L. (2007) 'Paradigms lost and pragmatism regained: Methodological implications of combining qualitative and quantitative methods', *Journal of Mixed Methods Research*, 1 (1): 48–76.

Näslund, D. (2002) 'Logistics needs qualitative research – especially action research', *International Journal of Physical Distribution & Logistics Management*, 32 (5): 321–338.

Patton, M.Q. (1991) *Qualitative Evaluation and Research Methods* (2nd edn). Newbury Park, CA: Sage.

Saunders, M., Lewis, P. and Thornhill, A. (2007) *Research Methods for Business Students* (4th edn). London: FT/Prentice Hall.

Somekh, B. and Lewin, C. (2005) *Research Methods in Social Sciences*. London: Sage.

Strauss, A. and Corbin, J. (1990) *Basics of Qualitative Research: Grounded Theory Procedures and Techniques*. London: Sage.

Tashakkori, A. and Teddlie, C. (1998) *Mixed Methodology: Combining Qualitative and Quantitative Approaches*, Applied Social Research Methods Series Volume 46. London: Sage.

Further Reading

Bell, J. (2010) *Doing Your Research Project: A Guide for First-Time Researchers in Education, Health and Social Science* (5th edn). Maidenhead: Open University Press.

Blumberg, B., Cooper, D.R. and Schindler, P.S. (2011) *Business Research Methods*. London: McGraw-Hill.

Bryman, A. (2012) *Social Research Methods* (4th edn). Oxford: Oxford University Press.

Collis, J. and Hussey, R. (2009) *Business Research: A Practical Guide for Undergraduate and Postgraduate Students*. Houndsmill: Palgrave Macmillan.

Easterby-Smith, M., Thorpe, R. and Jackson, P.R. (2012) *Management Research* (4th edn). London: Sage.

Molina-Azorin, J.F. (2011) 'The use and added value of mixed methods in management research', *Journal of Mixed Methods Research*, 5 (1): 7–24.

Robson, C. (2011) *Real World Research* (3rd edn). Chichester: John Wiley & Sons.

Saunders, M.N.K. and Lewis, P. (2011) *Doing Research in Business and Management: An Essential Guide to Planning Your Project*. London: Prentice Hall.

Thomas, G. (2009) *How to Do Your Research Project: A Guide for Students in Education and Applied Social Sciences*. London: Sage.

2
Developing a research topic

┌─ Learning Objectives ───┐

After reading this chapter, you should be able to:

- understand the criteria that need to be considered when choosing a research topic;
- know what makes a good research topic;
- recognize how to develop research questions;
- recognize how to develop objectives;
- evaluate your own research questions; and
- understand the relationship between theory, research questions and objectives.

└──┘

Introduction

The preceding chapter provided an introduction to business research. You are now ready to start thinking about your own research, in particular, your research topic. In business, a research topic is usually related to a particular organization and its respective industry. Research is often carried out in order to help improve company performance. For example, this may include consumer research so as to improve customer loyalty, competitor research to establish the potential threat of major rivals, or simply market research to establish if there is a market for a new product. In short, a practice-based researcher is unlikely to have the same flexibility when it comes to choosing a research topic as a student researcher. If you are studying on a general business and management course, most institutions simply specify that your topic must be business related. In principle, such a wide range of options sounds easy. In reality, it is usually anything but!

This chapter introduces you to arguably one of the most difficult stages of the research process – developing a research topic and a set of research questions. Or in other words, starting! By now, you should fully understand the nature of research, especially business research. The next step is to start thinking about a suitable topic. As most of you are studying on business-related programmes, naturally your topic must fall within the field of business and management. Unfortunately, a study on the breeding habits of the lesser-spotted eagle does not fall within the realms of business! However, in many cases a topic can always be given a 'business spin'. For example, 'Marketing the importance of protecting the lesser-spotted eagle' is more likely to be acceptable.

This chapter begins by discussing the nature of your topic, especially what is meant by the word 'topic' in the context of your research project. This is then followed by a section that examines the best time to decide on your area of research, along with the characteristics that best illustrate a good research topic. You may simply decide to choose a topic that you have a passion for. However, in truth, simply choosing something that you enjoy may not necessarily be the right choice. This section will help you to determine whether or not your choice of topic is a viable one.

Next, idea generation is explored. Above all, sources of ideas that can help you to decide on a possible topic preference. Our attention then turns to research questions. We examine: developing research questions, their importance, how to formulate researchable research questions and, finally, limitations that may impact your choice of research questions. Following this, aims and objectives are fully addressed, along with the role of theory. This time the chapter concludes with an additional case study to illustrate how topic, objectives and research questions link together.

Nature of Your Topic

Prior to discussing the nature of your topic it is worth reviewing what is actually meant by the word 'topic'. The majority of research begins with a topic. In relation to business and management, a *topic* can be defined as 'a business-related idea or issue'. A topic can be broken down into '*broad topic*' and '*specific topic*'. These are largely self-explanatory. Nevertheless, every year I encounter projects that adopt the former. This is disappointing. Basing your research on a broad topic can lead to all sorts of problems when carrying out your research. For instance, it can make in-depth analysis later on in your study all the more difficult. An example of a broad topic might be: 'Marketing in the construction sector'. Refining this subject into a specific topic may read: 'Relationship marketing within the UK construction sector'. The importance of being specific when deciding on your topic is covered later in this chapter.

When do I have to decide on my topic?

Before looking at the criteria that you need to consider when choosing your topic, it is essential that you know at what stage during your studies you need to select your project topic. Naturally, this depends on your course. For most undergraduate students this tends to be sometime towards the end of their second or the beginning of their third year. For some students the prospect of selecting a topic is a daunting task, while others know exactly what it is they want to study. If you think that you are likely to fall into the former group, don't panic! The ability to generate ideas is a key part to choosing your topic. You will find a useful guide on how to do this later in this chapter.

This next section is important as it sets out criteria that you need to consider when choosing your research topic. Although your area of research is business and management, the following criteria could almost apply to any academic discipline. In general, the characteristics of a good research topic include the following:

- your topic is achievable;
- your topic is specific;
- your topic is relevant;
- your topic satisfies project guidelines; and
- your topic is of interest to you.

Your topic is achievable

Previous modules studied during your course should provide some indication as to which topics you find easy and which ones are more difficult. Still, the extent to which your topic is *achievable* is not just dependent on your academic ability; other factors also impact your research. This includes access to data, the sensitivity of your chosen subject, the nature of your research questions and the achievability or, in other words, the level of *difficulty*, of your research. Devi Jankowicz (2005: 29) suggested that 'difficulty' can be broken down into the following six issues: (1) the level of qualification to which you are working; (2) the intrinsic complexity of the subject matter; (3) the availability of expertise on which you can draw; (4) the ease with which you can access data; (5) the financial costs involved; and (6) the time required to complete a project based on the topic in question.

- *The level of qualification to which you are working.* This relates to the type of degree that you're studying. For most of you, this is an undergraduate degree. Therefore your chosen topic should lend itself to an undergraduate degree. You do not need to 'make a contribution to knowledge'. This is something that tends to be a requirement for students undertaking a PhD. Nor do you need to reinvent the wheel! As a student researcher, it pays to be aware of your project requirements. Most readers are likely to be novice researchers. Therefore this will be reflected in the learning outcomes laid down by your academic institution.
- *The intrinsic complexity of the subject matter.* This concerns possible difficulties that you might face as a result of choosing a particularly complex topic. These may include: little published information in your university or college library; concepts and ideas that you may not have covered during your lectures; the contemporary nature of your topic may mean that the only information available is published in the commercial sector, thereby making it difficult to access.
- *The availability of expertise on which you can draw.* This concerns access to staff and resources. For example, if you intend studying entrepreneurship among UK small businesses, you will want access to a supervisor who specializes in this particular area. Similarly, you would also hope that your library computer resources hold relevant information on your area of research. Yet in some institutions it is not always easy to gain

access to a supervisor who is an expert in your chosen area. This is particularly the case in popular subjects such as Marketing.

- *The ease with which you can access data.* This depends on the nature of your topic. In some cases data may be too difficult to come by or simply too expensive, while in others it may take too long to acquire. The extent to which you are able to access data is an important consideration prior to going ahead with your research, as you do not want to encounter problems further down the line. Access to data is something that is clearly linked to ethical issues. For example, a director of a company may agree to provide you with invaluable information on condition that his or her identity is protected.

- *The financial costs involved.* While you may have ambitious ideas for a possible topic, they may not all be workable due to financial constraints. It is worth considering the financial cost and resources needed prior to commencing your research, as failure to do so might hinder your ability to address your objectives.

- *The time required to complete a project based on the topic in question.* Most students have a set timeframe for completing their research project. Typically, for undergraduate students this is the final year of their degree programme. Some students find the task of writing a project within this time period extremely challenging. The key to successfully completing any kind of project is planning. Having a set timetable to work to should ensure that you submit your project prior to your institution's deadline. However, remember that some aspects of your research, e.g. conducting interviews with company directors or travelling overseas to conduct interviews, may be susceptible to delays. Therefore, try to build a certain amount of flexibility into your planning.

Your topic is specific

Specific refers to the degree to which your research topic is focused and clear. The extent to which a research topic is specific depends on the clarity and number of words. Your topic is likely to start at a broad level. However, eventually you should end up with something that is specific enough for you to achieve within your research time period. As illustrated in Figure 2.1, 'Marketing' is a very broad topic that encompasses a number of different subdisciplines. These include consumer behaviour, market research and branding. Simply opting for marketing as your chosen topic would not allow you the necessary focus required to satisfactorily complete your project. On the other hand, the final box in Figure 2.1, 'Business marketing relationship between Cott Corporation and Tesco', provides the necessary focus required.

Your topic is relevant

Your college or university usually determines whether or not your topic is *relevant*. Obviously, for business students, it needs to be within the discipline of business and management. In general, this includes all functions of business. The main areas include marketing, finance, human resources and strategy. Those of you on courses based on specific areas of business, e.g. a BA (Hons) in Marketing, will undoubtedly select a topic that is relevant to marketing. This might include

FIGURE 2.1 Narrowing down your research topic

business marketing, consumer behaviour, international marketing, marketing communications or marketing research. Those of you on general business study programmes, however, are likely to have greater flexibility.

I have supervised many research students over the years, yet the variety of topics never ceases to amaze me. Nevertheless, there are certain topics that I would call 'hot topics' among students. These tend to come up on a frequent basis because the large number of sources available, plus familiarity with the subject, make it a relatively easy option. Examples often include case studies such as Coca-Cola, Tesco, Ikea and Marks & Spencer. In recent years there has also been a significant increase in submissions focusing on China. This can probably be attributed to China's rapid economic growth, accession to the World Trade Organization (WTO) in 2001 and Beijing's hosting of the 2008 Olympic Games. In essence, there is nothing wrong with choosing a popular topic, although most supervisors would probably like to see something a little more imaginative!

Finally, when considering the relevance of your chosen topic, it is worth taking a long-term view. In other words, what are your plans after completing your study? Let's say that you plan on working for one of the 'Big Four' accountancy firms. Then it makes sense to base your topic on something relevant to an area of accounting that fits with your career aspirations. For example, if you produce a project on auditing issues among UK SMEs, not only will this provide you with key transferable skills that can later be put to good use, but also the project itself may prove to be a useful 'selling tool' at interview.

Your topic satisfies project guidelines

Project guidelines are likely to be set out by your college or university. The flexibility governing your choice of topic typically varies between institutions; as a general rule, though, the main requirement is that the topic chosen 'fits' within the course of study. For example, if undertaking a degree in Human Resource Management, a study based on reward systems among independent food retailers obviously fits within the overall study programme.

You may have a sponsor or employer who requires you to focus on a particular topic. In some cases, the findings of your project may be implemented by your sponsor or employer. Usually, this is of great personal satisfaction to the student, although trying to fulfil your own academic achievements, while at the same time producing a piece of work that meets your employer's requirements, can be rather stressful to say the least!

Finally, your topic should satisfy ethical guidelines. Make sure that you understand your own institution's rules and regulations governing ethics.

Your topic is of interest to you

The key word here is *motivation*. Obviously, if your passion is finance, then opting for a marketing-based subject may not satisfy your interest. Sometimes a student may select a topic because it is perceived as an easy or 'soft' option. Also, choice may be influenced by the reputation of a project supervisor. In reality, these are often poor reasons for selecting a particular topic. I regularly advise students that choosing a subject of interest is far more likely to lead to higher levels of motivation towards your research. Table 2.1 shows some sample topics by area, field and aspect.

It is worth noting that occasionally some students decide to change their topic at some point during their research. For example, if you decide that several months into your research you have 'fallen out of love with finance', one option is to consider changing your topic. But, understand that the later into your research you decide to change, the more difficult it will be to complete your project prior to your deadline. An added complication if you decide to change from one discipline to another, e.g. from Human Resources to Finance, is that you may also require a new supervisor. This could prove problematic, considering that most supervisors will already have been appointed. Therefore, if you wish to change your topic, my advice is to try to keep within the same subject discipline.

TABLE 2.1 Sample topics by area, field and aspect

Area	Field	Aspect
Marketing	International marketing	An analysis of market entry methods
Human Resources	Employee retention	An analysis of employee retention in relation to Hawkins plc
Finance	Management accounting	Development of a Word-based financial system for the Royal London Hospital Accounting Department

What Makes a Good Research Topic?

While we have looked at the characteristics of a good research topic, what makes a good project in terms of ideas? First, you should now understand that you do not have to 'reinvent the wheel' to come up with a suitable idea. Your idea does not have to be original or unique, and may be similar to existing studies. Still, your final choice of topic is likely to come from your own idea or ideas, rather than someone else's.

Generating ideas in relation to your topic usually begins at a broad level, and then a natural progression is to refine your ideas, thereby making them more specific. In reality, this is not always straightforward. Actually coming up with a workable idea is a common concern among students.

Generating research ideas

So far in this chapter you have learned the criteria to consider when choosing a research topic. Naturally, the next step is to start thinking about *generating research ideas*. Ideas for a research project can come from a variety of sources. These may include a discussion with your supervisor or employer, brainstorming (perhaps as part of a research skills class with other students), through reading existing literature, scanning previous research projects or drawing mind maps or relevance trees. If you do not have a topic, or are struggling to find one, don't worry! Many students take time to select a suitable topic. In some cases, it may be because they have several ideas and find it difficult to select their preferred option, while others are perhaps hesitant to take that first step of the research process. Whatever the reasons, eventually a suitable topic is chosen. Deciding on a topic can often be made easier by using a variety of sources (see Figure 2.2). The following section explores some of these options in greater detail.

Discussion with your supervisor or employer

In all likelihood, your supervisor will be familiar with the broad topic area that you have chosen for your research, e.g. marketing, finance, human resources, strategy, etc. Typically, the role of the supervisor is not to tell a student what to study; however, they can certainly suggest possible topics. Also, they can perhaps recommend relevant books and/or articles that can help to stimulate ideas.

Consider, too, talking to other tutors within your college or university. While not directly involved in your research project, tapping into their experience and knowledge is also likely to stimulate ideas. However, be wary of the fact that tutors are often likely to recommend a topic closely linked to their own preference and area of research. As a result, their expectations of your work may be higher.

Topics such as human resources and marketing are particularly popular with students. This is especially true of the latter. Therefore, if you opt for a marketing-based topic, you may find yourself competing with a large number of students for a small number of potential supervisors. If this means the appointment

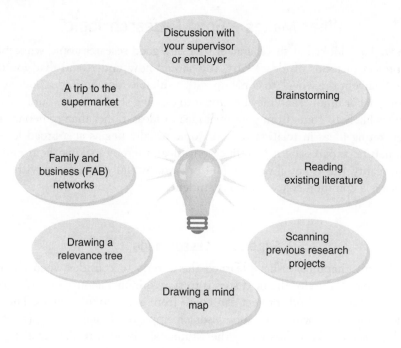

FIGURE 2.2 Sources of ideas

of a supervisor who does not teach your chosen topic, this is not a major concern. A key part to any project is structure. The main chapters, such as introduction, literature review, methodology and results will be familiar to your supervisor, irrespective of their specialism.

Many institutions also frequently hold research seminars and guest lectures. These can provide an insight into a diverse range of topics. In some cases guest lecturers working for local companies are usually happy to take questions during and after presentations. This may provide an interesting source of developing your ideas.

Part-time students may be in a fortunate position to discuss their research with their employer. In some cases employers see this as an opportunity to support the student in return for having access to their findings. I recall one particular student who worked part-time for an established independent hotel. Her employer was fully supportive and took a vested interest in her research. The student was able to carry out research into the hotel's operational procedures and had full access to staff, guests and hotel records. Upon completion of her study, management implemented a number of her recommendations. At the same time, the student found the whole experience extremely rewarding. This was reflected in her achieving an excellent mark for her efforts.

Not all students, of course, are fortunate enough to have the support of an employer. Still, it is worth considering discussing ideas with local firms. Often small companies in particular can be very supportive towards students.

Brainstorming

Students undertaking a research skills module are likely to participate in a *brainstorming* session as part of their module. Developed by a US advertising executive in the 1950s, brainstorming is a problem-solving technique conducted in a group environment. Adrian Furnham (2000: 22) suggested that a number of rules have been developed to ensure that a brainstorming session is properly conducted:

- *Group size should be about five to seven people.* If there are too few people, not enough suggestions are generated. If too many people participate, the session becomes uncontrolled and uncontrollable.
- *No criticism is allowed.* All suggestions should be welcome.
- *Freewheeling is encouraged.* The more outlandish the idea the better.
- *Quantity and variety are very important.* The more ideas put forth, the more likely is a breakthrough idea. The aim is to generate a long list of ideas.
- *Combinations and improvements are encouraged.* Building on the ideas of others, including combining them, is very productive.
- *Notes must be taken during the sessions.* Either manually or with an electronic recording device. The alternatives generated during the first part of the session should later be edited for duplication and categorizations.

The session should not be overstructured by following any of these rules too rigidly. Brainstorming is a spontaneous small-group process and is meant to be fun.

Students often much prefer to be able to talk to their peers about their topic, rather than just their supervisor. While brainstorming can be fun, it can also be highly productive by raising both positive and negative aspects associated with your research.

Reading existing literature

Among sources of ideas for a research project, perhaps the most important are textbooks and academic journals. These can be an excellent source of inspiration. As a student, you should already be reading these on a regular basis. Reading through academic or peer-reviewed journals will also give you some idea of the amount of available literature on a possible topic. Be careful here. Although a large amount of literature may prove very useful, it may also mean that a particular topic has been exhausted. In other words, it is already a well-trodden path. Similarly, a dearth of literature on a possible topic may make it difficult when writing your literature review.

Unfortunately, students often ignore the significance of academic journals. Not only can these be an excellent source of ideas, but they also contain many of the features associated with a research project, namely an introduction, literature review, methodology, data analysis, conclusion and referencing. It is worth familiarizing yourself with these features at an early stage as it can only help to better prepare you for your own research.

Scanning previous research projects

Scanning past projects within your university or college can be a useful way of generating ideas. In addition to differences in subject, previous research projects also differ in terms of approach. This can help you to start thinking about your own methodology as well as research topic. As a general rule, universities and colleges do not reveal marks of past projects. Therefore, in some cases it may prove difficult to determine the quality of work. Riley et al. (2000: 32) highlighted the advantages and disadvantages of referring to previous projects:

- *Advantages.* The possibility of advancing and/or developing a previous piece of research; and locating a piece of research where external contacts and respondents who participated in the research may be willing to help again.
- *Disadvantages.* A risk of relying too heavily on previous research and doing little original research to advance it; and settling on a dissertation or report that was originally weak in terms of topic choice, execution or some other criterion (to assist with this aspect, it may be possible to find out how 'good' such pieces of work were by talking to tutors).

Drawing a mind map

A *mind map* involves writing the name of a phrase or theme of your proposed research in the centre of the page. You then branch out with each sub-theme, further sub-themes, and so on (see Figure 2.3). The advantage of a mind map is that it can help you to develop links between ideas, it can stimulate further ideas, and it

FIGURE 2.3   An example of a mind map

Mind map of a successful future hand drawn on paper using felt pen.
© Luckyshot I Dreamstime.com / ID: 27292688

can help you to set boundaries when conducting your research. Producing a mind map involves a series of simple stages:

1. Arm yourself with a blank sheet of A3 or A4 paper and lots of coloured felt tip pens.
2. Relax, think 'creative'; you do not have to be an expert artist!
3. Select your key word or image, for example 'Business research', and write or mark it in the centre of the page.
4. Branch off any ideas related to this central theme, such as 'methodology', 'literature review' and 'research questions'. Include thoughts which may seem irrational or obscure – they will give you a fresh perspective on your subject.
5. Use one colour for each branch, with sub-branches flowing off from the centre continuing until you have exhausted all possible links.
6. Restrict your thoughts to one word per line, so you are free to make a greater number of connections.
7. Use images instead of words whenever possible, and draw boxes around, or otherwise high-light, important information. The more colourful your mind map the easier it will be to remember things.
8. When you think you have finished, edit and regroup your notes on a fresh sheet in order to produce your final mind map.

(Adapted from 'Mind Maps chart the way to business efficiency', 1998)

Drawing a relevance tree

A *relevance tree* is an alternative form of mind map, but it tends to be more ordered. Relevance trees provide structure to your literature search as well as generating boundaries. The headings and subheadings are often key words that can later be used electronically to aid your literature search. Relevance trees are often a logical next step following a brainstorming session.

To set out a relevance tree, you should:

- begin with your research question or objective at the top of the page;
- identify the key subject areas that you think are important;
- further subdivide each major subject area into sub-areas which you think are of relevance;
- further divide the sub-areas into more precise sub-areas that you think are of relevance;
- identify those areas on which you need to focus (your project will be of particular help here); and
- as your reading and reviewing progress, add new areas to your relevance tree.

Family and business networks

Family and business (FAB) networks relates to your own personal web of contacts. In general, the latter is probably less likely to apply to full-time students who have yet to gain employment. Mature and part-time students, however, may have built up a comprehensive network of business contacts. These contacts may be in a position to offer more than a range of ideas, such as sponsorship of your research.

As well as providing moral support and encouragement during your study, family may also be in a position to help with your research. And I don't mean writing it! I mean helping in other ways, such as older siblings who have gone through the research process and are able to provide their own first-hand views of what you can expect, family contacts who may make suitable interviewees as part of a sample; or you may even be in a position where a member of your family runs a business and is looking for your project to form the basis of their next strategic direction! No matter what the extent of your family's input, it is a potential source of ideas that should not be ignored.

A trip to the supermarket

No, I haven't gone mad! Think about it for a moment. For business and management students one potential source of stimulus is to look at what's going on in your local supermarket. Possible topics include product development, branding, consumer behaviour, pricing, customer service, sales promotion, corporate strategy – the list is almost endless. Because the likes of Tesco and Asda have diversified into other products and services, increased their number of stores and penetrated international markets, the scope for topics on which to write is huge.

Finally, the above sources of ideas are by no means exhaustive. Essentially, they give you an overview of how to generate and develop your ideas prior to beginning the next step: establishing a research problem.

Research problem

A research topic is not the same as a *research problem*. A research problem tends to be more specific. For example, a research topic may be concerned with the internationalization of German engineering companies, whereas a research problem leads to a more specific question, such as: 'What motivates German engineering companies to internationalize?' Basically, when you start to move from a general topic to a research problem, you are beginning to make progress in refining your research. Research questions are the tools that help you to answer your research problem. Yet, just how do you develop these research questions? And why are research questions so important? The answers to these questions are addressed in the following sections.

How to Develop Research Questions

Although some of you may have a pretty good idea of your chosen topic, at some point this needs to be broken down into *research questions*. If you already have a clear idea of your chosen topic, then you should find the next subsection beneficial as it deals with the important task of developing research questions.

The importance of developing a clear and focused set of research questions has already been stressed in Chapter 1, though at some point your research idea needs refining in order to develop research questions. A research question usually follows a *general research idea*. The majority of business and management students are expected to generate their own ideas and subsequent research questions. In this respect, it is probably the first time you have not been given a pre-set range of questions. A useful exercise is to ask yourself certain questions to help you clarify the nature of your research:

- What do you want to find out?
- Why do you want to research this topic?
- Why does this research need to be carried out? (Is there a gap in the literature, or does it contribute to existing theory and/or management practice?)
- What data/information already exists in other similar studies?

(Adapted from Wilkinson, 2000: 16)

First, try to define in no more than 12 words exactly what it is you wish to find out. In other words, sum up the nature of your research in no more than one sentence. This is a useful exercise as it helps you to clarify in your own mind what you intend to achieve from your research.

Second, try to provide reasons for choosing your particular topic. As mentioned earlier, for many students these include a topic that is of personal interest and related to your future career aspirations. In general, being able to explain why you wish to research your chosen topic area helps to justify your research, while at the same time should also help motivate you to undertake and finally complete your research.

A third key issue is to establish why it is important for your chosen research topic to be carried out. From your background reading you may have identified a gap that exists in the current literature on the subject area that requires further investigation. Whatever the reason, it is important that you understand the significance underlying your research.

With respect to what information currently exists elsewhere, students are often faced with either a wealth or dearth of information. A wealth of information is in some respects more difficult for a student. This is for two reasons: the literature review can be more time-consuming, and it can be challenging when it comes to identifying the most relevant literature. Sometimes, if a student is faced with a huge amount of literature to review, this can eat into valuable time required to carry out other stages of the research. Identifying the most relevant literature can be made easier by counting the number of citations: the more frequently a particular author is referred to by others often indicates the level of importance of that particular author's work.

A dearth of information can also be time-consuming, as some sources may prove difficult to access. For example, your university or college may not have access to some American journal articles essential to your study. These may need to be ordered, which obviously takes time.

In summary, the key questions highlighted above are a constructive exercise in helping to clarify your research. It provides a useful platform to help develop your research questions.

Why are research questions important?

Similar to your chosen topic, generally, your research question(s) should satisfy the following requirements: they must be achievable, specific, relevant, satisfy your institutions guidelines and, finally, perhaps above all, be of interest to you!

Arguably, research questions are the most important aspect to a project for the following reasons:

1. They help to set boundaries when conducting your literature review and help to identify the key literature.
2. They help propose a suitable methodology.
3. They help produce a refined set of results.
4. They allow easier analysis.
5. They help to draw together a reasonable set of conclusions and make reference to previous research.

Just as your topic needs to be specific, so do your research questions. In short, your research questions are the tools that help you to identify and narrow your literature to something that is manageable, and can be reviewed within your time constraints. However, to be able to do this, it is vital that you formulate a researchable set of research questions. The next section looks at how this can be achieved.

How to formulate a researchable research question

When formulating a research question it is perhaps worth considering the possible weaknesses. A number of weaknesses can be identified in relation to research questions. Common weaknesses that I tend to come across include: being too sensitive, not specific enough, being more appropriate to a longitudinal study, and simply not being measurable. Let us examine these points more closely.

First, certain subjects are taboo and others are sensitive. If your research includes questions on sensitive or embarrassing topics, there is every possibility that this will seriously impact your response rate. For example, questions concerning politics, demographics and education should be formulated with caution. In addition, if your research involves cross-cultural research, there is a greater likelihood that you will encounter problems over the formulation of questions. From my own experience of conducting cross-cultural research involving Western and Chinese participants, the best thing to do in an attempt to avoid such difficulties is to conduct joint research. In other words, researchers from different cultural backgrounds work together on a project, such as a US and a Chinese researcher working on a comparative study of brand loyalty in the US and Chinese automobile markets. Then again, as a student researcher, having a fellow researcher is not something that you are privileged to. For that reason, if the nature of your research is cross-cultural issues, the best way to proceed is to consult your supervisor, friends and family, and relevant literature on culture in order to avoid potential pitfalls when compiling your questions.

Second, the specific nature of research questions has already been addressed. Third, a *longitudinal study* is a piece of research conducted over an extended period of time. In some cases, your research questions may be better suited to this type of research. An example might be a study of the changes in consumer behaviour in the UK automobile market. Unlike the technology sector, major changes in the automobile market tend to occur over a reasonable period of time. Hence the need for a longitudinal study that identifies and measures the changes over time.

Lastly, you may have difficulty measuring your findings if your research question does not allow for access to information, or is too ambitious or poorly worded. Ideally, when formulating your research questions, the following issues need to be considered:

- your questions must not be too easy;
- they should allow for suitable analysis;
- they should provide a future perspective;
- they should allow the generation of new insights; and
- they should avoid common areas of research.

Of these, 'provide for a future perspective' is an area that is often overlooked by students. For example: 'What impact is the introduction of a minimum wage likely to have on the employment market over the short to medium term?' Notice that 'short to medium term' provides the future perspective. Incorporating a question of this nature allows for detailed analysis.

Recognizing limitations of a particular research question

It is important to recognize certain limitations when formulating your research questions. Most institutions require students to work to a strict timetable in terms of project submission. Obviously, this then rules out research questions centred on a longitudinal study. Common limitations linked to research questions include: a lack of focus, being too lengthy, being too optimistic and not being relevant.

One approach to formulating your research questions is to consider what I refer to as the 'broken vase' method. When attempting to put the pieces of a broken vase back together, you will find that some pieces are too big, too small, too fragmented, too sharp; too many pieces look alike; and finally there are the pieces that fit just right. Table 2.2 shows how this analogy can be applied to research questions.

Table 2.2 shows the last question to be the most suitable. By now, you should be in a position to understand why this question is suitable, as opposed to the other examples in the table. In general, Table 2.2 provides a useful guide when you come to develop your own research questions. However, research questions are only one aspect when it comes to explaining the direction of your research. Having a clear set of aims and objectives is just as important as your research questions.

How do I know if my research questions are just right and what are the criteria of judgement? On the first point, hopefully Table 2.2 is a helpful reference; you can

TABLE 2.2 Research questions and their relationship to the 'broken vase' method

Research question	Broken vase method
How does the introduction of a supermarket loyalty card generate loyalty and customer satisfaction among UK shoppers?	*Too big:* This question consists of too many words and would be difficult to achieve.
What is sustainable management?	*Too small:* Also having a single 'What' question is likely to produce an excessively descriptive piece of work.
What marketing communication tools do companies employ in the business-to-business sector, how effective are these, why are they employed?	Although you can argue that this is essentially too big, the main problem is that it is *too fragmented*. It actually comprises three research questions.
What are the levels of bribery and corruption within central government?	*Too sharp or sensitive.*
How do Chinese cultural values impact on management and leadership style?	*Look alike, too similar.*
How do cultural values influence Chinese management?	
How successful is Brampton plc in the Indonesian market?	*Just right.*

also consult your project supervisor for his or her views. In terms of criteria of judgement, to a certain extent deciding whether a research question is just right is a subjective one. Using other researchers' questions as a benchmark is a good starting point. One way to establish if their research questions are suitable is to read later stages of their research, such as the literature review and methodology. If their research questions are too big, then this will be reflected in the literature review. Quite simply, they will not have been able to cover all of the key literature, as their research questions lack focus.

Also, it is important to stress that your research questions are likely to result from reviewing the literature. The reasons for this are twofold. First, reading the research questions of experienced scholars provides a useful insight when it comes to developing your own set of research questions. Second, you will be able to identify the contribution that your study can make to the literature, thus your research questions will reflect this. Do not be too concerned with literature review at this stage, as I cover it at great length in Chapter 3.

How to Develop Aims and Objectives

Sometimes the words 'aims' and 'objectives' are used interchangeably. Yet there is a distinct difference. An *aim* can be described as a general statement of what the research sets out to achieve, while an *objective* is a more specific statement relating to the defined aim of your research. Quite simply, the aim is what you want to achieve, and the objective describes how you are going to achieve that aim. Both aims and objectives are equally important. Looking ahead to the conclusion of your project, you will need to assess to what extent you have achieved your set aims and objectives.

Although aims tend to be more general than objectives, the two should be very much interrelated. An objective is derived from an aim, has the same intention as an aim, but is more specific. Your number of research objectives should be limited to a convenient quantity. The more objectives you have, the less likely you will be able to achieve each one fully.

Consider the following examples, showing the 'link' between research questions and objectives. Examples of research questions:

1. How important are the various factors for evaluating staff performance?
2. How have sports celebrities contributed to the Gillette brand?
3. What attitudes do consumers have towards fair trade products?

Examples of research objectives:

1. Identify the reasons behind the company's expansion into the Dutch market.
2. To determine the best way our company can increase staff retention over the next financial year.
3. To establish the best way of introducing a sales training scheme.

In essence, an objective is a statement that sets out to define a particular problem, while a research question tends to be more specific about what it is you are trying to achieve. Finally, research questions also sometimes include a clear, well-written set of hypotheses. 'A *hypothesis* is an unproven proposition or possible solution to a problem. Hypothetical statements assert probable answers to research questions. A hypothesis is also a statement about the nature of the world, and in its simplest form it is a guess' (Zikmund, 2003: 99). For example, a marketing manager may hypothesize that an increase in advertising spend will lead to an increase in sales.

Basically, a hypothesis is concerned with the relationship between two variables. The hypothesis will predict the relationship between variables, and, through testing, may or may not support the theory. There are two types of variables associated with hypotheses – independent and dependent variables. *Independent variables* are those seen as a 'cause', while a *dependent variable* is seen as the 'effect' (outcome). This is often referred to as a cause-and-effect relationship. Using the example 'In Sino-UK joint ventures what is the effect of trust and commitment on joint venture performance?', the independent variable would be 'trust and commitment', and the dependent variable (or outcome) would be joint venture performance.

A hypothesis can also be stated as a null hypothesis. This states that there is no relationship between the independent and dependent variables, and is mainly used in research involving statistical analysis (see Chapter 9).

Why are objectives important?

We have established that objectives set out how you are going to achieve your aims. The important point, however, is that objectives allow you to set 'boundaries' prior to conducting your research. Similar to research questions, objectives provide a focus for your research. As mentioned, unlike research questions, objectives tend to be statements; they do not ask an outright question. The main thing that research questions and objectives have in common is that both seek to generate answers. Because of this, sometimes these words are used interchangeably to mean one and the same.

How to formulate researchable objectives

An easy way to formulate research objectives is to consider applying the widely used acronym 'SMART'. It stands for 'Specific, Measurable, Achievable, Relevant and Timed'.

- *Specific*. Are the objectives stated clearly? Are they focused and indicate what is to be achieved?
- *Measurable*. Can the stated objectives measure what is claimed?
- *Achievable*. Are your objectives achievable and attainable?
- *Relevant*. Objectives should also add value to your chosen topic and, above all, be applicable to your subject.
- *Timed*. Is there a time period within which the objectives will be accomplished?

Although SMART is a good starting point when formulating your objectives, it is also worth taking into account the factors that may contribute to a poor set of objectives. First, make sure that you do not fall into the trap of just repeating the same objectives, but in slightly different terms. In essence, there should be a clear distinction between each objective. Second, make sure that your objectives are structured in the correct way. Ideally this should be in bullet-point format, rather than as a list of 'issues' related to your chosen topic. Third, remember that your objectives need to be more specific than your aims. Therefore, spend time making sure that they are not too vague, overly ambitious or lack focus. Fourth, ensure that the objectives 'fit' within your chosen topic area and do not fall within another discipline. And finally, do not contradict yourself within your objectives, e.g. say that you intend doing one thing, while in another objective state the complete opposite.

In summary, we have now looked at four areas of research that are clearly inter-linked – problem, aims, objectives and research questions. By now, you should have an understanding of what is meant by each term, along with how, collectively, they form an important part of your research project. However, to make things clearer, Figure 2.4 shows each of these areas and the relationship between each one.

The example in Figure 2.4 is clearly linked to a business scenario. But, as a student researcher, you also need to be aware of how to arrive at a set of research questions that form the basis of your research project. Failure to do so is likely to lead to problems already cited in this chapter.

Problem: 'Loss of trade'

Aims: 'Increase trade'

Objective: 'To increase UK sales by 10% within the next 12 months'

Research question: 'How do we increase UK sales by 10% within the next 12 months?'

FIGURE 2.4   Relationship between problem, aims, objectives and questions

Theory, Research Questions and Objectives

It is important to understand theory when formulating your research questions and objectives. *Theory* is a word that many people recognize as having several meanings. As a student, I'm sure that you have come across the word on many occasions. For example, your lecturer may make reference to a 'lack of theoretical application' in one of your assignments. Fred N. Kerlinger (1986: 9) defined theory as 'a set of interrelated constructs (concepts), definitions, and propositions that present a systematic view of phenomena specifying relations among variables, with the purpose of explaining and predicting the phenomena'.

In short, theory is a set of principles devised to explain phenomena. In order to be able to explain phenomena, a theory needs to be applied (application); once applied, this will produce an outcome (result). For example, many business students are familiar with Michael Porter's Five Forces theory. In essence, the theory proposes that industries are influenced by five forces. The outcome of applying Porter's theory is dependent on a number of factors, e.g. time, industry and setting (national, international, global).

When formulating your research questions and objectives you need to consider how theory will feature in your research. For example, if you opt for a deductive approach, normally you would conduct a literature review in order to identify an appropriate theory and construct a hypothesis. On the other hand, if you decide on the inductive approach, your principles are likely to be based on the development of theory following your data collection.

Given the importance of choosing your topic, developing objectives and formulating research questions, the next section includes a student case that brings together much of what I have covered in this chapter. Remember that it is not so much the topic that is important, but the formulation of the objectives and research questions.

Alexander, a BA (Hons) Business Management student, decided to focus his research project on the 'Internationalization of small and medium sized enterprises (SMEs) based in the West of England'. The main objective of his proposed research was:

> to better understand the internationalization process and market entry methods of SMEs based in the West of England. The aim is not only to evaluate internationalization process and market entry methods, but also to analyze what types of strategy SMEs need to take in order to compete successfully in emerging international markets.

The objectives of his study were as follows:

- To understand what motivates SMEs to internationalize.
- To examine the internationalization strategies adopted by SMEs.
- To determine the market entry methods chosen by SMEs.
- To examine the strategies SMEs need to adopt in order to successfully compete in emerging international markets.

The main research questions to be addressed were:

- Why do SMEs decide to internationalize?
- What internationalization strategies do SMEs adopt?
- How do SMEs enter emerging international markets?
- What strategies do SMEs need to adopt in order to successfully compete in emerging international markets?

The rationale of undertaking his research was as follows:

> Although the internationalization of firms has been well documented, there is a lack of research into the internationalization process of SMEs, particularly those based in the West of England. The leading emerging markets of India and China have also received limited attention. In short, this is an area of research that remains under-explored. The majority of the literature has tended to focus on the internationalization of large multinational companies and market entry into developed markets such as the US and Europe. UK government initiatives to encourage UK SMEs to internationalize, especially in emerging markets such as India and China, mean that research in this area is both important and timely.

Notice how the objectives and research questions are very much related to one another. Also, the title is short and to the point. Finally, through reading the key literature on the subject, Alexander was able to identify a clear rationale for his study.

Are you happy?

At a cost of £2 million, the government's 'happiness survey' will be sent to 200,000 households per year until 2015. David Cameron, the British Prime Minister, chose to introduce a new 'happiness index' as a way of measuring well-being by means other than wealth and spending. The first results, published in July 2012, show that the average adult was rated 7.4 out of 10 for life satisfaction.

Perhaps unsurprisingly, results also show that those who have more money are a lot happier with their lives. It found that the poorest are the least happy, while those in the higher tax bracket are the most satisfied. Although most people are happy, traditional married families are happiest of all.

The 'happiness index' has its critics. Len McCluskey, the newly elected general secretary of the giant Unite union, said it was an attempt by the Coalition to 'pull the wool over people's eyes' and disguise the impact of spending cuts. While an article in *The Independent* newspaper (2011) suggested that we could all become happier, and that 'One way to achieve that, for most of us, would be by persuading the Government to stop wasting our ever-onerous taxes on entirely pointless surveys.' Some of the criticism centred on the research questions. For example, one question asked whether 'the things you do in your life are worthwhile'. However, for all its critics, the happiness survey is with us until 2015. The big question is: Will people be happier next year?

Although the above example cannot be described as 'business research', the reasons I have chosen the UK government's happiness survey are threefold. First, it illustrates the difficulty in measuring a broad, multifaceted topic like well-being. Second, it shows that formulating research questions to measure something as subjective as happiness is no easy task. Third, this case also demonstrates the importance of defining any terms used in research. The same applies to your own study. For example, let's say that you have the following research question: 'How successful are UK companies in the luxury brands market?' One of the key terms in this question is 'successful'. Success can be defined and measured in many different ways. Examples include profit, turnover, customer satisfaction and market share, to name but a few. It is important to make it clear which definition you will be using in your study. This is often explained in the literature review and may also be explained to respondents when collecting primary data (see Chapters 3 and 6 respectively). In a positivist study, it is essential to define key terms, as this will promote greater consistency and validity in your research. If you are undertaking an interpretivist study, then you are likely to be engaging in research of an exploratory nature. Thus, defining key terms might be more difficult as they are likely to be an outcome of the research.

Summary and Conclusion

This chapter has been about developing a suitable research topic, objectives and research questions. In it, we have looked at the characteristics of a good research topic, and how to formulate objectives and research questions. Here are the key points from this chapter:

- A topic can be broken down into 'broad topic' and 'specific topic'.
- The characteristics of a good research topic are that it must be achievable, specific, relevant, satisfy project guidelines and be of interest to you.
- Topic ideas can come from a number of sources, including brainstorming sessions, discussion with your supervisor, reading existing literature and family and business networks.
- Ask yourself certain issues that help to clarify the nature of your research, e.g. define what you want to find out.
- Research questions are important because they help to set boundaries when conducting your literature review.
- When formulating your research questions, they must not be too easy.
- An aim can be described as a general statement of what the research sets out to achieve, whereas an objective is a more specific statement relating to the defined aim of your research.
- A hypothesis is an unproven proposition or possible solution to a problem. Hypothetical statements assert probable answers to research questions.
- Theory is a set of principles devised to explain phenomena. In order to be able to explain phenomena, a theory needs to be applied (application); once applied, this will produce an outcome (result).

CASE STUDY | **Turning a Research Topic into Aims, Objectives and Research Questions**

Sandra was thrilled to have been chosen as a volunteer for the 2012 London Olympic Games. She was very much looking forward to the experience and considered it to be a strong 'selling point' when applying for graduate jobs. Due to commence the final year of a BA (Hons) Business Management degree in September 2012, Sandra also deemed the London Olympics as a possible topic for her undergraduate research project. She had already done some background reading on the London Olympics and had found a large amount of published material on all aspects of the games. This included research studies published in academic journals on everything from the tourism implications of the games to corporate sponsorship. In terms of the latter, Sandra was particularly interested in how the London Organising Committee of the Olympic and Paralympic Games (LOCOG) protected their sponsors' interests. More specifically, she wanted to know the preventative measures the committee took against the marketing strategy of associating a brand with the Olympics, when a brand has not paid for the right to be an official sponsor – otherwise known as 'ambush marketing'.

Sandra was pleased with her chosen area of research, but was unsure how to narrow down her selected topic into a set of aims, research objectives and research questions.

Case study question

- Can you help Sandra by suggesting a possible set of aims, objectives and research questions?

— YOU'RE THE SUPERVISOR —

You have received a number of research proposals from final-year Business Management students. Each proposal should set out the nature of the research topic, research aims, objectives and research questions. In addition, there should be a brief overview of the key literature, methodology and research timetable. One would expect to see a proposal contain a reasonably focused research topic. The nature of the topic should be specific, relevant and achievable. Four of the proposals you have received have raised concerns over the choice of research topic. Discuss the problems associated with each research topic.

Research topics

1. Promoting equal opportunities in the workplace.
2. Sources of finance for small businesses.
3. Measuring the future success of luxury brands.
4. Making sense of UK crime statistics.

COMMON QUESTIONS AND ANSWERS

1. At what point should I choose my research topic?

Answer: Your institution is likely to have a deadline at which point you should have chosen your research topic. Typically, the choice of research topic is submitted as part of a research proposal usually up to 12 months before the project deadline. However, this does not mean that you should wait until you are required to produce a research proposal before thinking about possible areas of research. From my own experience of supervising countless research projects, I tend to find that those students who decide on a topic before their final year are less likely to have difficulty in starting their research. If you do not give your choice of topic much thought early on, then you may find you 'panic' into choosing something. Ostensibly, this will lead to a greater likelihood that you will change your mind. This is primarily because you have not devoted sufficient time to thinking about the implications of choosing a particular research topic.

2. What factors should I consider when choosing my research topic?

Answer: As noted earlier in the chapter, you should choose a topic that is specific, relevant, satisfies project guidelines and is of interest to you. Furthermore, consider how your choice of topic might be of benefit in relation to your chosen career.

References

Furnham, A. (2000) 'The brainstorming myth', *Business Strategy Review*, 11: 21–28.

Jankowicz, A.D. (2005) *Business Research Projects* (4th edn). London: Thomson Learning.

Kerlinger, F.N. (1986) *Foundations of Behavioural Research* (3rd edn). New York: Holt, Rinehart & Winston.

'Mind Maps chart the way to business efficiency' (1998), *Education + Training*, 40 (4): 173–174.

Riley, M., Wood, R.C., Clark, M.A., Wilkie, E. and Szivas, E. (2000) *Researching and Writing Dissertations in Business and Management*. London: Thomson Learning.

The Independent (2011) 'Happiness is … the end of pointless surveys like this', http://www.independent.co.uk/voices/editorials/leading-article-happiness-is-the-end-of-pointless-surveys-like-this-6270648.html, accessed 2 August 2013.

Wilkinson, D. (2000) *The Researcher's Toolkit: The Complete Guide to Practitioner Research*. New York: Routledge.

Zikmund, W.G. (2003) *Business Research Methods* (7th edn). London: Thomson Learning.

Further Reading

Andrews, R. (2003) *Research Questions*. London: Continuum.

Bell. J. (2010) *Doing Your Research Project* (5th edn). Maidenhead: Open University Press.

Blumberg, B., Cooper, D.R. and Schindler, P.S. (2011) *Business Research Methods* (3rd edn). Maidenhead: McGraw-Hill.

Bryman, A. and Bell, E. (2012) *Business Research Methods* (3rd edn). Oxford: Oxford University Press.

Punch, K. (2006) *Developing Effective Research Proposals* (2nd edn). London: Sage Publications.

Quinlan, C. (2011) *Business Research Methods*. Andover: Cengage Learning.

Robson, C. (2011) *Real World Research* (3rd edn). Chichester: John Wiley & Sons.

White, P. (2008) *Developing Research Questions: A Guide for Social Scientists*. Basingstoke: Palgrave Macmillan.

3
Conducting a literature review

─Learning Objectives─

After reading this chapter, you should be able to:

- understand the nature of a literature review;
- be able to explain the importance of conducting a literature review;
- know the stages in the literature review process;
- plan a literature search and know various sources of literature;
- explain the typical structure of a literature review;
- know how to present a literature review; and
- understand the difference between a good and a poor literature review.

Introduction

This chapter is about how to conduct a literature review. When undertaking your research project it is essential that you are aware of and acknowledge existing research in your chosen area. Most student researchers therefore spend a considerable amount of time reviewing the literature: first, in order to identify possible gaps or ideas that can help refine their own research and, second, to examine relevant sources so as to become fully conversant with the literature.

This chapter starts by introducing the nature of a literature review and briefly stresses why it is an essential part to your research project. The next section aims to answer a common question among student researchers, namely, 'Why conduct a literature review?' This is then followed by a discussion on the literature review process, in particular the stages that you are likely to go through when searching the literature and conducting your review. Next, planning your literature search emphasizes the necessity of planning your review, while the section on sources of literature provides a relatively brief overview of the main places to look in order to determine what has been written on your chosen topic. These sources include books, journals,

Internet sites and abstracts. A key part of conducting a review is recognizing where to search. Therefore, this section sets out not only the process of searching the literature, but also the range of sources that can be accessed.

The ability to carry out a critical review of the literature remains a challenge for many students. The intention of the following section is to alleviate these concerns by discussing how to adopt a critical approach. Another common cause of concern for students is structuring and presenting the literature review. Therefore, an illustration of how to divide up the review section is provided, along with an example of an introduction. Next, our attention turns to what constitutes a good or a poor literature review. Although by no means exhaustive, I have included examples of good practice, along with the most frequent problems students encounter. Finally, the last part of the chapter serves as a reminder of the importance attached to a critical review of the literature. In short, how to write a good literature review is something that many students find particularly challenging. This chapter should help you to deal with this challenge as it explains the common issues that students typically face when undertaking this part of their research.

Nature of a Literature Review

In the context of your research, 'literature' means all sources of published material. A *literature review* can be described as 'identifying, evaluating and critically assessing' what has been published on your chosen topic. Reviewing the literature critically will allow you to develop an understanding of previous research that is relevant to your own study. In addition, it should allow you to understand how the literature has developed. An important part of conducting your literature review is to establish the current state of findings in your chosen area. For example, an environmental scientist studying climate change is unlikely to conduct research without first referring to previous studies into climate change. Similarly, as a student researcher you also need to be aware of existing research. Once you have chosen your topic, e.g. mergers and acquisitions involving UK companies, you then need to find out what has been written about it across a wide variety of media. This is likely to include books, textbooks, academic journals, government reports, trade magazines, Internet websites, newspaper articles and quite possibly unpublished dissertations.

Conducting a methodical review is not an easy task. To be sure, it is not something that you can do over the course of a weekend! In truth, your review is likely to take several months. The length of time that you spend on your review is usually dependent on three factors: (1) the amount of literature available; (2) the accuracy of data; and (3) access to data.

Jeffrey W. Knopf (2006: 127) suggested that a literature review has two key elements. First,

> it should concisely summarize the findings or claims that have emerged from prior research efforts on a subject. Second, a literature review should reach a conclusion about how accurate and complete that knowledge is; it should

present your considered judgements about what's right, what's wrong, what's inconclusive, and what's missing in the existing literature.

Why do I have to conduct a literature review?

Students have asked me on many occasions, 'Why do I have to conduct a literature review?' Understandably, for some students the process of conducting a literature review is totally alien to them. Often, these are international students who originate from countries with markedly different educational systems from that of the UK. However, in some instances UK students may also experience difficulty conducting the review. In short, conducting a thorough, critical literature review is no easy task for the novice researcher. Yet it forms an integral part of your research. Through compiling a literature review you are demonstrating an important set of skills.

> Undergraduates researching for their dissertation or thesis are expected to show familiarity with their topic. Usually, this takes the form of a summary of the literature, which not only demonstrates the skills to search and compile accurate and consistent bibliographies, but also summarizes your key ideas, showing a critical awareness. They are required to demonstrate, on the one hand, library and information skills, and on the other, the intellectual capability to justify decisions on the choice of relevant ideas and the ability to assess the value of those ideas in context. (Hart, 1998: 9)

Several reasons support the carrying out of a literature review. First, you should review the literature on your chosen topic because it can provide much-needed inspiration for research topic ideas. Second, although you may already have a significant level of knowledge on a particular topic, a review of the literature is likely to further this knowledge. Third, it can help to identify new and emerging research areas. Fourth, it can ensure that you are actually contributing to an area of research by avoiding what has been done already. Fifth, previous researchers often make explicit recommendations for further research. Sixth, by reviewing previous literature you are able to identify methods and approaches used by others in similar research areas, as well as identify gaps in knowledge. Finally, the review is a way of organizing your own thoughts. It is also a record of the evidence/material you have gathered.

Conducting a literature review can have several benefits:

- It can give you a general overview of a body of research with which you are not familiar.
- It can reveal what has already been done well, so that you do not waste time 'reinventing the wheel'.
- It can give you new ideas that you can use in your own research.
- It can help you to determine where there are problems or flaws in existing research.
- It can enable you to place your research in a larger context, so that you can show what new conclusions might result from your research.

(Knopf, 2006: 127)

Literature Review Process

The best way to think of the literature review is as a *process*. Each subsequent step builds on the previous one, building a solid understanding of the literature.

I am aware that you may decide not to follow each step to the letter. For example, it is likely that you may already have what you perceive as relevant literature. Therefore, you do not need to go out and actively search for your sources. Still, wherever possible, try to follow the process as closely as you can in order to ensure that you adopt a thorough, efficient approach to your literature review. The literature review process involves the following:

Research questions and objectives

By now you should be familiar with how to formulate research questions and objectives, as this is something that was covered in Chapter 2. Once you are confident that you have a suitable range of objectives and research questions, you are then ready to proceed to the next step of defining your parameters. At this stage, it is worth noting that your research questions and objectives will ultimately determine the literature that you will read and refer to in your literature review. For example, if one of your objectives is 'To determine the marketing metrics used by UK national newspapers', then one would expect to see reference to articles on different types of marketing metrics, as well as the UK newspaper industry. In simple terms, the marker of your project will be looking to see if there is a clear 'link' between your research questions and literature review.

Define parameters

Essentially, the term 'parameters' means you are setting *boundaries* to your study that help you to narrow down what it is that you intend to search. One way of doing this is establishing *key words* (see below). The ability to be clear about what it is that you are trying to study can help set your parameters. In some cases, parameters linked to a given topic are reasonably clear, particularly in relation to certain theories. On the other hand, you may find it difficult to set parameters. This is where reviewing existing articles can help, especially to determine parameters to similar studies and how these relate to your own work.

Key words

Both Internet search engines and search engines specific to applicable databases rely on *key words* to find relevant information. It is therefore essential that you are able to identify your topic, sub-topics, main variables, theories, key concepts, etc., in the form of key words. You will then be able to search for works by both single and combined key word searches (O'Leary, 2004: 70). An example of how to do a key word search is illustrated later in the chapter. For now, it is worth considering possible key words for your study. Ideally, you do not want to be in a position where you are unclear or have too many or too few key words, as this is likely to make your literature search all the more difficult.

Conduct search

A key part to conducting your search is identifying possible sources of literature. The majority of your search will involve reading through articles in academic journals. After all, your project is of an academic nature. The main thing to do at the beginning of your search is to identify the leading journals in your discipline. It is usually in leading and/or specific journals relating to your chosen topic that you will find the greatest wealth of information.

Jill Hussey and Roger Hussey (1997: 87) provide the following useful guide to conducting a literature search:

- It is very important to start exploring the literature as soon as possible. If, initially, your research project is still fairly unfocused, your search will be in general terms only.
- Decide the scope of your research and set your parameters accordingly (e.g. by period of time, geography or industry).
- Determine the key words, including alternative spellings, synonyms and differences in usage.
- Only collect articles, books, papers, etc. which are relevant to your research (e.g. in terms of subject matter, methodology, research instrument, theoretical discussion). Good research articles should review the literature, describe the research methodology used in the study, discuss the results and draw conclusions.
- Use the references given in the literature you have collected to guide you to other articles you should collect.
- When you start to recognize the references cited in other works, you are nearing the end of your first search.
- In order to keep up to date with the literature, it is important that you continue your literature search throughout your study.

Today, student researchers are in the fortunate position of having access to a wide range of electronic sources, in particular electronic databases that contain articles from academic journals. As a student, your library card is likely to offer you free access to a large number of articles relevant to your research project. Perhaps one of the more well-known electronic databases in the field of business and management is 'Emerald'. It is something that is certainly popular with my own students, largely because it is easy to access and holds full articles on many different business-related topics.

Basically, Emerald is an online database covering 24,000+ articles and 104+ journal titles. It covers mainly management and business subjects, e.g. marketing, human resources, finance, general management and strategy. Although there is no substitute for actually using Emerald, Table 3.1 gives you an insight into how to perform a *key word search*. The first column shows the words entered into the 'quick

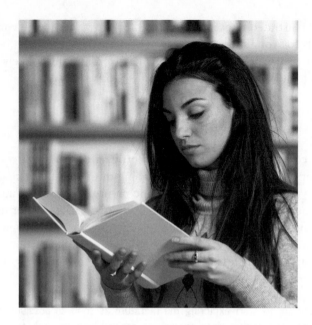

search' facility, while the right-hand column shows the actual number of 'hits' or, in other words, articles that contain the terms entered.

In Table 3.1, you can see that through experimenting with key words, the student has managed to refine their search to a manageable number of sources. Obviously, simply searching for just 'trust' or 'commitment' is far too general, and likely to encompass a wide range of articles. Table 3.2 shows the same search terms; however, this time an 'Advanced search' has been selected, followed by 'Content item title' in the 'All fields' box.

Clearly, searching the literature takes time. However, undertaking searches using the key words or themes set out in your research questions will ultimately help you to identify the most relevant and leading studies in your selected area of research.

TABLE 3.1 How important is trust and commitment in business-to-business relationships?

Search item	Hits
'Commitment'	43,607
'Trust'	35,169
'Business-to-business'	671
'Trust and commitment'	657
'Business-to-business relationships'	5
'Trust and business relationships'	3

TABLE 3.2 How important is trust and commitment in business-to-business relationships? (2)

Search item (Advanced search)	Hits
'Commitment'	593
'Trust'	796
'Business-to-business'	1
'Trust and commitment'	12
'Business-to-business relationships'	0
'Trust and business relationships'	0

What if I can't find any relevant sources?

'I can't find any literature on my research topic' tends to be an issue for those students who have not gone about their literature review in an appropriate, systematic way. Often, literature is always available. In general, if you experience problems finding literature on your chosen topic, it is probably due to the following causes:

- you are looking for the wrong type of source;
- you are looking in the wrong place;
- you have problems with the parameters or key words for your research; or
- you really have found an uncharted research area.

How do I plan my literature search?

When it comes to the best way to plan the literature search, there is no one definitive answer. Fundamentally, two key factors need to be considered – *organization* and *time*. In terms of the former, I have already stressed the importance of keeping an accurate record of your findings. It is also a good idea to plan when and where you intend to conduct your literature search. In terms of the latter, make sure that you allocate sufficient time to searching the literature. Personally, I find that it is the kind of task that very rarely can be undertaken in short time periods. Preferably, you should allocate a minimum of half a day to conduct an efficient review of key sources.

Obtain literature

Obviously, in order to do a literature review you need to obtain literature. Try to use a wide range of sources. Some students have a tendency to mainly use web-based sources when conducting their literature review. By only referring to a very narrow range of online literature, key studies in your chosen area are likely to be ignored. You will find that the majority of literature is accessible in your college or university library. By now, you should be familiar with the sources made available by your institution's library. These will almost certainly include textbooks, journals, reports, magazines, encyclopaedias and directories, to name but a few. Of course, in some cases these sources may only be available in hard copy or electronic format. Still, this should not detract from your ability to obtain the literature.

For part-time or mature students, a useful source of literature is often their employer. I have known several cases where students are actively encouraged by their employer to make use of all available literature within their place of work. Yet this support is usually because the employer has sponsored the student to base their research on the company.

Evaluate

Two key reasons exist why researchers use a wide range of sources when reviewing the literature. First, different sources are open to varying degrees of bias. For example, if you cite an article written in the UK's *Guardian* newspaper on government education policy, you will most probably get a largely critical viewpoint. In other words, being a left-wing newspaper, the journalist is more likely to write something that takes on a left-wing political bias. Obviously, as a researcher, you need to be aware of bias, as this will affect your own evaluation and interpretation of the findings. Second, different sources are aimed at different audiences. As a result, they go through a variety of processes prior to publication.

Recording the literature

At the beginning of your project, as soon as you are able to, get into the habit of *organizing* your literature. Ultimately, by the end of your project you will have gathered a wide range of sources. Each one that you refer to needs to be included in the bibliography section at the end of your project. Believe me, a situation where you are frantically searching for your sources at the last minute is best avoided! Therefore, it is a good idea to make a note of each source from the outset. Ideally, enter the full reference (Harvard system) and comments in Word. This is for the simple reason that you can do a 'cut and paste' when it comes to finalizing your references. In addition, organizing articles electronically is far less cumbersome than storing hard copies. Hussey and Hussey (1997: 102) recommended the following reasons for maintaining a database:

- You need to be able to identify the full and accurate reference in order to find or order the material.
- You can develop links among authors, topics, results and periods of time by re-sorting your database.
- It prevents duplication of effort.
- You will need to refer to your sources of information in your proposal and final research report.
- Others reading your finished work will be able to trace the original sources of information easily.

By the time you start your research project, you should have some experience of *referencing*. Basically, referencing your work involves two things. First, if you are citing a piece of work in the main text of your research, then you need to acknowledge within the text the source from which you have gathered the information. If you are using the *Harvard referencing system*, this involves citing within the main text (as opposed to footnotes). Some institutions may insist on an alternative referencing system that requires students to cite work within footnotes. Always check with the project guidelines published by your college or university to find out which referencing system you are required to follow.

Another aspect of referencing that tends to vary between institutions is use of the term 'references' and 'bibliography'. In general, *references* is a comprehensive list of sources that have been cited in the main text of a research project, whereas *bibliography* refers to those items that a student has read but not necessarily cited in the text. There appears to be no consensus between institutions as to the preferred method. For example, you may find that all references, both those consulted and cited, are required to be listed underneath the one heading of 'bibliography'. On the other hand, your project guidelines may require you to distinguish between bibliography and references. In short, it is best to consult your project guide or ask your project supervisor to determine what is required.

Using research management software to organize your literature search

There a number of *research management programs* available. These are designed to make it easier to organize and store literature in a searchable library. One that I have personally used and is ideal for students doing a research project is ReadCube which is a free academic software and reference manager for researchers. This can be downloaded at www.readcube.com. Alternatively, you could simply organize your journal articles on a thematic basis by creating a folder for each theme. For instance, if we use the earlier marketing metrics and UK national newspaper example, in the broadest terms, you could have one folder for 'Marketing metrics' and another folder for 'UK newspaper industry'. It is important to take an organized approach from the outset, otherwise you will find it difficult when it comes to locating literature and writing your review.

Start drafting review

If you are fully conversant with the literature and you have organized it into something that is manageable and easily accessible, then you are ready to begin drafting your literature review. Notice that I use the word 'draft'. This is because in all likelihood you will end up writing your literature review several times. Not only because you discover new literature that you wish to incorporate, but also because your supervisor may require you to rewrite it. On the other hand, you may simply wish to rewrite it several times until you hit upon a final version that you are comfortable with. Still, the main reason that you will write several drafts is because you should continue conducting your literature search up to a few weeks prior to submission.

Sources of Literature

Incorporating an eclectic mix of sources into your research project is likely to be deemed good practice by your supervisor and/or your marker. It illustrates that you have gone to great lengths when conducting your literature review.

Different sources of literature have different advantages and disadvantages. The important thing is that you are fully aware of these strengths and weaknesses, and that you refer to each one when conducting your review. This section examines the main sources that you are likely to draw on when reviewing the literature.

General reports

These may include *government reports*, *country data reports* such as those produced by the Economist Intelligence Unit (EIU), and market research reports such as those produced by Mintel. In some cases, these reports are difficult to access and can only be accessed by paying a subscription fee, although the majority of university and college libraries subscribe to the leading reports. Their usefulness should not be ignored, particularly if you are conducting research into a topic that may make use of macroeconomic data. You may find that market research reports produced, and commissioned, by different companies may contain conflicting data. This can make an interesting inclusion to your research.

Theses

These include major projects such as those associated with MPhil and PhD degrees. You may be able to access these in your own institution. Alternatively, the British Library keeps a large number of *theses*. The advantage of referring to research of this nature is that it may provide you with ideas for your own study. Generally, the structure is likely to be very similar to your own research project. For example, you will certainly see reference to some kind of introduction, methodology, data analysis, etc. But be wary of the fact that a thesis submitted for the award of an MPhil or PhD is usually in the region of 60,000–80,000 words. It will certainly be more in-depth and probably more theoretical than your own submission. Also, a PhD thesis needs to 'make a contribution to knowledge'. This is not the case for undergraduate studies.

Conference reports

The majority of *conferences* have a theme that is quite specific. For example, the Industrial Marketing and Purchasing (IMP) conference examines topics relating to interactions, relationships and networks in business-to-business markets, while the annual Association of Chartered Certified Accountants (ACCA) conference explores all areas of accounting and finance. An *academic conference* usually invites academics to write and present a paper based on a particular theme associated with the conference. In essence, it is largely an opportunity for academics to get together to discuss each other's research interests. How does this apply to student researchers? Well, in many cases, the entire body of papers presented at the conference are put on to the conference organizer's website. Some of these are available for public access free of charge. The IMP is such an example. More than 1,600 articles can be viewed free of charge at www.impgroup.org.

Newspapers

When considering *newspapers* as a possible source, make sure to review what is commonly referred to as the *business press*. For instance, the *Financial Times* is a great source for leading articles on company performance, mergers and acquisitions, the financial markets, and information on sectors ranging from construction to IT. Yet, although newspapers can be a useful source, remember that they are only likely to provide a practical insight into companies and markets. As you are conducting a research project that also requires reference to theory and possible theoretical application, you must not confine your sources just to newspapers. The majority of your theoretical content will come from academic journals.

Academic journals

An *academic journal* can be defined as 'a peer-reviewed periodical containing scholarly articles in a particular field of study'. Unlike newspaper articles, articles in academic journals are different both in terms of content and the process of publication. Table 3.3 summarizes the key differences between a newspaper article and an article featured in an academic journal. Academic journals are rated on their quality and standing within the academic community. In general, the leading research tends to be published in top journals that are rated four or five stars. Still, this should not dissuade you from reviewing the other journals. Even those rated as one star are of a sufficient standard for you to refer to them in your research project.

Of course, there are a large number of academic journals in the discipline of business and management. Table 3.4 provides examples of some of the academic journals you may consider referring to when undertaking your research. This has been divided on the basis of Marketing, Human Resources (HR), Strategy and Finance. I have purposely chosen these journals to illustrate the plethora of different areas of research within each discipline. For example, some journals focus on a

TABLE 3.3 A comparison of academic and newspaper articles

Academic article	Newspaper article
Authors: Usually academics who are experts in their field. Most are affiliated to an academic institution.	Authors: Journalists. Usually one journalist will write an article. Their credentials are often not supplied.
Bibliography: A detailed list of references using the Harvard referencing system at the end of the article.	Bibliography: Often not featured within the article.
Content/structure: Specialist content, research based. Typical structure includes an abstract, introduction, literature review, methodology, analysis and results, conclusion and bibliography.	Content/structure: Based on current affairs and topics of general interest. Often in line with the view of the target readership, and generally in narrative format.
Length: Longer articles (typically 5,000–8,000 words) based on an analytical approach.	Length: Short articles.
Peer review: Often peer-reviewed by experts in the field. Reviewers may accept an article outright, or accept it subject to modifications, or decline it outright.	Peer review: Reviewed by the editor or editorial board of the newspaper.

TABLE 3.4 Academic journals

Subject	Journals
Marketing	• *Journal of Marketing* • *Asia-Pacific Journal of Marketing and Logistics* • *European Journal of Marketing* • *Journal of Marketing Management*
Human Resources	• *Journal of Human Resources* • *Human Resources for Health* • *Asia-Pacific Journal of Human Resources* • *Advances in Developing Human Resources*
Strategy	• *Business Strategy and the Environment* • *Journal of Business Strategy* • *Journal of Economics & Management Strategy* • *Strategy & Leadership*
Finance	• *Journal of Property Finance* • *Managerial Finance* • *Pacific Accounting Review* • *Accounting Review*

particular geographical region, such as the *Asia-Pacific Journal of Marketing and Logistics*, while others may focus on one specific area of research within a broader discipline, such as the *Journal of Property Finance*.

Table 3.4 is by no means exhaustive and does not include journal rankings. My intention here is not to list the most prestigious journals in each subject area, but to provide you with an insight into some of the key journals that are likely to be relevant to your own research.

Textbooks

Textbooks need no introduction, as I know that you are likely to have read many different titles during the course of your study! As a potential source for your research project, they can prove invaluable. Yet you should still be careful when searching through the various titles covering your chosen topic. In short, make sure that you choose a good book. Jennifer Rowley and Frances Slack (2004: 33) propose that a good book should fulfil the following criteria:

- It should be relevant to the research topic.
- It should be written by an authoritative author; the bibliographical details given in the book will summarize the author's experiences in the field.
- It should be up to date, as signalled by the publication date.
- It should be published by a reputable publisher in the discipline.
- It should include extensive reference to other associated literature.
- It should be clearly structured, well presented and easy to read.

Certainly, textbooks can be a great source of information. By the time you begin working on your research project you should be very familiar with the layout, content and style of writing associated with textbooks. Of course, some textbooks tend to be more comprehensive than others. Typically, the larger texts that tend to focus on a broad discipline, such as Finance, Marketing or Human Resource Management, can be as long as nearly 1,000 pages. Although these may seem too general for your chosen topic, an interesting feature included in many of the leading textbooks is a glossary and company index. The former is helpful when generating key words associated with your study, while the latter can aid your research if you have decided to adopt a *case study approach*, i.e. you have chosen to research a particular company or companies.

Despite the obvious strengths associated with textbooks, the main downside is that they are unlikely to feature the latest innovative research. Moreover, textbooks do not always explore issues within a particular discipline in any great depth. In short, they are intended to cater for students engaged in a module over the course of one or two semesters, not as an aid to student researchers. Finally, remember that in some disciplines, especially those referring to the technology sector, material can soon become dated. Be wary of reviewing literature that may be deemed to be out of date, as this may impact on the credibility of your literature review.

Internet websites

In recent years, I have noticed an increasing number of students making reference to *Internet websites* within their research project. Given the growth in the Internet this is to be expected. Although Internet websites can provide ease of access to a wide range of sources, you still need to take a cautious approach when searching through various websites. In considering whether or not to use a particular web-based source, you should determine the *reliability* of the source and its perceived standing among the academic community. First, reliability can be relatively easy to determine. For instance, most students are familiar with *Wikipedia*. Although Wikipedia claims to be the biggest multilingual free-content encyclopaedia on the Internet, there are questions over its reliability. It is unable to guarantee the accuracy of the information appearing on its website. For this reason, several colleges and universities prefer students to refrain from quoting from Wikipedia. Similarly, some external examiners prefer not to see Wikipedia featured among references. If in doubt whether or not you are able to use Wikipedia, check with your college or university.

In brief, the web is likely to be your main tool for locating relevant literature. The majority of researchers use a technique known as 'snowballing' to help build a database of relevant literature that can be used as part of their literature review. Snowballing means reading through relevant article references in order to locate other sources, then reading through those sources' references, and so on. Eventually, you know you are making progress when authors' names become familiar to you or the same references appear on a regular basis. Although the Internet holds a wealth of information, how you access, record and recognize data is vitally important. Martin Brett Davies (2007: 40) makes the following valid points when searching via the web:

1. When you are carrying out a net search – which will lead you in all manner of directions – be sure to make notes of the interesting and useful items and sites that you come across. You can use a Word file to do so, but while you're actively net searching, you may find it more efficient to make hand-written notes and references.
2. When you come across quotable items that you might want to include in your report, copy and paste them to a file straight away.
3. Save any good websites that you come across to your Favourites.
4. Remember that there is a lot of rubbish on the net. When you are using a search engine, make sure that what comes up is useful, true and reliable. Be discriminating and selective in your choices.
5. If you are stuck, your academic library will have information specialists who are there to guide you in your net searches. Make sure you can tell them just what it is that you are seeking, and be prepared to listen to their advice.

Google Scholar is another useful search tool for students. Released in November 2004, it is a freely available service that includes the content of scholarly documentation from a wide variety of sources. Google Scholar covers journals, books, conference proceedings, dissertations, technical reports, preprints and postprints, and other scholarly documents (Neuhaus and Hans-Dieter, 2008: 200).

Abstracts

An *abstract* is a summary of an article. The abstract is designed to give the reader a 'snapshot' of the article content. The majority of articles in academic journals include an abstract. Essentially, it is a short overview (usually no more than 350 words) of the entire research. It is used as a helpful guide to researchers so that they can determine to what extent the article 'fits' with their own research. In short, it can be defined as a time-saving device: because it summarizes the study, the reader does not have to read the entire article. A search using key words within an abstract is a useful way of narrowing your search. If an abstract contains your key word, it is highly likely that the article is relevant to your research.

Catalogues

A *catalogue* contains a comprehensive list of sources held by a library. Increasingly, library catalogues tend to be electronic database systems. I have found that a useful source is copac.ac.uk (Copac, 2008). Copac is a freely available library catalogue, giving access to the merged online catalogues of many major UK and Irish academic and national libraries, as well as an increasing number of specialist libraries.

Dictionaries

A *dictionary* is a 'reference book containing words and other information'. Obviously, a dictionary, together with a thesaurus, is a very useful tool for any writer. A definition from a dictionary can be used if you intend defining a word or term for the benefit of your readers. As a general rule, the *Oxford English Dictionary* is the definitive dictionary. For example, if your intention was to critically review the body of literature on cultural theory, you may start by including a definition of culture from the *Oxford English Dictionary*. A range of definitions from established researchers in the field may then follow. There is no harm in consulting a range of dictionaries in order to get an eclectic mix of definitions.

Bibliographies

A *bibliography* is a comprehensive list of books, articles, Internet websites, magazines and other sources used in a particular study. A bibliography is often found towards the end of a book or journal. Its purpose is twofold: first, to acknowledge those authors whose work has been used when conducting the study, and second, to help other researchers engaged in a similar area of research. By including a bibliography, other researchers can save a great deal of time when conducting research.

Encyclopaedias

Quite simply, an *encyclopaedia* can be a book or more commonly a set of books that contains information on a wide range of topics. In this digital age, electronic versions tend to be more popular. As already mentioned, perhaps the most famous electronic encyclopaedia is Wikipedia. It remains a popular source of information for students, but, once again, reliability remains a concern. Although an encyclopaedia may provide relatively detailed information on your chosen topic, it is unlikely that this will go into any great depth. Moreover, material published on your chosen topic is likely to be the work of one particular author. Therefore, it may be subject to bias and is probably based on a limited range of sources. Quite simply, the purpose of an encyclopaedia is to provide material of a practical nature, so you will find few references to specialist studies.

Citation indices

These provide an indication of the quality and expert nature of a piece of research, by showing how many times the work has been cited. In brief, it can help you to identify the leading authors in your subject area by indicating how many times their work has been referred to. Scopus (2008) (available online only, www.info.scopus.com) is the largest abstract and citation database of research literature and quality web sources for the social sciences. Once again, your library should allow you to access this particular facility.

In sum, this section has examined a range of possible sources you can consult when doing your literature review. The next step is to consider what to actually do with the literature. In essence, this involves conducting a critical review.

Critical Review

A key skill in doing a literature review is to be able to read and review literature *critically*. By improving your knowledge of your topic through reading a wide range of sources you are more likely to familiarize yourself with the major issues surrounding your research. Some key questions that you may ask to help you to critically review an article include:

1. What is the main topic under review?
2. What are the results?
3. What methodology has the author(s) used? Is it appropriate?
4. What are the main issues raised by the author?
5. To what extent do the findings echo existing studies?
6. What questions are raised?
7. Is the article fair/biased?
8. How does the article relate to your own views?
9. Does the article display a contemporary view or are the findings/sources dated?
10. What are your own conclusions about the literature?

Certainly, the above questions should provide you with a useful guide when attempting to critically review an article. They can also be put to good use when you are actually writing your own literature review, and are comparing, contrasting and critically reviewing a range of literature within the review section of your research project. Personally, I have found that the critical nature of the literature review is something that some students find particularly difficult to grasp. Unfortunately, some fall into the trap of being overly descriptive. As a result, rather than ending up with a critical review, the final version of the review section ends up being an almost verbatim account of extracts from several different articles. This ultimately leads to a lower mark being awarded, as it falls some way short of actually critically reviewing the literature.

Structure of a Literature Review

Although adopting a critical approach is important, it is also essential that you structure your literature review in an appropriate way. Rowley and Slack (2004: 38) provide the following useful example of how to structure a literature review:

1. Include basic definitions, e.g. What is business process re-engineering (BPR)? What is e-government?
2. Discuss why the subject is of interest, e.g. What impact can BPR have on business success? Why are e-government applications important and what is their scope?
3. Discuss what research has already been undertaken on the topic, and whether there is any research on aspects of the topic that need to be investigated, e.g. the application of BPR to support the delivery of e-government applications.
4. Provide a clear summary of the research opportunities and objectives that emerge from the literature review.

A poorly structured literature review can be both irritating and confusing for the reader. In short, the structure of your literature review should include an introduction, the main body and a conclusion.

It can be argued that no one part of the review is more important than any other. However, I personally believe that it is important to start your literature review well by defining your topic, providing a clear rationale for selecting the topic, making clear your intentions, providing adequate background, and making reference to key authors.

Example of an introduction to a literature review

What follows is an example of an introduction to a literature review. Do not be too concerned about the nature of the topic. I have intentionally included an example that gives you an insight into content, thematic structure and referencing.

> This chapter discusses the development of research into relationships, inter-action and networks. There is a huge body of literature on this subject, and many theories have been used to describe relationships. Understanding relationships and their importance is of great significance in Chinese culture, and

has resulted in a growing Western literature on the subject (Vanhonacker, 1997; Strange, 1998; Child, 2000; Stuttard, 2000). First, a brief overview of the IMP Group's key empirical findings illustrates the work of IMP and how it links to this study. Second, relationships will be discussed. There are many definitions of relationship. It must be emphasized that this study focuses on interorganizational rather than interpersonal relationships. Third, interaction and networks will be examined, in particular work conducted by the IMP Group. Finally, FDI relationships and the key constructs of commitment, trust and cooperation will be considered.

Main body of the review

This is where you discuss the range of sources that you consider particularly relevant to your study. It is important that you adopt a critical approach to your review and organize it so that it follows a logical structure for the reader. In general, there are three options governing the structure of your review. First, you may decide to follow a thematic approach. In other words, your review takes particular themes in the literature and discusses each one in turn. Next, a methodological approach to your structure may analyze qualitative studies first, followed by quantitative studies. If some studies have adopted a mixed methods approach, this may be your final section. Or you may choose to structure your review chronologically. This involves reviewing changes in the literature over time. For instance, a timeline could be incorporated to show how a series of economic events have changed people's perception of government. Whichever option you choose, remember that your literature review needs to have a 'natural flow'.

Conclusion to the review

Your conclusion should summarize the leading articles in your chosen topic, evaluate the existing position within the area of your research, and identify gaps in and possible future areas of research. Above all, you should make the link between existing research studies and your own. For example, are you incorporating any aspects of existing research, e.g. in terms of methodology, and if so, why?

How to present your literature review

The above section should provide a useful guide in terms of structure, yet students are also frequently unsure of how to *present* their literature review. The simple answer is that there are no hard-and-fast rules on presentation. Personally, I like to see a bit of variation when it comes to presenting the review. Tables are a great way of summarizing existing key studies in your chosen area. They provide not only an interesting 'snapshot' for the reader, but also make it easier for other researchers wishing to review research of a similar nature. Table 3.5 is an excellent example of

TABLE 3.5 Comparing definitions of trust in inter-firm relationships

Author(s)	Definition	Type of relationship
Anderson and Weitz (1989)	'One party's belief that its needs will be fulfilled in the future by actions undertaken by the other party'	Sales agencies and manufacturers in the electronic components sector
Aulakh et al. (1996)	'Degree of confidence the individual partners have on the reliability and integrity of each other'	Interorganizational relationships
Chow and Holden (1997)	'The level of expectation or degree of certainty in the reliability and truth/honesty of a person or thing'	Buyer–seller in the circuit board industry
Doney and Cannon (1997)	'Perceived credibility and benevolence of a target of trust'	Buyer–seller in manufacturing
Ganeson (1994)	'Trust is the willingness to rely on an exchange partner in whom one has confidence'	Retail buyers and vendors from department store chains
Morgan and Hunt (1994)	'Trust exists when one party has confidence in an exchange partner's reliability and integrity'	Relationships between automobile tyre retailers and their suppliers
Sako and Helper (1998)	'An expectation held by an agent that its trading partner will behave in a mutually acceptable manner'	Supplier–manufacturer relationships in the auto industry

Source: Adapted from Raimondo (2000)

the type of table that can be incorporated into a literature review. As you can see, it includes all of the relevant information the reader would be interested in seeing, in this case: author(s), definitions and type of relationship.

Referencing under the Harvard system

I have already briefly mentioned the Harvard referencing system. In terms of referencing method, it remains the favoured choice for the majority of academic institutions. Following your own institution's guidelines on referencing is important as in some cases they may expect an alternative referencing system to be applied, or indeed, a slight variation on the Harvard system. Therefore, there is no excuse for not getting it right! Yet, perhaps surprisingly, poor referencing still appears to be a relatively common feature in student research projects. The next section should help you to overcome this problem by illustrating how to reference different sources within your references or bibliography.

Citing work using the Harvard system

How you cite your work in your references or bibliography is dependent on the source that you are referring to. However, no matter what the source, e.g. journal article, book, magazine or newspaper, all your references need to be laid out alphabetically, with the first named author's surname determining where each reference goes.

Examples of how to reference using the Harvard system:

- *For authored books*: Author's surname, initials (year of publication in brackets), *title of the book in italics*, place of publication, publisher.

For example: Jones, K. (2007). *Business Research*. London: Sage.

- *For journal articles*: Author's surname, initials (year of publication in brackets), 'title of the article in inverted commas', *title of the journal in italics*, **volume number in bold**, (issue number in brackets), page numbers.

For example: Henderson, T. (1995). 'International marketing: Cross-cultural issues'. *Journal of Marketing*, **24** (4): 212–224.

- *For papers published in edited books*: Author's surname, initials (year of publication in brackets), 'title of the paper in inverted commas', editor's surname, followed by the editor's initials, *title of the book in italics*, place of publication, publisher, page numbers where the paper can be found.

For example: Cole, A. (1996). 'Benchmarking in the UK retail sector', in Smith, L. (ed.) *International Business*. London: McGraw-Hill, pp. 12–19.

- *For newspaper articles*: Author, initials, (year). Title of article. *Full Title of Newspaper*, day and month of publication, page numbers and column line.

For example: Slapper, G., 2005. Corporate manslaughter: new issues for lawyers. *The Times*, 3 Sep. p. 4b.

- *Online newspaper articles*: Author and initials or corporate author, (year). Title of document or page. *Name of newspaper*, [type of medium] additional date information. Available at: include website address/URL (uniform resource locator) and additional details of access, such as the routing from the home page of the source [Accessed date].

For example: Chittenden, M., Rogers, L. and Smith, D., (2003). Focus: Targets Fail NHS. *Times Online*, [internet] 1 June. Available at: http://www.timesonline.co.uk/printFriendly/0..11-1506-669.html [Accessed 17 March 2005].

NB: the URL should be underlined.

It is good practice to keep a copy of the front page of any website you use.

- *Author's name cited in the text*: When making reference to an author's work in your text, their name is followed by the year of publication of their work, in brackets (parentheses), and forms part of the sentence:

For example: Cormack (1994, pp. 32–33) states that 'when writing for a professional readership, writers invariably make reference to already published works'.

- *More than two authors for a work*: Where there are several authors (more than two), only the first author should be used, followed by 'et al.' meaning 'and others':

For example: Green et al. (1995) found that the majority …
 Or indirectly: Recent research has found that the majority of … (Green et al., 1995).

- *More than one author cited in the text*: Where reference is made to more than one author in a sentence, and they are referred to directly, they are both cited:

For example: Jones (1946) and Smith (1948) have both shown …

What makes a good literature review?

By now, you should be familiar with the nature, approach and structure of a literature review. But what actually constitutes a good literature review? Zina O'Leary (2004: 81–82) cites a number of valid points that are worth considering when writing a good literature review. These are as follows:

- *Read a few good, relevant reviews.* There is no substitute for reading reviews produced in leading academic journals. By simply typing 'literature review' in the title search box of your search engine, you will probably find hundreds of articles that review literature within a particular topic.
- *Write critical annotations as you go.* If you begin sorting and organizing your annotations by themes, issues of concern, common shortcomings, etc., you may find that patterns begin to emerge. This can go a long way in helping you develop your own arguments.
- *Develop a structure.* We explored structure in the earlier section. Remember that your structure may alter as you discover new literature and your thinking evolves.
- *Write purposefully.* The literature review is driven by the researcher and needs to have and make a point. You can review literature without an agenda, but you cannot write a formal 'literature review' without one. Your audience should be able to readily identify the 'point' of each section of your review. If your audience does not know why you are telling them what you are telling them, you need to reconsider your approach.
- *Use the literature to back up your arguments.* It is important that when you make a statement or claim, you use supporting literature. For example, if you were to quote 'China is set to be the world's largest economy by the year 2020', then you must provide the source of the quote, e.g. 'China is set to be the world's largest economy by 2020' (Smith, 2005: 23).
- *Make doing the literature review an ongoing process.* As we have explored earlier, the literature review is a cyclical process. In reality, you should be conducting your review right up to a few weeks prior to your submission date.
- *Get plenty of feedback.* Writing a literature review is not an easy task, and your supervisor's expectations can vary widely. Don't wait until the last minute to begin the writing process or to get feedback. Be sure to pass a draft to your supervisor (although in some institutions this is not permitted), or anyone else willing to read it early on.
- *Be prepared to redraft.* It would be nice if first drafts and last drafts were the same draft. However, this is unlikely to be the case.

What makes a poor literature review?

You might think that what makes a poor literature review is essentially the opposite of what is listed above. That is certainly true to a point. Still, the following list of points are what I personally consider to be the more common mistakes made by students. Hopefully you will find these useful – not to copy, but to avoid at all costs!

- *No evidence of a literature review.* Thankfully this is somewhat of a rarity. Clearly, if you fail to include a literature review within your research project, it is likely to signal to your reader that you have failed to acknowledge work carried out by specialists in your chosen subject area. In addition, given that the literature review is a major part of your project, failure to include it will almost certainly mean a significant deduction in marks.
- *Poor length.* Your work is also likely to suffer if your review is of insufficient length. A question that I am often asked is 'How long should I make my literature review?' In general, this largely depends on your research approach – whether it is inductive or deductive. However, a useful guide is that your review is likely to be in the region of 25–30% of your overall word count.
- *Denser referencing required.* Although a review may be of sufficient length, sometimes a drawback is that a student has failed to include adequate reference to previous work in the main text. This suggests that the student has failed to examine the wide range of sources available to them. It also indicates that the student perhaps has not given enough time to carrying out their literature review.
- *The literature review is largely a verbatim reproduction of the original texts.* Unfortunately, sometimes students 'fall into the trap' of purely citing extracts from previous work in their subject area. As a result, the review becomes a very list-like style of writing. Of course, what they should be doing is adopting a critical approach to their review.
- *Poor structure.* A muddled, poorly structured review makes it difficult for the reader to fully grasp the nature of the research.
- *Literature does not correspond to research objectives.* Identifying and reviewing literature that is not relevant to a set of objectives shows poor understanding of the topic. In principle, if you fully understand your objectives, parameters and key words, then it should be easy to avoid citing work that is not relevant to your own study.

─RESEARCH IN ACTION─

Conducting a systematic literature review

The article below is taken from the *Journal of Knowledge Management*: 'Knowledge Management in SMEs: A literature review', Durst, S. and Edvardsson, I.R. (2012)

In this article, the authors undertake a systematic literature review of 36 refereed empirical articles on knowledge management and small and medium sized enterprises. The aim of the paper is to examine the current status of research in knowledge management (KM) in SMEs. The research questions are as follows:

- Which knowledge management topics are well researched and which are not?
- Which were the main findings of the studies?

- Which methods were used?
- How does the research handle the particular challenges small firms are facing regarding knowledge management?

The methodology of the literature review is explicitly set out within the paper. The methodology begins by explaining what is meant by a systematic review and the principles adopted when carrying out the review. In this case, the authors explain the process as beginning with mapping the field through a scoping review, followed by a comprehensive literature search, quality assessment, data extraction, synthesis and writing up.

First, the authors set out a research plan comprising the research questions, keywords, and details of inclusion and exclusion criteria. The inclusion criteria were: publications in the period of 2001–2011, empirical research papers, peer-reviewed, English language, SME focus on knowledge management and knowledge management processes, and ProQuest database. Conversely, any publications outside this timeframe, papers and reports that did not meet these criteria, and other databases were excluded from the review. The authors used an Excel data sheet to record the 'key elements' of each article. This consisted of the name of the author(s), year of publication, research aim/objectives, theoretical perspective/framework, method, main findings and name of the journal.

Second, the comprehensive literature search began with both authors accessing the ProQuest database to look for suitable articles. This process involved undertaking a key word search using 'knowledge management' and 'SMEs'. However, the researchers found that the search produced only a small number of publications. Refining the search to using 'KM' in combination with 'SMEs' resulted in 398 hits. This illustrates the importance of experimenting with a number of different key word searches when doing your own research. Durst and Edvardsson (2012) also included the highest ranked journals in their chosen area of research to make sure that the work by key authors was included in the review. In addition, three international journals in the field of small business were reviewed, thus resulting in an additional 697 hits.

Third, quality assessment entailed both authors reading through the abstracts and, if relevant, any other sections of the articles to make sure that they covered the pre-defined scope. This process yielded a final selection of 36 articles which fulfilled the criteria set and allowed for the analysis stage to be carried out.

Fourth, data extraction of the 36 papers was undertaken by dividing the papers among the two authors. Thus, each author read 18 papers. Both researchers then entered the relevant data regarding the research aim in the spreadsheet and jointly went through each data entry and discussed the content. If any of the authors had any reservations about one particular paper, then both authors went through the paper in question. The rationale behind this is to ensure consistency in terms of analysis and conclusions drawn.

Fifth, at the synthesis stage, the final Excel sheet was jointly discussed. This discussion enabled the authors to categorize the findings under KM themes, which, in turn, helped to clarify what is known about knowledge management in SMEs and to which KM areas the body of knowledge is limited.

Sixth, the final stage of the review process was devoted to writing up the findings.

The above article demonstrates one approach to conducting a literature review, and clearly shows the different steps that the authors went through when reviewing the literature. You will find many examples of literature-review-based articles on electronic databases such as Emerald and Business Source Premier. Irrespective of the topic, reading these types of articles will give you a good insight into how to conduct your own literature review, particularly in terms of structure and writing style.

A final reminder!

Remember that searching and critically reviewing the literature is likely to be a major part of your research project. After all, it is essential to acknowledge what has already been written. A thorough review will ensure that you have understood and identified the key authors who have published in your area.

Fundamentally, searching and reviewing the literature is a process that you should continue to undertake right up to a few weeks prior to submission. Moreover, make sure that you include a range of contemporary references. On occasion, I have read projects where the reference list contains little in the way of references post-2000. This illustrates a failure on the part of the student to actively seek the latest publications on their chosen topic.

Summary and Conclusion

In this chapter we have looked at various issues relating to conducting a literature review. The literature review is likely to be a major part of your research project. In essence, a literature review not only allows you to better understand your topic, but also allows you to identify 'gaps' and provides evidence of research. Here are the key points from this chapter:

- In the context of your research, 'literature' means all sources of published material.
- A literature review can be described as identifying, evaluating and critically assessing what has been published on your chosen topic.
- You are required to demonstrate library and information skills, the intellectual capability to justify decisions on the choice of relevant ideas, and the ability to assess the value of those ideas in context (Hart, 1998: 9).
- Think of the literature review as a process. Before you begin conducting your review of the literature you need to be clear about your objectives and research questions.
- When conducting your literature review, it is likely that you will use a wide source of literature.
- Reading journal articles is a great way to understand how to conduct a literature review.
- A key skill to doing a literature review is to be able to read and review literature critically.
- Searching the literature should be carried out until a few weeks prior to your submission date.

CASE STUDY — **Writing a Successful Literature Review**

Dirk has recently completed a workshop on how to write a literature review. Following the workshop, he felt a lot more confident in terms of how to approach the literature review for his own research project. He now realizes that key success factors include: reading relevant

---

sources, developing a coherent structure, reviewing the literature as an ongoing process, and being prepared to redraft. However, he is unable to recall other important factors that the lecturer highlighted during the workshop, in particular, how to approach presentation, structure and writing style.

Case study question

- What other factors does Dirk need to consider if he is going to write a successful literature review?

YOU'RE THE SUPERVISOR

Sarah has emailed you a draft of her literature review. The final paragraph of her review reads as follows:

> Henderson (2011) provides the most interesting study into leadership across cultures as it includes respondents from a range of different cultural backgrounds. His findings argue that cultural factors play a significant part in influencing leadership. I may make reference to this seminal piece of work later on in my own research.

Supervisor question

- What are the problems associated with finishing a literature review in this way and how would you advise Sarah to conclude her review?

COMMON QUESTIONS AND ANSWERS

1. How long should my literature review be?

Answer: This varies, and the word limit and views of your supervisor must be considered. For example, if you are working on the basis of a 10,000 word limit, then clearly one would expect to see a shorter literature review than if you were working towards completing a 15,000 word project. Your supervisor is likely to have his or her own opinions as to the appropriate length of your review. Also, noting the weighting of marks towards the literature review is a useful indicator. For instance, again, if you are working towards a 10,000 word project and 25% of the marks are allocated for literature review, then you can aim at writing in the region of 2,000–3,000 words. Finally, the amount of relevant literature and availability of sources are also factors. If you find that there is very little written on your subject, then perhaps your topic is too narrow. Conversely, if your topic is too broad, this will have a detrimental effect on your review because you will be unable to cover all relevant themes.

2. How do I write a literature review?

Answer: One of the most commonly asked questions by my project students is 'How do I write a literature review?' As noted earlier, the literature review is a process and should contain key features, such as: definitions of key terms; discuss why the subject is of interest; discuss research already undertaken; and provide a clear summary of the research opportunities and objectives that emerge from the literature review. Although you may know the structure and key features of a literature review, you may still feel apprehensive about actually writing your review. Although the likelihood is that you have been taught how to write a review as part of a workshop or research methods module, there is no substitute for reading literature reviews featured in leading academic journals. Literature review based articles give you an excellent insight into: structuring your literature review, adopting a critical approach, referencing your work, and summarizing and making a link to your own work. As a helpful guide, in the further reading section at the end of the chapter I have included details of three literature review articles. These have been purposely chosen as they are all on business-related topics and provide a basis in which you can learn how to form and develop your own review. Do not be too concerned if the topic does not fall into your chosen area of research. The important thing is to get a 'feel' for the writing style and how to produce a good literature review.

3. How many chapters shall I devote to my literature review?

Answer: This is often a matter of personal choice. However, I suggest that you seek advice on this from your project supervisor. In most cases, the majority of my students tend to devote one chapter to the literature review. This is generally for two reasons. First, the 10,000 word limit means that devoting more than one chapter to the review may mean that other sections of the project do not receive adequate attention. Second, the thematic nature of the chosen topic can easily be covered within one chapter. Sometimes a literature review may be based on two chapters. This might be because one chapter focuses on a more practical element, e.g. a case study, while the second chapter reviews relevant theoretical content. Again, if in doubt, discuss with your project supervisor.

4. What type and how many sources do I need to include in my literature review?

Answer: As you are conducting an academic piece of work there must be a certain number of academic sources within your research project, and this includes material from academic journals. Using other sources such as newspapers, magazines and websites is fine, as long as you also include academic sources such as academic journals and textbooks. In terms of websites, try to avoid obscure websites as the information they provide is likely to be unreliable. Moreover, try to avoid over-reliance on web-based sources. In short, it is best to use a range of sources when writing your literature review, although one would expect the majority of these sources to be 'academic based'. In terms of number of sources, this is difficult to answer as it depends on several factors; for example, amount of literature, chosen topic, university regulations, etc. Your referencing should be relatively dense and not rely too heavily on a small number of sources.

References

Anderson, E. and Weitz, B. (1989) 'Determinants of continuity in conventional industrial channel dyads', *Marketing Science*, 8 (Fall): 310–323.

Aulakh, P., Kotabe, M. and Sahay, A. (1996) 'Trust and performance in cross-border marketing partnerships: A behavioural approach', *Journal of International Business Studies*, 27 (5): 1005–1032.

Child, J. (2000) 'Management and organisations in China: Key trends and issues', in J.T. Li, A. Tsui and E. Weldon (eds), *Management and Organisations in the Chinese Context*. Basingstoke: Macmillan, 33–62.

Chow, S. and Holden, R. (1997) 'Toward an understanding of loyalty: The moderating role of trust', *Journal of Managerial Issues*, 9 (3): 275–298.

Copac (2008) 'Copac academic and library catalogue', online source: copac.ac.uk/, accessed 10 September 2008.

Davies, M.B. (2007) *Doing a Successful Research Project: Using Qualitative or Quantitative Methods*. Basingstoke: Palgrave Macmillan.

Doney, P.M. and Cannon, J.P. (1997) 'An examination of the nature of trust in buyer–seller relationships', *Journal of Marketing*, 61 (April): 35–51.

Durst, S. and Edvardsson, I.R. (2012) 'Knowledge Management in SMEs: A literature review', *Journal of Knowledge Management*, 16 (6): 879–903.

Ganeson, S. (1994) 'Determinants of long-term orientation in buyer–seller relationships', *Journal of Marketing*, 58 (2): 1–19.

Hart, C. (1998) *Doing a Literature Review: Releasing the Social Science Research Imagination*. Thousand Oaks, CA: Sage.

Hussey, J. and Hussey, R. (1997) *Business Research: A Practical Guide for Undergraduate and Postgraduate Students*. Basingstoke: Macmillan.

Knopf, J.W. (2006) 'Doing a literature review', *Political Science & Politics*, 39 (1): 127–132.

Morgan, R.M. and Hunt, S.D. (1994) 'The commitment–trust theory of relationship marketing', *Journal of Marketing*, 58 (3), July: 24–38.

Neuhaus, C. and Hans-Dieter, D. (2008) 'Data sources for performing citation analysis: An overview', *Journal of Documentation*, 64 (2): 193–210.

O'Leary, Z. (2004) *The Essential Guide to Doing Research*. London: Sage.

Raimondo, M. (2000) 'The measurement of trust in marketing studies: A review of models and methodologies', *Proceedings of the 16th Annual IMP International Conference*, Bath, September.

Rowley, J. and Slack, F. (2004) 'Conducting a literature review', *Management Research News*, 27 (6): 31–39.

Sako, M. and Helper, S. (1998) 'Determinants of trust in supplier relations: Evidence from the automotive industry in Japan and the United States', *Journal of Economic Behaviour and Organization*, 34: 387–417.

Scopus (2008) online source: www.info.scopus.com, accessed 15 September 2008.

Strange, R. (1998) *Management in China: The Experience of Foreign Businesses*. London: Frank Cass.

Stuttard, J.B. (2000) *The New Silk Road*. London: John Wiley & Sons.

Vanhonacker, W. (1997) 'Entering China: An unconventional approach', *Harvard Business Review*, March–April: 130–140.

Further Reading

Bruce, C. (1994) 'Research students' early experiences of the dissertation literature review', *Studies in Higher Education*, 19 (2): 217–229.

Cooper, H.M. (1998) *Synthesizing Research: A Guide for Literature Reviews*. Thousand Oaks, CA: Sage.

Fink, A. (2009) *Conducting Research Literature Reviews: From the Internet to Paper* (3rd edn). Thousand Oaks, CA: Sage.

Ismail, A.R., Melewar, T.C., Lim, L. and Woodside, A. (2011) 'Customer experiences with brands: Literature review and research directions', *The Marketing Review*, 11 (3): 205–225.

Nabi, G., Holden, R. and Walmsley, A. (2006) 'Graduate career-making and business start-up: A literature review', *Education + Training*, 48 (5): 373–385.

Oliver, P. (2012) *Succeeding with your Literature Review*. Maidenhead: Open University Press.

Ridley, D. (2008) *The Literature Review: A Step-by-Step Guide for Students*. Thousand Oaks, CA: Sage.

Soltani, E., Gennard, J. and van der Meer, R.B. (2004) 'HR performance evaluation in the context of TQM: A review of the literature', *International Journal of Quality & Reliability Management*, 21 (4): 377–396.

4
Addressing ethical issues

┌─Learning Objectives─┐

After reading this chapter, you should be able to:

- understand the nature of business ethics;
- appreciate the importance of ethics in business;
- know how to address ethical issues;
- recognize how ethics can be interpreted across cultures;
- realize why your research needs ethical approval;
- be aware of the role of the university or college research ethics committee;
- be aware of the consequences of not following ethical guidelines; and
- be familiar with how to negotiate access when conducting your research.

Introduction

This chapter discusses the importance of ethical issues facing the student researcher. As a researcher, you have a moral responsibility to carry out your research in an accurate and honest way. Adhering to ethical concerns is something that you should adopt right at the beginning of your research. For instance, if you decide to study the influence of networking on company performance, it is likely that you would find the collection of data, analysis and interpretation of results relatively straightforward. Yet, what would you do if some of your respondents commented that a vital part of maintaining their personal networks involved corruption? You then need to decide if it is morally appropriate for you to continue carrying out the research.

Many colleges and universities now require that students who undertake a research project concerning human subjects must obtain ethical approval for their work. This usually involves the completion of an ethical approval form. Subsequent approval is then required from a departmental or institutional ethics committee before the student is able to proceed with their research. It was once the case that only medical research raised ethical concerns. But it is now widely recognized that anyone conducting research involving human participants, whether in medical science or the social sciences, needs to consider ethical issues.

This chapter begins by discussing the nature of ethics. It sets out by defining ethics, analyzing it in the context of business research, and explains why ethical issues require the attention of both the student researcher and research practitioner. The chapter then examines the role ethics plays in business. HSBC and CIS Bank are used as illustrative case examples of how the promotion of ethical values can be a particular source of competitive advantage for companies.

As a student researcher you need to address a large number of ethical issues. The next section provides a comprehensive overview of the main ethical concerns that you will need to consider throughout the research process. It considers ethical concerns from the perspective of all those stakeholders with a vested interest in your research.

In some respects, the nature of ethics, and how it is interpreted, is likely to be alien to many students. For example, if you are an Asian student studying in a UK institution, the importance and interpretation you place on ethics may well differ from that of your university or college. Similarly, if conducting cross-cultural research, it is essential that you clearly define what is meant by ethics to your research participants. In short, cultural differences are likely to affect how individuals perceive ethics. The section 'Ethics across cultures' addresses this point by looking at the cultural impact on ethical concerns.

Next, we explore the increasing importance of ethics approval. This includes the approval process and the role of the ethics committee. Conversely, we also look at the consequences of not following ethical guidelines. The last section discusses how to negotiate access to individuals and data, taking account of ethical issues in the process.

The Nature of Ethics

Reports of ethical conduct, or misconduct, are common in the leading business press. Business ethics is a well-explored subject in business and management. As a result, there are a large number of definitions available to the researcher. However, one thing that the majority of definitions have in common is that they consider ethics from a stakeholder perspective. In other words, ethics is not just considered from the point of view of the researcher, but also from the viewpoint of those with a vested interest in the research, namely individuals, organizations and governments. A definition that underlines this view is that of Linda Treviño and Katherine Nelson (1999: 12). They defined *ethics* as: 'the principles, norms, and standards of conduct governing an individual or group'.

The terms 'ethics' and 'social responsibility' are often used synonymously. However, there is a key difference. *Social responsibility* relates to the public's expectations of companies to act in a manner that is socially responsible, while ethics relates to morality rather than society's interests. What is perceived as moral is down to an individual's perception of what is right or wrong.

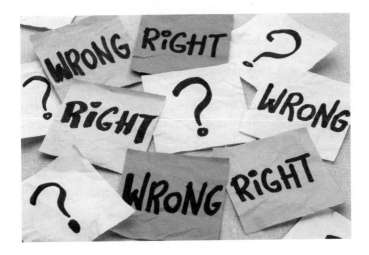

Figure 4.1 illustrates your possible research stakeholders. Fundamentally, these are individuals and groups that are likely to be influenced by your research. Therefore, you need to address ethical issues in relation to each and every one of them. Only when you have fully addressed these ethical considerations will you appreciate the extent to which ethics directly impacts on how you conduct your research. The role of each of the research stakeholders highlighted in Figure 4.1 is explained later in this chapter, but for now we will continue examining the nature of ethics and how it relates to business.

Generally, a key aspect of ethical issues is that you have a moral responsibility to carry out your research in an accurate and honest way. This includes respecting the

FIGURE 4.1 Research stakeholders

wishes of your participants. Rowley (2004: 210) suggested that 'conducting research ethically is concerned with respecting privacy and confidentiality, and being transparent about the use of research data. Ethical practices hinge on respect and trust and approaches that seek to build, rather than demolish, relationships.'

Personally, I consider Rowley's former point, that of 'respect and trust', to be particularly important when conducting research. The building of both respect and trust with your participants can only strengthen your credibility as a researcher. Moreover, it is likely to lead to a greater willingness to collaborate in your research project.

In sum, ethical issues are of concern to all of your research stakeholders. Not respecting privacy and confidentiality not only has a negative impact on your credibility as a researcher, but also may influence the reputation of participants and/or sponsors.

Ethics in business

In general, the same ethical principles apply to both the student researcher and research practitioner. Even so, a research practitioner working for a market research agency has an additional consideration. He or she needs to take into account obligations to their clients. According to Tony Proctor (2000: 20), the obligations a market researcher must undertake are as follows:

- Methods used and results obtained must be accurately represented. Researchers must use effective research procedures in obtaining and analyzing the data. There is an obligation to tell clients when they make ill-advised research requests. The researcher must also inform the client of any critical weakness or limitation in the collected data, especially those that could lead to major errors if the information is acted upon without reservation.
- The client's identity as well as the information obtained must be held in confidence. Any actual or prospective client approaching or using a research firm has the right to expect that what is revealed to the firm as part of this relationship is confidential.
- Research should not be undertaken for a client's competitor if such research will jeopardize the confidential nature of the client–researcher relationship.

Russ-Eft et al. (1999) suggested that when conducting business management research, your work should be professional and responsible, use an appropriate means of data collection, involve informed consent, carefully control deception and be carefully interpreted. In order to achieve this, many companies now have their own *code of ethics*. One such example is the leading multinational banking giant HSBC. The following provides some of the expectations included in HSBC's *Ethical Code of Conduct* in respect of its relationships with its suppliers:

Suppliers must embed basic business principles in a Code of Business Standards or a similar policy, including such items as adherence to local laws and a stand against bribery and corruption. Suppliers must abide by all legislation and regulations related to the protection of the environmental and the handling of dangerous and hazardous materials. Suppliers must treat all employees fairly and not discriminate against any group in its employment practices. Suppliers should have reasonable payment policies with their own suppliers and subcontractors. To work actively to improve the environment and proactively to pursue any initiatives that bring about that improvement. (Ethical Code of Conduct, 2013)

Another bank that prides itself on its ethical approach is the Co-operative Bank. The Co-operative Bank is well known to many UK consumers. Its 'ethical policy' is a common feature of both its advertising campaign and promotional literature. An extract from the company's website illustrates the importance it places on ethical concerns:

The Co-operative Bank's Ethical Policy is based on extensive consultation with customers and reflects their ethical concerns surrounding how their money should and should not be invested. It also informs the Co-operative Bank's choice of partners and suppliers.

The policy covers the following issues:

- Human Rights
- The Arms Trade
- Corporate Responsibility and Global Trade
- Genetic Modification
- Social Enterprise
- Ecological Impact
- Animal Welfare

During 2005, the Co-operative Bank turned away some 30 businesses whose activities were in conflict with their customers' ethical concerns. As a result, income worth some £10 million was denied to the bank. At the same time, significant monies were directed to businesses whose activities were support-ive of the Bank's customer's ethical priorities. (Co-operative Bank, 2013)

One might perceive the Co-operative Bank's ethical policy as a form of competitive advantage. To be sure, many ethical consumers are interested in ethical banking and finance. Yet ethical considerations apply to all sectors of the economy, not just banking and finance. For example, supermarkets need to address a whole range of ethical issues. These include everything from using recycled packaging materials to food content.

So far we have largely examined ethical practice from a corporate perspective. Each business function also needs to consider ethical practice, as collectively they help to form consumer opinion about a company as a whole. Hence, ethical practice is undoubtedly essential to all functions of business. The next section illustrates some of the key business functions and their ethical considerations.

Ethics and marketing

Much interest in marketing ethics is motivated by the basic premise that employees' unethical activities may have negative consequences for the well-being of the firm by eroding consumer trust (Mascarenhas, 1995). For example, consumers may distinguish between brands based on their own ethical judgement.

In their 1985 study into ethics and marketing management, Lawrence B. Chonko and Shelby D. Hunt came to the following five major conclusions:

- The most often mentioned ethical problem faced by marketers is bribery. Five other issues (fairness, honesty, pricing strategy, product strategy and personnel decisions) were also frequently cited as difficult ethical problems.
- The primary ethical conflict reported by marketing managers involved balancing demands of the corporation against customer needs.
- Marketing managers perceive many opportunities in their firms and industries to engage in unethical behaviour. However, they reported that few managers engaged in such behaviours.
- Marketing managers do not believe that unethical behaviours in general lead to success. However, many believe that successful marketing managers do engage in certain specific unethical behaviours.
- When top management reprimands unethical behaviour, the ethical problems perceived by marketing managers seem to be unrelated to the extent of unethical problems in marketing management.

Ethics and accounting

Obviously, ethical values are not just important to marketers, but also to accountants. If, for example, you are studying for an Accounting degree, then it is essential that you understand that society has extremely high ethical expectations of accounting professionals. In recent years a number of high-profile cases of 'cheating' have been reported in the world's press.

Perhaps the most publicized was that of the American energy giant Enron. Cheating in the form of grossly overstating revenue caused the demise of Enron, which resulted in a loss of approximately $60 billion. While increasing revenue to maintain an 'apparent constant rate of growth' was the bottom-line result, Enron's errors were far broader than simply overstating revenue. Enron's energy traders did what they could get away with to increase their apparent sales volume, even to the extent of shutting down energy generating plants in California. This culture of deceit was so endemic that the leaders of Enron actually viewed themselves as 'heroes' for maintaining Enron's apparent viability in the face of imminent disaster. Enron's corporate culture epitomized 'a need to succeed' at all costs.

Ethics and other business functions

Of course, ethics is not just applicable to marketing and finance. Ethical values need to be considered in relation to *all* business functions. For instance, human-resources managers need to ensure that their company has in place a form of employee assessment that is fair to all employees, while those working in research and development need to make sure that materials are sourced from ethical suppliers. Supplier-based ethical issues may include working pay and conditions, employee rights and the use of child labour.

In sum, ethical considerations can be viewed from a number of different perspectives. These include *consumer* perspectives, *corporate* perspectives and each respective internal *business function*.

Why Do I Need to Learn About Ethics?

Although engaging in ethical practice is clearly important for businesses, it also forms an important part of your own work as a student researcher. There are two main reasons why it is so vital for you to learn about ethics in the context of your research project. First, when undertaking your research project, you will need to be aware of a range of ethical issues that impact a wide variety of research participants. These are fully explored in the next section. However, for now, it is worth noting that failure to address ethical issues can lead to potentially quite serious consequences. These include damage to your credibility as a researcher and possibly the integrity of your participants.

Second, learning about business ethics can give you transferable skills that can be used in the workplace. For example, a study by Purcell (1977) found that those US MBA students who participated in a seminar on business ethics were still positively influenced by the contents of the seminar many years later. In other words, the content had a positive impact on their ethical views.

Ethical Responsibilities to Research Stakeholders

Earlier in this chapter we briefly looked at the research stakeholders who need to be considered when you are conducting your research (Figure 4.1). This section provides you with a comprehensive guide to the main ethical responsibilities that you have to each research stakeholder. It is important that you check with all those involved in the research that you are satisfying your ethical commitments throughout the entire research process.

Individual participants

A key question for the researcher is 'How are participants going to be selected?' Certainly, it is not ethical to approach friends and family and ask questions that they are not qualified to answer. However, in some cases friends and family may understandably form part of your sample. Of course, this is largely dependent on your objectives. In essence, all participants taking part in your study need to be fully briefed on the nature of your research and understand the implications of taking part. Ideally, this process should involve completion of a consent form. However, participants must always be given the option to withdraw at any stage of the research without recrimination. In short, your responsibilities towards research participants are primarily to offer the level of protection that participants expect.

Next, we examine in closer detail some of the ethical considerations relating to individual participants.

Protection of participants

As a researcher it is your responsibility to ensure the welfare of *all* your research participants. This includes both their physical and mental well-being. Protection of participants should be based on the same thorough, professional process, irrespective of age, gender or ethnic background. Knowing who your research participants are can help to better protect their well-being, although sometimes there is a fine line between protecting their well-being and asking unethical questions. In the area of business and management there are examples of research that may impact on subjects. For example, the Stanley Milgram experiment of 1963 is an example. On some occasions you might find that respondents are only too happy to divulge highly sensitive information. Just because they have divulged it does not mean that it should be written up or published. Sometimes as a researcher you may need to make a judgement as to the potential consequences of publishing highly sensitive information. In short, discretion may well be called for on your part.

Safety of the researcher

At first, you may think that your own safety is unlikely to be compromised as a result of carrying out your research. In principle, you're right. Nevertheless, your own welfare is something that you need to consider when undertaking your research design. Remember that potential risks are not only physical, but also psychological. Research into sensitive subjects, such as child abuse or prostitution, may carry a greater likelihood of psychological risk. You need to take into account such safety issues when conducting your research in order to reduce the risk to your own welfare. Ideally, procedures to deal with safety issues should be clearly set out with your project supervisor. In some cases, your research may require insurance cover to protect against any unforeseen eventuality. This may include travel insurance (e.g. if you are doing cross-cultural research) or personal liability insurance.

Recruitment and informed consent

Recruitment relates to the process of inviting people to take part in your research. How you recruit your research participants can be done in a number of different ways, although it largely depends on your sampling method. We examine sampling in Chapter 8.

Consent can be defined as 'seeking permission for something to happen or for something to be done'. Another important aspect of consent is informed consent. This means that it is the responsibility of the researcher to accurately explain the nature of the research and the role the individual is likely to play in it. Participants are only able to give informed consent on the basis that they have a full understanding of the nature of the research. According to O'Leary (2004: 53), informed consent implies that participants are:

- *Competent.* They have the intellectual capacity and psychological maturity necessary to understand the nature of the research and their involvement in the study.
- *Autonomous.* They are making self-directed and self-determined choices. Others, such as parents or guardians, cannot make the decision to participate for them.
- *Involved voluntarily.* They must be made aware of the research being conducted. Research 'on them' cannot be conducted without their knowledge and consent.
- *Aware of the right to discontinue.* Participants are under no obligation to continue their involvement, and pressure to continue should not be applied.
- *Not deceived.* Researchers need to be honest about the nature of their research, about the affiliation or professional standing, and the intended use of their study.
- *Not coerced.* Positions of power should not be used to get individuals to participate in a study, as can happen when employers or teachers apply pressure on their charges to engage in research.
- *Not induced.* An offer of money or some other reward that entices individuals to participate in research that they would otherwise avoid is considered an inducement. While it may be acceptable to compensate individuals for their time and effort, it should not be to an extent where it compromises a potential participant's judgement.

Informed consent forms (an example is illustrated later in this chapter) are often used to make things clearer to research participants. The following list provides examples of the type of information that most informed consent forms include:

- Information about the nature and purpose of the research.
- A statement that participation is voluntary, including the choice to opt out at any time.
- Information about the data collection methods and the option to agree/refuse to being recorded (if applicable).
- A description of the extent to which confidentiality will be maintained and an option to choose anonymity.
- A description of any possible risks or discomforts to participants.
- A description of any possible benefits to participants or others.
- Contact addresses, emails and/or telephone numbers for any questions about the research.
- A description of the intended uses of, and disposal/storage and documentation procedures for, data, including an option to agree/disagree with these procedures.
- Finally, an option to agree or refuse to participate (signature of participant, date, signature of witness/researcher).

(Burns and Burns, 2008: 35)

Anonymity

You should offer all respondents taking part in your research the option to remain anonymous. If a respondent wants *anonymity*, then this means that he or she does not wish to reveal their name. In short, they do not want their name to be linked with their opinions provided in your study.

If you are conducting a questionnaire survey with a large sample size, anonymity is perhaps not such an issue. However, under certain circumstances you may find that a large number of your respondents prefer to remain anonymous. This tends to be the case if the subject is of a sensitive nature. For instance, asking respondents to express their views on politics, sexual behaviour or immigration is likely to lead to more requests for anonymity. Similarly, if your study involves interviewing respondents of a senior status, e.g. managing directors of multinational companies, then you must have permission to reveal their identity. If respondents make clear that they will only take part if anonymity is enforced, then obviously you must abide by their wishes.

Confidentiality

Confidentiality focuses on the data collected. If a company provides you with information on the basis that it will be treated in the strictest confidence, then this is something that you must adhere to.

In reality, dealing with participants who insist on data being treated in confidence is common to both academic and student researchers. Dealing with the issue of confidentiality is usually relatively straightforward. For instance, let's say that you have conducted research into staff retention among five leading European companies. Now, this is clearly a sensitive subject, so it is perhaps unsurprising to find that all five companies wish data provided to be treated in the strictest confidence. How do you overcome this problem? Well, the best option is to refer to each company either on the basis of their respective industry or country of origin, e.g. 'the construction company' or 'the Dutch company'. This is usually enough to satisfy participants concerned with confidentiality.

Even so, in some instances, respondents may not agree to such an approach for fear that the reader is still able to identify their company. In this case, a last resort is to advise the participant that the only individuals to view your work will be your research supervisor, a second marker and possibly an external examiner. In other words, a copy will not be put into the public domain (normally this is your college or university library). I have found that participants are usually happy with this approach, although it does mean checking with your institution to see if it will concur. If it does, final clarification should be made at the point of submission.

Data Protection Act 1998

The *Data Protection Act 1998* was passed by Parliament to control the way data are handled, to give rights to people who have information stored about them. The Act works in two ways. First, it states that anyone who processes personal information must comply with eight principles, which make sure that personal information is:

- fairly and lawfully processed;
- processed for limited purposes;
- adequate, relevant and not excessive;

- accurate and up to date;
- not kept for longer than is necessary;
- processed in line with your rights;
- secure; and
- not transferred to other countries without adequate protection.

(Information Commissioner's Office, 2009)

The second area covered by the Act provides individuals with important rights, including the right to find out what personal information is held on computer and in paper records (www.ico.gov.uk).

Although the Data Protection Act only applies to the UK, other European countries have similar laws governing the use of data.

Advice to participants

It is important that you *fully brief* your participants prior, during and after your research. Arguably, the most important of these is prior to conducting your research. Your participants are likely to want to know the nature of your research, how the information they provide will be used, and to what extent it will be made public. Misleading participants from the outset is only likely to create problems later on. Ideally, aim to 'sell' the merits of your research in an honest, open and professional manner. Moreover, establish a close working relationship with your participants, built on trust and commitment. By doing so, you will undoubtedly find that your research is a great deal more rewarding.

I believe that it is essential to fully brief your participants throughout, as many of them are likely to show a keen interest in your research. I know from my own experience that actively engaging participants can also help to develop key networks suitable for further research projects.

Responsibility to other researchers and the wider community

Although you are likely to be a novice researcher, you still have a responsibility to the wider research community and other researchers associated with your chosen subject. Failure to acknowledge the work of other researchers is of course highly unethical. Also, plagiarism and manipulating other researchers' work so that it meets your own ends are equally unethical. Even if you have no intention of publishing your work, it is important to get into the habit of accurately acknowledging and representing the work of others. The following section addresses some of the specific areas of responsibility you have to other researchers and the wider community.

Plagiarism

Plagiarism is viewed as a serious offence both in academia and business. *Plagiarism* is the deliberate copying of someone else's work and presenting it as one's own. The consequences of plagiarism are widely published to students. Many universities and colleges now use a range of ways to deter and prevent plagiarism, including using detection software such as Turnitin. However, for all the preventative measures installed by institutions, plagiarism still takes place. One might argue that plagiarism is more widespread today than ever before. Unsurprisingly, the Internet has made it easier to plagiarize work produced by someone else. Often, material such as conference papers, journal articles, business reports and theses are easily accessible via the Internet. This provides those with a view to plagiarizing data both easy access and the ability to copy the work in a relatively straightforward manner.

'Plagiarism' is a rather broad term. One might argue that varying degrees of plagiarism exist depending on the extent to which something is copied, and the source that it is being copied from. More specific examples of plagiarism include:

- The verbatim copying of another person's work without acknowledging it.
- The close paraphrasing of another person's work by simply changing a few words or altering the order of presentation without acknowledging it.
- The unacknowledged quotation of phrases from another person's work and/or the presentation of another person's idea(s) as one's own.
- Plagiarized work may belong to another student or be from a published source such as a book, report, journal or material available on the Internet.

(Anglia Ruskin University, 2007)

Self-plagiarism

Unlike plagiarism, self-plagiarism is perhaps less well known to students. *Self-plagiarism* is including work in your research project that you have already submitted as part of a previous piece of assessment. In some instances, students choose a topic that they have researched previously. In principle, choosing the same subject is fine. However, if you incorporate a significant amount of a previous piece of work into your research project, this could be construed as self-plagiarism. The simplest way to avoid self-plagiarism is to choose a topic that you have not addressed in any of your modules, but if you want to research a topic you have covered in the earlier stage of your course, then you need to be aware of the dangers of self-plagiarism and avoid it at all costs.

Rules governing the submission of previously submitted work and self-plagiarism tend to vary among institutions. If in doubt, check with your college or university before considering including work that may have been submitted as part of an earlier piece of assessment.

Project supervisor

In any supervised research project, it is unethical to be secretive and dishonest about your research with your supervisor. Remember that your supervisor is there to support you throughout the research process. As you can imagine, your supervisor only has your word that you are undertaking a particular type of research. The relationship between the supervisor and research student is built on trust. Failure on the part of the student to follow a set of ethical principles, such as submitting plagiarized work, will undoubtedly break this trust. Of course, it can also have serious consequences in terms of your academic progression.

University/college

As well as your supervisor, it is equally important that you consider your university or college when conducting your research. As an 'ambassador' for your institution, you need to conduct yourself in a manner that follows the highest ethical standards (often set out by your institution's 'Ethical Code of Practice'). A worst-case scenario is that failure to do so may lead to negative publicity against both yourself and your institution, thereby damaging its reputation in the education marketplace.

Employer

If you are working and studying part-time, then there is a possibility that your employer may form a crucial part of your research. This can provide real benefits. For instance, it can give you access to important data, key personnel, and perhaps even financial support while you are carrying out your research. Still, remember that you have a responsibility to your employer to conduct your research in accordance with their ethical requirements. The important thing here is to fully brief your employer on the nature of your research and seek appropriate consent prior to including them in your study.

If you receive their informed consent to participate, make sure it is from the right individual and keep your employer regularly informed of your progress. And remember that if their consent comes with conditions attached, you must comply with those conditions. One example is providing management with a full report of your research findings.

Organizational participants

As a business researcher, there is a strong likelihood that in your research you may include participants who work for an external organization. Similar to conducting research on your own organization, it is ethical to inform these participants of the purpose of the research and to gain their informed consent prior to their participation. One of the problems associated with informing participants is that their actions may change as a result of being involved in your research project.

Professional standards

To indicate the professional standards required of you as a researcher, seven factors will be briefly covered:

Personal conduct

Your own personal conduct when conducting your research must be professional, honest and transparent. It is not only your own reputation at stake, but also that of your institution. Remember that when you mention you are conducting research, you need to explain the purpose and how the findings will be disseminated.

Deception

In some cases, a researcher may create a false impression in order to disguise the true purpose of the research, for example, if the topic is of a particularly sensitive nature, e.g. employees' views of management within a particular organization. Honesty is essential to all research. Myers (2009: 47) provided the following illustration of the possible implications of engaging in deception:

> Imagine if a researcher was able to publish a paper that contained fictitious data and lies about the research methods. What would this do to the reputation of the journal in which the paper appeared? As soon as it became public knowledge, the reputation of the journal in question would be in tatters. It is also very likely that the very field itself would be brought into disrepute.

You are unlikely to go on to publish your work in peer-reviewed journals, but it is essential that you do not set out to deceive any of the stakeholders involved in your research. You must be honest about all aspects of your data – collection, analysis, interpretation of findings, and conclusions.

Respect

Respect means that researchers should consider the feelings and rights of all those participating in their research. In reality, respect is likely to be developed over time, but if you adopt a professional manner from the outset and throughout your research, your participants are far more likely to show respect towards you as a researcher.

Conflict of interest

An example of a conflict of interest would be if you were conducting research into career progression within your own organization, and your position within your firm was that of Human Resources Manager. This is perhaps an obvious example. However, it illustrates the difficulty in attempting to take an objective stance if there is a potential for conflict of interest. Objectivity means that as a researcher you should not allow your own biases or perceived values to impact your study. Objectivity is certainly essential. Without objectivity, the credibility of your research is likely to be called into question.

Dissemination

Dissemination relates to the publication of your research following completion. For example, are those respondents who have contributed to your work happy for it to be turned into academic journal articles, presented at conferences, produced in magazines or even put on your college or university website? The ideal way of dealing with this issue is to seek consent about dissemination from the outset. As far as possible, participants need to be fully aware of what, where and when you intend to disseminate your work.

Debriefing

Debriefing is talking to participants following their role in the research. For instance, it is often important to provide participants with any additional information they need to develop their understanding of the research after the data have been collected. In some cases, participants may also be interested in a summary of the research findings to see how their role in the research compares to that of others.

Debriefing is also very important in qualitative research to make sure that you have correctly interpreted your participant's comments. Asking a participant to read through your interview notes can help to clarify their comments, but it can also result in the participant making alterations to their earlier comments because, in hindsight, they deem them to be inappropriate. If this happens, it is best to make the changes so as to maintain trust with the participant, and if so required, ensure confidentiality.

Collusion

Collusion occurs when two or more individuals cooperate to produce a research project that is presented as the work of one student alone. Your research project must usually be an individual piece of work. In other words, joint authorship is not permitted. If your project guidelines do not allow collaboration, then you must submit an individual piece of work. Evidence to the contrary is likely to lead to a fail at the very least.

Ethics Across Cultures

Applying ethical guidelines is all very well, but to what extent are ethics in one particular culture the same in another? The 'ethical relativist' maintains that nothing is 'really' or 'simply' good or bad; it is only good or bad in relation to the moral code of a given culture or historical era.

If you are considering conducting cross-cultural research, how ethical principles are interpreted across cultures could directly impact all areas of your research. Generally speaking, when conducting research across cultures, it is important to consider a number of points. First, as a researcher you need to show respect and willingness to adapt to different cultures. Second, be prepared to follow 'written' and 'unwritten' codes of conduct. Third, understand sensitive issues when compiling questionnaire surveys. And finally, respect varying degrees of confidentiality and anonymity.

Ethical Approval for Research Involving Human Subjects

Many universities and colleges now require that researchers seek ethical approval if conducting research involving human subjects. Ethical approval for research with human subjects is required for the following reasons:

- To protect the rights and welfare of participants and minimize the risk of physical and mental discomfort, harm and danger from research procedures.
- To protect your rights as a researcher to carry out legitimate investigation as well as the reputation of the university for research conducted and sponsored by it.
- To minimize the potential for claims of negligence made against you, the university and any collaborating individual or organization.
- Because, increasingly, external funding bodies and refereed journals require a statement of ethical practice in applications for research funds and as a precondition of publication.

According to Michael Jay Polonsky (1998: 1227) an understanding of ethical issues is important to your research for the following reasons:

- Business students are increasingly undertaking research that involves human intervention in various business-related courses. Some firms, especially small businesses, may see student research projects as a form of 'cheap' consulting. Where academics 'require' students to interact with the business community, they [the academics] become responsible not only for student learning process, but staff must also ensure that participants in the wider community are protected.
- Students' understanding of business ethics should be demonstrated in their ability to identify and address key ethical issues in 'real' research activities. Providing complete subjects on business ethics or the inclusion of discussions of ethical issues within a given subject does not necessarily assist students in identifying the ethical dilemmas that they may face when they are business practitioners.
- The incorporation of an ethical evaluation of students' research projects may serve as a useful teaching tool to inculcate ethical reasoning.
- Lastly, formal ethics clearance processes may serve as a useful mechanism to protect students, staff and the university (Hart et al., 1992).

Ethical codes

Various disciplines within business have established their own codes of ethics, including the Chartered Institute of Marketing (CIM) which has its own code, of 'Professional standards, ethics and disciplinary procedures' (CIM, 2012). Below is a summary of the main points. The full version can be accessed from the CIM website (www.cim.co.uk).

1. A member shall at all times conduct himself with integrity in such a way as to bring credit to the profession of marketing and the Chartered Institute of Marketing.
2. A member shall not, by unfair or unprofessional practice, injure the business, reputation or interest of any other member of the Institute.
3. Members shall, at all times, act honestly in their professional dealings with customers and clients (actual and potential), employers and employees.
4. A member shall not, knowingly or recklessly, disseminate any false or misleading information, either on his own behalf or on behalf of anyone else.
5. A member shall keep abreast of current marketing practice and act competently and diligently and be encouraged to register for the Institute's scheme of Continuing Professional Development.

(CIM, 2012)

The university or college research ethics committee

As previously stated, many universities and colleges now require that researchers seek ethical approval if conducting research involving human subjects. For undergraduate students, this may require the completion of an ethics checklist. If the checklist confirms that research will be carried out with human participants, then ethical approval is often required from a department or faculty ethics committee. This usually requires student researchers to submit the following documents to seek ethical approval: the ethics review checklist, the ethics application form, a detailed research proposal clearly outlining the methodological approach, and the participation consent form. First, the purpose of the ethics review checklist is to see if further ethical approval is required. This typically contains questions such as 'Does your research involve human participants?' and 'Does your research involve accessing confidential data?' Second, the ethics application form (see Figure 4.2) includes information on the researcher's details, project aims and objectives, research methodology, ethical issues and consent. Third, a detailed research proposal includes information on the research background, research questions, methodology, key literature and proposed research timetable. Finally, the participation consent form (see Figure 4.3) consists of brief background on the research, the role of the participant and what will happen to the data following collection.

Even if your own institution does not insist on an ethics application, my advice is to complete one for your own personal use. This helps you to address your own ethical concerns by putting them in writing. Above all, it gives you piece of mind that you have taken into consideration the ethical concerns of all relevant research stakeholders. Figures 4.2 and 4.3 give examples of an ethics approval form and an informed consent form respectively. To be honest, there really is no substitute for putting everything in writing. By adopting this method, you are far less likely to come across ethically related problems later in your research.

Saxon University

Ethics Application Form

SECTION A: Project/Researcher details

Title of Project:

Name of Student Researcher:

Student Number:

Project Supervisor:

Is this research sponsored by any external organization by either the provision of access to data or by funding in cash or in kind?

Will the research be carried out on the premises of another organization? (If so, please attach written consent from this organization.)

SECTION B: Project aims and objectives

Please include a brief outline of your research project. Please make clear the rationale and benefits of the project. In addition, please include whether or not your research will make reference to your affiliation to the college.

Does the project involve the direct participation of individuals other than your research supervisor? If no, please go to the last section (SECTION F). If yes, please continue.

SECTION C: Research methodology

Please provide details of when you intend to commence your project and indicate the likely duration. In addition, please provide details of the proposed methodology.

SECTION D: Ethical issues

Risk – Does the proposed research place any of the participants at risk of physical, psychological or emotional harm? If yes, please provide details and how you intend to deal with this.

Confidentiality and anonymity – Does the proposed research raise issues relating to confidentiality and anonymity? If yes, please provide details of how you intend to deal with this issue.

Sponsorship – Is the project sponsored by an individual or external organization? If so, will the project require the signing of a confidentiality agreement with an external organization? (If so, this needs to be agreed by the college's research office.)

Will the sponsor need to see the data that you have collected or the report of your research findings? If so, please provide details.

Are there any other ethical issues that you wish to highlight to the research ethics committee?

SECTION E: Consent

It is essential that all those who participate in your research do so of their own free will. For consent to be valid, participants must be informed about the nature of the research, and they must be competent to understand the implications of their participation.

Please provide details of how it is intended that informed consent be obtained from the participants. Copies of relevant documentation should be included, especially any explanatory material given to participants and the consent form.

Discuss the procedures you intend to undertake for gaining permission from participants who are unable to give informed consent. If you intend conducting research without informed consent of participants, detailed reasons must be provided.

Finally, give a detailed account of how you will comply with the Data Protection Act 1998.

SECTION F: Signatures

Student:

Supervisor:

Director of Research:

Date:

FIGURE 4.2   Ethics application form

Saxon University

Participant Consent Form

NAME OF PARTICIPANT:

Title of the research project:

Main investigator and contact details:

Members of the research team:

I confirm that I agree to take part in the above research. I have read the Participant Information Sheet which is attached to this form. I understand what my role will be in this research project, and all my questions have been answered to my satisfaction.

I understand that I am free to withdraw from the research at any time, for any reason and without prejudice.

I have been informed that the confidentiality of the information I provide will be safeguarded.

I am free to ask any questions at any time before and during the study.

I have been provided with a copy of this form and the Participant Information Sheet.

Data Protection: I agree to Saxon University processing personal data which I have supplied. I agree to the processing of such data for any purposes connected with the Research Project as outlined to me.*

***Note to researchers: please amend or add to this clause as necessary to ensure that it conforms with the relevant data protection legislation in your country**.

Name of participant (print) .... Signed .... Date ....

YOU WILL BE GIVEN A COPY OF THIS FORM TO KEEP

(Continued)

If you would like to withdraw from the research, please complete the form below and return to the main investigator named above.

Title of Project:

I WISH TO WITHDRAW FROM THIS STUDY

Signed: _____   Date: _____

FIGURE 4.3   Participant consent form

Negotiating access

Of course, an important part of your research is gaining access to potential participants. It goes without saying that this also needs to be done in an ethical manner. Negotiating access to respondents can be a difficult task for student researchers. If you are a full-time student, you may find it is particularly difficult given that you do not have the benefit of a network of business colleagues. Still, there are certain tactics that you can use in order to gain access to your intended respondents. The following list provides a useful guide to gaining access:

- *Use all available contacts.* This includes family, friends and your research supervisor. The latter can be particularly useful as he or she is likely to have contacts that may be relevant to your own research.
- *Use a key individual as part of 'snowball sampling'.* This is useful if you only know one or two individuals. If that individual has several contacts, then they can target others through their own business networks.
- *Provide a clear overview of your research.* Potential participants are far more likely to be willing to take part in your research if they fully understand the rationale behind it. In addition, ensuring that the nature of your research is relevant to an individual is likely to lead to a willingness to take part.
- *Answer the 'What's in it for me?' question.* In other words, how will your participants benefit from your research? I have found that promising your participants a written summary of your findings upon completion of your research can be a major selling point. In short, through receiving something that acknowledges their participation, potential respondents are far more likely to show a willingness to take part in your research.
- *Do not take 'no' straight away.* Clearly, do not harass potential participants, but try to sell the merits of your research. Often, 'name dropping' can help to encourage potential participants to take part. In other words, if you were conducting research on local construction companies, mentioning that the largest company in the area is taking part may 'encourage' others to participate. However, remember that in order to do this, your existing participants need to be consulted!
- *Build relationships.* I have already briefly mentioned the importance of networks. Essentially, developing relationships and networks with individuals and companies can help to 'open doors'. For example, I recently had a student who conducted research into one of the UK's

largest supermarket chains. This involved interviewing one of the company's directors. How did he manage to gain access to such a high ranking individual? It just so happens that the director is a friend of his father!

─RESEARCH IN ACTION─

Ethical issues and your employer

The Research in Action example in this chapter highlights some of the ethical issues students may face if they decide to base their research project on their employer. Both part-time and work-based degree students often select a research topic that is in some way connected to their company. For the student, a research project on their employer has the advantage of overcoming problems associated with access to data. However, there are potential ethical difficulties with this type of research, as is illustrated below.

Darren worked part-time for an international telecommunications company, while also studying on a part-time undergraduate degree in Business Management. Darren had decided to focus his research project on his employer. The area of his research concentrated on employee motivation and retention rates. He intended to carry out semi-structured interviews with employees across different departments. As Darren was conducting research with human participants, he was required to gain ethics approval from his University's Research Ethics Committee (REC). Given the sensitivity of his chosen topic, he also realized the importance attached to gaining ethics approval from his employer.

Following approval by the REC, Darren proceeded with his planned data collection. In his application, he made it clear how he would deal with informed consent, anonymity, confidentiality and any potential risks. As part of his application he also included a letter from his manager confirming that he had permission to carry out his research. His manager included two important caveats in the letter. First, that all respondents must remain anonymous, and second, all information must remain confidential. In terms of the latter, the only people that were permitted to view the findings were Darren, his manager and his research project supervisor.

Darren's data collection involved interviewing employees responsible for different areas of the business. Questions centred on levels of motivation and why there had been a sudden increase in staff turnover. He was satisfied with his findings and presented many of the results using verbatim quotations within the main body of his research project. On completing his study, Darren was so pleased with his project that he decided to send a copy to the Chief Executive Officer (CEO) of the organization. Unfortunately, the response from the CEO was highly critical of Darren's research and questioned why he was granted permission to carry out a study of this nature. Moreover, the CEO commented that he was disappointed at the feedback from employees, and would be taking this up with management.

In Darren's research project above, the ethical issues appear to have been addressed. However, clearly a concern for the CEO is the content of Darren's research project and why he was given permission in the first place. Thus, this case raises three important points, namely, making sure to follow the ethics procedure as set out in your ethics application, permission, and disclosure. Let's look at each of these in turn. First, in his ethics application to the REC, Darren made it clear that all findings would remain confidential and only be seen by him, his manager and his research supervisor. He did not make any reference to the CEO of the company. Second, although Darren had permission from the company, it appears that he did not gain authorization from the right person. The manager in question did not seek to ensure that he had the authority to grant consent for Darren's project. Finally, the response from the CEO suggests that Darren's project contains highly sensitive information. As a researcher, Darren should have made a judgement as to what to include and what to exclude within his final project. In other words, even though he guaranteed anonymity and confidentiality, his manager is still able to read through the findings and may decide to take action at a departmental level, based on those findings. Darren needed to make an important decision as to how much sensitive information he should disclose. This is often a difficult choice to make for any researcher and is a balance between what is interesting and the welfare of the participant.

Summary and Conclusion

This chapter has addressed the ethical issues associated with your research project. It has introduced what is meant by business ethics. Consideration has been given to the importance of ethics in business and how to address ethical issues. Recognizing that ethics can be interpreted differently across cultures has also been a feature. Here are the key points from this chapter:

- Ethics can be defined as 'the principles, norms and standards of conduct governing an individual or group'.
- When conducting business management research, your work should be professional and responsible, use appropriate means of data collection, involve informed consent, carefully control deception and be carefully interpreted.
- You have an ethical responsibility to all research stakeholders.
- When conducting research across cultures, it is important to show respect and a willingness to adapt to different cultures. Be prepared to follow 'written' and 'unwritten' codes of conduct, understand sensitive issues when compiling questionnaire surveys, and respect varying degrees of confidentiality and anonymity.
- Completing an ethical approval form helps you to address your own ethical concerns by putting them in writing. Above all, it gives you peace of mind that you have taken into consideration the ethical concerns of all relevant research stakeholders.

CASE STUDY — **Ethical Issues Prior to Conducting Research**

Wang Hao has decided to base his research topic on leadership in the Chinese construction industry. Wang Hao's father is the Chief Executive of a large Chinese construction company and has agreed for him to interview some of the workers to gain their views on leadership.

Wang Hao's father is very supportive of his son's study and has allowed him unlimited access to both employees and senior management within the company. Wang Hao has decided

---

to use the company's employee database to contact staff via email and telephone. Following this, he intends carrying out a number of in-depth interviews with employees to gauge their views on leadership within the company. He intends to publish a summary of his research findings in the company's monthly newsletter. Given that his father is CEO of the company, Wang Hao does not envisage any problems in developing a suitably sized sample of employees to take part in his study.

Case study question

- What are some of the ethical concerns raised by Wang Hao's research?

YOU'RE THE SUPERVISOR

Roy, a final-year BA (Hons) Tourism student, has emailed you a copy of his research proposal. Roy's chosen topic is on Green Tourism in the UK. Having read through the proposal, it is clear that he has based his area of research on a recent article published in the magazine *Tourism in Europe*. To be sure, many sections of his proposal appear to have been lifted verbatim from the article.

Supervisor question

- What action would you take in this situation?

COMMON QUESTIONS AND ANSWERS

1. Although I am keen on undertaking primary research, a problem I have is not being able to negotiate access. What steps can I take here?

Answer: You can take a number of steps to improve your ability to negotiate access. First, use all available contacts. There is no substitute for personal networks when trying to gain access. Second, similar to personal networks, consider snowball sampling. By using one or a small number of individuals to tell others about your research, the hope is that your sample size will grow as a result of the personal recommendation. Finally, again, on a personal level, try to build relationships with those respondents that you intend including in your study. An important point to remember when attempting to negotiate access is not to take 'no' straight away. In short, be persistent.

2. What is the process for gaining ethical approval?

Answer: This really depends on the institution. Certainly in UK universities you will find that all of them have some kind of ethics policy. Some of them are more formal than others. For example, sometimes ethics approval might be required from an ethics panel rather than left to the discretion of the research supervisor, while in other institutions all research involving human participants must go to either a department, or in some cases, a faculty panel for approval.

Typically, research projects that focus purely on secondary data do not require ethics approval, while those involving human participants require an ethics checklist to be undertaken.

3. Why does my university insist that I run my dissertation through Turnitin software?

Answer: The growth of the Internet has meant that it is now much easier to plagiarize other people's work. As a result, an increasing number of institutions now require students to submit their work to some kind of plagiarism detection software. Several universities and colleges in the UK now use Turnitin as a web-based tool for deterring and detecting plagiarism. Turnitin is designed to scan students' work against a large database of books, journal articles, web pages and previously submitted assignments. It then matches a student's work by producing a similarity score and an originality report. A similarity score identifies how much of the submitted work Turnitin can detect as being matched to another source, while an Originality Report identifies each match in more detail and allows a more thorough investigation of the original source. The Originality Report does not indicate that a piece of work has or has not been plagiarized. In essence, the outputs from Turnitin provide guidance in considering whether work has been correctly referenced or plagiarized. There is no magic percentage figure that indicates plagiarism. This remains an academic decision. The best way to avoid plagiarism is to reference your work correctly.

References

Anglia Ruskin University (2007) *Presentation and Submission of Major Projects and Dissertations for Taught Higher Degrees* (5th edn), September. Cambridge: Anglia Ruskin University.

Burns, R.B. and Burns, R.A. (2008) *Business Research Methods and Statistics Using SPSS*. London: Sage.

CIM (Chartered Institute of Marketing) (2012) 'Professional standards, ethics and disciplinary procedures in accordance with Royal Charter bye-laws', online source: www.cim.co.uk/Files/codeofprofessionalstandards10.pdf

Chonko, L.B. and Hunt, S.D. (1985) 'Ethics and marketing management: An empirical examination', *Journal of Business Research*, 13: 339–359.

Co-operative Bank (2009) 'Ethics at the Co-operative Bank', online source: www.co-operativebankinggroup.co.uk/servlet/Satellite?c=Page&cid=1169627027831&pagename=Corp/Page/tplCorp, accessed 20 September 2013.

Hart, B., Irvine, R. and Williams, A. (1992) 'The problem and prospects of a Health Research Ethics Committee for undergraduate students', *Bioethics News*, 12 (3) (Ethics Committee Supplement): 4–10.

HSBC (2009) 'Corporate governance', online source: https://hsbc.aecglobal.com/code_conduct_full.aspx, accessed 20 September 2013.

Information Commissioner's Office (2009) 'Data Protection Act', online source: www.ico.gov.uk/what_we_cover/data_protection.aspx, accessed 4 May 2009.

Mascarenhas, O.A.J. (1995) 'Exonerating unethical marketing executive behaviours: A diagnostic framework', *Journal of Marketing*, 59 (April): 43–57.

Myers, M.D. (2009) *Qualitative Research in Business and Management*. London: Sage.

O'Leary, Z. (2004) *The Essential Guide to Doing Research*. London: Sage.

Polonsky, M.J. (1998) 'Incorporating ethics into business students' research projects: A process approach', *Journal of Business Ethics*, 17 (11): 1227–1241.

Proctor, T. (2000) *Essentials of Marketing Research*. Harlow: FT/Prentice Hall.

Purcell, T.S.J. (1977) 'Do courses in business ethics pay off?', *California Management Review*, 19 (4): 150–158.

Rowley, J. (2004) 'Researching people and organizations', *Library Management*, 15 (4/5): 208–215.

Russ-Eft, D., Burns, P.J., Hatcher, T., Otte, F.L. and Peskill, H. (1999) 'Standards on ethics and integrity', *Performance Improvement Quarterly*, 12 (3): 5–30.

Treviño, L. and Nelson, K. (1999) *Managing Business Ethics: Straight Talk About How To Do It Right*. New York: John Wiley & Sons.

Further Reading

Blumberg, B., Cooper, D.R. and Schindler, P.S. (2005) *Business Research Methods*. Maidenhead: McGraw-Hill.

Bryman, A. and Bell, E. (2007) *Business Research Methods* (2nd edn). Oxford: Oxford University Press.

Collis, J. and Hussey, R. (2009) *Business Research: A Practical Guide for Undergraduate and Postgraduate Students* (3rd edn). Houndsmill: Palgrave Macmillan.

Journal of Business Ethics, Springer.

Oliver, P. (2010) *The Students' Guide to Research Ethics* (2nd edn). Maidenhead: Open University Press.

Wiles, R. (2013) *What are Qualitative Research Ethics?* London: Bloomsbury.

5
Establishing a research design

┌─ Learning Objectives ───┐

After reading this chapter, you should be able to:

- know what is meant by the term research design, and why it is important to the student researcher;
- explain the different types of research design;
- understand the impact of time horizons on research;
- explain what is meant by reliability and why it is important to researchers;
- know the different types of validity;
- produce an outline research proposal; and
- appreciate the role of your project supervisor when undertaking your research proposal.

└───┘

Introduction

This chapter is concerned primarily with the fourth segment of the Honeycomb of Research Methodology: research design (Figure 5.1). A *research design* is a detailed framework or plan that helps to guide you through the research process, allowing a greater likelihood of achieving your research objectives. The emphasis in this chapter is very much on different types of research design. As with any kind of research, issues of validity and reliability also need to be addressed. Hence, the latter part of this chapter fully explores these issues.

First, this chapter examines the nature of research design. This is followed by a brief discussion on the difference between research design and research methods. Although the terminology used in business research can sound strikingly similar, often there are quite distinct differences. Then, we undertake a detailed overview of the main research design options available to the student researcher. These include: case study, experimental, archival, comparative, cross-sectional and longitudinal design. Understanding the various types is all very well, but how does one determine which is the most appropriate? In short, a number of factors are likely to determine your research design. Once we have explored these, you should have a clear idea of the extent to which these factors are likely to impact on your own choice.

An important aspect of your research is making sure that you measure what you intend to measure. In essence, what I am referring to here is validity. Broadly speaking, there are three types of validity – content, construct and external validity. I shall examine all three of these later in this chapter. After that, we explore reliability. This refers to the credibility of your findings and enables findings to be replicated. This chapter illustrates how you can aim to ensure higher levels of both reliability and validity. Following this, an outline research proposal is included to show you how a plan from the outset can help you when it comes to starting your actual study. Next, I reflect on the main topics covered in this chapter, in particular, the relationship between research designs, types of research and research strategy.

Nature of Your Research Design

In Chapter 1, readers were first introduced to the Honeycomb of Research Methodology (see Figure 5.1). You will recall from our analysis of the model that there exists a relationship between the first three of these elements, the key concepts of research, in that your choice of research philosophy is likely to influence both choice of research approach and research strategy. Similarly, your choice of research philosophy underpins your choice of research design. As mentioned, Mark Easterby-Smith et al. (2002) suggest that there are three reasons why an understanding of philosophical issues is very useful. First, it can help to clarify *research designs*. This entails considering the type of evidence required and how it is to be collected and interpreted. Second, knowledge of philosophy can help the researcher to recognize which designs work best. Finally, knowledge of philosophy can help the researcher identify and adapt research designs according to the constraints of different subject or knowledge structures.

In the first part of this chapter we examine research design (see Figure 5.1). Essentially, research designs are detailed plans to focus and guide the research process. They can be formalized as research proposals and are influenced by both technical and contextual considerations. According to Rowley (2002: 19), a research design has the following components:

- the study's questions;
- the study's propositions;
- the study's units of analysis;
- the logic linking the data to the propositions; and
- the criteria for interpreting findings.

Blumberg et al. (2005: 195) cite the essentials of research design as follows:

- the design is an activity- and time-based plan;
- the design is always based on the research question;
- the design guides the selection of sources and types of information;
- the design is a framework for specifying the relationships among the study's variables; and
- the design outlines procedures for every research activity.

Epistemology: Positivism,
Interpretivism, Pragmatism
Ontology: Objectivism, Subjectivism
Axiology: Value-free, Biased

Research
philosophy
1

Descriptive statistics
Inferential statistics
Grounded theory
Narrative analysis
Discourse analysis
Visual analysis
Content analysis

Data analysis
techniques
6

Research
Methodology

Research
approach
2

Inductive
Deductive

Data collection
5

Research
strategy
3

Quantitative
Qualitative
Combining quantitative and
qualitative strategies
(multi-strategy research)

Interviews
Questionnaires
Observation
Secondary data

Research
design
4

Action research
Case study
Experimental
Longitudinal
Cross-sectional
Archival analysis
Comparative

FIGURE 5.1   The Honeycomb of Research Methodology (©2013 Jonathan Wilson)

There exists a general consensus among leading authors that research design is concerned with producing a 'plan' that guides the research process. In addition, Blumberg et al. (2005) also highlighted the fact that an essential part of research design is that of a time-based plan. For some students, when it comes to timing, they simply wish to complete their project as quickly as possible! However, time also plays a part in relation to unit(s) of analysis. In other words, over what period of time do you intend to conduct your analysis? The issue of time horizon is explored later in this chapter.

A number of research design options are available to you. These are listed in Figure 5.1. It is worth noting that this list is by no means exhaustive, but contains the more commonly chosen research designs among student researchers. Before we move on to look at some of these options in closer detail, the next sections briefly clarify the types of research studies and the distinction between 'research design' and 'research methods'.

Types of Research Study

Your choice of research study largely depends on the purpose of your research. For example, do you intend to conduct research into a subject that has been neglected among researchers? Or perhaps you are interested in determining how one variable impacts on another? Ultimately, your choice of research study will directly influence your choice of research design.

Exploratory research

Exploratory research follows an inductive approach. In exploratory research the researcher conducts research into a research problem where there currently exists very little, if any, earlier work to refer to. Hence, where there is a lack of published research and a lack of knowledge about a given topic, then exploratory research is a viable research design. The aim of this type of research is to develop a better insight into a particular topic, leading to the development of a set of hypotheses. This set of hypotheses can be tested at a later date.

By way of illustration, Cathy Hart and Belinda Dewsnap (2001) provided an interesting example of exploratory research in their study of consumer behaviour in the fashion industry. Having recognized that the vast majority of research into consumer decision-making tended to focus on outer clothing, the authors set about conducting research into inner apparel, the main emphasis being on the purchasing of bras and lingerie. Given the dearth of literature on their chosen topic, the authors established that their research was exploratory in nature.

Exploratory designs are largely qualitative, and typically employ focus groups, in-depth interviews, historical analysis and observation. As a result, exploratory research seldom provides conclusive answers to research problems, but helps to generate future research direction.

Descriptive research

Descriptive research is carried out to describe existing or past phenomena. More specifically, it sets out to describe a subject using observation. For example, a marketer interested in understanding the buying habits of a certain consumer group may observe the group's buying habits. This is likely to be conducted within the buyer's own natural shopping environment.

Descriptive research can be either qualitative or quantitative. Typically, a survey is used to gather data that can later be analyzed using a range of descriptive statistics. Similar to exploratory research, descriptive studies are often preliminary studies that lead to further research. The types of research question used in descriptive studies perhaps best illustrate the nature of descriptive research. Illustrative examples of research questions in descriptive studies are as follows:

- What is the employee turnover in ABC Ltd?
- What are the feelings of bank workers regarding the current financial crisis?
- What type of 'additional extras' for a motor vehicle do consumers prefer?
- What are the views of different socio-economic groups on global warming?
- How many teenagers play football in the UK compared with teenagers in Brazil?

Given that they are descriptive in nature, the above questions begin with either 'what' or 'how'. Of course, the examples cited above lack clarity and certainly require greater focus. For example, even something that may sound fairly simplistic, such as determining employee turnover (the ABC Ltd example), requires elucidation of the departments within the organization, the time period covered and, more specifically, the role and responsibilities of those employees being examined.

On a positive note, descriptive studies tend to provide accurate information, and help to form the basis of simple decision-making by setting out to provide answers to what, how, when, who or where questions. However, they do not determine cause-and-effect relationships.

Causal research

In contrast to descriptive research, *causal research* is solely concerned with learning why. By way of illustration, research on a firm's advertising is descriptive if it measures advertising spend, where advertising was placed, when advertisements were placed and how the advertisements were produced. On the other hand, a causal study may set out to determine whether an increase in advertising spend (cause) leads to an increase in sales (effect). A researcher engaged in causal research aims to determine cause-and-effect relationships. According to Gavin Dick et al. (2008: 695), causality is usually accepted in empirical research as requiring three conditions:

1. There is an association between variables that logically might influence one another.
2. The causal variable must produce its influence before the outcome occurs.
3. Other possible explanations must be eliminated, such as a third variable that influences both variables.

What is the difference between research design and research methods?

At this point, I believe that it is worth making the distinction between 'research design' and 'research methods'. Sometimes students use these two terms interchangeably, yet there is a distinct difference between the two.

As noted earlier, a research design is a framework or plan for the collection and analysis of data. This is not to be confused with research methods that are, quite simply, the different techniques for collecting data. Examples include unstructured interviews, an email questionnaire or a focus group where a researcher records the verbal and non-verbal communication of those taking part in the group. Research methods are examined in Chapters 6 and 7.

Types of Research Design

By now, you should have a firm grasp of what is meant by research design. The next step is to begin to understand the various research design options available to you.

In this section, we shall explore each one in detail. A number of research designs are available to the student researcher. These include:

- action research (how);
- case study (how, why);
- experimental (how, why);
- longitudinal (who, what, where, how many, how much);
- cross-sectional (who, what, where, how many, how much);
- archival analysis (who, what, where, how many, how much); and
- comparative (how, why, what).

The types of question associated with each research design are shown in brackets.

Action research design

The term 'action research' was first coined by the social psychologist Kurt Lewin in 1946. In essence, *action research* involves the researcher taking on an active role in the research, as opposed to being purely an 'outside observer'. Unlike traditional research, where findings may lead to recommendations of future actions, action research produces both an outcome and actions.

Although there is no definitive approach to action research, the general consensus among researchers is that it usually consists of a group of people. These 'research participants' may include employees, managers and consultants. Moreover, action research projects traditionally involve spiralling cycles of action and research (Lewin, 1946). There are four elements associated with this cycle:

1. Planning – a collaborative process that should involve all members of the action research group.
2. Action – at this stage, plans are implemented.
3. Observation – at this stage, actions are observed to assess how they perform.
4. Reflection – at this stage, reflection involves evaluating whether or not the actions were appropriate and how they might influence any future planning.

Given the cyclical nature of action research, the 'reflection' stage is followed by a 'revision' stage. This is likely to involve making changes to the original plan as a result of the initial research findings. The revisions will then be put into 'action', and will be 'observed' again, and so on. By now, you should recognize that the exploratory nature of this design means that action research lends itself particularly well to answering 'how' research questions.

Action research is often associated with organizational change and can be a useful approach for organizations intent on continuous improvement. For example, employees trying to assess why there has been an increase in customer complaints might use action research. They would then collectively formulate their own plan of action to improve levels of customer service. On a positive note, employees may feel more 'valued' by taking on such responsibility. Conversely, there are ethical implications of researching within your own workplace, as well as knowing when to stop your research.

Unfortunately, action research has its limitations for some students. These include:

- Difficulty in accessing key individuals within an organization.
- The student is not in a position to instigate organizational change.
- The project deadline does not allow a sufficient timeframe in which to carry out action research.

Case study design

While many students are familiar with the terms 'case' or 'case study', few have an understanding of what is actually meant by these terms, especially the nature of *case study* design.

Robert Yin (2003: 13) defined case study research as follows: 'A case is an empirical enquiry that investigates a contemporary phenomenon within its real-life context, especially when the boundaries between phenomenon and context are not clearly evident.' In business research, case study design often involves an in-depth analysis of an individual, a group of individuals, an organization or a particular sector. In short, the case study provides an in-depth analysis of a specific problem.

Case study research can be divided on the basis of single and multiple case studies. The former involves research that examines a single case, while the latter analyzes several cases. Case study research can also be categorized on the basis of analysis. The researcher has two options here – holistic (single unit of analysis) or embedded (multiple units of analysis). Figure 5.2 illustrates the four options available to the student researcher.

As Figure 5.2 illustrates, case study research may be broad or narrow in scope. First, I will discuss the choice of scope in case study design – single case versus multiple cases. Then I will discuss the methods of analysis – holistic versus embedded analysis.

Case designs – scope

		Narrow	Broad
Analysis	Narrow	Single case designs (holistic analysis)	Multiple case designs (holistic analysis)
	Broad	Single case designs (embedded analysis)	Multiple case designs (embedded analysis)

FIGURE 5.2 Case study research designs

Single case designs

Single cases can be viewed as single experiments. A number of reasons exist as to why you may opt for a single case study. For example, your chosen case may be regarded as an extreme example or possibly a unique case. An illustration of this would be the events surrounding 9/11 – this was the first time such extreme terrorism occurred on US soil. A single case study may also be a suitable method when critically testing a long-standing theory. Single case studies may also be used as part of a pilot study prior to extending the research to a multiple set of cases. Finally, selecting a single case may allow you to conduct an in-depth study. This usually involves using a wide range of information and possibly several different units of analysis. Researchers engaged in in-depth case study research are often in a position to claim expert status on their chosen case.

Multiple case designs

Multiple cases can be viewed as multiple experiments. The more cases that can be marshalled to establish or refute a theory, the more robust are the research outcomes. A frequent question is how many cases should be included in a multiple study. There is no simple answer to this question. Cases need to be carefully selected so that they either produce similar results (literal replication), or produce contrasting results but for predictable reasons (theoretical replication). Typically, six to ten cases might achieve literal replication, whereas more cases might be needed to examine other patterns of theoretical replication (Rowley, 2002: 21–2).

A potentially interesting multiple case study could be the UK banking sector. For instance, research could be conducted into the extent to which the 2008/09 credit crunch has impacted on UK banks. This is likely to produce contrasting results as some banks were more heavily exposed to the American sub-prime mortgage market than others.

Holistic analysis

Holistic cases examine the case as one unit. From the outset of your research, it is important that you are clear on what it is exactly that you intend to analyze. Certainly your supervisor and the readers of your research project need evidence of clarity in your unit of analysis. Typical units of analysis in business case study research include an organization, business function, strategic implementation or possibly an individual, for example the Finance Director for a leading multinational company.

In essence, your unit of analysis helps you to set the boundaries in your research. All of your analysis must focus on the 'unit'. Unfortunately, I have found that failure to illustrate the unit of analysis clearly is relatively common among student researchers. Remember, you may be fully aware of what it is that you are analyzing, but do not forget to make explicit reference to this when writing up your research!

Embedded analysis

An embedded case study is a case study containing more than one sub-unit of analysis (Yin, 2003). Whereas single designs focus on one unit of analysis, embedded studies pay attention to a number of units of analysis. For example, rather than analyzing Finance Directors (single case), you may also focus on Marketing Directors, Human Resource Directors and Chief Executives (multiple cases). By way of illustration, a single case study and embedded analysis may involve a university (case), and the units of analysis might include various levels of management, e.g. Heads of Department, Deans and Pro-Vice-Chancellors.

Of course, your analysis is largely dependent on your case selection. As we have established, a case study can represent a number of different things. Figure 5.3 illustrates some of the case selection options available to the student researcher.

Idiographic and nomothetic case studies

Some researchers make a distinction between cases on the basis of idiographic and nomothetic. First, idiographic involves investigating case studies which focus in-depth on one case to achieve a unique understanding of the individual or possibly an event; for example, why the American energy giant Enron failed. Your entire research, including observations and measurement, is on the single case. Conversely, nomothetic investigates large groups of cases in order to find general laws of behaviour that apply to everyone.

FIGURE 5.3 Examples of case selection options

When choosing your case(s), a distinction can be made between organization-, process- and event-based cases. First, *organization-based* cases relate to an organization or are organization-related. For example, this could extend to actors within a company, e.g. management and employees, or possibly even a sector that an organization operates in. Second, *process-based* cases relate to the processes that an organization may go through. This may include organizational restructuring or perhaps financial process improvement. Finally, *event-based* options focus on a particular circumstance within business and management. Often, these are seminal events, such as China's accession to the World Trade Organization in December 2001.

Experimental design

An *experimental design* posits that experiments are conducted along the lines of the natural sciences, i.e. in a laboratory or in a natural setting, in a systematic way. Experimental studies allow causal relationships to be identified. The aim is to manipulate the independent variable (e.g. a reduction in price) in order to observe the effect on the dependent variable (e.g. sales levels of a Sunday newspaper).

Saunders et al. (2007: 138) provide a useful illustration of a classic experiment. Two groups are established and members are assigned at random to each group. This means that the two groups will be similar in all aspects relevant to the research whether or not they are exposed to the planned intervention or manipulation. In the first of these groups, the *experimental group*, some form of planned intervention or manipulation is made, such as a 'buy two, get one free' promotion. In the other group, the *control group*, no such intervention is made. The dependent variable, in this example purchasing behaviour, is measured before and after the manipulation of the independent variable (the use of the 'buy two, get one free' promotion) for both the experimental group and control group. This means that a before and after comparison can be undertaken. On the basis of this comparison, any difference between the experimental and control groups for the dependent variable (purchasing behaviour) is attributed to the intervention, in this example the 'buy two, get one free' promotion.

The time horizon

In terms of the time dimension associated with your study, we must distinguish between longitudinal and cross-sectional designs. The former is not often a viable option for many student researchers, for reasons that will become apparent below.

Longitudinal design

A *longitudinal design* is a study over a long period of time of a particular case or a group of cases. Typically, this involves several years of research. The aim of the research is to examine changes that take place over time. These changes can be on a number of levels, e.g. social, demographic, political and economic. Perhaps unsurprisingly, a longitudinal design is not a common choice among business students! Many are restricted by tight submission deadlines and are therefore unable to carry out research over such a long period.

Longitudinal studies lend themselves better to health and sociological studies. Still, this does not mean that longitudinal studies should be neglected altogether. A great deal of secondary data is available that examines changes over time, in particular data published by the government on various social, political and economic issues. Multilateral organizations also publish interesting country data online. For example, the World Trade Organization (WTO) publishes economic data on all member states.

Matlay and Carey (2007: 256) provide an interesting example that combines case study and longitudinal research design:

> Comparative longitudinal case study methods were used to collate, cross tabulate and analyze in-depth qualitative data relating to entrepreneurship education in the UK. A matched sample of case studies involving 40 new and established universities in the UK was selected and contacted on an annual basis during a period of ten years, between 1995 and 2004. The relevant annual research information was tabulated, analyzed and mapped, in order to provide comparative data for 20 new and 20 established universities located in England, Scotland and Wales.

As you can see, the above illustration explicitly mentions 'longitudinal case study methods'. In addition, the authors summarize the nature of their research design in a clear and concise manner. A number of limitations are associated with longitudinal research. For example, respondents may withdraw from the study prior to completion. This could ultimately impact on the research findings. Also, researchers engaged in the study need to be committed over the long term. A change in researcher, research team and/or research funding can all have a negative impact on longitudinal research.

Cross-sectional design

A *cross-sectional design* involves the collection of data from a number of cases. It is also referred to as a survey design. Another important feature of a cross-sectional design is that data is collected at a *single point in time*. As a result, research can be completed over a relatively short period. The design is less time-consuming and less expensive than a longitudinal study. However, cross-sectional design does have its limitations, the main one being that certain topics may not be appropriate for cross-sectional design. For instance, conducting research into consumers' views on a new games console may produce very positive feedback. Yet, new technology dates very quickly and conducting the same study on a longitudinal basis will almost certainly produce a different set of results.

Another problem facing researchers is trying to compare studies that adopt different time-based designs. In other words, it is difficult to compare a 2008 study into unemployment in the UK construction industry (cross-sectional) with that of a similar study undertaken during 1995–2008 (longitudinal).

Which time-based design is best? As we have established, the short answer is that there is no one 'best' design. Both longitudinal and cross-sectional designs have their limitations. In some respects, students are often left with no option but to select cross-sectional design because completion of their project is governed by strict submission deadlines. Still, longitudinal design should not be completely discounted. If you start your research early enough, this might just be an option!

Archival design

Archival design relates to public records or documents. It is sometimes referred to as raw data. Archival data are a type of secondary data that exist in the form in which they were originally intended. For example, this may include business reports, country reports, staff records or minutes for a local community group.

Archival design is a favoured research design among historians. Although archival design is unlikely to be your preferred choice of research design, you may wish to make use of archival data. Reasons for this may include the following:

- Archival analysis is a favoured design in your subject area, e.g. human resource management.
- You intend to carry out archival analysis as part of an exploratory study prior to conducting more detailed research.
- You may combine this with a case study design, allowing you to access company documents such as staff records.

Comparative design

A *comparative research design* compares two or more groups on one variable. A *variable* is a characteristic that can be measured. By way of illustration, comparing the profits (variable) of German companies to the profits (variable) of British companies can be interpreted as a comparative research design. The variable in this case is 'profit', while the two groups are 'German companies' and 'British companies'. Of course, this could be extended to include analyzing the profits of companies from other countries of origin. A comparative design can produce an interesting set of findings. It is particularly useful if your intention is to compare like for like and draw conclusions from your group findings.

One of the potential problems with a comparative design is ensuring that the variable in your study is interpreted the same way by your chosen groups. This can be particularly problematic when comparing groups across distinctly different cultures. Let us say that your chosen variable is trust and you wish to compare trust between cultural groups from Germany, Japan, France and the UK. How do you know that the concept of trust is interpreted in the same way across these respective cultures? In short, *cross-cultural research* may make the ability to measure comparisons extremely challenging.

How do I know which research design to choose?

A number of factors are likely to determine your choice of research design. According to Bryman (2004: 27):

> A choice of research design reflects decisions about the priority being given to a range of dimensions of the research process. These include the importance attached to:
>
> expressing causal connections between variables;
>
> generalizing to larger groups of individuals than those actually forming part of the investigation;
>
> understanding behaviour and the meaning of that behaviour in its specific social context; and
>
> having a temporal (i.e. over time) appreciation of social phenomena and their interconnections.

Having supervised countless research projects over the years, undoubtedly case study research design tends to be the favoured option among business and management students. More specifically, they are cases that are usually based on single or multiple organizations. Why? Quite simply, many students may have a passion for a particular firm, currently work for the organization, have a view to a career with a potential organization(s) or have aspirations to work in a particular sector upon leaving their place of study.

Can I combine research designs?

In principle, there is no reason why you cannot combine research designs, though you need to be sure that going down this route works in practice and, above all, addresses your overriding research problem. As mentioned above, students tend to favour case study research design when carrying out their research. Case study research lends itself well not only to the testing of existing theory, but also to applications in organizations or individuals and groups engaged in business practice. Sometimes case study design is combined with survey design, although the two are not mutually exclusive. Another alternative is the combination of a causal–comparative research design. A number of possibilities exist when it comes to combining research designs. Your choice of design(s) is of course dependent on a number of factors. These include the purpose of your research, the timeframe, the research approach and the availability of data.

Examples of combined research designs

To give you an idea of how a combination of research designs can be applied in practice, what follows is a selection of examples from academic journal articles. Each example is based on a different subject discipline within the field of business and management.

Finance

A study by Gabrielsson et al. (2004: 596–597) looked at the influence of financial strategies and finance capabilities on the globalization of Born Global companies. The authors carried out analysis based on *longitudinal design* on the firm's finance records and knowledge accumulation processes when globalizing their operations. *Multiple case study research* was also selected. This involved interviewing different respondents among 30 companies based in Finland. Finally, the authors supplemented this with *archival material* such as newspaper articles, press releases and the company material.

Tourism

Suosheng Wang and Hailin Qu (2004) carried out *comparative research* of Chinese domestic tourism and that in the USA. The *case studies* involved in the study were from the USA and China. The authors argued that domestic tourism comparisons between China and the USA would generate some important issues on perspectives which could be useful to China's tourism authorities, and domestic and international travel-related companies. Comparisons were made in the following categories:

- tourists' sources of information;
- transportation;
- accommodation;
- tourists' travel activities;
- tourists' spending patterns; and
- government involvement in domestic tourism.

To conduct their comparative research, the authors consulted *archival data* such as tourism associations from each respective country.

Human resources management

The nature of Nikandrou et al.'s (2005) study was to examine HRM strategies and practices within organizations in various cultural, economic and socio-political contexts from a *longitudinal* perspective. The authors used a longitudinal design to *compare* changes and trends in HRM issues among 18 European countries (*multiple case studies*). In this instance, each country was a unit of analysis. In other words, authors used multiple case studies with holistic analysis.

Marketing

Darling and Puetz (2002) conducted a study into the changes in consumer attitudes towards the products of England, France, Germany and the USA (*multiple case studies*), from 1975 to 2000. The authors examined the attitudes of Finnish consumers towards the 'Made in' label and other information indicating a product's national origin. This required analysis into studies carried out in 1980, 1985, 1990, 1995 and 2000. These replicated an earlier study originally conducted in 1975, utilizing the same questionnaire and similarly selected random samples of consumers. These repeated cross-sectional studies permitted the measurement and *comparison* of consumer attitudes over time (*longitudinal*).

In sum, you can see that research designs can be combined in a number of different ways. Article extracts such as those cited can be an excellent source of information, not least for developing your own ideas governing research design.

Testing the Quality of Research

The ability to test the quality of your research is essential. Without addressing issues of validity and reliability your research is unlikely to carry much credibility. In other words, if you do not mention in your research that you have considered the overall quality of your work, the reader will undoubtedly begin to ask questions as to why quality issues have not been tackled.

This section sets out to discuss the two main issues that will impinge upon the quality of your work unless confronted: namely reliability and validity.

Reliability

Reliability concerns the extent to which a measurement of a phenomenon provides stable and consistent results (Carmines and Zeller, 1979). Reliability is also concerned with repeatability. For example, a scale or test is said to be reliable if repeat measurements made by it under constant conditions will give the same result (Moser and Kalton, 1989: 353). Although reliability is important to your study, it is not sufficient unless combined with validity. In other words, for a test to be reliable, it also needs to be valid. By way of illustration, let us say that you time yourself on the way to college every morning. If your watch is 10 minutes fast, when you note your time of arrival, it will be in excess of 10 minutes. The time measurement in this case is reliable as it records a time in excess of 10 minutes every day. However, it is not valid for the simple reason that it adds 10 minutes to your actual arrival time. We explore validity in the next section, but first, let us examine the three main types of reliability: inter-judgemental reliability, testing and retesting reliability, and parallel forms of reliability.

Inter-judgemental reliability

Inter-judgemental reliability is used to determine the extent to which individuals with the required skills and/or authority agree in their assessment decisions. Inter-judgemental reliability is particularly applicable for studies of a subjective nature. For example, this type of reliability would be useful if you required assessment of qualitative findings taken from explorative interviews. In this case, judgement could be sought from your supervisor, other academics and possibly participants in your research.

Testing and retesting reliability

Testing and retesting reliability relates to the measurement of the same reliability test on more than one occasion. This is conducted over a particular period of time to the same group of participants. For example, a questionnaire designed to assess workers' views on health and safety in the workplace can be administered on two occasions – say one month apart. The feedback from time 1 (T1) and time 2 (T2) can then be correlated to see if there is a relationship between them.

Parallel forms of reliability

Parallel forms of reliability is a method of measuring reliability that uses two different types of assessment tool. Each tool must contain items that are intended to measure the same things. It must also be carried out on the same group of individuals. The scores from the two versions can then be correlated in order to evaluate the consistency of results across alternative versions. By way of illustration, if you wanted to test the reliability of a financial knowledge assessment, you may develop a large set of items that all apply to financial knowledge and then randomly divide the questions up into two sets, which would represent the parallel forms.

Threats to reliability

There are several potential threats to reliability. These include time error, subject error and observer influence. Let us examine these more closely.

Time error

Time error may lead to your data being unreliable. By way of illustration, let us say that you decided to carry out a study into levels of commitment among employees. Your measurement in this instance is the number of working hours over one working day – a Friday. This may sound fine in principle, but in the UK it is not uncommon for employees to leave work on time so as to 'unwind' at the local pub! Obviously, this means that those employees who would normally work longer hours prefer not to on a Friday. In order to reduce the likelihood of time error, it would be better to choose different times of the day and week on which to examine the population under study.

Subject error

As well as considering the potential for time error when carrying out research, a researcher also needs to be aware of the nature of the subjects being observed. For example, let us say that you conducted a study into the buying habits of new property buyers. This may involve observing individuals at a major new development recently launched within your local area. If your intention is to observe new potential buyers, then perhaps the focus of your study is professional families. This may sound straightforward in principle. Yet, if you happen to choose a day on which a major architectural firm (interested in the development) visits, then this would lead to subject error – rather than observing families, your observation is mainly focused on employees of the architectural company.

Another form of subject error relates to bias. Using the same example, let us say that you visited the site on the day when the majority of the developer's employees were celebrating the launch. If the purpose of your research was to gauge the public's opinion of the development, then obviously questioning employees is liable to lead to subject bias. This is a consequence of poor sampling technique.

Observer influence

You are concerned with the observation of directors within a small retail company. If the subjects (namely the directors) are aware of your presence, there is a likelihood that they will change their behaviour. Observer influence can change the behaviour of those being observed. It can also impact on reliability because of the researcher's own beliefs and attitudes.

During the 1980s, observer influence was a key concern for some Members of the UK Houses of Parliament. Arguments for and against televising the proceedings of the House were discussed in various debates on the subject. Members against the idea expressed concerns that the traditional character of the Chamber might be altered, with some Members being tempted to speak to the public at large, and that the nature of debating would not be understood. Yet, despite these concerns, broadcasting eventually began towards the end of 1989 (www.parliament.uk) (House of Commons Information Office, 2010).

Perhaps one answer to this fear of a change in behaviour is to take on the role of a covert observer. In other words, you observe the subjects in the research setting, but do so without their knowledge. As noted in Chapter 4, ethical issues need to be taken into consideration when carrying out your research, and covert observation can certainly be construed as being 'unethical'. A more ethical approach is to advise those subjects that you are observing them, and will do so over a long period of time. This is in the hope that over time they will become familiar with your presence and will be more likely to maintain their 'normal' behaviour.

Observer influence can also relate to possible bias on the part of the researcher. Let us say that you are studying the role of management within your own family business. Your observations may suggest a possible positive bias towards those managers who are family members. In all fairness, this may be something that has arisen subconsciously. However, it is something that you certainly need to think about.

How to improve reliability

Yin (2003) suggested adopting the following three principles in order to help deal with the problems of establishing the reliability of a case study:

1. *Use multiple sources of evidence.* A major strength of case study data collection is the opportunity it gives you to use many different sources of evidence. The use of multiple sources of evidence in case studies allows an investigator to address a broader range of historical, attitudinal and behavioural issues. Thus, any finding or conclusion in a case study is likely to be much more convincing and accurate if it is based on several different sources of information.
2. *Create a case study database.* Every case study project should strive to develop a formal, presentable database, so that, in principle, other investigators can review the evidence directly and not be limited to the written reports.
3. *Maintain a chain of evidence.* This increases reliability by allowing an external observer to follow the derivation of any evidence from initial research questions to ultimate case study conclusions. The external observer should be able to trace the steps in either direction (from conclusions back to initial research questions or from questions to conclusions).

Validity

We saw in the last section of this chapter that reliability is concerned with the extent to which a measure provides stable and consistent results. This is only one aspect of testing the quality of your research. Researchers are also concerned with *validity*. About validity, Frankfort-Nachmias and Nachmias (1992: 158) asked: 'Is one measuring what one intends to measure?' In other words, it refers to the relationship between a construct and its indicators. In business research, multiple indicators are often used when measuring a particular construct. What do I mean by this? Well, let us say that your employer wanted to measure your level of commitment to your job. They could look at your level of absenteeism as an indicator of your commitment. This is of course perhaps rather unfair, especially as you may have taken time off work through ill health. Ideally, multiple indicators could be used, e.g. the number of sales you have made, customer feedback, management skills, communication skills, etc. Hence, by using multiple indicators the aim is to create a measure that covers the construct (in this case, 'commitment') in its entirety.

We can view validity on the basis of *internal* and *external* validity (see Figure 5.4). The two main types of internal validity are *content* and *construct*, whereas we deal with external validity in a holistic way. Let us look at each of these in turn.

FIGURE 5.4   Internal and external validity

Internal validity (content)

There are two types of content validity: face validity and sampling validity. First, *face validity* concerns the extent to which an instrument measures what it is supposed to measure. For example, in order to ensure face validity for a questionnaire to both Japanese and Western respondents a number of specialists may view the questions prior to compiling a final version. These may include a research supervisor or business manager. Both may have extensive research experience, while one may speak both Japanese and English. Ultimately, there needs to be agreement among the specialists that the questionnaire has face validity.

Some of the validity problems associated with cross-cultural research can be addressed using back translation as a form of face validity.

> This procedure helps to identify probable translation errors. One translator translates from the source language (S) into a target language (T). Then another translator, ignorant of the source-language text, translates the first translator's target language text back into the source language (S'). Then the two source-language versions, S and S', are compared. (Usunier, 2000: 218)

Sampling validity ensures that your measure includes all areas within the nature of your study. For example, if you decided to measure company performance among UK SMEs, it would not be appropriate to restrict your measurement to profit. Other performance measures, such as sales, market share and consumer feedback, should also be included. As we have established, your measurement should not take on a 'narrow' view, but examine the entire subject (in this case, 'company performance').

Internal validity (construct)

Construct validity is particularly important in quantitative research. Yin (2003: 34) defined it as 'establishing correct operational measures for the concepts being studied'. A construct is valid to the extent that it measures what it is supposed to measure. Using questions that have been pre-tested using a pilot study, and are also based on relevant literature, is one method of aiming for construct validity.

Triangulation is another way to aim for construct validity. Using data triangulation addresses the potential problems of construct validity because the multiple sources of evidence essentially provide multiple measures of the same phenomenon (Yin, 2003).

External validity

External validity is the extent to which the findings from your study can be generalized to other cases or settings. External validity tends to be more important to those researchers who have adopted a positivist approach to their study. A positivist researcher will often strive to claim generalizability of their results. This is where sampling becomes important; the aim is to achieve a representative sample. For those researchers who tend to adopt an interpretivist approach, particularly through case study research design, the intention is often not to generalize. The purpose of the research is to explain a particular case in the context of one particular research setting. This is often to provide new insights that can later be followed up with research that looks at the potential to generalize.

Threats to validity

There are various potential threats to validity. The following list, adapted from Robson (1993), highlights the main considerations.

History

You may decide to study the opinions of local people about the incumbent government party. However, if the research is carried out shortly after a major tax increase, this is likely to have a significant impact, and a quite spurious effect, on the findings.

Effects of pre-testing

Let us say that your research involves measuring the number of monthly client visits among sales staff. If you conduct a pre-test prior to your main study, then this may impact on the results of your actual research as participants are concerned with the consequences of not performing to a 'required' level.

Mortality

This refers to participants dropping out of a research study. You may find that there is a greater likelihood of this happening if your participants are engaged in demanding jobs, e.g. those in management positions. If your research is based on a longitudinal design, there is a greater risk of higher drop-out rates.

Instrumentation

Once again using the sales staff example, the sales staff may have received an instruction (possibly from management) that they are to take every opportunity to increase the number of sales visits between the times you tested the first group and second group of salespeople. Consequently, the number of sales calls is likely to be greater.

Maturation

You concentrate on a longitudinal design into the 12-month sales performance of a local independent supermarket. The supermarket realizes the need to advertise in the local press in order to increase its customer base. If, following the campaign, it succeeds in doing this, is this down to the newspaper campaign? It might be explained by other factors, e.g. the closure of a nearby competitor or the completion of a new housing development within a mile radius of the store.

Ambiguity about the direction of causal influence

It is not always possible to determine a straightforward cause-and-effect relationship. For instance, you determine a positive association between stress in the workplace and alcohol consumption. Does alcohol consumption lead to greater stress in the workplace? Or does stress in the workplace lead to greater alcohol consumption?

How to improve validity?

In the last section we looked at various threats to validity. This is all very well, but equally important is an understanding of how to improve validity. In general, you can improve validity in the following ways:

- Ensure that your research questions and objectives are clearly defined, understood and workable.
- Fully engage your research stakeholders (e.g. ask participants to look over your questions and measures).
- Make sure that your measures are related to your research questions and objectives.
- Ideally, compare your measures with those of previous research.

Mays and Pope (2000) recommended the following ways to improve validity when conducting qualitative research:

1. *Methodological triangulation.* This compares the results from either two or more different methods of data collection or two or more data sources. The researcher looks for patterns of convergence in the data to develop or substantiate an overall interpretation.
2. *Respondent validation.* This includes techniques in which the researcher's account is compared with those of the research participants to establish the level of correspondence between the two sets. Research participants' reactions to the analyses are then incorporated into the research findings. This also generates further original data, which in turn requires interpretation.
3. *Clear exposition of data collection and analysis.* It is important to have a clear account of the process of data collection and analysis. In particular, how early classification evolved into more detailed coding structures.
4. *Reflexivity.* This is defined as sensitivity to the ways in which the researcher and the research process have shaped the collected data, including the role of prior assumptions and experience. Any personal and intellectual biases need to be clearly stated at the beginning of the research in order to enhance the credibility of findings.
5. *Attention to negative cases.* Qualitative research can be improved by searching for and discussing elements in the data that contradict, or seem to contradict, the emerging explanation of the phenomenon under study.
6. *Fair dealing.* It is important to ensure that the research design explicitly incorporates a wide range of different perspectives so that the viewpoint of one group never dominates the findings, but rather that these results represent the whole truth about a situation.

The Research Proposal

Once you have determined your research design, you will be in a position to formulate your *research proposal*. In many respects, a research proposal follows a similar structure to your final research project. For example, it must include a title, an introduction, a literature review and your methodology. A research proposal sets out your research design in a structured, concise manner.

The majority of institutions require that students submit a research proposal so that a supervisor who specializes in the student's chosen area of study can be allocated. In some cases, those students who undertake a research-skills-based module are also required to submit a formal research proposal as a form of assessment. The typical structure of a research proposal is as follows.

Title

The title of your proposed research must fulfil a number of set criteria. First, it must reflect the nature of your study. For example, if you intend studying a particular firm's financial performance, then something to this effect must be stressed in your proposed title. Second, it must be concise. Ideally, try not to exceed more than

10–12 words. Third, try to avoid unnecessary terms such as 'case study approach'. Your research design can be fully explained within your introductory chapter. Finally, try to keep your title clear and easy to understand. In other words, consider it from the layperson's point of view. Remember that the title is the first thing that your supervisor will see when reading your work, so make sure that they understand the nature of your study!

Research problem

The research problem or the main focus of your research should be clearly set out within the introductory section of your proposal. As noted earlier, it is important that the nature of your topic is clear and easy to understand.

Your introductory section should provide the background to your study as well as define any key words or terms. Ideally, brief reference should also be made to existing studies that are relevant to your own work, of course making sure that the Harvard referencing system is applied in the correct way.

Research objective/questions

In Chapter 2 we looked at how to formulate research objectives and research questions. Remember, the key thing here is to recognize certain limitations when developing your research questions, while an easy way to formulate your research objectives is to consider applying SMART.

Key literature

This involves a shortened literature review that critically analyzes the work of leading authors relevant to your own research issue. In Chapter 3 we examined how to write a literature review. In short, it must be critical and not overly descriptive. The verbatim copying of previous studies provides no evidence of how existing work 'links' to your own study. Remember that at some point you also need to say how your own research fits into the current literature. This usually comes somewhere towards the end of your preliminary review.

Methodology

This part of the proposal should classify your research design. Include the rationale behind your chosen research strategy, along with methods for collecting and analyzing your data. This is, of course, dependent on your research approach. Aim to provide support for your choice of methodology. This can be done on the basis of using academic references or referring to previous work that also used a methodology similar to your own. Clear support for the latter option is the ability to compare your findings with those of previous studies.

We have already established in this chapter the importance of validity and reliability, so these aspects should also feature in your proposal. In addition, use this as an opportunity to cite any potential limitations that you foresee with your research. *Limitations* are constraints in your research. For example, for most researchers, financial and time constraints are potential limitations.

Research timetable

The proposal is also where you develop your own research timetable. If you prefer to work in an *ad hoc* manner, you might question the purpose of a timetable. However, while every researcher works in their 'own' way, I can tell you from experience that the vast majority of students prefer to work towards a set timetable. Setting out clear tasks, along with start and completion dates, can help you to work towards a set research schedule. A Gantt chart often works best. However, remember that, when allocating time, it is better to be conservative rather than too ambitious.

References

Your research proposal should finish with all those references that you have cited in your text. You are unlikely to have a large number of references; however, these should be referenced using the Harvard referencing system. Getting into the habit of correctly applying Harvard referencing in your proposal is good practice for when you come to write up your research project.

What follows is an example of a research proposal; although it is rather lengthy and perhaps not on your chosen subject, it provides a good example of how to develop a proposal.

──┤RESEARCH IN ACTION├──────────────────

The internationalization and brand development of Chinese firms

Research problem

A number of internal and external factors have resulted in many Chinese firms becoming involved in the internationalization process. Increased domestic competition, along with an easing of regulations under the World Trade Organization (WTO), have allowed Chinese firms to penetrate international markets. This has resulted in a dramatic increase in Chinese outward investment. However, there currently exists a limited amount of research on the internationalization of Chinese firms (Child and Rodrigues, 2005; 2007a; Deng, 2007b). The majority of research focuses on inward, as opposed to outward, foreign direct investment (FDI). Therefore, a gap needs to be filled that explores the reasons why Chinese firms internationalize, as well as how they currently penetrate international markets.

An important aspect of internationalization is how an organization develops its brand when penetrating international markets. For example, a key question is to what extent should we adapt our brand attributes? Often viewed as 'the workshop of the world', China has yet to develop a single brand that can be described as truly global. 'Building brands fits with the Chinese government's strategy of consolidating strategic industries in order to create national champions that can hold their own in global markets, and is viewed as one more way for the country to restore its imperial glory' (Shenkar, 2006: 158).

Reasons for China developing global brands are that the home market is fiendishly competitive and puts constant pressure on prices; branded products can be more profitable than those of original equipment manufacturers (OEMs); and competing in foreign markets forces companies to innovate and improve, thus helping them to move away from their image as producers of cheap goods (Gao et al., 2003).

According to one of the world's leading brand consultants, Interbrand, Chinese enterprises such as Haier, Lenovo, TCL and Huawei Technologies are ready to compete on a world stage (Interbrand, 2007). Although Chinese brands have made evident and impressive progress in terms of internationalization, they still have far to go to compete with their global rivals, and the gaps are even widening in some respects. This is demonstrated by the revenue of China's largest consumer appliance company, Haier, which in 2002 amounted to only about 10% of Sony's total electronic sales (Fan, 2006: 367).

Interestingly, the current 2007 list of Interbrand's top 25 Chinese brands includes a total of seven that feature 'China' in their name. Much research has shown that country of origin (COO) affects consumers' perceptions of brand image and consumer behaviour (Hong and Wyer, 1995; Peterson and Jolibert, 1995). Chinese products are typically perceived as being 'cheap' and of 'low quality'. Therefore, one would postulate that in order to establish a global brand, reference to China might not help with global ambitions. Even China's East Asian neighbours have brands featured in the top 100. Japan has eight brands listed (positions in brackets) – Toyota (6), Honda (19), Sony (25), Canon (36), Nintendo (44), Panasonic (78), Lexus (92) and Nissan (98) – while the Republic of Korea has three brands listed – Samsung (21), Hyundai (72) and LG (97). These Japanese and South Korean companies made the transition from national to global brands; however, this took some years to achieve.

The development of Chinese brands has received limited attention from researchers (Fan, 2006). Therefore, a gap in the literature exists to explore reasons behind the lack of truly global Chinese brands, and to determine the steps Chinese firms need to take in order to achieve global brand status. In sum, the nature of this research project is to examine the internationalization and brand development of Chinese firms.

Research objective/questions

The main objective of the proposed research is to better understand the internationalization and brand development of Chinese firms. The aim is not only to evaluate internationalization and the reasons China lacks a truly global brand, but also to analyze what types of strategy Chinese brands need to take in order to achieve 'global brand' status.

The objectives for this study are as follows:

- To understand what motivates Chinese firms to internationalize.
- To examine the internationalization strategies adopted by Chinese firms.

(Continued)

(Continued)

- To determine the reasons behind China's lack of truly global brands.
- To examine the strategies Chinese firms need to adopt in order to develop global brands.

The main research questions to be addressed are:

- Why do Chinese firms decide to internationalize?
- What are the internationalization strategies adopted by Chinese firms?
- Why doesn't China currently have a major global brand?
- What strategies do Chinese brands need to adopt in order to achieve global brand status?
- How can Chinese firms compete in global markets?

Key literature

There has been a call from a number of researchers to examine the internationalization of emerging market multinationals (EMMs), especially those originating from China (see Fan, 2008: 357). Research into FDI in China is now a 'well-trodden path'. However, there exists a limited body of literature into China's outward investment, particularly in relation to the internationalization process of Chinese firms. Child and Rodrigues' (2005) article is one of the few studies that explore internationalization from a Chinese perspective. Obviously, the growing dominance of China on the global stage is justification for a better understanding of the internationalization of Chinese firms. Although there have recently been a number of high-profile cases, e.g. Lenovo's acquisition of IBM's PC division, the actual process of internationalization of Chinese firms, and the reasons behind it, have still not been fully explored.

According to Hulland (1999), the source country of brands can be seen as an important determinant of brand choice. Given China's reputation as the 'workshop of the world', it is difficult to find anything these days that is not produced in China. Although many of the world's top global brands, such as Nike, Nokia and Gap, are produced in China and other developing countries, consumers often view these brands on the basis of the origin of the brand, as opposed to the country of manufacture. Recently, the 'Made in China' label has proven to be a headache for marketers of Chinese brands. An article in *Business Week* (September 24, 2007) highlights this by stressing that:

> After a year of massive toy recalls, tainted toothpaste scares, and poisonous pet food incidents, consumers around the globe are thinking twice – or more – before buying Chinese-made goods. Indeed, in a new survey of marketing and business professionals worldwide, 69% of respondents said the phrase 'Made in China' hurts mainland brands. The word most frequently associated with Chinese products? 'Cheap.'

Methodology

This study will use a range of secondary sources; 'Secondary data is data which already exists' (Hussey and Hussey, 1997). For this study, this includes annual reports, promotional material, company documentation, published case descriptions, magazine and newspaper reports, as well as government-printed sources. Multiple sources of data are used in case studies to increase validity and reliability (Yin, 1989). It should be stressed that the secondary data in this research are largely limited to data presented in English. As a non-Chinese speaker, this is an obvious limitation since it is restricting the volume of data available for analysis. However, it is a common problem for individual researchers conducting cross-cultural research.

This study follows a qualitative approach by principally analyzing relatively qualitative information and is based on comparisons between cases. Its intention is exploratory in nature, and is aimed at advancing tentative propositions rather than drawing generalized inferences (Child and Yan, 2003).

Research timetable

It is envisaged that this entire research project will be completed within a period of 18–24 months. At first, this may seem like an extremely short period of time in which to complete such an in-depth study. However, it must be noted that the student has already collected a significant amount of secondary data on the subject. In addition, the student has close contacts in a Sino-UK joint venture and therefore has an excellent insight into the logistics of operating such a venture. He is also very familiar with existing relevant sources and has access to data.

RESEARCH TIMETABLE

Task	Start date	Completion date
Meet supervisor to discuss proposal	May 2011	May 2011
Conduct literature review	May 2011	Continue up to 2 weeks prior to submission
Formulate research questions	June 2011	June 2011
Data collection	June 2011	September 2011
Data analysis	September 2011	December 2011
Writing up	January 2012	March 2012
Submission	April 2012	

References

Business Week (2007) 'China's brands: damaged goods', online source: www.businessweek.com/magazine/content/07–39/64051053.htm, accessed 10 March 2009.

Child, J. and Rodrigues, S.B. (2005) 'The internationalization of Chinese firms: A case for theoretical extension', *Management and Organization Review*, 1 (3): 381–410.

Child, J. and Yan, Y. (2003) 'National and transitional effects in international joint ventures: Indications from Sino-foreign joint ventures', *Management International Review*, 41 (1): 53–75.

Deng, P. (2007a) 'Investing for strategic resources and its rationale: The case of outward FDI from Chinese companies', *Business Horizons*, 50 (1): 71–81.

Deng, P. (2007b) 'Outward investment by Chinese MNCs: Motivations and implications', *Business Horizons*, 47 (3): 8–16.

Fan, Y. (2006) 'The globalisation of Chinese brands', *Marketing Intelligence & Planning*, 24 (4): 365–379.

Fan, Y. (2008) 'The rise of emerging multinationals and the impact on marketing', *Marketing Intelligence & Planning*, 26 (4): Viewpoint.

Gao, P., Woetzel, J.R. and Wu, Y. (2003) 'Can Chinese brands make it abroad?', *The Mckinsey Quarterly*, Special Edition: Global directions, (4): 54–65.

Hong, S. and Wyer, R.S. (1995) 'Effects of country-of-origin and product attribute information on product evaluation: An information processing perspective', *Journal of Consumer Research*, 16 (2): 175–187.

(Continued)

(Continued)

Hulland, J. (1999) 'The effect of country-of-brand and brand name on product evaluation and consideration: A cross-country comparison', *Journal of International Consumer Marketing*, 11 (1): 23–40.

Hussey, J. and Hussey, R. (1997) *Business Research*. Basingstoke: Macmillan.

Interbrand (2007) 'Made in China: 2007 Brand Survey', online source: www.ourfishbowl.com/images/surveys/Interbrand_Made_In_China_2007.pdf, accessed 10 July 2008.

Peterson, R.A. and Jolibert, A.J.P. (1995) 'A meta-analysis country-of-origin effects', *Journal of International Business Studies*, 26 (4): 883–901.

Shenkar, O. (2006) *The Chinese Century*. Upper Saddle River, NJ: Wharton School Publishing.

Yin, R.K. (1989) *Case Study Research: Design and Methods*. Newbury Park, CA: Sage.

The research proposal illustrates the importance of having a clear plan prior to commencing your actual research. Although the research timetable is perhaps lacking in detail, it aims to set out clear start and completion dates for each relevant task. In many respects, certain elements of your plan are likely to change during your research. For example, you may realize that you have been overly ambitious in your selection of research design. However, in essence, the broad topic area often remains the same.

Your project supervisor and the research proposal

By now, you should hopefully recognize the importance of making effective use of your project supervisor. The research proposal is no exception. Your supervisor is on hand to help you to formulate a proposal that will set the 'foundation' for your research.

It is vitally important that you work closely with your supervisor when developing your research proposal. Effectively, your research proposal is the plan for your research project. Its intention is to lay down a clear set of guidelines. Remember that your supervisor is no stranger to the research proposal. They will no doubt have a wealth of experience as to what constitutes an appropriately structured proposal. I always think that there are comparisons to be made between building a house and completing a research project. Each one is a time-consuming task, often challenging and at times frustrating! Ask yourself: Would you build a house without a detailed set of plans? No. So make sure that your research project is no different.

The Relationship Between Research Design and Research Strategy

How does research strategy relate to the purpose of research and research design? Let us explore the extent to which these issues are interrelated. Table 5.1 provides a clear overview of how the purpose of research, research design and research strategy are interconnected.

The first thing to stress about Table 5.1 is that its purpose is to serve as an indicator of the preferred options between each respective research design, type of

Research design	Type of research	Research strategy
Action research	Exploratory	Qualitative and quantitative
Case study	Exploratory	Qualitative
Experimental	Causal	Quantitative
Comparative	Descriptive	Quantitative
Archival	Descriptive	Qualitative
Cross-sectional	Descriptive	Quantitative
Longitudinal	Causal	Qualitative

research and research strategy. This does not mean that each one is mutually exclusive. As noted earlier, case study research design lends itself to exploratory study, typically using a qualitative approach in order to answer 'how' and 'why' questions, whereas archival design is largely historical and lends itself to descriptive qualitative research. Nevertheless, remember that just as research strategies can be combined, so can different types of research question and research design. The important thing is that you support your reasons for using a 'mixed' approach.

The 'Research in Action' feature in this chapter discusses a journal article which is based on a holistic case study research design.

⎯RESEARCH IN ACTION⎯

Online branding – The case of McDonald's

In this article (Rowley, 2004), the author uses a case study research design to explore the approaches to the delivery of brand messages through a website. The focus is on one single case study – McDonald's. The author analyzes the Internet presence of McDonald's and reviews some of the devices the company uses to develop the brand through this channel.

In the methodology, Rowley (2004) provides support for using a case study research design. First, she argues that the understanding of online branding is relatively undeveloped. Second, case study research is recognized to be suited to new research areas. And finally, case studies are particularly appropriate when asking 'how' or 'why' questions. The author uses a holistic single case design and provides justification for the choice of McDonald's based on the fact that it is a global brand, market leader and one of the world's top ten most valuable brands.

The author begins by analyzing the way in which the various elements of the McDonald's website are used to reinforce brand message, image and identity. Following this, analysis focuses on other elements of branding strategy. In the article, the author analyzes all of the different communication tools associated with the McDonald's website. This includes: the logo, graphics, text and copy, currency and news, colour, shapes, layout and combination of images, wallpapers and screensavers. Rowley (2004) analyzes how each of these elements is designed to communicate the overall brand message of a fun experience. After reviewing the different elements of the website, the author concludes that although branding may be worldwide, preferences are local.

(Continued)

(Continued)

Evidence from the research findings suggests that McDonald's recognizes this, as it has a corporate website and a website for each of the countries in which it operates.

Rowley (2004) goes on to conduct comparative analysis between the McDonald's websites for the UK, Australia and Hong Kong. Results illustrate that there are only subtle differences between the UK and Australia, whereas Hong Kong shows blatant differences in terms of ethnicity of people in pictures, language and prices in Hong Kong dollars.

One conclusion the author draws from her analysis is the importance of community and how this is communicated via McDonald's online presence. The author states that McDonald's use their website to 'promote and communicate McDonald's values around community involvement and environmental and social responsibility' (p. 234). In addition, the findings show that McDonald's does not rely solely on one channel to communicate its brand, but adopts channel integration. The researcher uses McDonald's in Australia as an illustration by citing the fact that the company has implanted a number of campaigns designed to drive audiences from one channel to another. Examples of these campaigns are provided within the paper.

The author reports that for McDonald's, the online channel is strictly a marketing communications channel with delivery through restaurants, while a key aspect of the website is to engage with the local community and that the integration of online branding has been promoted by campaigns designed to drive customers between channels. Finally, Rowley (2004) suggests that any future research should address one fundamental question, namely: 'How can online branding help to raise awareness and promote customer relationships and identification with the brand?'

One of the notable strengths of the above article is that the author provides clear justification for using a case study research design. Moreover, there is an outline of the chosen case, McDonald's, and explicit details of how in-depth analysis was carried out. These are important considerations if you decide to choose a case study research design for your own research project.

Summary and Conclusion

In this chapter we have addressed a range of issues concerning research design. Focus has been drawn to different types of research design, validity, reliability, and the research proposal. Here are the key points from this chapter:

- The purpose of your research may include exploratory, descriptive or causal research questions.
- Research designs are detailed plans to focus and guide the research process. They can be formalized as research proposals and are influenced by both technical and contextual considerations.
- A research design is a framework or plan for the collection and analysis of data. This is not to be confused with research methods, which are quite simply different techniques for collecting data.
- Types of research design include case study, experimental, archival, comparative and time-based (namely cross-sectional and longitudinal) designs.
- Research design does not have to be mutually exclusive; different designs can be combined.
- Validity is the ability of an instrument to measure what it is designed to measure. There are three types of validity – content validity, construct validity and external validity.

- Reliability concerns the extent to which a measurement of a phenomenon provides stable and consistent results.
- A research proposal sets out your research design in a structured, concise manner.

CASE STUDY — **Case Analysis Options**

Allison, a final-year Business Management student, has decided to adopt a case study research design for her research project. The nature of Allison's study is corporate social responsibility among UK small and medium sized enterprises (SMEs). She has negotiated access to a number of companies, but is unsure whether to adopt a single or a multiple case design. Allison is familiar with case study research, having been taught it as part of a research skills module, but is unsure which approach to case study research she should adopt.

Case study questions

1. Discuss how Allison might decide whether to do a single or multiple case study design.
2. Allison is also considering conducting a comparative design. What is one of the potential problems associated with adopting this type of research design?

YOU'RE THE SUPERVISOR

Anne, a BA (Hons) student in International Business Strategy, intends to base her research project on the automobile manufacturer Volkswagen. Anne is in a fortunate position in that she undertook an internship in the company's marketing department for three months as part of her degree programme. Hence, she has developed an excellent understanding of how the company's marketing department operates, along with a useful number of contacts who are willing to participate in her research.

Having taught Anne International Marketing, you recognize that she is a particularly well-organized, hard-working and highly motivated student. Indeed, Anne has come to discuss her research ideas with you on the same day she has received notification of her research supervisor.

Although Anne has completed a research skills module as part of her degree, she remains undecided as to how to address 'reliability issues' for her study. During your meeting with Anne, she raises the issue of reliability.

Supervisor question

- Given the above information, what steps can Anne take in order to improve levels of reliability?

COMMON QUESTIONS AND ANSWERS

1. What is validity and why does this need to be considered when carrying out my research?

Answer: Validity can be defined as 'Is one measuring what one intends to measure?' In short, the three types of validity are: content validity, construct validity and external validity. Content validity includes face validity and sampling validity. First, face validity concerns the extent to which an instrument measures what it is supposed to measure, while sampling validity ensures that your measure includes all areas within the nature of your study. Construct validity means 'establishing correct operational measures for the concepts being studied'. External validity is the extent to which the findings from your study can be generalized to other cases or settings.

2. What are the 'key features' of a research proposal?

Answer: A research proposal follows a similar structure to your final research project. For example, it must include a title, an introduction, a literature review, proposed research methodology and research timetable. In short, a research proposal sets out your research design in a structured, concise manner.

References

Blumberg, B., Cooper, D.R. and Schindler, P.S. (2005) *Business Research Methods*. Maidenhead: McGraw-Hill.

Bryman, A. (2004) *Social Research Methods* (2nd edn). London: Oxford University Press.

Carmines, E.G. and Zeller, R.A. (1979) *Reliability and Validity Assessment*. Newbury Park, CA: Sage.

Darling, J.R. and Puetz, J.E. (2002) 'Analysis of changes in consumer attitudes towards the products of England, France, Germany and the USA, 1975–2000', *European Business Review*, 14 (3): 170–183.

Dick, G.P.M., Heras, I. and Casadesús, M. (2008) 'Shedding light on causation between ISO 9001 and improved business performance', *International Journal of Operations Management*, 28 (7): 687–708.

Easterby-Smith, M.P.V., Thorpe, R. and Lowe, A. (2002) *Management Research: An Introduction* (2nd edn). London: Sage.

Frankfort-Nachmias, C. and Nachmias, D. (1992) *Research Methods in the Social Sciences* (4th edn). London: St Martin's Press.

Gabrielsson, M., Sasi, V. and Darling, J. (2004) 'Finance of rapidly growing Finnish SMEs: Born internationals and born globals', *European Business Review*, 16 (6): 590–604.

Hart, C. and Dewsnap, B. (2001) 'An exploratory study of the consumer decision process for intimate apparel', *Journal of Fashion Marketing and Management*, 5 (2): 108–119.

House of Commons Information Office (2003) 'Broadcasting Proceedings of the House', online source: http://www.parliament.uk/documents/commons-information-office/g05.pdf, accessed 19 September 2013.

Lewin, K. (1946) 'Action research and minority problems', in G.W. Lewin (ed.), *Researching Social Conflicts: Selected Papers on Group Dynamics*. New York: Harpers, pp. 201–216.

Matlay, H. and Carey, C. (2007) 'Entrepreneurship education in the UK: A longitudinal perspective', *Journal of Small Business and Enterprise Development*, 14 (2): 252–263.

Mays, N. and Pope, C. (2000) 'Qualitative research in healthcare: Addressing quality in qualitative research', *British Medical Journal*, 320 (1st Jan): 50–52.

Moser, C.A. and Kalton, G. (1989) *Survey Methods in Social Investigation*. Aldershot: Gower.

Nikandrou, I., Apospori, E. and Papalexandris, N. (2005) 'Changes in HRM in Europe: A longitudinal comparative study among 18 European countries', *Journal of European Industrial Training*, 29 (7): 541–560.

Robson, C. (1993) *Real World Research*. Oxford: Blackwell.

Rowley, J. (2002) 'Using case studies in research', *Management Research News*, 25 (1): 16–27.

Rowley, J. (2004) 'Online branding: The case of McDonald's', *British Food Journal*, 106 (3): 228–237.

Saunders, M., Lewis, P. and Thornhill, A. (2007) *Research Methods for Business Students* (4th edn). Harlow: FT/Prentice Hall.

Usunier, J. (2000) *Marketing across Cultures*. Harlow: FT/Prentice Hall.

Wang, S. and Qu, H. (2004) 'A comparison study of Chinese domestic tourism: China vs the USA', *International Journal of Contemporary Hospitality Management*, 16 (2): 108–115.

Yin, R.K. (2003) *Case Study Research, Design and Methods* (3rd edn). Newbury Park, CA: Sage.

Further Reading

Creswell, J.W. (2008) *Qualitative, Quantitative and Mixed Methods Approaches* (3rd edn). Thousand Oaks, CA: Sage.

Farquhar, J.D. (2012) *Case Study Research for Business*. London: Sage.

Hakim, C. (2000) *Research Design: Successful Designs for Social and Economic Research* (2nd edn). London: Routledge.

Maxwell, J.A. (2005) *Qualitative Research Design* (2nd edn). Newbury Park, CA: Sage.

Punch, K.F. (2006) *Developing Effective Research Proposals* (2nd edn). Thousand Oaks, CA: Sage.

Robson, C. (2011) *Real World Research* (3rd edn). Chichester: John Wiley & Sons.

Thomas, G. (2011) *How to do your Case Study: A Guide for Students and Researchers*. London: Sage.

White, B. (2000) *Dissertation Skills for Business and Management Students*. London: Thomson.

6
Primary Data Collection

┌─ Learning Objectives ───┐

After reading this chapter, you should be able to:

- know what primary data are;
- understand the different primary data options;
- appreciate how to conduct interviews;
- appreciate how to record primary data;
- understand the range of observational techniques;
- know how to conduct fieldwork within one's own organization;
- identify the importance of understanding cultural issues when collecting data; and
- understand triangulation of data collection.

└──┘

Introduction

So far in this book we have largely focused on the concepts surrounding business research. Once you are familiar with these concepts and have a clearly defined topic and research objectives, the next step is to consider data collection. In essence, there are two types of data. The first are *primary data*, which are information gathered for the purpose of your own study. And the second are *secondary data*, which are data that have already been published. In this chapter I will discuss primary data, while Chapter 7 focuses on secondary data.

The main aim of this chapter is to describe and explain the various primary data collection methods that you may consider when undertaking your research project. Primary data are defined, followed by a detailed overview of each of the main types of primary data collection tool. Broadly speaking, these include interviews, questionnaires and observation (see Figure 6.1). The Honeycomb of Research Methodology shows data collection as the fifth step in the typical structure of a research methodology chapter. However, in terms of the thought process of conducting research, it is often a starting point for students. For example, some students are set on 'doing interviews' or 'carrying out a questionnaire survey'. However, choice of research methods should be considered in the context of other elements of research methodology.

Interviews are a common tool for data collection among business and management students. There are effectively three different types of interview method that you may wish to consider when gathering data. Each one is fully explained in this chapter. Questionnaires are also a valuable tool for collecting data. However, a number of potential problems are associated with questionnaires. These include time constraints, the formulation of a suitable set of questions, and using appropriate questioning techniques. These points are examined using examples of questioning techniques and steps that can be taken to manage your time better when compiling and administering a questionnaire. Observation is the third primary data collection tool that we shall look at. Observation is a qualitative research method that involves the observation and recording of the subjects under study. Although not a prevalent choice among business students, observation can provide an interesting insight into a whole range of topics, in particular those relating to consumer behaviour. There are several different approaches to observation. We explore each one, highlighting the advantages and disadvantages of each.

Next, we examine how to conduct fieldwork within one's own organization. This is particularly aimed at those students who are working and studying and/or those who are conducting research on behalf of their sponsor's organization.

All researchers need to be aware of the implications of cultural factors on primary data collection – not only those undertaking cross-cultural research. For example, I have found that many of my own international students choose to focus on a UK-related topic. Culturally, this may not be such an issue for European

FIGURE 6.1   The Honeycomb of Research Methodology (©2013 Jonathan Wilson)

students, but those outside Europe may experience difficulties with their research if they do not have a clear understanding of cultural differences. An example of this may be a low response rate to a questionnaire survey because of overly sensitive questions.

If you are considering cross-cultural research, you are likely to encounter a whole new set of potential problems. Don't worry! The nature of these problems and how they can be overcome are fully addressed later in this chapter. Next, we examine online research methods. Increasingly, students are using online survey tools to collect data. In this section the main data collection instruments such as Survey Monkey are discussed, along with the ethical challenges associated with using web-based surveys. Finally, I have included a section on data triangulation to primary data collection. The intention here is to illustrate how different collection methods can be combined, and how they can be applied to your study.

What Are Primary Data?

In primary data collection, you collect data yourself using a range of collection tools such as interviews, observation and questionnaires, rather than simply relying on existing data sources. In other words, the data are unique to your own particular study. In general, there are three reasons that support the use of primary data. First, when existing secondary data are unavailable. This is likely to be the case if you have chosen a contemporary topic that has only recently come to the attention of researchers. At the time of writing, the current global economic crisis is a perfect example. Although the subject has received blanket coverage across the world's media, the number of academic articles written on the subject is still rather 'limited'. Second, existing secondary data may not be appropriate to your study. For example, I recently had a student who wished to analyze China's relations with Sudan. Although secondary sources are available, they tend to focus on Africa rather than individual states. So he decided to focus his study on primary research by conducting interviews. Finally, some institutions require students to undertake primary research, whereas in others it may not be a necessity. If you are unsure about this, check with your institution's submission requirements. Certainly, with postgraduate study it tends to be a necessity.

Primary data collection can be quite challenging for students. Establishing a suitably sized sample and gathering the data can be both time-consuming and often frustrating. Still, it can also generate an interesting set of findings that can make a significant contribution to your overall research.

Lastly, my own personal opinion is that even though you may not be required to conduct primary research, it is always good to see a student who has included primary findings. It often indicates that he or she has gone that little bit further to investigate their topic. Yet, one appreciates that primary data collection is not always possible, given time or financial constraints or an inability to access subjects. Those students who rely only on secondary data are often still capable of producing an excellent piece of work.

Primary Data Collection Options

A range of primary data collection options are available to you. As noted earlier, the three main data collection tools include interviews, questionnaires and observation. These data collection tools can be carried out using a variety of different survey methods (see Figure 6.2). We shall examine each of these survey methods later in this chapter.

Figure 6.2 is intended to illustrate how data collection tools are typically linked with different types of survey method. For example, the questionnaire data collection tool is often associated with postal, email and fax survey methods. Similarly, data collection tools are often associated with either qualitative or quantitative research. However, these associations are by no means immutable. For example, qualitative data from personal interviews can also be analyzed using content analysis. This is a quantitative technique used for discovering themes and patterns in text and will be examined in Chapter 10. In addition, more than one type of data collection method can be used in a research project. We examine mixed methods of data collection later in this chapter.

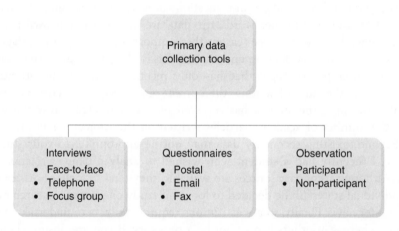

FIGURE 6.2   Primary data collection tools and survey methods

Introduction to Questionnaires and Interviews

Prior to examining the three different types of primary data collection, it is worth noting the distinction between questionnaires and interviews. Sometimes students use the terms interchangeably. However, there is a difference. Quite simply, the difference between a questionnaire and an interview is that an interview requires the presence of an interviewer. In other words, if a survey is self-administered, then this is a questionnaire. A *self-administered* questionnaire means that the respondent completes it without the assistance of an interviewer. Conversely, if the interviewer administers the survey, then this is regarded as an interview. Table 6.1 highlights the differences between questionnaire and interview.

TABLE 6.1 Differences between questionnaire and interview

Administered by	Survey method	Type of data collection
Interviewer	Face-to-face	Face-to-face interview
Interviewer	Telephone	Telephone interview
Interviewer	Focus group	Focus group interview
Self-administered	Postal	Postal questionnaire
Self-administered	Fax	Fax questionnaire
Self-administered	Email	Email questionnaire

Although some of the above types of data collection are more popular than others, the type selected should help to achieve your research questions. Each type has its advantages and disadvantages.

Interviews

Interviews are more commonly associated with a qualitative research strategy. Interviewing allows the researcher to gain an insight into a person's beliefs and attitudes towards a particular subject. In some types of interview a key advantage is that it permits you to examine both verbal and non-verbal communication. Obviously, with questionnaires administered via the post or email, the researcher only gains an understanding of the respondents' views expressed in words.

Ideally, when conducting an interview, you should aim for a location that is quiet, comfortable and where you are unlikely to be interrupted. Unfortunately for the researcher, the choice of venue is often dependent on the respondent. For example, I remember conducting an interview in a fast-food restaurant at London's Heathrow Airport! Why? Because I considered the respondent to be an integral part of my research, and it was the only time I could get an appointment!

Face-to-face interviews

A face-to-face interview is a direct meeting between an interviewer (often the researcher) and an interviewee or interviewees. Given the personal nature of face-to-face interviews, they are also sometimes referred to as *personal interviews*.

Several advantages are associated with face-to-face interviews. Among the most salient are:

- the ability to engage in verbal and non-verbal communication;
- the respondent's feedback can often be recorded, thereby providing accurate information;
- the greater flexibility regarding the delivery of questions; and
- completion is immediate and straightforward.

Verbal and non-verbal communication can provide interesting insights into your respondent's feedback and their general behaviour. Verbal communication often allows the respondent to answer a question in an in-depth way, and also permits them to elaborate on specific questions or key themes. This is certainly an advantage over non-personal data collection methods such as a postal survey. Non-verbal communication can provide you with extra information that is not available in written form. By analyzing your respondent's hand gestures, for example, you may be able to gain a clearer insight into their perceptions towards a particular subject. However, non-verbal communication can be misinterpreted. In cross-cultural research, a lack of understanding of cultural differences can make this especially difficult for researchers.

Recording interviews is an effective way to preserve respondent feedback compared to the sometimes onerous task of making hand-written notes. In reality, recording your respondents should not be viewed as an alternative to taking notes. Even the best recording equipment can fail at the wrong time! Therefore, note-taking should always be undertaken as a back-up.

Some interviewing techniques permit greater flexibility in the delivery of questions. This allows the researcher to explore particular themes that might arise as a result of the respondent's feedback. For instance, let's say that you interviewed a human resources manager about staff turnover. Rather than asking a structured set of questions focusing on your own presumed views, you encouraged the respondent to talk openly on the subject. The result was not only a wider exploration of the theme, but also the discovery of an underlying cause of staff turnover that you had not envisaged when compiling your questions.

The final advantage of face-to-face interviews is that they are immediate and generally straightforward to complete. The time taken to conduct an interview usually varies depending on the nature of the research. However, typically they can last anywhere between 20 minutes and two hours. The bulk of the time associated with interviews is in the transcribing and interpreting of data. We consider this in Chapter 10.

Although there is no denying the advantages of face-to-face interviews, they also raise a number of disadvantages. For example:

- Setting up and carrying out the interview can be problematic.
- Some questions may be perceived as embarrassing and highly sensitive by respondents. This can be a particular problem when conducting cross-cultural research.
- Transcribing and analyzing data is time-consuming and subjective.
- There may be unwillingness on the part of the respondent to answer questions.

Another drawback is that most students lack interviewing skills. Therefore, developing your credibility as a researcher and perfecting your interviewing technique are things you have to work on. One way to tackle this problem is to carry out a pilot or preliminary study prior to your main research.

The types of question delivered in face-to-face interviews can also generate problems. Although respondents have indicated a willingness to take part in your study, they are likely to be reluctant to answer sensitive or embarrassing questions. Certain questions may not appear to be sensitive or embarrassing to you, but your respondent may beg to differ. Remember that he or she may well have a different set of beliefs and attitudes towards your topic. Once again, cultural differences cannot be ignored. Sensitive questions are more likely to be an issue with cross-cultural research. How can one address this issue? Asking your supervisor to check over your questions, conducting a pilot study or incorporating questions from similar studies are all ways that can help to reduce the likelihood of inappropriate questions.

Transcribing and analyzing personal interview data can be a particularly laborious task. If possible, try to get someone with experience to transcribe for you.

Finally, unwillingness by the respondent to answer questions can be avoided to a certain extent by asking the right questions, recognizing potentially sensitive questions and staying within your chosen topic. Where a respondent indicates that they do not wish to answer a question, obviously this is their right. They should in no way be put under pressure to answer.

How to conduct a face-to-face interview

There are a number of factors to consider when conducting face-to-face interviews. Although I have highlighted some of these in the previous section, ideally you need to be aware of where these fall within the interview planning process. Figure 6.3 highlights the stages in this planning process.

Although the stages may seem self-explanatory, you need to realize the factors that need to be taken into account during each stage. First, during the planning stage, you need to make sure that you are clear on the type of information that you require. At this point, it is worth looking over your research objectives. This will help you to clarify the information that you require from your respondent. Next, select the type of interview that you wish to conduct – *structured, unstructured* or *semi-structured* – followed by your research questions. After this, it is a good idea to arrange a meeting with your project supervisor so as to check the suitability of your questions. Moreover, conducting a pilot study can help to improve the validity of your questions. Finally, arrange an appointment with your research participant.

Stage 1: Pre-interview (planning)
Stage 2: Day of the interview
Stage 3: Arrival
Stage 4: Start of the interview
Stage 5: During the interview
Stage 6: End of the interview

FIGURE 6.3   Stages in the interview process

Remember that the greater your flexibility in relation to time and venue, the greater the likelihood that the interview will take place.

On the day of the interview make sure that you take with you all necessary information. This includes the name and contact details of the participant, the venue address (map), your questions, paper, pens, dictaphone (if the respondent has agreed to being recorded), mobile phone, money and possibly business cards. Of course, it is also important to present yourself in a professional manner. Smart attire or a suit is usually best, although I remember one interview I conducted at the head office of a multinational supermarket group where all of the staff wore casual clothes. Why? Because the company implemented a dress-down Friday scheme where employees are encouraged to attend work on Fridays in casual clothes. Still, it is often better to be overdressed!

Upon arrival at your interview location you should have enough time to go over your questions and above all make sure that you know where your respondent is located. Ideally, ask to see your respondent approximately 10 minutes before your scheduled appointment. This can help to create a good impression and enforce your credibility as a serious researcher. Once you meet your respondent, a nice firm handshake, followed by a little small talk (e.g. 'Are you busy at the moment?') can help to settle your nerves.

Start your interview by clearly explaining the nature of your study, the purpose of the interview, the types of question that you will be asking, and how long the interview is likely to take. Remember that it may have been some time since your participant read through the details of your study. If you provide clear clarification of your questions, this will make your participant feel less apprehensive about what is to follow. Next, clarify the situation regarding anonymity and confidentiality. Finally, if your participant has agreed to be recorded, set up your recording equipment.

During the interview, ask your questions in a clear, professional manner. Give your respondent time to answer and try to avoid constantly interrupting them. Not only can this irritate a respondent, it can also mean that you end up losing vital data. The nature of your questions will ultimately depend on the type of interview you have chosen. Try to make sure that you gather the required information to address your original set of research questions.

At the end of the interview it is important to thank your participant for their time and contribution to your research. Preferably, try to stress that you will continue to make contact with your participant. From my experience, most participants are very interested to learn about research outcomes. As noted earlier, providing a summary of your findings for each participant can help to increase the 'perceived value' of the input from those research participants.

In sum, the above stages are intended as a useful guide to conducting a personal interview. Of course, there may be other considerations to take into account when carrying out interviews. Examples include cultural issues, the use of a translator and the interview environment.

In this section we have examined the advantages and disadvantages of conducting face-to-face interviews. Next, we will look at telephone interviews.

Telephone interviews

A telephone interview can be used as part of both a qualitative and quantitative research strategy. Quite simply, a telephone interview is an interview conducted over the telephone. It is certainly a viable alternative to face-to-face interviews although, perhaps surprisingly, I have found it a relatively uncommon choice among business students.

Numerous advantages are associated with the telephone interview. The main ones include the following:

- It can be a relatively quick and low-cost means of collecting data.
- It requires minimal organization.
- It is ideal for a wide geographical coverage, and often linked to cross-cultural research.
- It can often develop a large sample size.
- Interviews can be recorded.

Unlike face-to-face interviews, a telephone interview can be relatively easy and inexpensive to administer. For example, whether or not a respondent has a telephone is really no longer an issue for researchers. Also, a plethora of telephone providers also means that the cost of telephone calls has come down in recent years. So much so, in fact, that conducting international research via the telephone is not an option just for professional researchers. Cheap international phone cards mean that students can also engage in telephone interviews with respondents from around the world. Also, a series of telephone interviews can generally be administered over a short period of time.

The minimal effort required to organize a telephone interview is also attractive to a researcher. Whereas a face-to-face interview may involve planning detailed travel arrangements, telephone interviews only require an interviewee's consent and access to a telephone.

The fact that telephone interviews are now markedly easier to undertake makes them an ideal research method for cross-cultural research. Moreover, the relative ease and low cost associated with telephone interviews means that a larger sample size can often be generated.

Finally, like face-to-face interviews, telephone interviews also allow for the possibility of recording, provided that you have received consent from your respondent.

Given that most people have been targeted through telephone interviews, the associated disadvantages are all too apparent. These can be summarized as follows:

- They are often perceived as intrusive and linked to hard selling.
- It is difficult to explain complex questions over the telephone.
- It can be particularly problematic trying to get past the 'gatekeeper' and gain access.
- It can be time-consuming when attempting to contact the right person.

The first disadvantage is that they generally have a poor reputation. This is largely due to their association with hard selling. What is more, telephone interviews are often seen as intrusive. In particular, the practice of 'cold calling' is often viewed as an invasion of privacy and for this reason tends to produce low response rates.

Second, the researcher may find it difficult to explain more complex questions over the telephone. One danger of having to constantly explain questions to respondents is that they may become impatient and cut the interview short. Furthermore, a lack of clarity in the questioning may lead to inaccurate answers. Perhaps the best way to overcome this problem is to deliver clear, concise questions.

Third, a particular problem when trying to contact senior management or directors by telephone is the 'gatekeeper' – the individual or individuals who come between you and your intended respondent. Often, the gatekeeper is a personal assistant (PA) to a manager or director whose job it is to 'weed out' unnecessary calls. Overcoming this problem can be especially testing for student researchers. However, there are certain steps that can be taken. These include: selling the importance of your research to the gatekeeper in the hope that he or she will put you through; seeking confirmation from your respondent to participate in your research prior to making the telephone call; and using any potential contacts who may know your respondent to explain the merits of your research.

Lastly, it can be a time-consuming process trying to make contact with your respondent via telephone. This is especially true if you intend interviewing management or company directors. The likelihood is that they are likely to be extremely busy, and perhaps divide their time across several different sites, or even countries!

How to conduct a telephone interview

As we have established, ideally it is preferable to have sought agreement from a respondent prior to undertaking a telephone interview. By doing this, the respondent is aware of the nature of your research, is likely to view you as a credible researcher and, above all, has consented to taking part in a telephone interview.

Approaching telephone interviews through cold calling is not really appropriate for the reasons highlighted in the previous section. Consequently, seeking consent through other means of communication, such as email, post or through a contact, is arguably the best means of approaching a telephone interview. In reality, the steps involved in conducting a telephone interview are very similar to those of a face-to-face interview. You still need to engage in a certain amount of planning prior to carrying out your telephone interview. The key difference is time. The time spent engaged in the telephone interview process can make it an attractive alternative to face-to-face interviews.

Focus group interviews

Focus groups are typically associated with a qualitative research strategy. A *focus group* is an interview carried out by a trained researcher whose role is to both ask questions and observe participants within the group. Generally, the focus group is made up of a relatively small number of individuals (usually 8–10), who are asked questions about a particularly topic. Focus groups are commonly used in marketing as a method of establishing people's attitudes towards a product or service. They are especially useful if a company is considering launching a new product and is keen to determine consumers' views on the product. In short, a focus group is a group discussion.

Claes and Heymans (2008: 97) provided an excellent example of how a focus group can be used in research. Their study looked into human resource professionals' views on work motivation and retention of older workers:

> Three focus groups were conducted in September 2006 with the second author as a moderator. They lasted an average of two hours and took place at a quiet location within the university that was convenient and neutral for all participants. To ensure accuracy of information, the focus group was recorded on video and one observer per focus group took notes.
>
> A focus group interview guide was used as the main tool for data collection. The second author acted as a moderator in the three focus groups. Being a researcher, she was familiar with the topic while her training as an organizational psychologist enabled her to develop competencies in interviewing skills and the understanding of group processes. Her role during the focus group was to put participants at ease, to lead the interaction, to compare and contrast participants' views, and to ensure the necessary information was obtained by asking questions. After the HR professionals had left, she met briefly with the observer to debrief each focus group session.

Zikmund (1997) offers a number of advantages of such group discussions, which can be summarized as the '10 Ss':

- *Synergy* – the group process generates a wider range of information than would accrue from a comparable number of in-depth interviews.
- *Snowballing* – respondent interaction creates a chain of thoughts and ideas.
- *Serendipity* – a great idea can drop out of the blue.
- *Stimulation* – respondents' views are brought out by the group process.
- *Security* – respondents' views are more likely to be candid as there will probably be other similar people there and there is less individual pressure than in an in-depth interview.
- *Spontaneity* – because no one individual is required to respond to a question, this encourages a spontaneous response when people have a definite point of view.
- *Specialization* – a trained moderator can interview more respondents in a given session.
- *Structure* – it is easier for the moderator to reintroduce a topic not adequately covered before than in an in-depth interview.
- *Speed* – focus groups are quicker than individual interviews.
- *Scrutiny* – the group can be observed by members of the research team.

The key advantage of the focus group is that the researcher can observe how a group interacts, thereby examining both the verbal and non-verbal communication that goes beyond a single response.

The main disadvantage, however, is largely organizational. In truth, I have not come across many students who have used focus groups. The reasons for this include: an inability to acquire a suitable venue in which to conduct the interview; difficulty in attracting suitable participants; and a lack of experience in organizing and carrying out the interview. Those students who have conducted focus group interviews tend to use fellow students for the purpose of data collection. This helps to overcome the limitations discussed above.

How to conduct a focus group interview

Claes and Heymans' (2008) example should give you some indication of the necessary steps involved in conducting a focus group interview. However, we now explore this in a little more detail. Hussey and Hussey (1997: 155) offer a useful summary of the main stages involved in forming a focus group:

- Invite a group of people whom you consider have sufficient experiences in common on the topic to meet at a neutral location.
- Introduce the group members and discuss the purpose of the study and what will happen in the focus group.
- If possible, give visual examples of the subject matter. For example, if you want the group to discuss the merits of different brands of toothpaste, have the products on display.
- Start the session with a broad, open question. This can be displayed using a flip chart or overhead projector.
- Allow the group to discuss the topics among themselves, but intervene to ensure that all participants have an opportunity to contribute.
- Use a prepared list of topics and intervene to ensure that all topics are covered.
- Enlist the help of two observers and, if possible, record the proceedings on video.

Elite interviewing

For the majority of undergraduate students, gaining access to business elites is extremely challenging. This is because *elite interviewing* refers to 'conducting interviews with key decision makers and/or those in high-ranked positions, e.g. politicians, company directors or leading academics'. In a business context, elite interviewing means setting up and conducting interviews with high-level business executives. This could be directors or a CEO of a multinational company. Why would you want to engage in elite interviewing? Well, let's say that you were interested in studying corporate strategy among the UK's leading companies. You may decide that those individuals best positioned to comment on strategic direction are company directors. Thus, the aim would be to interview directors of your chosen companies or cases.

One of the earliest studies on elite interviewing is that by Kincaid and Bright (1957). The authors carried out interviews with high-ranking business executives in 37 large organizations. Although their interviews with high-level executives were conducted during the 1950s, many of the concerns that the scholars encountered are equally applicable today. These are some of the issues that the authors raise when conducting elite interviewing:

- Consider access: interviews with top-level executives should be requested using letters to the chief executive, which include the aims, details of the study and the reasons for requesting an interview with a high executive.

- A request is likely to be successful if it stresses the practical aspects of the research problem and relates them to the company's own particular interests.
- An excellent means of getting entrance to a corporation is through persons in a well-established business school who have personal acquaintances among business people.
- Research such as this can be slow moving and rather expensive. For example, arranging the interviews, preparation and writing up limit the number of interviews.
- Careful attention must be given to the respondent's conception of his or her role in the interview. This is because respondents may speak more as a company spokesperson on company policy.
- Respondents are likely to consider carefully the qualifications of the interviewer.
- Enlisting the cooperation of large organizations requires careful planning.

Clearly, students who intend carrying out elite interviewing face a number of challenges. In reality, you will often find that high-level executives may be interested in your research, but simply do not have time to see you. I remember writing to the CEO of a leading UK company asking for an interview to discuss the firm's internationalization strategy. Although I didn't get an interview, he kindly forwarded my request to the European Corporate Affairs Manager, who kindly offered to participate in the interview. Despite these difficulties, the whole process can be extremely rewarding. Not least for the satisfaction that comes with gaining consent from high-level executives. Also, the relationships that you develop during your research may prove useful when it comes to finding a job on completion of your studies.

Interview methods

Essentially, there are three different types of interview method: structured, unstructured and semi-structured (see Figure 6.4). Each type of interview has advantages and

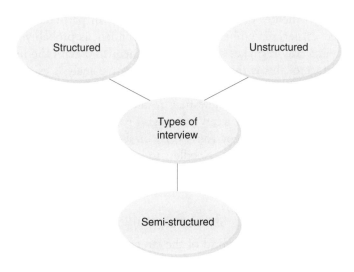

FIGURE 6.4   Interview methods

disadvantages for the student researcher. Of these methods, the semi-structured interview tends to be the favoured choice of researchers, for reasons explained below.

Structured

A *structured interview* is based on a rigid set of interview questions. In some cases these may produce short answers that allow for easier comparative analysis between respondents. An advantage of the structured approach is that it usually permits a greater number of questions to be answered. This is because the respondents are required to provide short, concise answers to questions. However, the disadvantage of adopting such an approach is that it may annoy respondents who want to elaborate on their answers. Bear in mind that generally the people you interview are likely to be experts on your chosen topic. Not allowing them the opportunity to elaborate or even introduce their own questions is a real disadvantage of a structured interview. Moreover, it may mean that potentially interesting data are not divulged to the interviewer.

Unstructured

An *unstructured interview* is also sometimes referred to as an *in-depth interview*. With an unstructured interview approach, the interviewer usually begins the interview with a broad question. The respondent then discusses this in a general, open manner. The interviewer's questions are very much dependent on the answers given by the respondent. The interviewer does not always ask direct questions, but invites the respondent to discuss a particular 'theme'. For example, 'What are your views on the current economic crisis?' The respondent's reply may lead the interviewer to 'probe' for further information.

The advantage of the unstructured approach is that it allows a respondent the freedom to discuss themes or raise questions that are of particular importance to them. As noted earlier, remember that your respondent is probably an expert on their topic, so in a way it makes sense to allow them to dictate the interview. The major disadvantage of this is that it makes comparative analysis especially difficult because there is no consistency in the answers being delivered. Furthermore, the unstructured nature of the interview may result in you 'drifting' away from the topic under study. For example, a few years ago I conducted an unstructured interview with an advertising manager. Fairly early on it became apparent that we both supported the same football team. Needless to say that we spent most of the time discussing football rather than focusing on the topic in question!

Semi-structured

A *semi-structured interview* is a hybrid of the structured and unstructured approach. The interview is based on a set of structured questions, but at the same time provides scope for the respondent to elaborate on certain points and raise particular questions or themes. The interviewer has greater flexibility and may introduce certain questions depending on the respondent's answer. The combination of set questions and flexibility is appealing to researchers and respondents alike. For this reason, it is no surprise that semi-structured tends to be the favoured choice for focus group interviews.

Recording interviews

Irrespective of your choice of interview method, each one provides the opportunity of recording your respondents. The decision to record interviews is always a difficult one for researchers. It is always better to record the feedback from respondents because this ensures that you can gather their verbatim answers, you don't lose any data and it makes the task of analysis easier. However, there are a number of counter-arguments against the recording of interviews. The interviewee may feel uncomfortable being recorded (even if he or she agrees, they may still feel uncomfortable!). For example, a few years ago I remember interviewing a joint venture manager about cultural issues between management and employees. At the time, he agreed to be recorded, although with some hesitation. However, it soon became apparent that he was uncomfortable with being tape-recorded. I decided to switch off the tape recorder and subsequently he began to divulge both very interesting and highly sensitive information! On this basis, one might argue that it is better not to record your respondents. Nonetheless, the ability to generate word-for-word answers and accurate information, thereby improving validity, perhaps outweighs the disadvantages. The main disadvantages are the costs in time and money. The latter certainly applies if employing a transcriber to transcribe interviews.

Questionnaires

A questionnaire is a method of data collection that comprises a set of questions designed to generate data suitable for achieving the objectives of a research project. It can be used to gather both qualitative and quantitative data.

The questionnaire is a popular data collection tool among student researchers engaged in primary research. By incorporating different questioning techniques within the questionnaire, the researcher is able to gather a wide range of data. A number of advantages and disadvantages are associated with questionnaires. First, we shall consider the advantages.

The advantages of using a questionnaire

The advantages of using a questionnaire are as follows:

- They allow you to obtain accurate information.
- They provide a cost-effective and reliable means of gathering feedback that can be qualitative as well as quantitative.

- A survey questionnaire can provide accurate and relevant data through thoughtful design, testing and detailed administration.

(McClelland, 1994: 22)

A well-produced questionnaire is capable of generating effective and accurate data. In order to facilitate the collection of accurate information, the researcher needs to take into account two key issues. First, an appropriate set of questions needs to be included within the main body of the questionnaire. These questions can be delivered using a range of techniques that can allow both qualitative and quantitative analysis to take place. We shall examine these techniques later in this chapter.

Second, the questionnaire must be aimed at the right target audience. A poorly selected sample can lead not only to a set of biased results, but also to a high non-response rate. Ultimately, this will have implications for your analysis.

Dillman (1978) describes how best to maximize the response rate of participants in questionnaire and telephone surveys.

1. Cooperation is in some sense rewarding for them.
2. The rewards outweigh the costs to them, in terms of money, time and effort.
3. They are convinced that they can trust you to keep your side of the transaction.

A questionnaire can also be relatively inexpensive to conduct. For this reason, email and postal surveys tend to be favoured methods of administering questionnaires.

The thoughtful design, testing and administration of your questionnaire can all contribute to the generation of accurate data. Arguably, the most important of these is testing. Many researchers conduct a pilot or preliminary study before a full-scale questionnaire is administered. This is simply to test that the questionnaire is understood by respondents, that it measures what it is intended to measure, and that it generates accurate data.

The disadvantages of using a questionnaire

Although the advantages outweigh the disadvantages, there are some potential problems with questionnaires. First, unlike personal interviews, the way that questionnaires are administered often means that they are impersonal. If a participant is unsure about a particular question, or simply requires clarification on a particular point, the researcher is not on hand to clarify. The consequences may be inaccurate data or the respondent fails to answer the question.

A second potential problem with questionnaires is that if the respondent misinterprets a question, that response cannot be included in the final analysis. In most cases, this is not the fault of the respondent, but is the consequence of a poorly designed questionnaire or the researcher's inability to explain the question clearly. For example, some questionnaires are composed of a large number of closed questions that can result in what I call 'tick box syndrome'. In other words, if there is a clear pattern in the answers, the respondent 'ticks' each subsequent box without

TABLE 6.2 Examples of reverse questions

Question	Yes / No (please circle)
Do you have a heart condition?	Yes / No
Have you been in hospital this year?	Yes / No
Have you suffered from kidney failure?	Yes / No
Do you eat fruit?	Yes / No
Have you ever contracted rabies?	Yes / No

reading the question, as they presume the same pattern of answers will continue throughout the questionnaire. An example is often found in medical questionnaires. Typically, the majority of respondents are not affected by any of the ailments listed on the questionnaire. They may therefore engage in tick box syndrome. How do researchers overcome this problem? One way is to include what is referred to as a *reverse question*. Table 6.2 illustrates an extract from a hypothetical medical questionnaire that includes a reverse question (question 4).

Of course, most respondents would answer 'No' to all of the questions, except question 4 (the reverse question). By including a question such as this the intention is to avoid tick box syndrome. Although the opposite can sometimes happen! A respondent engaged in tick box syndrome may also fail to read the reverse question. Hence, this can potentially lead to inaccurate data.

Sometimes, respondents may want to impress upon the researcher. For this reason, they may elaborate their answers. In some instances, this particular problem can be avoided by adopting the right questioning technique. For example, rather than asking 'How much do you earn?' a category question can be used (see Table 6.3).

Even a category question such as that shown in Table 6.3 can lead to a respondent exaggerating their answer. However, by adopting this approach, there is less likelihood that a respondent will elaborate on the truth because they do not have to provide a specific answer.

Finally, perhaps the leading disadvantage of using a questionnaire is the difficulty associated with questionnaire design. We fully explore this in the next section.

TABLE 6.3 Example of a category question

Please indicate your salary by ticking the relevant box below (£):			
£18,000 ☐	£18,001 – £29,000 ☐	£29,001 – £30,000 ☐	£30,001+ ☐

Designing a questionnaire

Designing a questionnaire is not easy. Prior to designing your questionnaire you need to think carefully about a number of factors. These can be summarized as follows:

- What is the purpose of your questionnaire?
- How can you ensure reliability and validity?
- How will the questions help you to answer your research objectives?
- What length should your questionnaire be?

We shall examine all of the above points in the next section, with the exception of reliability and validity. How to address reliability and validity in relation to interviews, questionnaires and observation is explored towards the end of this chapter.

Things to consider when designing a questionnaire

When designing your questionnaire, it is essential that you take into account a number of key factors, for example, question order, layout and length. Failure to note these important points is likely to have serious implications when it comes to response rate, analysis and the interpretation of your results. Factors to consider prior to administering your questionnaire are summarized below.

Theme/what to ask   Prior to formulating your questions, you must have a clear understanding of the general theme of your research. By the time you reach this stage of your research, your reading of the key literature means that you should have no problem in identifying the main theme and specific purpose of your study. You then need to formulate a clear set of research questions using questioning techniques that allow you to address each of your respective research questions.

Layout   Your questionnaire needs to be structured in a logical and clear manner. Questionnaires that are both poorly structured and poorly presented may seriously reduce your response rate. Each section of your questionnaire should be based on a particular theme. Let us say that you want to administer a questionnaire to retail managers. The first section may relate to personal details, followed by company background, then performance criteria, and so on.

Length   Establishing an ideal length for your questionnaire is always difficult. On the one hand, you do not want to deter respondents by making your questionnaire too long. On the other hand, it must be long enough so as to generate a sufficient amount of data. In essence, two things can be done to determine an appropriate length. First, look at questionnaires implemented by previous researchers in your chosen subject area. Second, conducting a pilot study can also prove useful.

Question order   Your questions must be in a logical order. Of course, questions relating to a specific topic must fall within the same themed section. Generally, more sensitive questions are best placed towards the end of the questionnaire. The logic behind this is that respondents are more likely to complete the questionnaire if they have already answered the majority of the questions.

Coding Codes are symbols, usually numbers, which are used to identify particular responses, or types of response, in questionnaires and similar instruments (Robson, 1993: 256). Coding is used as part of your questionnaire in order to help process and analyze your data. Most of your data will involve quantitative analysis. For this reason, data will need to be entered into a computer software package that allows them to be analyzed. The most commonly used statistical package among student researchers is SPSS (Statistical Package for Social Sciences).

Covering letter

Irrespective of your chosen survey method, it is vital that you include a covering letter with your questionnaire. A covering letter should set out the nature of your research, what it hopes to achieve, address any ethical issues and, above all, state how it is likely to benefit the respondent. Effectively, a covering letter is your 'sales tool' – it is intended to encourage a potential participant to take part. A well-written covering letter can certainly increase your response rate. Conversely, those that are poorly written are likely to lead to a low number of replies. An example of a covering letter is as follows:

─RESEARCH IN ACTION─

Dear Mrs Henderson,

My name is Jim Watson and I am a BA (Hons) Business and Management student at Brampton University. I am conducting research into the impact of the current economic crisis on estate agents in the Bloomfield area. There are many studies on the impact of the economic crisis on a nationwide basis, but nothing at present that specifically focuses on the area of Bloomfield. Therefore, I am inviting you to participate in this study. The questionnaire should take you no more than 10 minutes to complete, and includes questions on:

* the background of your company;
* number of employees;
* level of sales and market share; and
* future predictions concerning the housing market in the Bloomfield area.

I'm sure that you will agree that this is an important piece of research. The advantages of taking part in this study are as follows:

* It will contribute to research that carries regional significance;
* It will improve our understanding of the current and future housing market in the Bloomfield area; and
* All participants will receive a full report summarizing the findings of the study.

I can assure you that all data collected in this study will be treated in the strictest of confidence. I would therefore be grateful if you could please complete the questionnaire and return it in the

(Continued)

(Continued)

enclosed self-addressed envelope. Alternatively, if you would like to complete an electronic version, please email me at the address below:

J.Watson@brampton.ac.uk

Yours sincerely,

Jim Watson – BA (Hons) Business and Management student, Brampton University

Thanks

Make sure that you thank your participants for their time and cooperation. It is also worth inviting them to comment on any aspect of your research. This can sometimes provide useful information and lead to additional questions that might otherwise have been overlooked by the researcher.

Pilot study

As noted earlier, a pilot study is a small-scale study that is carried out prior to the main survey. The purpose of a pilot study is to try to increase levels of reliability and validity prior to the main survey. For example, I remember conducting a pilot study on a group of 25 business delegates in South-East Asia. Typically, my questionnaire included different types of question. However, upon analyzing the results, I realized that the majority had failed to correctly answer the Likert-scale questions. I had presumed that they would be familiar with this type of questioning technique. However, a Likert-scale question is essentially a Western questioning technique. Thus, the majority of respondents had no experience of completing Likert questions. Thankfully, the pilot study allowed me to alter the questions to make them more self-explanatory – something I would not have been able to do had the main survey gone ahead in the first instance.

Evaluation

The majority of the above factors are ultimately going to affect how you evaluate your questionnaire findings. For example, questioning techniques may influence the type of quantitative analysis you undertake. So let us turn to this subject next.

Questioning techniques

Earlier we looked at the main advantages of a questionnaire, along with general design issues such as length and testing. This is all very well, but the most important aspect of your questionnaire design is the formulation of questions through the application of questioning techniques. These questioning techniques are the different ways of asking a question to extract the information you need. They are important because they dictate the analytical techniques that can later be applied when analyzing your findings.

Open questions

An *open question* is one in which the respondent does not have to indicate a specific response. Open questions have a tendency to generate lengthy answers. Often, respondents see open questions as an opportunity to respond to a question in detail. If the topic is something that the respondent is particularly passionate about, one can expect some very lengthy answers!

The advantage of open questions is that they allow the respondent to provide an answer that is not restricted to a select view. In addition, open questions can provide some very interesting qualitative findings that may lead to new insights, or possibly help to develop future research ideas. Open questions are particularly useful when conducting exploratory research. For example, let us say that you are conducting research into company benefits. Open questions may include 'Why are company benefits important to you?' or 'How have company benefits changed over the last five years?'

There are two disadvantages associated with open questions. First, too many open questions can make the analysis and interpretation of your findings extremely time-consuming. Second, it can make a comparative analysis of qualitative answers difficult.

Closed questions

A *closed question* is one in which a respondent has to choose from a limited number of potential answers. Usually this is a straightforward yes or no. Other closed questions may require the respondent to choose from multiple response options. Table 6.4 includes some examples of (yes/no) closed questions, while Table 6.5 demonstrates multiple choice questions.

TABLE 6.4 Examples of closed questions

Question	Yes/No (please circle)
Do you like chocolate?	Yes/No
Do you buy a bar of chocolate every day?	Yes/No
Do you find chocolate expensive?	Yes/No
Do you enjoy receiving chocolate as a gift?	Yes/No

TABLE 6.5 Examples of multiple choice questions

Questions

1. Which of the following relates to the Marketing Mix?
   A. Product, price, place, promotion
   B. Product, price, place, package
   C. People, product, price, post
   D. Place, people, product, price
2. In finance, what is meant by the term ROI?
   A. Rate of investment
   B. Return on investment
   C. Risk of investment
   D. Rely on interest

Multiple choice questions

Multiple choice questions should be written so that the selection of answers directly corresponds to the question being asked. Each response must be mutually exclusive of the others so as not to cause an overlap in the choice (McClelland, 1994: 24).

Multiple choice questions are commonly associated with multiple choice examinations, but student researchers can also consider them in their project questionnaires.

Likert scale

Developed by the American psychologist Rensis Likert, a Likert-scale question is an 'attitude question' that seeks to determine a respondent's attitude towards a particular subject. Usually the respondent is required to read a particular statement, then 'tick' the response that best reflects their opinion. For example, let us say you are conducting a study into customer service in your local banks. You may include a Likert-scale question such as that in Table 6.6, which shows a five-point scale. A seven-point scale is also sometimes used, although most researchers tend to prefer the former as it works better with smaller samples.

TABLE 6.6   Example of a Likert-scale question

Statement	Strongly agree	Agree	Neither agree nor disagree	Disagree	Strongly disagree
ABC Bank provides excellent customer service					

Rank order questions

Another type of attitude-based question is a rank order question. Rank order requires the respondent to rank an attitude statement in their order of preference. Let us say that you are carrying out a study into consumers' perceptions of breakfast cereal. Your questionnaire may feature the following question: *Which is your favourite brand of chocolate? (Indicate your TOP three favourite brands, with 1 being your first choice, 2 your second, and 3 your third choice)*. Table 6.7 illustrates how this question may look in your questionnaire; you can see that the respondent has indicated Dairy Milk as their first choice, followed by Mars and Twix respectively.

TABLE 6.7 Example of a completed rank order question

Dairy Milk	[1]
Kit Kat	
Mars	[2]
Twix	[3]
Aero	
Other	

Semantic differential scale

A semantic differential scale intends to see how strongly the respondent holds an attitude. These scales include a progression from one extreme to another. Circling a number usually indicates the response. For example, Figure 6.5 provides an illustration of a semantic differential question.

Research skills is (please circle the appropriate number)						
Difficult	1	2	3	④	5	Easy
Enjoyable	1	2	③	4	5	Boring
Relevant	1	②	3	4	5	Irrelevant

FIGURE 6.5 Example of a completed semantic differential question

Sensitive questions

Sometimes it can be difficult to gauge the sensitivity of a question. In some respects, this might be influenced by cultural differences. For instance, in Chinese culture it is not unusual to ask direct questions such as 'How much do you earn?' or 'How much did you pay for your house?' Obviously, in other cultures these types of questions would be viewed as wholly inappropriate for inclusion within a questionnaire survey.

How to administer a questionnaire

A number of options are available to you when it comes to administering or carrying out your questionnaire. The methods are referred to as a 'survey'. A *survey* can be defined as a method of collecting information from a well-defined sample.

Postal questionnaire

A postal questionnaire involves the researcher sending out questionnaires to the addresses of research respondents. These respondents within your sample may be 'cold' or have already agreed or expressed an interest in your research. If you are posting questionnaires to respondents 'cold', then you have no previous contact with the respondent. This can lead to a low response rate as the recipient of your questionnaire has no knowledge of your research or your credibility as a researcher.

A telephone call to a potential respondent followed by a postal questionnaire can often work better. By making a telephone call you are seeking their agreement to take part in your study, prior to posting the questionnaire. Postal questionnaires remain a popular method of collecting data. Advantages are that they can be highly targeted, are inexpensive to administer and respondents may give a more honest reply to questions given that they are free from an interviewer's presence.

Fax

Even with the introduction of email, the fax machine is still a widely used communication tool. However, when it comes to relying on the fax machine as a tool for collecting data, its limitations are obvious. The slow, cumbersome, paper-dominated process of sending multiple faxes is certainly less favourable than sending repeat emails.

Schaefer and Dillman (1998) compared paper (i.e. fax or printed surveys) versus email surveys and found that response rates were not considerably different for the two methods. However, they did obtain more complete returned questionnaires when email was used. Email is also favourable compared to fax because it can be sent direct to a respondent and facilitates a quick reply. Certainly, when sending a fax there is no guarantee that it will find its way to your intended recipient. In addition, sometimes a fax is illegible or is received incomplete due to problems in transmission; or the machine runs out of paper, or pages may be lost internally. Thus, this is perhaps the reason why Schaefer and Dillman (1998) received more completed questionnaires via email.

Finally, fax tends not to be used by student researchers as the vast majority do not have access to a fax machine. In reality, email has largely replaced the fax when it comes to everyday communication. Today, it is mainly reserved for the sending of important documents by business organizations.

Email

Email surveys are conducted by sending questionnaires via email to respondents; these are then returned by email to the researcher.

It has been argued that many respondents feel they can be much more candid in emails for the same reasons they are candid in other self-administered questionnaires. It has been suggested that email questionnaires arouse curiosity because they are novel and because they reach respondents when users are more likely to answer, i.e. as they are opening their email they are prepared to interact (Zikmund, 1997). However, an increasing amount of email traffic is now considered to be junk mail. Therefore, the subject box is an important tool in trying to arouse interest when sending email.

Tse (1998) suggests that email surveys are best suited to situations where:

- the population under study has universal or nearly universal email account ownership;
- there is no need to incorporate high-quality image or colour in the questionnaire; and
- the inclusion of incentives will not greatly facilitate response rate and response quality.

Recording questionnaire data

Once you have a sufficient number of completed questionnaires, the next step is to record your questionnaire data. The hard copies of your questionnaire should be in an organized file ready for data entry. A number of user-friendly software packages, which permit the accurate recording of data, are readily available to student researchers. These include Microsoft Word and Excel, and specialized software packages such as SPSS and NVivo. SPSS is ideal if you have adopted a range of questioning techniques suitable for statistical analysis, while NVivo is aimed at qualitative research.

Example of a questionnaire using coding

The following short questionnaire incorporates many of the questioning techniques discussed above. In addition, a coding system ('For office use only') has been applied to make things easier when analyzing the data using a statistical software package such as SPSS.

Consumer behaviour and own-label brands		For office use only
Personal details		
1. Gender: Male	Female	1–2
2. Nationality: British	German	3–9
Japanese	Chinese	
Dutch	South African	
Other		
3. Age: 18–26 27–36 37–46 47–56 57+		10–14

Questions about own-label brands

4. Please indicate with a tick how important own-label brands are when buying your grocery items.

Very important	Important	Neither important nor unimportant	15–19
Unimportant	Very unimportant		

5. Please rank the top three phrases that you feel best describe own-label 20–24 brands (1 = first choice, 2 = second choice, 3 = third choice)

Quality	Cost	Poor standard
Poor brand image	Taste different from branded goods	

(Continued)

(Continued)

Consumer behaviour and own-label brands			For office use only
6. Do you buy own-label brands?			25–27
Yes	No	Don't know	
Other personal details			
7. What is your occupation?			28
8. What is your salary?			29
Many thanks for your cooperation.			

Observation

Observation is normally associated with a qualitative research strategy and involves recording the behaviour of your research subject. In general, there are two things to consider when conducting observational research. The first relates to the extent to which you wish your research subject(s) to be aware of your presence as a researcher. The second relates to the level of interaction with your research subject.

Disguised observation

In disguised or covert observation, research subjects are unaware that they are being observed. The advantage of this is that research subjects are more likely to carry out their tasks in a natural way. From the researcher's point of view, you are observing your research subjects in their natural setting without making them aware of your presence. Disguise can be achieved by hiding or, increasingly, using sophisticated technology such as hidden cameras. However, this approach raises significant ethical concerns, and can certainly affect the credibility of the researcher.

Undisguised observation

In undisguised observation, research subjects are aware that they are being observed. Although this avoids some of the ethical concerns, there is a possibility that research subjects may behave differently because they are being observed.

If you do decide to carry out undisguised observation, you need to establish whether or not to actively participate or be part of the group under investigation. We explore participation in the next section.

Participant observation

Participant observation involves the researcher interacting and being a part of the group under investigation. Participant observation can be undertaken in either a disguised or undisguised way.

A participant observer may join an organization or particular group in order to observe as a direct participant. For example, you may be interested in studying the influence, interaction between members and general operation of a local community group. By joining the group and making members aware of your research, you are able to gain a first-hand insight into these issues.

A limitation associated with observation is that the observer may be influenced by his or her own values and attitudes towards the subject. These values and attitudes may of course change through being part of your chosen group. Subsequently, this can make it hard for an observer to form an impartial view.

In general, a number of factors need to be considered when undertaking participant observation. According to Collis and Hussey (2009: 154), these include:

- purpose of the research;
- cost of the research;
- extent to which access can be gained;
- extent to which the researcher would be comfortable in the role; and
- amount of time the researcher has available.

Non-participant observation

In *non-participant observation* the researcher does not interact with the research subject(s). Non-participant observation may be disguised or undisguised. For example, a teaching inspector observing how a teacher delivers a class is a non-participant observer. Typically, this is undisguised. Hotel inspectors are also non-participant observers, yet their remit is usually based on disguised or covert observation. This approach allows them to gain an accurate everyday experience of the hotel's customer service, standards, quality of food, etc.

Recording observation data

Prior to recording observational data, you need to be clear on the following points:

- What you are observing and the units of analysis.
- When the observation is likely to take place.
- How the data will be observed.
- Where the data will be observed.
- How the data will be recorded.

First, make sure that you are clear on exactly what it is that you are observing. For example, if conducting observation in the workplace, are you observing all employees, all management or one particular individual? Also, consider units of analysis. Will this feature both verbal and non-verbal communication, or possibly board meetings only?

Second, consider when the observation will take place. You may only intend observing your research subject for 15 minutes each day. However, this may not give you a true indication of how they react in their natural setting. So you will need to choose a sufficient period of time that allows you to do this.

Third, when considering how the data will be observed, you may wish to use video equipment, other researchers or a camera, although there is no substitute for the 'human element' of observation. In other words, make sure that you are present when observing your participants.

Next, consider where the data will be observed. Typically, this is often in the research subject's natural setting. If observing employees in the workplace, observation will of course take place in their everyday working environment.

Finally, you need to consider how you will record your data. A video camera can be used for observing and recording. You can also use a dictaphone to create a verbal record of the subject's actions. However, there is no substitute for taking accurate notes. A diary-type system that includes the date, time, location, observed activity and comments on your observation is an excellent way to record your data.

How to Conduct Fieldwork within Your Own Organization

If you are currently combining your study with work, then you may be in a position to conduct primary data collection within your own organization. All of the primary data collection methods are an option to you. Ostensibly, the one that lends itself particularly well is observation. For example, those researchers intent on observing employees within the natural setting are likely to find it difficult if they do not have any direct relationship with the respective organization. As noted in the previous section, make sure that you fully understand what you want to observe, along with units of analysis and how you will make an accurate recording of the data.

Conducting fieldwork within one's own organization can make for a very interesting research project. Of course, this means that you are likely to engage in participant observation which should take an undisguised approach. The first step in undertaking this type of research is to contact your immediate superior and fully explain the nature of your research and how it may benefit the company. Above all, you must first seek approval.

Cultural Issues and Data Collection

The most important issue when conducting international or cross-cultural research is to note the impact of cultural differences on your questionnaire design. Failure to do so could seriously affect both the reliability and validity of your research.

Concepts such as 'transport', 'trust' and 'family' may have different meanings in the UK, India or China. By way of illustration, let us say that you administered a questionnaire to both Chinese and British respondents that included the question 'How many members are there in your family?' In the UK, this is likely to be interpreted as immediate family. However, the same question directed to Chinese respondents may well be interpreted as also including extended family, such as aunts, uncles, cousins, etc. It is therefore vital that the researcher clearly explains such concepts if they are to generate accurate and clear answers.

Cross-cultural research

Brislin (1986) offers the following advice when undertaking cross-cultural research:

1. Use short sentences with one dominant idea per sentence.
2. Avoid metaphors and colloquialisms.
3. Use specific rather than general terms.
4. Avoid vague terms to describe a certain object or event.

Yu et al. (1993) illustrate the importance of methodological issues when conducting cross-cultural research. These methodological issues fall into six categories: functional equivalence, conceptual equivalence, instrument equivalence, sample selection, data collection methods and data analysis:

- *Functional equivalence.* All variables under investigation must perform the same functions in the different nations being studied. For example, Westerners may view cycling as a leisure activity; Chinese people may see it as a way of getting to work.
- *Conceptual equivalence.* Many concepts are culture bound. Obviously, these concepts are inappropriate for use on a cross-national basis. For example, the concept of *mianzi* (face) is arguably culturally specific to China.
- *Instrument equivalence.* When conducting cross-cultural research it is very difficult to develop equivalence in cross-cultural instruments. These are divided into two categories: etic (culture free) and emic (culture bound). Etic instruments can be employed in all or a number of nations, whereas emic instruments can only be used to study a phenomenon within the context of a single society. Emic is broken down into measurement and vocabulary equivalence:

  i. *Measurement.* Equally valid measures need to be employed. For example, instruments may have to be modified to take into account differences in demographics and literacy rates of respondents.
  ii. *Vocabulary equivalence.* The translation must be equivalent to the original language in which the instrument was developed.

- *Sample selection.* Cross-national research requires samples that are as closely comparable as possible. These samples should be matched on basic socio-economic, organizational and other vital characteristics, which may affect research findings.
- *Data collection methods.* These include the following issues:

(a) *Response equivalence*. Researchers should adopt uniform procedures in different countries in order to minimize variance due to data collection procedures.

(b) *Timing*. For purposes of comparison, data must be collected in different countries either simultaneously or within a reasonable timeframe.

(c) *Status and psychological issues*. In some cultures, the status discrepancy between interviewers and respondents may result in response bias.

(d) *Longitudinal versus cross-sectional data*. Most data collection is cross-sectional, or collected at the same point of time, as opposed to longitudinal, or gathered over a long period of time. This applies not only to cross-cultural research, but also to research in general.

- *Data analysis*. A more sophisticated range of analytical techniques have now been developed, and researchers must, if appropriate, apply those which can capture subtle differences in how concepts are recognized in different cultures.

Data Collection Using Online Methods

There are two main methods for collecting data online – email surveys and web-based surveys (Granello and Wheaton, 2004). The former we examined earlier in the chapter. In relation to *web-based surveys*, sometimes referred to as Internet survey instruments, I have seen a noticeable increase in the number of students using this approach to data collection. This is because web-based surveys offer a number of advantages. These include lower cost than other methods, ease of data entry, an increasing number of recipients likely to accept the format, and reduced response time. In addition, Anderson and Kanuka (2003) argued that online surveys offer a range of advantages over paper and telephone surveys. These include enhanced

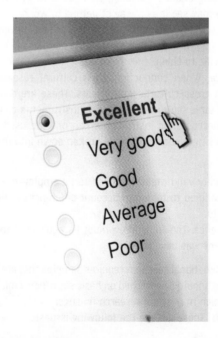

TABLE 6.8 Comparing online survey tools and the services they offer

Online survey tools	Questions per survey	Responses per survey	Number of question types	Price
SurveyMonkey	10	100	15	Free
SurveyGizmo	Unlimited	500 responses per month	19	Free
QuestionPro	10	100	N/A	Free

Source: www.surveymonkey.com, www.surveygizmo.com, www.questionpro.com (correct as of 6 August 2013).

presentation and higher response rates, while potential drawbacks include the following: response rates are affected by technical difficulties; representativeness of the sample is affected as not all respondents have access to or are able to complete the survey; security; and, finally, the number of respondents might be limited within the conditions of the agreement from the survey provider.

One of the most commonly used web-based survey applications is *SurveyMonkey*. For the majority of students, the free or 'Basic' plan is ideal as it allows up to a total of 100 responses to be viewed and ten questions per survey. Anything over 100 responses, then SurveyMonkey requires that you upgrade to a paid plan to view all of the responses. Features of the Basic plan include: up to 10 questions per survey, 100 viewable responses per survey, 15 types of questions, collect responses via web link, collect responses via email, embed survey on Facebook, view results as they are recorded, supports any language.

Many of the web-based survey applications offer free versions, although these tend to be limited in terms of the number of respondents and the features available. Table 6.8 provides a clear comparison of three of the more commonly used free web-based survey tools, the already discussed SurveyMonkey, SurveyGizmo and QuestionPro.

The likes of SurveyMonkey take away many of the time-consuming activities associated with more traditional data collection tools. They enable users to design surveys, collect responses and analyze survey results for free on the web. As indicated in Table 6.8, they also allow flexibility when it comes to types of questions. These include: rating scales, drop-down menus, multiple choice questions and open-ended queries. The layout of the survey and questions is also controllable by the user (Maxymuk, 2009).

Having conducted a cursory review of a number of online survey tools, those highlighted in Table 6.8 appear to be ideal for the majority of student researchers. Not only are they free, but they also allow for a reasonable number of responses per survey before charges are made. The majority of online web-based tools require users to sign up for a 7-day or 14-day free trial. Clearly, the advantage of those highlighted in the table is that there is no time restriction on free usage.

Online surveys are also being increasingly adopted by academic researchers. For example, Donelan et al. (2009) used the SurveyMonkey online tool when conducting a study on how women working in science, engineering and technology use online networking for career and professional development purposes. Interestingly, the authors considered a number of online tools before deciding to choose Survey-Monkey. Their reasons for choosing SurveyMonkey over alternative online tools included: a superior interface, for both designer and participant; it incorporated more features that assisted in the analysis of the data collected and encryption options to ensure confidentiality of the data; ease of use; it allowed anyone to participate who was emailed the relevant URL; and, finally, the tool automatically collated responses, enabled full responses or summaries to be viewed, and allowed them to be filtered as desired (Donelan et al., 2009: 98).

Ethical challenges associated with using web-based surveys

Even though carrying out a web-based survey has its advantages, you need to be aware of a number of ethical issues associated with this type of data collection. Although we examined ethics in Chapter 4, there are certain additional ethical concerns that need to be noted when conducting a web-based survey:

- Make sure to obtain consent from participants prior to study participation. For example, this can be achieved by asking them to tick a box linked to a statement that they agree to take part in the study and that they are over 18 years of age.
- Always provide participants with a 'submit data' button when the study is complete to make sure they understand and consent to their answers being submitted to the researcher.
- After the participant has submitted their responses, include a 'closing page' that includes the contact details of the researcher so that the participant can make contact should they have any outstanding issues.
- Assure all participants of the confidentiality of their responses, and take appropriate data storage security measures to reduce the possibility of any unauthorized people gaining access to the data.
- Make it clear how and where the research findings will be published.

(Adapted from Hewson, 2003: 293)

CASE STUDY — **Samsung and SurveyMonkey**

Increasingly, organizations are using online survey instruments such as SurveyMonkey. A number of leading multinational companies are using the services provided by SurveyMonkey. For example, Samsung, the Korean electronics giant, has teamed up with SurveyMonkey to undertake the *Samsung Electronics Social Media Satisfaction Survey*. The relatively short survey asks customers questions on social media:

1. Based on your recent social media experience are you more likely to contact Samsung support online instead of contacting 1-800-SAMSUNG?
   Yes   No
2. How would you rate your overall satisfaction in regards to your experience with Samsung social media? (Not product or service related issues.)
   Very satisfied / Satisfied / Average / Dissatisfied / Very dissatisfied

As you can see, this is a very short survey and is designed simply to gauge feedback on customers' experience with social media. In summary, there are a large number of online survey tools available to the student researcher. For a review of some of the leading tools, see Technology Tidbits (2010).

Triangulation of Data Collection

In this chapter we have examined the three main primary data collection methods in turn. Yet, as explained in Chapter 1, this does not mean that each one should be chosen in isolation. There is no reason why you cannot use data triangulation methods when gathering primary data. Triangulation has several advantages when conducting complex research. Denzin (1970) defined triangulation as 'collecting information from a diverse range of individuals and settings, using a variety of methods'. Easterby-Smith et al. (1991) identify four types of triangulation:

- *Data triangulation*, where data are collected at different times or from different sources in the study of a phenomenon.
- *Investigator triangulation*, where different researchers independently collect data on the same phenomenon and compare the results.
- *Methodological triangulation*, where both quantitative and qualitative methods of data collection are used.
- *Triangulation of theories*, where a theory is taken from one discipline and used to explain a phenomenon in another discipline.

A triangulation approach to data collection can reduce the risk of chance associations and of systematic biases (Strauss, 1987). Studies that use only one method are more vulnerable to errors linked to that particular method (e.g. loaded interview questions, or biased or untrue responses), whereas studies that use multiple methods, in which different types of data are collected, provide cross-data validity checks.

Finally, your decision to engage in data triangulation is likely to depend on your general research approach, access to data, previous research, and time and financial constraints.

Your Project Supervisor and Primary Data Collection

As always, your project supervisor should not be neglected when you are engaged in the process of collecting primary data. At this stage of your research you may be confronted by a number of issues, such as knowing how to formulate a suitable set of questions within a questionnaire, learning how to increase response rates, understanding how to deal with cultural differences, and simply deciding on which primary data collection method is the most appropriate for your particular study.

Your supervisor has probably supervised many students, so make sure you use his or her knowledge to your advantage. There are at least two reasons for seeking support and advice from your supervisor at this stage of your research: (1) you need to find the most appropriate data collection method(s), and (2) you need to check the suitability of your questions. The latter is particularly important. Very rarely do I come across a student with an ideal set of questions, whether for interview or questionnaire. Moreover, response rate is something that is usually considered in a reactive, rather than a proactive, way by students. For example, only when few replies to a questionnaire survey are generated do students consider why their response rate is so low. Your supervisor is there to help you to overcome these difficulties.

RESEARCH IN ACTION

British Airways plc

British Airways is one of the world's leading airlines. Given the competitive nature of the airlines market, customer satisfaction and the opinion of its stakeholders is key to defining British Airways' success. The company monitors customer satisfaction by a comprehensive and detailed survey, the Global Performance Monitor (GPM), which measures reaction to all aspects of its service throughout the entire journey experience. The survey was piloted extensively before it was fully launched to make sure that it was easy to understand and relevant to customers.

BA uses the on-board survey on all major routes across its network, including its franchises and subsidiaries. An indicator of the importance attached to the on-board survey is the response rate. Each year, British Airways receives over 70,000 customer comments – and it reads every one. The data gathered from the survey provides the company with invaluable information on customer satisfaction issues.

What happens to the data once it has been collected? British Airways recognizes the importance attached to disseminating customer feedback to all employees in the organization. For example, the results are available on the company's intranet, in its research library and through electronic presentations and display boards. In addition, customer insight is presented regularly to the directors and managers throughout the company. These are not the only research findings that are presented to senior management. British Airways also engages in research that measures customer satisfaction over time, the effectiveness of its advertising (advertising tracking), and performance issues across all functions of the business.

Finally, in order to ensure that their results are accurate, British Airways carefully plans the distribution of the survey to ensure that a random but fully representative sample of customers is achieved. One of the ways that the company checks this is to undertake follow-up interviews with customers.

Source: Adapted from www.BritishAirways.com

Questions

1. Why is it important for a company like British Airways to carry out customer research?
2. Why does British Airways need to continually carry out customer research?
3. In addition to customers, what other stakeholders do you think that British Airways should question? Give reasons for your answer.
4. Why is it important for British Airways to carry out customer research across all of its main routes?

Summary and Conclusion

In this chapter we have looked at primary data collection tools. The key points from this chapter are as follows:

- Primary data collection is collecting data yourself, rather than simply relying on existing data sources.
- The three main data collection tools include interviews, questionnaires and observation. These data collection tools can be carried out using a variety of different survey methods.
- There are three different types of interview method: structured, unstructured and semi-structured.
- There are two things to consider when conducting observational research. The first relates to the extent to which you wish your research subject(s) to be aware of your presence as a researcher. The second to make relates to the level of interaction with your research subject.
- The most important issue when conducting international or cross-cultural research is to note the impact of cultural differences in your questionnaire design.
- A triangulation approach to data collection can reduce the risk of chance associations and of systematic biases.

CASE STUDY — Types of Interview

Stephanie is a final-year International Business student. The focus of her research is on how charities are able to maintain donation levels during the current economic downturn. Stephanie is in the fortunate position of being able to interview six charity shop managers. These shops are located in a nearby local town, so minimal travel costs would be incurred. Stephanie believes that an exploratory study is appropriate for helping to answer her initial research questions. She has decided to carry out interviews with the shop managers and has made sure that ethical issues such as anonymity, confidentiality and informed consent have been addressed. Stephanie is aware that there are three different types of interview method, yet she is unsure which type will be the most appropriate for her chosen area of research.

Case study question

- Which type of interview is the most appropriate for Stephanie? Give reasons for your answer.

Trevor's broad research topic is consumer behaviour. More specifically, he intends to find out the process that consumers go through when they buy green products. A local supermarket has given Trevor permission to observe consumers' shopping habits during one Saturday afternoon's trading. However, although he is pleased to have been given access, Trevor is unsure about how he should go about observing shoppers. Direct observation will allow him to see at first hand the buying process that shoppers go through, although Trevor has yet to decide the extent to which he wishes his research subjects to be aware of his presence as a researcher. In addition, he is not clear on the extent to which he should interact with his research subjects.

Supervisor questions

1. Identify the observation options available to Trevor.
2. What are the advantages and disadvantages of each of these options?

COMMON QUESTIONS AND ANSWERS

1. How many interviews do I need to conduct in order to answer my research questions?

Answer: The number of interviews depends on the nature of your research approach and your research questions. For example, if you intend finding out employee satisfaction among employees in different departments, simply carrying out two interviews is not enough. Conversely, an in-depth case study on a small company may only require 3–5 interviews. This is because the firm may only employ a small number of staff.

2. How much time do I need to devote to collecting my data?

Answer: This depends on a number of factors. First, the type of data collection tools you are using. Remember that with qualitative research such as conducting interviews, it can take a great deal of time to gain informed consent from participants and to prepare for the interview. Conducting a questionnaire survey also takes time.

3. Can I use students to make up my sample?

Answer: This is fine in principle, but it largely depends on the nature of your study. For example, let's say that you wanted to conduct research on higher education in the UK. By using a sample made up of university students, your sample is not representative of society as a whole and could lead to biased feedback. On the other hand, students are often a convenient, inexpensive way of conducting research. So the possible application of this type of research method is not something that should be discounted altogether. Once again, if your objective is not to generalize to the wider population, but to carry out a pilot study or perhaps an in-depth case study, then this may provide justification for using a student sample.

References

Anderson, T. and Kanuka, H. (2003) *e-Research: Methods, Strategies and Issues*. Boston, MA: Allyn & Bacon.

Brislin, R.W. (1986) 'A culture general assimilator: Preparation for various types of sojourns', *International Journal of Intercultural Relations*, 10 (2): 215–234.

Claes, R. and Heymans, M. (2008) 'HR professionals' views on work motivation and retention of older workers: A focus group study', *Career Development International*, 3 (2): 95–111.

Collis, J. and Hussey, R. (2009) *Business Research* (3rd edn). Basingstoke: Palgrave Macmillan.

Denzin, N.K. (1970) *The Research Act: A Theoretical Introduction to Sociological Methods*. Chicago: Aldine.

Dillman, D.A. (1978) *Mail and Telephone Surveys: The Total Design Method*. New York: John Wiley & Sons.

Donelan, H., Herman, C. and Kear, K. (2009) 'Patterns of online networking for women's career development', *Career Development*, 24 (2): 92–111.

Easterby-Smith, M., Thorpe, R. and Lowe, A. (1991) *Management Research: An Introduction*. London: Sage.

Granello, D.H. and Wheaton, J.E. (2004) 'Online data collection: Strategies for research', *Journal of Counselling & Development*, 82 (4): 382–393.

Hewson, C. (2003) 'Conducting research on the internet', *The Psychologist*, 16 (6): 290–293.

Hussey, J. and Hussey, R. (1997) *Business Research*. Basingstoke: Macmillan.

Kincaid, H.W. and Bright, M. (1957) 'Interviewing the business elite', *American Journal of Sociology*, 63 (3), Nov: 304–311.

McClelland, S.B. (1994) 'Training needs assessment data-gathering methods: Part 1, survey questionnaires', *Journal of European Industrial Training*, 18 (1): 22–26.

Maxymuk, J. (2009) 'Online tools', *The Bottom Line: Managing Library Finances*, 22 (4): 135–138.

Robson, C. (1993) *Real World Research*. Oxford: Blackwell.

Schaefer, D.R. and Dillman, D.A. (1998) 'Development of a standard e-mail methodology: Results of an experiment', *Public Opinion Quarterly*, 62: 378–397.

Strauss, A. (1987) *Qualitative Analysis for Social Scientists*. Cambridge: Cambridge University Press.

Technology Tidbits (2010) 'Top 10 sites for creating surveys/polls', http://cyber-kap.blogspot.co.uk/2010/08/top-10-sites-for-creating-surveyspolls.html, accessed 6 August 2013.

Tse, A.C.B. (1998) 'Comparing response rate, response speed and response quality of two methods of sending questionnaires: E-mail vs mail', *Journal of the Marketing Research Society*, 40 (1): 353–361.

Yu, J., Keown, C.F. and Jacobs, C.W. (1993) 'Attitude scale methodology: Cross-cultural implications', *Journal of International Consumer Marketing*, 6 (2): 45–64.

Zikmund, W.G. (1997) *Business Research Methods* (5th edn). Fort Worth, TX: The Dryden Press.

Further Reading

Fielding, N., Lee, R.M. and Blank, G. (2008) *The SAGE Handbook of Online Research Methods*. London: Sage, pp. 177–194.

Goldie, J. and Pritchard, J. (1981) 'Interview methodology – comparison of three types of interview: One-to-one, group and telephone interviews', *Aslib Proceedings*, 33 (2): 62–66.

King, N. and Horrocks, C. (2012) *Interviews in Qualitative Research*. London: Sage.

Mikecz, R. (2012) 'Interviewing elites: Addressing methodological issues', *Qualitative Inquiry*, 18 (6): 482–493.

Quinlan, C. (2011) *Business Research Methods*. Andover: Cengage Learning.

Saunders, M.N.K. and Lewis, P. (2011) *Doing Research in Business and Management: An Essential Guide to Planning Your Project*. Harlow: Prentice Hall.

7
Using secondary data

Introduction

In the preceding chapter we looked at primary data and associated collection methods. In this chapter we continue the theme of data collection, by examining secondary data.

In contrast to primary data, secondary data are data that have been collected by other researchers. Secondary data encompass a range of different sources. We explored some of these sources in Chapter 3 – general reports, theses, newspapers, academic journals, textbooks, Internet websites, abstracts, catalogues, dictionaries, bibliographies, encyclopaedias and citation indices.

Most Business and Management students rely heavily on secondary data when conducting their research. To be sure, in some cases it can be used exclusively within a research project. Conversely, other students may prefer their project to be dominated by primary data collection, with secondary data receiving limited attention. How does one make a decision on the application of secondary data? Well, a key aim of this chapter is to help you to evaluate the extent to which secondary data may feature in your research.

This chapter begins by defining the nature of secondary data. I then examine reasons that may lead you to base your project entirely on secondary data. At one level, this is often determined by the assessment regulations laid down by your university or college. However, other factors may also influence your decision. We examine these later on in the chapter. Next, the advantages and disadvantages of secondary data are presented. Unsurprisingly, time is cited as a major advantage. The plethora of electronic sources available has made searching for secondary data all the easier. Nevertheless, there are notable disadvantages, and these receive similar attention.

Non-native English speakers and those who are able to read languages other than English will be able to use foreign language sources. This of course applies to many international students. Thus, I have included a section in the chapter that highlights some of the issues surrounding the usage of foreign language sources.

The availability of secondary data is a real concern to student researchers. Undoubtedly, your institution's library will contain a wealth of sources. The degree to which these correspond with your research depends on the nature of your topic. In some cases, you may need to access more specialized data. I will therefore make recommendations as to how this can be achieved.

The concluding part of the chapter examines the evaluation and presentation of secondary data. The ability to evaluate secondary data is essential, not least to determine the degree of reliability. Also, if you have amassed a huge amount of data, how do you know what to include and what to omit? One way is to consider the following data evaluation factors – purpose, scope, authority, audience and format. Addressing questions associated with each of these five factors should make the evaluation process easier. Next, I provide a relatively brief overview of how to present secondary data. Often, it can be presented in its original form, or you may wish to present the data in your own way. As there is very little distinction between presenting secondary and primary data, I pay greater attention to presenting data in Chapters 9 and 10. Finally, we examine how to link primary data with secondary data.

What Are Secondary Data?

As noted earlier, secondary data are data that have been collected by other researchers. Of course, the researchers could be an individual, a group or a body working on behalf of an organization. Secondary data include everything from annual reports, promotional material, parent company documentation, published case descriptions, magazines, journal articles and newspaper reports to government printed sources.

Most research begins with secondary data analysis. The outcome of this analysis usually dictates whether or not the researcher will engage in primary research. For example, if you determine that there is a limited amount of secondary data on your chosen topic, you may be more inclined to conduct primary research. Conversely, if a plethora of data exists, then you may not feel the need to engage in primary data collection. The amount of existing data available is just one reason that may influence your decision to focus solely on secondary data. I discuss other reasons in the next section.

Reasons for Basing Your Research Project Entirely on Secondary Data

There are two main reasons that may lead you to base your entire research project on secondary data – the nature of your topic and your institution's assessment regulations.

Certain research topics are more likely to warrant a greater emphasis on secondary data. For example, let us say that you intend conducting a comparative study into gross domestic product (GDP) growth rates among European Union states. Given the large amount of secondary data on this particular topic, the likelihood is that you may not feel the necessity to collect primary data. You may argue that you are perfectly capable of producing a comprehensive piece of research without the need for primary research. This may be true. Nevertheless, your intentions may not be workable due to your institution's assessment regulations.

Some universities and colleges insist that primary data must feature within a research project, although this tends to be more applicable to postgraduate rather than undergraduate programmes. Therefore, if your institution permits projects solely based on secondary data, this may influence you to go down this route. If in doubt, check with your academic institution.

There are other reasons that may influence your decision. Arguably, these are less significant, but they still need to be considered. These can be summarized as:

- your choice of research design;
- whether you are undertaking international or cross-cultural research; and
- whether you are unable to conduct primary research.

First, your choice of research design may influence your decision whether or not to conduct a project based exclusively on secondary data. If, for example, you plan on undertaking a longitudinal study over several years, this will not be feasible using primary research. However, you may find that there are existing longitudinal studies relevant to your chosen topic. This would allow analysis, perhaps even comparative analysis, of existing studies.

Another example is using a case study research design based entirely on secondary data. Let us say that you are concerned with a comparative analysis of the internationalization strategies of two of the UK's leading supermarkets – Tesco and Sainsbury's. You may argue that existing comparative studies have already been undertaken by other researchers, in which case the nature of your research is to compare and contrast existing data.

Realistically, financial and time constraints make undertaking international or cross-cultural research difficult for student researchers. Nevertheless, this does not mean that it has to be ruled out altogether. An abundance of existing secondary sources (perhaps across different countries) may mean that you are in a position to conduct your research. However, you need to be cautious of potential differences in how studies are conducted and analyzed across cultures.

You may feel that an inability to collect primary data means that you have no option but to focus entirely on secondary data. For example, a primary study into pay awards among multinational company directors is likely to be beyond even the most dedicated student! Yet, if several organizations publish these data, you might ask yourself – 'Why do I need to conduct primary research?'

Finally, I am of the view that a perfectly good undergraduate research project can be written based solely on secondary data. True, certain topics are best suited to primary data. But if a suitable amount of secondary data exists, there is no reason why a project based exclusively on secondary data cannot be undertaken. This does not mean that using completely secondary sources is a 'soft option'. The real challenge for students is collecting, analyzing and interpreting someone else's data so that it corresponds to their own research problem.

Business and Secondary Data

Organizations also need to decide how to incorporate secondary data into their research. For example, if a company is about to launch a new product, it will run a market survey to collect primary data and gauge customer reactions; if it wants to evaluate general economic activity in an area, it will use secondary data prepared by the government (Waters, 1997: 73).

In business, there are two broad classifications of secondary data – *internal* and *external* data. Examples of internal sources include customer records, sales invoices, previous market research reports and minutes from board meetings. External sources tend to be more varied. These include everything from competitors' promotional brochures to government reports.

Classifying secondary data on the basis of internal and external sources makes sense when considering an organizational perspective. Yet, how does this relate to the student researcher? Arguably, a one-size-fits-all definition is neither practical nor possible. The majority of students do not have the privilege of access to internal company data. Moreover, not all students engage in organizationally based research. Therefore, I propose a 'student-based' classification of secondary data later in this chapter.

Small organizations have a propensity to use mainly secondary data when conducting market research. For example, this may include information from trade magazines, articles in the local press and internal data. One of the reasons for this is that many do not have the resources to engage in primary research. Where primary research is undertaken, this tends to be conducted on an informal basis.

Unlike small firms, large organizations often buy in secondary data, or mailing lists, from specialized agencies. To illustrate, let us say that a tyre manufacturer wishes to promote their tyres to French car dealers. If no published data are available, then one option is to buy the data from a specialized agency. This is costly, of course, and does not guarantee a high response rate. Other potential problems are associated with buying in data. First, secondary data soon become out of date. This is also a concern with internal data such as customer records. Relying on such data can help maintain close customer relationships, but it needs to be updated regularly.

Second, although buying in data can be potentially rewarding, the data have to be correct. There are likely to be literally thousands of data lists available. Companies that fail to buy from a reputable source may find that the data do not meet their expectations, particularly in terms of reliability and validity.

Third, secondary data bought for the purpose of direct marketing activities are unlikely to be exclusive to one organization. This is especially true in business-to-business markets, where several companies compete for a small number of customers.

In sum, for many organizations intent on promoting their products and services, secondary data can be a useful way to target potential customers. However, such data have several limitations: they soon become dated; it is sometimes difficult to verify the credibility of a source; and competitors have access to the same data.

Reliance on the Internet as a Secondary Data Source

In the last section we looked at how businesses might use secondary data. Of course, often an important source of secondary data for both businesses and students is the Internet. First, businesses may use it as a vehicle for gathering information from competitors' websites, accessing industry data or assessing potential environmental threats to the business. Most businesses are also aware of the importance of not overly relying on the Internet. Other, more traditional, secondary sources are equally important. These may include printed business directories, government reports and, of course, internal data.

Similarly, I am certain that the Internet is already an important source of information in your research. An increasingly common theme I have witnessed in research projects is overemphasis on Internet-based sources. This over-reliance is likely to have a negative impact on the reliability of your research, especially if your chosen sources are unknown and cannot be tested for their credibility. As we have established, the Internet has brought many benefits to researchers, but the increasing emphasis on Internet sources by some students is a concern. Not only does it mean that attention is being paid to potentially unreliable websites, but also that more traditional sources, such as books, are sometimes being excluded from their research.

The Distinction Between Literature Review and Secondary Data Analysis

By now, you should be aware of the role that secondary sources play in conducting your literature review. However, secondary data can also form a major, if not exclusive, part of your analysis. For those of you focusing your research entirely on secondary data, you need to make a clear distinction in your research between your literature review and analysis. Students sometimes find this difficult. In essence, your literature review is likely to be one or two chapters and will come before your secondary analysis. Unlike your literature review, secondary data analysis may involve using previously published survey data as the focal point for your analysis. Alternatively, the main focus might be on a particular case or multiple cases which could also feature published survey data. In short, either of these approaches is helpful in maintaining a distinction between the literature review and analysis chapters.

Whereas your literature review may *describe* your chosen survey, and compare and contrast similar studies, your secondary analysis is likely to involve a detailed analysis of your chosen survey. Typically, this might form the basis of one chapter – namely your analysis and results.

Remember to justify your choice of survey. Reasons might include: the reputation of the source, the contemporary nature of the study, the sample size, or simply that it is the only recognizable study conducted in your area of research.

Classifying Secondary Data

Secondary data can be classified in a number of different ways. A distinction can be made on the basis of format and intended audience. First, secondary data can be classified into electronic and written formats. Although this distinction has become blurred in recent years, it still applies to the majority of students engaged in research. Second, these groups can be further divided into subgroups according to their intended target audience. Usually, this means an exclusively academic or commercial audience. Figure 7.1 illustrates the classification of secondary data. Although

FIGURE 7.1 Classification of secondary data

it is by no means exhaustive, it classifies the main sources of secondary data used by students. Now, let us begin to look at each of these classifications in turn, starting with electronic data.

Electronic format

'Electronic data' refers to data presented in electronic format, such as Internet websites. As noted in this chapter, Internet websites are an increasingly popular source of literature for students, but the Internet is by no means the only source of electronic data. Other potential sources for you to consider are DVDs, videos and audio media. These can include an organization's in-house training video, promotional materials for a multinational company, an audio recording of a radio interview with a company director or even an audio book. Although the latter may seem an unlikely source for your research, occasionally you may find invaluable data that are only available in one particular format.

The main advantages of electronic data are that they save time because they are easily accessible, and can be easily stored. Indeed, gone are the days when student researchers were forced to keep several lever arch files of relevant articles. I remember them well!

Table 7.1 provides a list of useful government websites, multilateral organizations and general business-related sites that prove popular with business students. In addition, the American Marketing Association (2013) provides a comprehensive list of electronic data sources.

Electronic format – commercial audience

Electronic sources geared towards a commercial audience include multilateral organization and government websites. The former are particularly useful for students

TABLE 7.1 Useful electronic data sources

Source	Web address	Summary of information
World Trade Organization	www.wto.org	Data on WTO member states
OECD	www.oecd.org	Statistics on member states
International Monetary Fund	www.imf.org	Publishes a range of commercial and financial data
European Union	www.europa.eu	Statistical information on member states
Financial Times	www.ft.com	Information on financial markets
The Economist	www.economist.com	Economic data and articles
Business Week	www.businessweek.com	Provider of global business news
British Broadcasting Corporation	www.bbc.co.uk/news	Daily news on the UK and worldwide
Dun & Bradstreet	www.dnb.com	Provides global information on businesses
World Bank	www.worldbank.org	Country data and analysis on the global economy
The Guardian	www.guardian.co.uk	A leading UK newspaper

engaged in research on economics, the business environment and international trade. For instance, the WTO site contains a wealth of information on these and many other subjects.

Electronic format – academic audience

Electronic data targeted at a mainly academic audience include academic journal articles and conference papers. These are an invaluable source of data for students for the simple reason that they are aimed at a predominantly academic audience and are likely to contain many of the sections that will feature in your research project, e.g. literature review, methodology, conclusion, and so on.

Written format

Written data refer to data that are printed in hard-copy format. The main examples of secondary data are the more 'traditional' published sources, such as textbooks and academic journals. Ostensibly, we will continue to see a shift away from traditional publishing to electronic formats. This has certainly been the case in terms of publishing and accessing academic journals in recent years. Although your university or college library is likely to hold both electronic and hard copies of academic journals, once again accessing them electronically saves time and is easier to organize.

Written format – commercial audience

Written data produced for a commercial audience are generally published for convenient and functional purposes. For example, a building firm is likely to produce sales invoices, customer records and sales figures. Although the company is legally required to keep such data for accounting purposes, it is also a convenient way to develop customer relationships through direct marketing and advertising. Furthermore, such internal data can aid the organization with strategic development over the short, medium and long term.

Business data are also produced by publishers such as Dun & Bradstreet. Although such data tend to be produced in both hard-copy and electronic format, many companies still prefer hard copy. Organizations and governments can use the data produced to target potential customers and/or business partners.

Written format – academic audience

Academic data in written format still tend to include textbooks and lecture notes. The former are an essential source of data for students, as modules are often structured on a particular key text. Both textbooks and lecture notes can make worthy contributions to your research. For example, many textbooks feature contemporary case studies. You may decide that information from these cases can be used as part of your secondary analysis.

The Advantages of Secondary Data

There are several advantages of using secondary data. First, you will find that the majority of data are available through your institution's library at no or very little cost. Second, in contrast to primary data, secondary data can be relatively straightforward to collect. Detailed advantages include:

Less resource-intensive

In general, secondary data are a convenient and cost-effective source of information for the student researcher. Given that much of your secondary data are likely to be readily available, accessing information this way will save time when it comes to analyzing and interpreting your findings. Obviously, conducting primary research involves a great deal of time to prepare, implement, collect and interpret results. By focusing on secondary data, you may be able to collect and analyze much larger data sets, like those published by an organization such as Mintel.

Can allow for comparative analysis

Another advantage of secondary data is that they can be compared to your primary findings. By comparing your primary data with your secondary sources, you can determine the extent to which you agree or disagree with existing studies. For example, if you consider a study into car ownership, you may find that a national study suggests a possible downturn in the market. However, a questionnaire survey of car owners in your area may generate contradictory data.

Secondary data also enable cross-cultural or international comparative research, as they help to overcome the obvious limitations associated with primary data collection. The Economist Intelligence Unit (EIU) provides country data that can be used exclusively or on a comparative basis.

Ideal for longitudinal studies

I have already noted that secondary sources provide students with an opportunity to engage in longitudinal research. This is a clear advantage. Much of the data collected by governments are compiled over several decades. For instance, census data and data published on the Retail Price Index (RPI) can be analyzed over many years. This lends itself well to a longitudinal study. On the other hand, you still need to be wary of how such data relate to your research problem. For example, census data are ideal if the nature of your research is to examine demographic change and/or population growth, but are unsuitable if you want to explore customers' purchasing decisions, for instance.

Easily accessible for other researchers

Finally, secondary data facilitate access for other researchers interested in your area of research. Many researchers rely on secondary data. Therefore, by making reference to secondary sources you are likely to aid other researchers engaged in developing their own research.

The Disadvantages of Secondary Data

There are numerous disadvantages associated with secondary data. The main thing to consider is that secondary data should not be used exclusively simply as a means of saving time and money! Also: data may be outdated, there may be a dearth of data relating to your study, and the data may be unreliable.

Access is difficult and costly

Often, you will find that high-quality and reliable secondary data are difficult to access. Examples include certain types of government data and internally produced organizational data. The main reason that access to this type of data is generally restricted is largely due to its sensitive nature. Normally, the only way to get hold of such valuable data is if you work for the organization that produces them. Even then, accessing such data can still prove difficult!

The cost of accessing data is also a disadvantage to student researchers. On many occasions students have told me that they have found an excellent report online, but obtaining a copy usually involves a subscription fee or a sizeable one-off payment.

May not match your research problem

You may find it problematic to find secondary data that correspond to your study. For instance, I remember supervising a student who wished to analyze the development of ecotourism in Zanzibar. Needless to say, the amount of secondary data on the subject can best be described as 'narrow'. In circumstances like these, where the nature of the topic is highly specialized, it is often essential to conduct primary research.

Another problem is that although data may appear to correspond to your research, sometimes you may find quite distinct differences in how key variables have been defined. Similarly, a different set of measures may have been employed.

You may believe you have a sufficient amount of data, but remember that secondary data are data that have been collected by other individuals or organizations for their own purposes. Such data may not therefore answer your research questions.

Difficult to verify reliability

In general, the ability to determine whether or not secondary data are reliable is largely down to the source. Certainly, academic journals offer high levels of reliability, as do established business publications such as the *Harvard Business Review* and *The Economist*. The main problem tends to be with the more obscure publications and websites.

Sometimes, it can be argued, the limitation associated with reliability can be overcome by using a varied range of secondary sources. By way of illustration, in their article into annual working hours in Britain, Gall and Allsop (2007: 801) justify the use of secondary data by making reference to the absence of standardized and longitudinal data. In addition, the authors also include a wide range of secondary sources:

> The material for this research is derived from a number of secondary sources, such as the publications of the Advisory, Conciliation and Arbitration Service (ACAS), Incomes Data Services (IDS), Industrial Relations Services (IRS), Labour Research Department (LRD) and the Institute of Personnel Management (IPM)/Chartered Institute of Personnel Management (CIPD) as well as coverage of salient developments in the quality press like the *Financial Times* and *The Guardian* and among regional daily broadsheets. Whilst there are a number of weaknesses in the robustness of the data generated using such a method, this data can help supplement other data – which itself is not without weaknesses – so that a fuller, multi-component picture of annual hours can be built up.

The secondary data cited in Gall and Allsop's article may not be familiar to you. These include publications from public sector bodies, professional bodies, and regional and national newspapers.

Not in a manageable form

Data that have experienced little, if any, processing are referred to as *raw data*, whereas data that have received some form of processing or summarizing are known as compiled or *cooked data*. For example, a successful dot.com company selling books and music CDs online might collect huge volumes of sales-related raw data each day, but such data are not very useful until they have been analyzed, interpreted and presented in a manageable form. Once processed, this type of data might be used for analyzing sales trends, launching a targeted sales promotion campaign or simply analyzing the most profitable lines. Tables 7.2 and 7.3 show raw data and cooked data respectively.

TABLE 7.2 An example of raw data

Transaction no.	Amount (£)
101293	42.96
101294	20.99
101295	11.50
101296	13.75

TABLE 7.3 An example of processed (cooked) data

Date	Daily sales achieved (£)	Daily sales target (£)	Difference (+/−)
Mon 23 March	35,000	34,750	+250
Tues 24 March	18,345	22,950	−4,605
Weds 25 March	17,234	14,750	+2,484
Thurs 26 March	29,108	28,250	+858
Fri 27 March	22,400	21,750	+650
Sat 28 March	39,100	38,250	+850
Sun 29 March	12,240	11,500	+740
TOTAL for week	173,427	172,200	+1,227

A disadvantage of raw data is that researchers need to allocate time to processing and summarizing the data. On the other hand, a major advantage is that the data can be processed in a way that suits the researcher. Table 7.2 is an extract from a daily list of sales transactions for an independent food retailer. Obviously, in its current, unprocessed, form it provides very little information for the retailer. Clearly, the only information that the list does provide is the value of each transaction, and its respective transaction number. Table 7.3 shows how the food retailer might process weekly sales transactions. As you can see, the data have been presented in a much more manageable form. Moreover, it features some interesting information that can be used to aid inventory levels, marketing and budgeting. The most notable feature is the extent to which sales have fluctuated over the course of the week, and of course the fact that the retailer has exceeded its weekly target.

Comparability

One final disadvantage with secondary data is comparability. I have already mentioned that an advantage of using secondary data is that data can be compared with your primary findings. However, if you are engaged in exclusively secondary data, then this option is not open to you. Of course, your secondary data may include both qualitative and quantitative data, e.g. a country report published by the World Trade Organization that includes quantitative statistical data such as GDP figures *and* qualitative analysis in the form of quotations from leading economics experts.

In one sense, applying a wide range of secondary sources is a good thing, but you must ensure that you can compare your findings on an equal footing. Comparability is often a problem when integrating and examining data from different sources. Differences may occur in the following aspects:

- *The reliability of the information.* In developing countries, where a substantial proportion of the population may be illiterate or difficult to access, population or economic data may be based on estimates or rudimentary data collection procedures.
- *The frequency of studies.* The frequency with which surveys are undertaken may also vary from country to country. While in the UK a population census is undertaken every 10 years, in some countries it may be more than 30 years since a complete census was undertaken.
- *Measurement units.* These are not necessarily equivalent from country to country.
- *Differences in circumstance.* Even where data may seem comparable, there may be differences in the circumstances that lie behind the data. If a researcher was to undertake a comparison of GNP (gross national product) per capita data from Sweden and the UK, the information may prove misleading. The high per capita income figures for Sweden, which suggest a high standard of living, do not take account of the much higher levels of Swedish taxation linked to the state's provision of social services.

(Wilson, 2006: 58)

The Usage of Foreign Language Sources

If you have the capability of reading foreign language sources, then this is clearly an advantage as it allows you to consult a wider range of secondary sources. In addition, if you are an international student, then you are likely to be familiar with secondary sources in your home country that might prove useful for your research. For example, given that one of my areas of research is the internationalization of Chinese brands, I tend to supervise several Chinese students. I always stress to them the importance of consulting both English and Chinese sources. This is partly because some secondary sources from different countries make for an interesting comparison, but also using secondary data from different countries can help to improve the validity of your results.

How do I reference foreign language sources? To some extent, conventions here vary depending on the referencing system. Often, non-English sources are treated the same, with direct quotes translated into English. If you are translating the text yourself, one way to illustrate this is by inserting 'translation by the author' in brackets after the quote. For example: 'Wong, 2012: 14, translation by the author.' Again, you will probably find that there are subtle variations of this approach, so if in doubt check with your project supervisor. In terms of how to reference the source in your reference list, typically, the reference will include the title of the book or article in the original language, followed by the English translation in brackets.

Evaluating Secondary Data

You may be in the position of having gathered an abundance of secondary data. Yet, on what basis do you decide what to include and what to omit from your research? Blumberg et al. (2008: 319) list five factors that should be taken into account when evaluating secondary data – purpose, scope, authority, audience and format. Table 7.4 summarizes the critical questions that a researcher might ask when evaluating secondary information sources. The questions are associated with each of these factors.

Purpose

The main point to consider here is the extent to which the purpose relates to your own research. It does not necessarily have to be a 'perfect fit'. If, for example, you are conducting research into cultural differences between Japanese and US consumers, you may find that a similar study focusing on US and South Korean consumers may be of relevance. One might argue that as South Korea and Japan are both South-East

TABLE 7.4   Evaluating information sources (adapted from Blumberg et al., 2008: 315)

Evaluating factor	Questions
Purpose	• Why does the information exist? • What is its purpose? • Does it achieve its purpose? • How does its purpose affect the type and bias of the information presented? • How does it relate to the purpose of my own research?
Scope	• How old is the information? • How often is it updated? • How much information is available? • What are the criteria for inclusion? • If applicable, what geographic area, time period or language does it cover? • How does the information presented compare with similar information sources?
Authority	• What are the credentials of the author, institution or organization sponsoring the information?
Audience	• To whom is the information targeted? • What level of knowledge or experience is assumed? • How does the intended audience affect the type and bias of the information?
Format	• How quickly can you find the required information? • How easy to use is the information source? • Is there an index? • Is the information downloadable into a spreadsheet or word-processing program if desired?

Asian states, there may be cultural similarities. Hence, you may not wish to discard the research in the first instance.

Scope

Scope covers such qualities as the age and the amount of data available, whether the information is up to date, how frequently data are updated, what period of time they cover, how information is presented, etc.

Authority

A more well-known and credible authority on a topic is likely to be more reliable than an unknown source. Assessing the credibility of the authority will allow you to determine whether or not the data warrant inclusion in your research.

Audience

The intended audience is a good indicator of the nature and quality of the data. Classifying your data on the basis of commercial and academic content can help you to form a judgement as to its appropriateness for your research.

Format

The format of the data (e.g. whether on hard copy or in an electronic version) dictates the ease with which you can access and interpret the data. Does the layout make it easy for you to find what you need, for example? Can you consult an index? Of course, if the data are vital to your research, you will want to use them irrespective of format.

In sum, it is sometimes difficult to evaluate secondary data. The source may be relatively unknown – even your supervisor may not be aware of its existence! My advice is to try to use secondary data from established sources, which can be verified in some way. In general, if a source is unknown and cannot be verified, then it is probably best avoided.

Presenting Secondary Data

Essentially, two factors are likely to determine how you present your secondary data within your research project. First, whether your data are qualitative or quantitative. Second, whether your data are raw data, or cooked data. If the latter, then you may be in a position to present the data in their original format. For example, if the

TABLE 7.5   FDI by type of investment

Type of investment	1999		2002	
	No. of projects	Value (£m)	No. of projects	Value (£m)
Joint venture	60,253	65,128.5	72,821	88,456.3
WFOE*	5,430	18,676.2	9,073	27,710.5
Total	65,683	83,804.7	81,894	116,166.8

*Wholly foreign-owned enterprise

Financial Times published a pie chart showing a breakdown of the UK's exports by industry, you could probably reproduce this in its original format, providing it is properly sourced, of course. However, if the article only quotes export figures, then you would need to consider presenting the data in your own way.

Table 7.5 illustrates the use of secondary data in its original format. You do not need to concern yourself with the actual topic. The point I am trying to make here is that tables, charts and graphs are ideally suited to many research projects. Indeed, they can form an important part of your secondary analysis.

Presenting secondary data also includes qualitative data. Let us say that you intend analyzing secondary data in the form of leading economists' views on the global economy. As you are analyzing qualitative secondary data, you may illustrate their views by quoting them directly.

There are numerous ways of analyzing qualitative and quantitative secondary data. In reality, many of these techniques are equally applicable to primary data analysis. I will therefore devote greater attention to this topic in Chapters 9 and 10.

Your Project Supervisor and Secondary Data

When a student wishes to see me to discuss concerns over secondary data, it is usually for one of two reasons. First, the student has been unable to locate sufficient secondary sources. Second, they have gathered copious amounts of data but are unsure what to give prominence to in their research. In this chapter, I have covered both these points at some length.

By now, you should be aware of just how important your supervisor is to your research project. This includes their advice on overcoming potential difficulties with secondary data. Your supervisor can provide invaluable advice on how to evaluate your data, and may also be able to recommend secondary sources that you have not yet considered. Moreover, if they feel that your topic provides access to a sparse amount of secondary data, they may be able to offer suggestions about primary data collection. Once again, when you feel yourself 'hitting a brick wall' with your research, do not forget to consult your project supervisor.

How to Link Primary and Secondary Data

If you intend including primary and secondary data in your research project, then it can sometimes be difficult to know how to link these two main sources of data. As previously noted, one way is to compare your primary data with secondary data from books, journal articles, published statistics and other sources. Part of this comparison should involve the analysis and interpretation of data. For example, let us say a UK Government report states that the main reason why joint ventures in China fail is due to cultural differences. Yet, analysis of your primary findings indicates that the leading cause is due to a failure to agree strategic objectives. The key question here is why the difference between the primary and secondary data? To be a good researcher you must compare, analyze and interpret both primary and secondary data and not fall into the trap of simply describing the data.

Secondary data can also be used to increase the credibility of your primary research findings. For instance, if your primary findings support the view of leading authors in the field, one argument that you could make is that your results are likely to be both valid and credible.

──Research in Action ─────────────────────────

Examining sources of secondary data

In the academic article detailed below, an overview is provided on the sources of secondary data used in business ethics research. Irrespective of the topic, much of the content is very useful as it examines sources of secondary data which could equally apply to other areas of business research.

Cowton, C.J. (1998) 'The use of secondary data in business ethics research', *Journal of Business Ethics*, 17 (4): 423–434

The aim of Cowton's (1998) paper is to promote the interest of business ethics researchers in using secondary data, either in place of or as a complement to primary data. The article examines both sources and usage of secondary data, although the details below centre on sources of secondary data. In short, the author is making a call to business ethicists to pay greater consideration to secondary data.

In the article, Cowton highlights a number of sources of secondary data, namely: *governmental and regulatory bodies, the press, companies, other academic researchers* and *private sources*. First, the author suggests that a source of material of considerable interest to business ethicists is the legal system. Examples given here include published legal judgments, while regulatory bodies such as the Advertising Standards Authority (ASA) in the UK publish reports which are often easily accessible to the researcher.

In terms of companies, the researcher stresses that much material is publicly available, particularly in the annual report and accounts. This includes the Chairman's statement that can be analyzed using tools such as content analysis (this is something we cover in Chapter 10). Reference is made to quantitative, particularly company financial, data as an easily accessible source, as this information is now published on a number of databases.

(Continued)

(Continued)

The researcher suggests that both the press and media in general are useful sources of data. Newspaper articles can be used as sources. Also, in some articles you will find opinion polls; the advantage of these is that they distance the researcher from the evaluations. However, it is worth noting that newspaper articles should be treated with care as they have not gone through a peer review process.

Other academic researchers include data by other scholars. Unlike newspaper articles, academic articles are peer reviewed. In addition, there is scope to undertake meta-analysis. This is 'quantitative analysis of a group of studies that investigates the same research questions'. One of the benefits of meta-analysis is that it generates a large sample. One issue for the researcher, though, is the need to perhaps negotiate with the original researcher in order to gain access to the dataset.

Finally, private sources are another potential source of secondary data. Here, the author suggests that these include companies' internal reports and memoranda; this is in addition to organizational archives. However, for the student researcher there are clearly obvious difficulties in accessing such sources. Cowton makes a similar point by acknowledging the potential difficulty of negotiating access.

Cowton's (1998) article is helpful to researchers as it considers a number of different sources of secondary data. A useful exercise would be to look at the entire article, as it also discusses using secondary data. Once again, although the paper focuses on business ethics, many of the author's points are equally applicable to other areas of business.

Summary and Conclusion

This chapter has examined how secondary data can be incorporated into your study. It defined what is meant by secondary data and considered the advantages and disadvantages of using secondary data in your research. It also examined how to evaluate and present secondary data. Here are the key points from this chapter:

- Secondary data are data that have been collected by other researchers.
- Secondary data can be classified into electronic and written formats, and subdivided into commercial and academic purposes.
- The main advantage of secondary data is that such data save time and money for the researcher. The main disadvantages include the potential difficulty in verifying the reliability of the data and whether the data are applicable to your research problem.
- If you have the capability of reading foreign language sources, then this is clearly an advantage as it allows you to consult a wider range of secondary sources.
- Secondary data can be evaluated by considering its purpose, scope, authority, audience and format.
- Your university or college library is likely to contain the majority of secondary data you will need. However, consult your supervisor if you need more specialized data.
- Cooked data can often be presented in its original format, whereas raw data needs to be processed by the researcher.

Helen's chosen topic for her research project is mergers and acquisitions in the European banking sector. As a BSc (Hons) Finance student, Helen has learned that the market has experienced consolidation in recent years, and she is keen to examine the impact of mergers and acquisition (M&A) on the banking sector workforce. She has chosen a case study research design, and intends to analyze two high-profile mergers and one acquisition. All of these took place within the last 12 months.

Helen is fortunate in that her research supervisor's main area of research is similar to her own proposed research topic. She has therefore sought advice from her supervisor on numerous occasions. One of the suggestions her supervisor has made is for her to include a question that examines whether or not the bout of recent mergers and acquisitions looks set to continue.

Fortunately, Helen's topic has received detailed coverage across both the business press and wider media. In addition, in recent months several empirical studies have been published in leading academic journals. Helen also has a list of all the mergers and acquisitions that have taken place in Europe since 2000, including those in the banking sector. The main problem she faces is that this is simply a list from a specialist trade magazine; it provides no detailed analysis or discussion on the companies involved.

Case study questions

1. Suggest an approach that Helen could adopt to evaluate the suitability of the secondary data she has collected.
2. Discuss the potential problems Helen might encounter by only using secondary sources.

YOU'RE THE SUPERVISOR

Pauline has decided to base her research topic on 'key changes in British family life over the last 30 years'. Although this may not seem like a business-related topic, she is interested to see how key changes, particularly household demands, might influence the marketing of certain goods and services. In the first instance, Pauline was very keen to adopt a longitudinal research design, but she now realizes that this is not a realistic option given that her project needs to be fully completed inside 12 months.

Consequently, Pauline has decided to base her entire project on secondary data. She is especially pleased to have discovered the General Household Survey (GHS), and intends using this as her exclusive secondary source of analysis. The GHS includes figures on car ownership, pensions, sport participation and the use of health services. Pauline believes the GHS is ideal for her research as it fully addresses her research problem. The GHS is described thus:

> The General Household Survey (GHS) has been providing key data on life in modern Britain for over 30 years. The annual *Living in Britain* report, the printed and online document that brings its main findings to a wide audience of researchers, students, decision-makers, media and more, adds an extra dimension of explanation, insight and analysis. (National Statistics, 2002)

(Continued)

(Continued)

Much as Pauline would like to carry out primary research, she feels that this is not a viable option due to time constraints. She believes it would be impossible to generate a sample the size of the GHS. Pauline has also ruled out using other secondary data analysis because she believes the GHS fully addresses her research problem. Still, as her research supervisor, Pauline has met you to seek clarification that you share her views in relation to the GHS.

Supervisor question

- Do you agree with Pauline that the GHS should be used exclusively? Give reasons for your answer.

COMMON QUESTIONS AND ANSWERS

1. You have decided to base your research project on the current economic crisis. Your leading research question is 'How has the current economic crisis impacted on trade between the UK and USA?' Suggest possible sources of secondary data that you might use to answer this question.

Answer: Figure 7.1 provides an eclectic range of secondary sources. The majority of these are likely to be ideal for the above topic. Moreover, you may also find that each country's respective Chamber of Commerce and Embassy websites offer useful information. The important thing here is to try to consult a wide range of secondary data. At the time of writing, the global financial crisis continues to dominate daily news. Consequently, you should have no trouble in finding an abundance of information. Remember that the main advantage in consulting a wide range of secondary data is the likelihood of greater reliability.

2. Can I base my research project entirely on secondary data?

Answer: Some universities and colleges insist that primary data must also feature in a research project. However, this tends to be more applicable to postgraduate rather than undergraduate programmes. If in doubt, check with your research supervisor. If you decide to only refer to secondary data, then it is worth considering explaining to the reader why you have opted not to undertake primary research. For instance, one reason might be that there is already a plethora of data on your chosen subject so you do not feel the need to include primary data.

If you are permitted to conduct your research using purely secondary data, consider the following questions:

- Can my research problem be addressed by simply including secondary data?
- How significant might the contribution of primary data be to my research?

3. Can I use foreign language sources in my research project?

Answer: The short answer is yes. This is clearly an advantage for the student researcher as it allows access to a wider range of sources. However, one drawback is the time it takes to consult both English and foreign language sources. Hence the importance attached to considering the five factors when evaluating secondary data – purpose, scope, authority, audience and format.

4. Suggest the possible advantages of using secondary data in an electronic format.

Answer: There are two key advantages associated with using secondary data in electronic format – time and organization. The ability to access an extensive range of articles electronically will save you a great deal of time, which you can then spend on accessing a wider range of sources or analyzing your findings in greater depth. The organization of your findings can also be more easily achieved using electronic sources. For example, a vast amount of data can now be transported manually on a single USB memory stick.

References

American Marketing Association (2013) 'Secondary data sources', http://www.marketingpower.com/Community/ARC/Pages/Research/SecondaryData/default.aspx, accessed 7 August 2013.

Blumberg, B., Cooper, D.R. and Schindler, P.S. (2008) *Business Research Methods* (2nd edn). Maidenhead: McGraw-Hill.

Cowton, C.J. (1998) 'The use of secondary data in business ethics research', *Journal of Business Ethics*, 17 (4): 423–434.

Gall, G. and Allsop, D. (2007) 'Annual hours working in Britain', *Personnel Review*, 36 (5): 800–814.

National Statistics (2002) 'Living in Britain: Results from the General Household Survey', online source: http://webarchive.nationalarchives.gov.uk/20100520011438/statistics.gov.uk/lib2002/default.asp, accessed 19 September 2013.

Waters, D. (1997) *Quantitative Methods for Business* (2nd edn). Harlow: Addison Wesley Longman.

Wilson, A. (2006) *Marketing Research: An Integrated Approach* (2nd edn). Harlow: Prentice Hall.

Further Reading

Bryman, A. and Bell, E. (2011) *Business Research Methods* (3rd edn). Oxford: Oxford University Press.

Cooper, D.R. and Schindler, P. (2008) *Business Research Methods* (10th edn). Maidenhead: McGraw-Hill.

Quinlan, C. (2001) *Business Research Methods*. Andover: Cengage Learning.

Saunders, M.N.K., Lewis, P. and Thornhill, A. (2012) *Research Methods for Business Students* (6th edn). Harlow: Prentice Hall.

Stewart, D.W. and Kamins, M.A. (1993) *Secondary Research: Information Sources and Methods* (2nd edn). Newbury Park, CA: Sage.

8
Sampling

┌─ Learning Objectives ─────────────────────────────────────┐

After reading this chapter, you should be able to:

- know the stages in the sampling process;
- understand the reasons for sampling;
- recognize the differences between probability and non-probability sampling;
- apply a range of sampling techniques;
- appreciate the combining of sampling techniques;
- know how to determine sample size; and
- recognize issues associated with response and non-response.

└───┘

Introduction

In the preceding two chapters we have concentrated our attention on data collection methods. An important part of primary data collection is sampling. In general, there are two fundamental questions often associated with sampling – 'How do I know *which* sampling technique to use?' and 'What is an appropriate sample size?' This chapter sets out to answer these questions.

As noted in Chapter 6, when undertaking your research, the likelihood is that you will need to collect primary data. However, in order to answer your research questions, it is doubtful that you will be able to collect data from all cases. Therefore, you will need to select a sample. The entire set of cases from which your sample is drawn is called the population. In reality, most researchers neither have the time nor the resources to analyze the entire population. Fortunately, a range of sampling techniques allows you to reduce the number of cases taking part in your study.

The sampling techniques(s) you select largely depend on whether or not you wish to infer that your findings apply to the wider population. However, you may not wish to generalize, but aim to provide a 'snapshot' of one particular case, e.g. asking business customers what they think of one particular delivery process to one particular supplier, rather than to all suppliers.

This chapter begins by describing the series of stages involved in the sampling process. During the early stages I make clear the distinction between commonly used terms in sampling; these include population, sampling frame and sampling itself. Then we explore the reasons for engaging in sampling and how you set about selecting your sampling frame. Next, we examine sampling techniques. There are basically two broad types of sampling: probability (also referred to as random) sampling and non-probability (also referred to as non-random) sampling. Each sampling method is clearly defined and the main methods are illustrated with case examples.

You do not necessarily have to restrict yourself to one type of sampling technique. Many students combine different types of sampling technique to answer their research problem. Yet, whatever method you select, it is essential that you explain the rationale behind your choice. A number of factors are explored that might lead you to combine sampling techniques. This section concludes with a summary of the strengths and weaknesses of each sampling technique.

Following this, I deal with a key issue in sampling – that of sample size. Various factors influence sample size. In essence, these factors can be divided on the basis of either subjective or statistical methods.

Your choice of sampling technique can directly impact on your response rate. Usually, non-probability sampling techniques are associated with higher response rates. However, this has to be balanced with the quality of the response, and not just numbers. The concluding part of this chapter addresses how to deal with poor response rates, and how in some instances it may require the introduction of a substitute sample.

Stages in the Sampling Process

Figure 8.1 illustrates the stages that you are likely to go through when conducting your sampling. In reality, sampling is not always a straightforward linear process, as will become apparent later on in this chapter. Still, Figure 8.1 provides a useful template from which to work when choosing and implementing your sampling method(s).

Throughout the chapter I will discuss each respective stage in the sampling process, concluding with advice on how to assess your response rates.

Stage 1: Clearly Define Your Target Population

Your first stage in the sampling process is to clearly define your target population.

Population is commonly related to the number of people living in a particular country. However, population does not just relate to individuals. A *population* is also a clearly defined group of research subjects that is being sampled. For example, in the electronics sector, the population might include all electronics manufacturers in Japan (one particular country). Similarly, if you considered doing research on

FIGURE 8.1 Stages in the sampling process

tourism development in London, you may consider the population as all tourist attractions located within the London area.

Defining a population is not always straightforward. It largely depends on your research questions and the context with which you wish to study. When defining your population, you need to establish the types of case that make up your population, e.g. individuals, firms, households, etc.

In essence, a population can often be broken down by moving from the general to more specific. For instance, the population of a country such as the UK can be sub-divided as follows: East Anglia, Cambridge, area in Cambridge. Most students do not have the time or resources to target a large population, and therefore need to target a smaller population or consider sampling. However, you might find that the size of your population is small enough for you to target the entire population. Let us say that you wanted to target manufacturers of large passenger aircraft. In the main, the population consists of two companies – Airbus and Boeing. So, you may decide to target the entire population. For this reason, Figure 8.1 shows an arrow leading from 'clearly define your target population' to 'collect data'. Effectively, you are bypassing the stages concerned with sampling, as you are targeting the whole population.

Stage 2: Select Your Sampling Frame

A *sampling frame* is a list of the actual cases from which your sample will be drawn. The sampling frame must be representative of the population. However, in reality it is difficult to know when a sample is unrepresentative and should not be used.

An important aspect of your sampling frame is to consider how such a list of people or organizations can be located. For example, if you intend surveying local building firms in your area, you may identify your population as all those firms within a ten-mile radius of your address. At first, locating a list of building firms may seem relatively simple. An obvious source is your local telephone directory, although bear in mind that not all firms are likely to publish their details in the phone book. Therefore, how do you know that those firms in the directory are representative of the population? We will come back to this point later in this chapter.

Some researchers do not have access to a sampling frame such as a definitive directory providing company details. If you find yourself in this position, you will need to develop your own sampling frame. This can be a time-consuming and challenging process. Moreover, you are faced with the problem of trying to ensure that your sampling frame is representative of the population. In some respects, this can be achieved by referring to earlier studies that might illustrate key characteristics of the population.

Once you have established your sampling frame, the next stage is to consider sampling and sampling techniques.

Stage 3: Choose Your Sampling Technique(s)

Prior to examining the various types of sampling method, it is worth noting what is meant by 'sampling', along with reasons why you are likely to select a *sample*.

Taking a subset from your chosen sampling frame or entire population is called *sampling*. Sampling can be used to make inferences about a population or to make generalizations in relation to existing theory. In essence, this depends on your choice of sampling technique.

Figure 8.2 illustrates the relationship between population, sampling frame and sample. The large circle represents the entire population, the inner circle the sampling frame, and the centre circle the sample. The size of each circle represents the number of cases. For example, the population might be 1,000, a list of some of the cases might represent 500, while the sample might be 250 (a subset of the sampling frame). Each case is represented by a small circle.

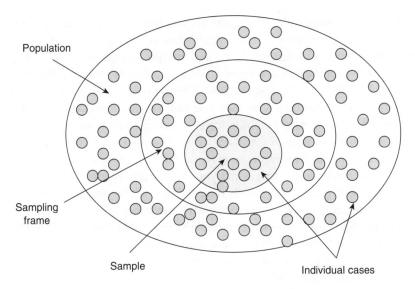

Population

Sampling
frame

Sample

Individual cases

FIGURE 8.2 Relationship between population, sampling frame and sample

Why do I need to select a sample?

Before we examine factors that might lead you to engage in sampling, it is worth noting that businesses also use sampling techniques when conducting research. Suppose, for instance, a car manufacturer is in the process of launching a new model in Germany and wants some data about possible sales. Essentially, there are two ways of finding this:

1. It could ask every person in Germany who might buy the car whether or not they will actually buy it, and how much they would be prepared to pay.
2. It could take a sample of people, ask them whether or not they will buy the new model, and then estimate the likely demand from the population as a whole.

Obviously, the first option is both costly and time-consuming. Furthermore, the car manufacturer would be unlikely to contact the entire population of Germany, as not all people drive or are interested in buying a new car. In short, it is not feasible to conduct research on such a large scale, especially as it is not targeted to those potential purchasers of the new car. Option 2 is far more feasible as sampling can be used to generate dependable results, rather than focusing on the whole population.

In addition, it is impracticable to even attempt to survey the entire population. These impracticalities include the following:

- there is no time to survey the entire population;
- there are not the resources, particularly the budget, to survey the entire population;
- the skills to collect all of the data and interpret findings are lacking;
- the size of the population is too large;
- it is too difficult to access the entire population; and
- you wish to compare your research to that of previous studies.

First, an obvious impracticality that prevents you from surveying the entire population is time. Even if your population is within close geographical proximity, it can still be time-consuming contacting, analyzing and interpreting the findings of each case.

Second, a general lack of resources is likely to prevent you targeting the entire population. In particular, the cost involved. The main cost is associated with administering your data collection. Whether you opt for interviews or a questionnaire survey, associated costs might include travel, accommodation, postage, etc.

Third, your lack of skills as a researcher may hamper your ability to survey the entire population. If, for example, your study involves international research, then your lack of language skills may restrict your ability to target the entire population. Similarly, you may not have the skills required to analyze large volumes of data or to allow for the production of a simple, clearly interpreted set of findings.

Fourth, the size of the population means that it is wholly unrealistic to target the entire population. Examples include populations of countries or regions within a country. Moreover, targeting companies within certain sectors, e.g. small businesses in France, is similarly unrealistic.

Fifth, you might find it difficult to access the entire population. Instances that might restrict your access include: a sensitive topic, a lack of published data on the whole population, and a general unwillingness of participants to take part in your research.

Finally, perhaps not so much an impracticality but a preferred choice is your intention to compare your research with that of earlier studies. In order to be able to compare like-for-like data your intention might be to adopt the same sampling method as other researchers.

In this section we have explored a number of reasons for selecting a sample. The next stage is to consider what constitutes a suitable sample size.

Sampling techniques

In general, sampling techniques can be divided into two types:

- probability or random sampling; and
- non-probability or non-random sampling.

Before choosing your specific type(s) of sampling technique, you need to decide your broad sampling technique. The reasons that I have referred to sampling in both the singular and the plural is because in some cases you may wish to adopt more than one sampling method. We explore reasons for this later on.

Figure 8.3 shows the various types of sampling technique. These can be categorized on the basis of probability or non-probability sampling.

Probability sampling

Probability sampling means that every item in the population has an equal chance of being included in your sample. One way to undertake random sampling would

FIGURE 8.3   Sampling techniques

be if you were to construct a sampling frame first and then use a random number generation computer program to pick a sample from the sampling frame.

'Probability or random sampling has the greatest freedom from bias but may represent the most costly sample in terms of time and energy for a given level of sampling error' (Brown, 1947: 337). In addition, it is not always appropriate for those students who are interested in doing case study research. There are several different types of probability sampling technique. We shall now examine each one in turn.

Simple random sampling   The simple random sample means that every case of the population has an equal probability of inclusion in your sample. For example, let us say that you want to survey 250 members of a sports club. If the total membership is 1,000, the probability of inclusion in the sample is:

$$P(\text{inclusion}) = \frac{\text{sports club members}}{\text{total membership}} = \frac{250}{1,000} = 0.25 \text{ (i.e. 1 in 4)}$$

Disadvantages associated with simple random sampling include:

- a complete frame (a list of all units in the whole population) is needed;
- in some studies, e.g. surveys by personal interviews, the costs of obtaining the sample can be high if the units are geographically widely scattered; and
- the standard errors of estimators can be high.

(Ghauri and Grønhaug, 2005: 149)

Systematic sampling   Systematic sampling is where every nth case after a random start is selected. For example, if surveying a sample of consumers, every fifth consumer may be selected from your sample. You need to ensure that there is no regular pattern in the population, which, if it coincided with the *sampling interval*, or in other words distance between your chosen cases, might lead to a biased sample. In addition, the subjects in the population need to be ordered in some way. For example, supermarket stock that are ordered on a shelf; names of businesses ordered in a business directory; names of health club members ordered alphabetically on the company database; or addresses ordered on the basis of postcodes.

Referring to the earlier sports club example, we know that we are to select one member in four. With a systematic sample, we would make a random start between one and four inclusively, possibly by using the last two digits in a table of random numbers.

The advantage of this sampling technique is its simplicity. Moreover, a sampling frame is not always required. The main downside is the potential for a regularly occurring anomaly impacting on the quality of the data. By way of illustration, let us say that a manufacturer of luxury ornaments decides to implement a system of total quality management (TQM). A main feature of their TQM strategy is regular quality control checks of their finest bone china range. Adopting a systematic sampling method may sound fine in principle. Yet, what if the machine painting the ornaments develops a fault? If this fault leads to the paint supply running out at regular intervals, these may generate wildly inaccurate data as to the overall quality of the production output. One way to overcome this problem is to have random rather than systematic checks.

Stratified random sampling   Stratified sampling is where the population is divided into strata (or subgroups) and a random sample is taken from each subgroup. A subgroup is a natural set of items. Subgroups might be based on company size, gender or occupation (to name but a few).

Stratified sampling is often used where there is a great deal of variation within a population. Its purpose is to ensure that every stratum is adequately represented. Hence, the number of items chosen from each subgroup may be proportionate to the size of the stratum in relation to the population. For this reason, when making inferences in relation to the wider population, stratified sampling usually has a smaller sampling error than simple random sampling. This higher level of precision is a key advantage of stratified sampling. Still, it can sometimes be difficult to get hold of detailed information on your entire sampling frame, thereby making it problematic when it comes to identifying your strata.

A systematic approach can be taken when conducting stratified sampling. The stages involved are shown in Figure 8.4.

The following example illustrates how stratified sampling might work in practice. A retailer employs a total of 2,000 people. Using a sampling frame of 1,000 (50% of the total workforce), your intention is to conduct research into absence in the workplace. You have identified the following strata – gender and occupation. The total workforce is made up of 300 male and 400 female managers, and 800 male and 500 female employees respectively. Using stratified sampling, your sample of 1,000 would consist of 150 male and 200 female managers, and 400 male and 250 female employees (see Figure 8.5).

FIGURE 8.4 Stages to stratified sampling

	Males			Females			Total		
	S	R	%	S	R	%	S	R	%
Management	150	95	63	200	102	51	350	197	56
Employees	400	263	66	250	92	37	650	355	55

S = sample; R = response rate

FIGURE 8.5 An example of stratified sampling

Cluster sampling   Cluster sampling is where the whole population is divided into clusters or groups. Subsequently, a random sample is taken from these clusters, all of which are used in the final sample.

Cluster sampling is advantageous for those researchers whose subjects are fragmented over a large geographical area, as it saves time and money. If, for example, you wish to examine healthcare provision among hospitals in the UK, rather than targeting the entire population, you can use cluster sampling. You may start by recognizing regional NHS (National Health Service) Trusts as clusters. Subsequently, a sample of these Trusts can be chosen at random, with all hospitals in each Trust included in the final sample.

The stages to cluster sampling can be summarized as follows:

- Choose cluster grouping for your sampling frame, e.g. type of company or geographical region.
- Number each of the clusters.
- Select your sample using random sampling.

In the earlier cited example, the main advantage of cluster sampling is that it saves the researcher the time and money of having to travel to every hospital in the UK.

Multi-stage sampling   Multi-stage sampling is a process of moving from a broad to a narrow sample, using a step-by-step process. If, for example, a French publisher of a pet food magazine were to conduct a survey, it could simply take a random sample of dog owners within the entire French population. Obviously, this is both expensive and time-consuming. A cheaper alternative would be to use multi-stage sampling.

In essence, this would involve dividing France into a number of geographical regions. Subsequently, some of these regions are chosen at random, and then subdivisions are made, perhaps based on local authority areas. Next, some of these are again chosen at random and then divided into smaller areas, e.g. towns or cities. The main purpose of multi-stage sampling is to select samples which are concentrated in a few geographical regions. Once again, this saves time and money.

Non-probability sampling

If, for example, you decided to use a non-probability sample in your research, then the probability of each case being selected from your total population is not known. Thus, it is not possible for you to make statistical inferences in relation to the wider population.

Non-probability sampling is often associated with case study research design and qualitative research. With regards to the latter, case studies tend to focus on small samples and are intended to examine a real-life phenomenon, not to make statistical inferences in relation to the wider population. A sample of participants or cases does not need to be representative, or random, but a clear rationale is needed for the inclusion of some cases or individuals rather than others.

There are several advantages and disadvantages associated with non-probability sampling. We shall examine these in relation to each of the respective non-probability sampling techniques. These are now explored.

Quota sampling   Quota sampling is a non-random sampling technique in which participants are chosen on the basis of predetermined characteristics so that the total sample will have the same distribution of characteristics as the wider population. One problem associated with quota sampling is the difficulty of gaining information on the characteristics of those in your intended sample. In addition, as a non-probability sampling method you are unable to infer from your results to the wider population.

Snowball sampling   Snowball sampling is a non-random sampling method that uses a few cases to help encourage other cases to take part in the study, thereby increasing sample size. 'This approach is most applicable in small populations that are difficult to access due to their "closed" nature, e.g. secret societies and inaccessible professions' (Brewerton and Millward, 2001).

If, for example, you want to interview managing directors of local companies, you may find it difficult accessing a sufficient number of directors. Snowball sampling allows you to perhaps overcome this problem by using the directors you do know to contact other directors within their business network. How can this be achieved? Well, often you tend to find that people in senior management positions are members of various professional bodies, business associations and, in general, of a wide business network. In essence, you can use a few of these key individuals to contact their wider business network about your research.

The advantage of snowball sampling is that other individuals can do much of the work for you in developing your sample size. In addition, some of these individuals may be crucial to your research. The disadvantages with snowball sampling are that they provide the researcher with very little control over the cases within the sample. For example, individuals are likely to contact close friends, who may share similar views. Hence, there is the possibility of obtaining a biased, unrepresentative number of cases.

Convenience sampling   Convenience sampling is selecting participants because they are often readily and easily available. Typically, convenience sampling tends to be a favoured sampling technique among students as it is inexpensive and an 'easy option' compared to other sampling techniques. Convenience sampling often helps to overcome many of the limitations associated with research. For example, using friends or family as part of your sample is easier than targeting unknown individuals.

A key limitation connected with convenience sampling is the potential for high levels of bias as well as the inability to make generalizations across the wider population. In short, convenience sampling can be defined as a non-random sampling technique that is chosen by the researcher for its practicality.

Purposive or judgemental sampling   Purposive or judgemental sampling is a strategy in which particular settings, persons or events are selected deliberately in order to provide important information that cannot be obtained from other choices (Patton, 1990; Maxwell, 1996). It is where the researcher includes cases or participants in the sample because they believe that they warrant inclusion. In other words, inclusion is based on your own personal judgement. A number of reasons may exist for your deciding to include certain cases but exclude others. These can be summarized as:

- a unique case;
- a critical case; and
- a focus on heterogeneous or homogeneous groups.

A unique case is one that displays a characteristic that is not shared by other cases. To illustrate, let us say that you are conducting a study into the world's leading brands. In general, these are dominated by the USA and Japan. However, if one

European brand – let's say Nokia – was the only one representing Europe in the top ten, this might be interpreted as a unique case. By including a unique case, the intention is to compare and contrast findings with other cases in your sample. The inclusion of a unique case can often provide interesting findings that can be further explored in later studies.

A critical case is one that is essential to your research. For example, the USA would be viewed as a critical case in the context of research into the world's leading economies. In other words, failure to include the USA in your research is likely to have a negative impact on the credibility of your results.

Finally, you may wish to examine either heterogeneous or homogeneous groups. The former might comprise student participants from different countries, whereas the latter would focus on a group of students from one particular country.

One of the drawbacks associated with purposive sampling is the potential for sampling bias. Moreover, you are unable to generalize your research findings to the wider population.

Can I combine sampling techniques?

You do not necessarily have to restrict yourself to one type of sampling technique. Many researchers combine various methods when conducting their research. Of course, you will need to justify your reasons for combining your chosen methods within your research. First, you might argue that similar studies have combined sampling techniques. Therefore, in order to compare findings, you wish to make a case for combining methods. Second, you might be using methodological triangulation as part of your study. Therefore, in order to increase levels of reliability and validity, you may wish to make the case for combining sampling methods. Finally, you may simply argue that combining methods means that you are better placed to answer your research problem.

In general, certain sampling techniques are better combined than others. For instance, if using convenience sampling, it seems natural to perhaps include cases within your sample that are crucial to your research (judgement sampling). While using probability and non-probability methods for the same population can be undertaken, it is often time-consuming and costly for the researcher.

Table 8.1 illustrates strengths and weaknesses associated with each respective sampling technique. By now, you should be aware that there is no one 'best' sampling method. As noted, a number of factors are likely to dictate your choice of sampling technique. However, Table 8.1 acts as a useful starting point.

Stage 4: Determine Your Sample Size

'How large does my sample size need to be?' Students have confronted me with this question on countless occasions. In short, there is no easy answer. A number of factors influence your choice of sample size. However, remember that before you make your choice, you should have already established two important sets of criteria. First, you are able to clearly define your population and, second, you have determined your sampling frame.

TABLE 8.1 Strengths and weaknesses of sampling techniques

Technique	Strengths	Weaknesses
Convenience sampling	Least expensive, least time-consuming, most convenient	Selection bias, sample not representative, not recommended for descriptive or causal research
Judgement sampling	Low-cost, convenient, not time-consuming, ideal for exploratory research designs	Does not allow generalization, subjective
Quota sampling	Sample can be controlled for certain characteristics	Selection bias, no assurance of representativeness
Snowball sampling	Can estimate rare characteristics	Time-consuming
Simple random sampling	Easily understood, results projectable	Difficult to construct sampling frame, expensive, lower precision, no assurance of representativeness
Systematic sampling	Can increase representativeness, easier to implement than simple random sampling, sampling frame not always necessary	Can decrease representativeness
Stratified sampling	Includes all important sub-populations, precision	Difficult to select relevant stratification variables, not feasible to stratify on many variables, expensive
Cluster sampling	Easy to implement, cost-effective	Imprecise, difficult to compute and interpret results

Source: Malhotra and Birks (2006: 374)

In some respects, the size of your sample is likely to be determined by the nature of your research philosophy. If you have adopted a positivist stance, then the likelihood is that you are interested in generating a large sample that permits statistical analysis. On the other hand, if you decide to engage in an interpretivist approach to your research, then you are likely to be concerned with a smaller sample. In summary, your choice of sample size depends on:

- the confidence you need to have in your data, i.e. the level of certainty that the characteristics of the data collected will represent the characteristics of the total population;
- the comparative sample size of earlier studies;
- the margin of error that you can tolerate, i.e. the precision you require for any estimates made from your sample;
- the types of analysis you are going to undertake, in particular the number of categories into which you wish to subdivide your data, as many statistical techniques have a minimum threshold of data cases for each cell;
- the size of the total population from which your sample is being drawn; and
- using formulas and published tables.

First, if you wish to make an inference to the wider population, as a 'rule of thumb' the sample size should consist of at least 30 cases. Ideally, where the population is less than 30, the entire population should be included in the study, although this also depends on the extent to which a sample is homogeneous. In general, the more heterogeneous a population, the larger the sample required to acquire a representative sample, while the more homogeneous, the less *variability* in the distribution of the characteristics in the population. The *confidence level* is expressed as a percentage, typically 95% or 99%. It is how confident you are that a *parameter* falls within a specific range of values. A parameter is a population characteristic such as a proportion (P) or mean. For example, if you adopt a 95% confidence level, then you expect 95 out of 100 samples will have the true population value within the range of precision, e.g. ±5 per cent.

Second, you may wish to base your sample size on earlier, similar studies in your chosen field. The advantage of this is that it can allow for direct comparative analysis with previous research. Yet the downside is that reviewing these earlier studies does not always reveal the sampling techniques used by researchers. Thus, although your sample may be of similar size, it is unlikely that you will adopt the same sampling method and/or cases.

Third, the level of precision or *sampling error* is the range in which the 'true' population value is estimated to be. This range is typically illustrated using percentages, e.g. ±5 per cent. For example, if a researcher finds that 80% of consumers engage in recycling activities with a precision rate of ±5%, then the researcher can conclude that between 75% and 85% of consumers in the population have engaged in recycling activities.

Every sample statistic you calculate from a sample will have sampling error, no matter which sampling technique you use. Ultimately, the lower the sampling error required, the larger the probability sample needs to be. The only way to eliminate sampling error is to undertake a census of the entire population.

Fourth, if you are adopting a case study research design, then the likelihood is that you are examining a real-life phenomenon, perhaps an in-depth case. Hence, the sample size may be one. Conversely, if you are conducting quantitative research and are intending to use inferential statistics, then you need to consider your sample size carefully. In particular, subdividing your data into various categories will impact on the types of data analysis technique you can use.

Fifth, if the population is small, e.g. less than 150, then you may be in a position to carry out a census of the entire population. The advantage of being able to do this is that it eliminates sampling error data on all individuals. Still, as we have established, it can be both costly and time-consuming targeting the entire population.

Finally, there are several different formulas and tables used for determining sample size. The range of methods is beyond the scope of this book. For a more in-depth discussion on sampling methods see Cochran (1977). However, below is an example from Yamane (1967). This formula is used to calculate the sample sizes in Table 8.2. The table shows the size of population and the required sample size for ±5% precision levels, where the confidence level is 95% and P = .5, which is the estimated proportion of a characteristic that is present in the population.

Example

Yamane (1967: 886) suggests the following way to calculate sample size:

$$n = \frac{N}{1+N(e)^2}$$

$$\frac{400}{1+400(.05)^2}$$

where:

n = sample size
N = population size
e = precision (sampling error)

By way of illustration, if you know the population size to be 300 managers and wish to know the sample size in order that 95% of the sample values are within 2 standard deviations of the true population mean, the above formula would read as follows:

$$n = \frac{300}{1+300(.05)^2}$$

A sample size of 172 managers from a population of 300 corresponds to the final set of figures given in Table 8.2.

As mentioned, there are several methods used to calculate sample size. The criteria of precision (sampling error), variability and confidence level are important considerations when thinking about sample size in your own research project. Remember that your calculated sample size does not allow for non-responses. Ideally, you need to increase your sample size by at least 30% in order to overcome this problem.

Calculating sample size is typically associated with probability sampling, involving quantitative analysis. Deciding on sample size for a qualitative study might seem simple, as you are not necessarily making inferences in relation to the wider population. However, in some respects it is more difficult because there are no rules that

TABLE 8.2 Sample size for $\pm 5\%$ precision levels where confidence level is 95% and P = .5

Size of population	Sample size (n) for precision (e) of +5%
100	80
125	96
150	110
175	122
200	134
225	144
250	154
275	163
300	172
325	180

Source: Yamane (1967: 886)

govern sample selection. In some respects, the final sample size is almost always a matter of judgement rather than calculation (Hoinville and Jowell, 1985).

Stage 5: Collect Your Data

Once you have established your target population, sampling frame, sampling technique(s) and sample size, the next step is to collect your data. As noted in Chapter 6, there are numerous primary data collection methods. Your chosen method(s) are likely to impact on your choice of sampling techniques. Participant observation is typically associated with non-probability sampling, whereas you are more likely to use probability techniques if you are conducting a questionnaire survey.

Once you start to collect your data, a key concern is achieving a suitable number of responses. Ideally, your sample size should be large enough to accommodate non-responses. We examine the issue of response rates in the next section.

Stage 6: Assess Your Response Rate

Your response rate is the number of cases agreeing to take part in your study. These cases are taken from your original sample. Your response rate can, of course, be represented as a percentage or actual number. For example, if we consider the former, let us say that you have 200 cases in your sample and a total of 40 participants take part. Then our response rate equates to:

$$40/200 \times 100 = 20\% \text{ (response rate)}$$

In reality, most researchers never achieve a 100% response rate. Reasons for this might include refusal to respond, ineligibility to respond, inability to respond, or the respondent has been located but you are unable to make contact. Response rate is important because each non-response is liable to bias your final sample. If, for example, you decided to conduct an email survey into working practices and received a response rate of 60%, this could be interpreted as an excellent response. Yet, closer examination of your findings might indicate that the majority of respondents are those in full-time employment and working from home, while those in part-time employment generated a low number of responses. You might then conclude that this bias is possibly due to the fact that those in part-time employment have limited access to the Internet. Therefore, your sample is not representative of the entire population.

A high response rate is essential if you wish to infer from your results to the wider population. If you do generate a low response rate then the greater the likelihood for sample bias. For example, response rates as low as 5–20% increase the likelihood of the sample being unrepresentative. To illustrate, suppose you conduct research into keeping pets using a random sampling method of people in your area. If you receive a response rate of only 25%, this might be because only those respondents who have a pet or an interest in pets responded. This is because those people with an interest in pets are more likely to return their completed questionnaire.

For these reasons, it is vital to keep track of responses. If you do experience a low response rate, do not feel too despondent. A low response rate may be in keeping with previous research studies. If so, this can make for interesting comparative analysis. Through conducting your literature review, you should be familiar with what constitutes a 'typical' response rate in your chosen subject.

A key factor in increasing your response rate is always to involve a 'chase-up' stage. This basically involves contacting participants again so as to 'encourage' them to take part in your research. If all else fails, a reserve sample can always be placed on standby – if your population is large enough to allow you to have a reserve sample, that is!

In sum, response rate is important because each non-response is liable to bias your final sample. Clearly defining your sample, employing the right sampling technique, and generating a large sample in some respects can help to reduce the likelihood of sample bias.

Choosing an inappropriate sampling technique is something that you will probably realize in hindsight. A key indication of a poor choice of sampling method is a low response rate. Certain methods, such as convenience sampling, are unlikely to pose a problem in terms of response. Conversely, stratified random sampling is often more problematic because of its very nature.

Generally, you should be confident that you have chosen the right sampling method prior to collecting your data. Your choice of sampling method may be dependent on how much accuracy is needed. Let us say that you have an important problem to address. There is therefore a greater need for an unbiased sample with a measurable sampling error. The best technique would be a probability sample. On the other hand, if the findings relate to a less important decision, a judgement sample may be justified (Peterson and O'Dell, 1950).

RESEARCH IN ACTION

Innocent Drinks

Four years after finishing university, former Cambridge graduates Richard Reed, Adam Balon and Jon Wright decided to work together on pursuing their business idea. With a background in management consultancy and advertising, the three budding entrepreneurs certainly had the knowledge required to start their own business. Their intention was to develop the 'best fresh drinks in the whole world'. Yet, although they believed in the essence of their idea, they still did not have a product.

In 1998, after six months of trying out recipes on friends, they spent £500 on fruit, turned it into smoothies, and sold them at a small music festival in London. Next to their stall, they

(Continued)

(Continued)

put up a large sign saying 'Do you think we should give up our jobs to make these smoothies?' They put out a bin saying 'YES' and a bin saying 'NO' and asked festival goers to put their empty bottle in one of the bins. Richard, Adam and Jon were no doubt pleased to find that the 'YES' bin was full because they did not hesitate in resigning from their jobs the following day! Innocent Drinks was born.

Given their financial constraints, they continued with their sampling by taking several bottles at a time into local retailers one day and returning the next day to see if the shop owner wanted to sell more. With the help of a capital injection of £250,000 from an American investor, the company has grown from strength to strength. Products include a wide range of fruit drinks, all of which are made of 100% natural ingredients.

Interestingly, although not particularly scientific, some might argue that a key factor in the company's success was the relentless sampling undertaken by the entrepreneurs at the beginning of the venture.

Questions

1. What type of sampling technique do you think Richard, Adam and Jon adopted?
2. What are the advantages and disadvantages of their chosen technique?
3. Discuss the alternative sampling techniques the three entrepreneurs could have adopted. Give reasons for your answer.

Sources: Innocent Drinks (2009); *Marketing Week* (2005)

Summary and Conclusion

In this chapter we have examined a number of sampling-related issues. In particular, why sampling is often undertaken by researchers, the process involved in selecting a sample, and the range of sampling techniques available to researchers. Here are the key points from this chapter:

- The sampling method(s) you choose largely depend on whether or not you wish to infer that your findings apply to the wider population.
- A population is a clearly defined group of research subjects that is being sampled.
- You need to consider a number of factors when considering your sample size. These include: the confidence that you have in your data, earlier studies, the margin of error you can tolerate, the types of analysis you are going to undertake, the size of the total population, and using formulas and published tables.
- In general, sampling techniques can be divided into two types: probability or random sampling and non-probability or non-random sampling.
- A high response rate is essential if you wish to infer from your results to the wider population. If you generate a low response rate, then there is a greater likelihood for sample bias.

Miriam, a final year Finance student, has decided to base her research on the relationship between the marketing and finance function in accounting practices. Miriam is a part-time student, and divides her time between studying and working in a local accountancy practice. Several of her colleagues are members of the professional accountancy organization, the Association of Chartered Certified Accountants (ACCA). Miriam has asked her colleagues to speak to fellow ACCA members to see if they would be interested in participating in her study. In essence, Miriam has opted for a non-probability sampling method – snowball sampling. She is confident of generating a suitably sized sample as she has the full support of her colleagues.

Miriam's rationale for choosing snowball sampling is that several existing studies have used the same sampling technique. Hence, she wishes to compare her findings with those of existing studies.

Supervisor questions

1. Discuss the advantages and disadvantages associated with snowball sampling.
2. Describe the sampling design process Miriam is likely to go through.
3. What are the options available to Miriam if she fails to achieve a suitably sized sample?
4. In general, why are non-probability samples popular among students?

YOU'RE THE SUPERVISOR

Determining sample size

Richard's research focuses on student satisfaction within his own university. He has chosen to undertake a single case study research design. Given that Richard is interested in the opinions of his fellow students, he believes that a convenience sampling technique is the obvious choice for his study. As an active member of his Student Union, Richard is in the fortunate position of having access to a large number of his peer group. However, although the number of participants does not appear to be a problem, Richard is unsure how large a sample size is required. Richard has arranged a meeting with you to discuss your views as to an appropriate sample size.

Case study question

- Can you suggest a suitably sized sample for Richard?

COMMON QUESTIONS AND ANSWERS

1. What sampling technique shall I use for my research?

Answer: You need to consider a number of factors when considering your sample size. These include: the confidence that you have in your data, earlier studies, the margin of error you can

(Continued)

tolerate, the types of analysis you are going to undertake, the size of the total population, and using formulas and published tables. In addition, if opting for a qualitative research strategy, then the size of your sample may not be such an issue. This is because the aim of your research is not to make inferences in relation to the wider population, but to analyze a real-life phenomenon.

2. Can I use more than one sampling technique?

Answer: Do not feel that you have to restrict your research to one sampling technique. However, bear in mind that certain sampling techniques are perhaps better suited than others. Combining judgement and convenience is not unusual. Both are non-probability sampling methods, and there is a clear similarity between the two. If, for example, you were concerned with studying the financial performance of SMEs in your region, you may decide to choose those within a five-mile radius of your home (convenience). However, if you are in the fortunate position of having many businesses within close proximity, you would choose those that, in your judgement, were perhaps likely to provide the most interesting findings (judgement sampling).

3. How do I identify my population?

Answer: This can be difficult. You may find that there is no one definitive directory of all companies, consumers or managers that make up your population. This is a problem I found when researching UK companies that had established joint ventures in China. Although the number stands at somewhere around 4,000, at the time of my research, there did not exist one definitive directory containing all 4,000 joint ventures. Needless to say, I spent a great deal of time trying to compile my own sampling frame. This involved using a wide range of sources. In order to ensure that my sample was representative of the population, I took into account a number of factors, namely company size, type of joint venture, number of years established and type of industry. These were largely based on earlier studies.

4. I am finding it difficult to generate a suitably sized sample. Can I use friends and family?

Answer: To some extent, this depends on your research questions and chosen methodological approach. If you decide to use convenience sampling, then note the lack of representative people within the study. Also, you may get a biased set of answers because your respondents do not come from different demographic backgrounds. Students do sometimes include friends and family as part of their chosen sample. If you decide to do this, it is important that you highlight your reasons for adopting convenience sampling and address the issue of possible bias in your methodology. One argument for using a small sample based on convenience sampling is that your research is intended as a pilot study, prior to conducting a large-scale piece of research.

References

Brewerton, P. and Millward, L. (2001) *Organisational Research Methods*. London: Sage.
Brown, G.H. (1947) 'A comparison of sampling methods', *Journal of Marketing*, April, XI (4): 331–337.

Cochran, W.G. (1977) *Sampling Techniques* (3rd edn). New York: Wiley.

Ghauri, P. and Grønhaug, K. (2005) *Research Methods in Business Studies*. Harlow: FT/Prentice Hall.

Hoinville, G. and Jowell, R. (1985) *Survey Research Practice*. Aldershot: Gower.

Innocent Drinks (2009) 'Our story', online source: www.innocentdrinks.co.uk/us/?Page=our_story, accessed 10 April 2009.

Malhotra, N.K. and Birks, D.F. (2006) *Marketing Research: An Applied Approach* (2nd edn). Harlow: FT/Prentice Hall.

Marketing Week (2005) 'A loss of innocence', online source: www.marketingweek.co.uk/home/a-loss-of-innocence?/2004552.article, accessed 10 April 2009.

Maxwell, J.A. (1996) *Qualitative Research Design: An Interactive Approach*. Applied Social Research Methods Series. London: Sage.

Patton, M.Q. (1990) *Qualitative Evaluation and Research Methods*. Newbury Park, CA: Sage.

Peterson, P.G. and O'Dell, W.F. (1950) 'Selecting sampling methods in commercial research', *Journal of Marketing*, 15 (2): 182–189.

Yamane, T. (1967) *Statistics: An Introductory Analysis*. New York: Harper & Row.

Further Reading

Barnett, V. (1991) *Sample Survey Principles and Methods*. London: Edward Arnold.

Bryman, A. and Bell, E. (2007) *Business Research Methods* (3rd edn). Oxford: Oxford University Press.

Cochran, W.G. (1977) *Sampling Techniques* (3rd edn). New York: John Wiley & Sons.

Henry, G.T. (1990) *Practical Sampling*. Newbury Park, CA: Sage.

Robson, C. (2011) *Real World Research* (3rd edn). Chichester: John Wiley & Sons.

9
Analyzing quantitative data

Introduction

In the preceding three chapters, we have looked at issues surrounding the gathering of data. Once you have completed your data collection, the next step is to begin analyzing your data.

This chapter is the first of two that explore data analysis. The chapter aims to provide you with a solid grounding in the different methods you can use to analyze quantitative data. An in-depth discussion of the numerous methods associated with quantitative data analysis is beyond the scope of this book, although I have included a number of sources dedicated to quantitative methods in the 'Further reading' section at the end of this chapter.

The chapter begins by considering the nature of quantitative analysis and goes on to describe the various methods you may consider when analyzing your data. The methods you choose largely depend on the purpose of your research. Moreover, certain conditions need to be met before choosing your methods of analysis. For example, the number and types of variable you are looking to analyze will ultimately influence your choice of quantitative methods.

A good starting point in your analysis is the summarizing of your data. Frequency tables can be very useful here. They provide you with a brief overview of your findings, and can help you to determine your approach in undertaking more complex statistical analyses, such as tests of association. Illustrative examples show how you might wish to incorporate frequency tables into your study.

I then explore the various ways of describing your data. Possible methods here come under the broad headings of 'measures of central tendency' or 'measures of dispersion'. Although business students tend to have a varying degree of mathematical ability, many are likely to be familiar with at least some of these methods. This section provides a useful overview, including examples, along with the advantages and disadvantages of each measure.

The next section examines slightly more complex methods of quantitative data analysis. These relate to measures of association, measures of difference, and regression analysis. Once again, your choice of analysis depends on the characteristics associated with your data. We shall explore these characteristics, and how to determine your choice of methods later on.

Data analysis is now typically undertaken using statistical software. Thus, the final part of the chapter provides a brief guide to using the Statistical Package for Social Sciences (SPSS). This covers naming and defining the properties of your variables, entering data and presenting descriptive statistics.

What is Quantitative Data Analysis?

Statistics is a branch of mathematics that is applied to quantitative data in order to draw conclusions and make predictions. Statistics are used in all walks of life. In fact, you probably come across a whole range of statistics every day without realizing it. Examples include government surveys, inflation figures, company sales figures, unemployment figures, interest rates, and so on. Statistics can be used in connection with economic, political, environmental and social issues. Moreover, they can be used to analyze past and current data, and forecast future projections.

If you have undertaken a positivist research philosophy, you will have gathered mainly, if not exclusively, quantitative data. Your *quantitative data* involves data that is numerical in nature. Those researchers who have adopted an interpretivist philosophy may also use quantitative data. For example, content analysis, which is a quantitative form of analysis, is typically associated with qualitative data.

A range of quantitative analytical techniques can be used to analyze and interpret your data. These include everything from simple tables to summarize your data, to multivariate tests to determine the strength of relationships between variables.

Thankfully, the introduction of statistical software packages such as SPSS means that the time taken to prepare, conduct and interpret quantitative data has been markedly reduced. This is important for those students who are concerned about having to manually carry out calculations and who perhaps cite their 'fear' of statistics as reasons for not incorporating quantitative analysis into their study. In some cases, students may recognize the value of statistics, but they fail to consider quantitative data analysis because they believe that the following concerns apply to them:

1. I am no good at mathematics, and do not have the time to learn.
2. I need a large sample for quantitative analysis.

With regards to the first point, certainly some statistical methods used to analyze quantitative data are extremely difficult to learn, although methods used to describe data and make inferences to the wider population are mostly basic. Do not feel obligated to using complex methods to analyze your data. Essentially, the quality of your data and the clarity of your analysis are more important than using complicated analytical tools. Moreover, it is essential that you understand the rules of application and know how to interpret your results.

The second point tends to be more important for quantitative research strategy as you are likely to make inferences in relation to the wider population. In order to do this, you need a representative sample, although this does not necessarily need to be large in size (see Chapter 8). It is not always necessary to have large quantities of data for analysis.

In Figure 9.1 we return to the Honeycomb of Research Methodology. The highlighted element (6) shows the data analysis techniques that you may consider when undertaking your research methodology. In this chapter we look at quantitative analysis, while Chapter 10 examines qualitative analysis. The statistical procedures used to analyze quantitative data can be divided into two branches, namely: *descriptive statistics* and *inferential statistics*.

The majority of textbooks on quantitative analysis tend to make a distinction between *descriptive statistics* and *inferential statistics*. The former is used to summarize

FIGURE 9.1   The Honeycomb of Research Methodology (©2013 Jonathan Wilson)

and describe data, while the latter is used to make inferences in relation to a wider population. Inferential statistics can also be subdivided on the basis of *non-parametric* and *parametric tests*.

Parametric tests are regarded as more powerful as they assume that the observed data follows a *normal distribution* (we examine this later in the chapter). Parametric methods are used when you are able to estimate the parameters of distribution in the population. Two of the main parameters are the *mean* and *standard deviation*. Non-parametric methods are used where a normal distribution cannot be ascertained. In other words, when you know nothing about the parameters and have a small sample size, then non-parametric tests must be used.

When conducting your quantitative analysis, it can be viewed as a process that involves the following stages:

- preparing your data for analysis;
- summarizing and presenting your data using tables and graphs;
- describing your data using suitable statistical methods; and
- examining relationships and trends between variables.

We shall now explore each of the above stages in turn.

Preparing Your Data for Analysis

The first step in quantitative data analysis is organizing your data so that it is ready for analysis. Typically, this involves entering your data into a specialized software package such as SPSS. When entering your data, you will start by creating a spreadsheet or matrix. Each column in your spreadsheet should represent a variable, and each row represents a case (see Figure 9.2).

Figure 9.2 is only a brief example. In reality, you may have a large number of cases, and thus a very large spreadsheet. The first column indicates the 'case number'. As noted in Chapter 5, a single case might be a company, individual or possibly an event. The 'age' column is self-explanatory. The final three columns representing 'gender', 'nationality' and 'highest level of qualification' are given numerical values rather than text. This is because most software packages are programmed to analyze data in this way. Hence, all data should be given a numerical value.

Ideally, you should have assigned your codes when collecting your data. For example, allocating codes to respective questions within a questionnaire will make

Case number	Age	Gender	Nationality	Highest level of qualification
001	34	1	1	2
002	45	2	3	3
003	26	2	5	3

FIGURE 9.2   Example of an extract from a data spreadsheet

the task of preparing your data for analysis much easier. When assigning your codes it is important to consider the following points (Bryman, 2004: 146):

- the categories that are produced must not overlap;
- the list of data must take into account all possibilities. This includes missing data and answers to open questions that might come under the heading 'other'; and
- there should be a clear set of rules governing how codes are applied. This is to ensure that coding is consistent over time.

Types of data

The likelihood is that not all of the data that you have collected will be the same. In order to select appropriate methods for analyzing your data, it is important that you understand the different types of data. There are four main types of data:

- nominal;
- ordinal;
- interval; and
- ratio.

Nominal

Nominal data are data that cannot be measured numerically. In other words, it is named data and includes values that can be classified into categories. If, for example, you conduct a questionnaire survey into employee promotion, you may be interested in placing employees into categories. Thus, 'trainee' may be coded as 1, 'supervisor' 2, 'manager' 3, and so on. There are a limited number of methods that can be used to analyze nominal data. Typical methods include frequency counts and finding the *mode*.

Ordinal

Like nominal, *ordinal data* are another type of *categorical data*. However, the main difference is that unlike nominal data, ordinal data can be rank-ordered. Let us say that you are interested in finding out the extent to which customer service is important among a sample of consumers. Using a Likert-scale question, perceived importance may be ranked from 1 to 5, where 1 = very important, 2 = important, 3 = neither important nor unimportant, 4 = unimportant, 5 = very unimportant. Examples of types of analysis suitable for ordinal data include frequency counts and percentages from a set of *ranked data*. Note that the distance across your set of categories might not be equal. Regarding the customer service example, we cannot say that those consumers who consider customer service as very important judge it to be 5 times more important than those who give a 1 – although we can say what percentage of respondents tick each box on our 5-point Likert-scale question.

Interval

Interval data have been achieved when the distance between the numbers are equal across the range. For example, the difference between 5 and 6 is 1. This is equal to the difference between 6 and 7. The temperature scales of Fahrenheit and Celsius are typical examples of interval scales in that the zero in both scales is arbitrary. So, you cannot say that 30 °C is twice as warm as 15 °C. When dealing with interval data you need to be very careful not to make such claims. The *mean, mode* and *median* can be used to describe interval data.

Ratio

Ratio data are very similar to interval data. The distinction between the two is that ratio data have a fixed zero point. Examples of ratio data include income, weight and height. Interval and ratio data allow for more precise levels of measurement than categorical data (nominal and ordinal). For example, a director's salary might be given in exact figures (ratio), or listed in relation to other directors within the company (ranked). Interval and ratio data also offer a greater number of options when it comes to data analysis. We explore some of these options later in the chapter.

Number of variables

Just as the types of data influence your choice of analytical tool, the same can be said of the number of variables. In essence, statistical methods can be based on the following numbers of variables: univariate (one), bivariate (two) or multivariate (three or more). The majority of methods associated with descriptive statistics are based on univariate data. Conversely, inferential statistics are typically associated with bivariate or multivariate data.

Coding

We came across coding in Chapter 6. All types of data should be coded numerically. For example, the *dichotomous variable* 'gender' is usually coded '1' and '2' when using statistical analysis software. The advantage of coding is that it will ultimately make your analysis easier and less confusing. Moreover, it is essential for most statistical software packages.

Coding during data collection

If you have adopted a deductive approach to your research and already have a set of predetermined categories, then you will most probably code your categories on your questionnaire survey. Certainly the advantage of coding at this stage is that it will save time later when carrying out your analysis.

Coding following data collection

If you are uncertain of the number and complexity of your responses, you may decide to implement your coding scheme after data collection, although for a collection tool such as a questionnaire survey, a predetermined set of codes for each question can make data entry and analysis less time-consuming.

Missing data

It is essential that you also code any missing data. Failure to do so is likely to impact on the interpretation of your results. A missing data code can be used to illustrate why data are missing. For example, a non-response might be indicated by a '0'. Coding missing data is required if you wish them to be excluded from your analysis.

Missing data may arise for a number of reasons. These include: a question is irrelevant to a respondent; a question is left blank as the respondent did not wish to complete it; or a question is not answered because the respondent did not understand it. The latter is sometimes a problem when conducting international or cross-cultural research.

Summarizing and Presenting Your Data

Summarizing and presenting your data is likely to be the first step in your analysis. It comes under the broad heading of descriptive statistics (see Table 9.1). Undertaking descriptive statistics not only allows you to describe your data, but also to present it in a number of different ways. Almost certainly you will be familiar with some of the techniques used to present descriptive statistics. These include frequency tables, bar charts, pie charts and graphs. Many studies that engage in statistical analysis use descriptive statistics as a starting point. The main advantage of summarizing the data in this way is that it provides the reader with a simple overview of your data prior to more detailed analysis.

Table 9.1 shows the various methods that can be used when describing your data. Column two highlights the purpose of each method, while column three shows a brief example of how each method might be applied. The application of each of the methods depends on a number of factors. These include the number of variables, the type of data and the purpose. I will now discuss each of the methods listed in Table 9.1 in more detail, including the advantages and disadvantages of each one.

Frequency tables

A good starting point when analyzing your data is to look at the *frequency distribution* for each variable in your study. A *frequency* is a numerical value that illustrates the number of counts for an observed variable. For instance, you might be interested in the number of cars company directors have.

TABLE 9.1 Examples of descriptive statistics

Method	Purpose	Examples of application
Frequency tables	Summarizing data	Number and percentage of employees in each firm
Graphs and charts	Summarizing data	Advertising spend on different types of media
Mean, median, mode	Measuring central tendency	Analyzing exam scores from a finance exam
Standard deviation	Measuring dispersion	Analyzing the standard deviations from a finance exam
Range and interquartile range	Measuring dispersion	Analyzing the range from a finance exam
Index numbers	Describing change	Changes to retail prices
Cross-tabulations	Frequency distribution	A preference for a brand of cereal based on gender
Scatter diagrams	Frequency distribution	Exploring the link between car mileage and petrol consumption
Multiple bar charts	Frequency distribution	Comparing the output for three different computer manufacturers over a five-year period

When constructing a frequency table, data are arranged in rows and columns. There are numerous ways to present a frequency table. Indeed, you probably come across a variety of examples on an almost daily basis. Examples include everything from school to football league tables!

A table is also a good starting point for both presenting and summarizing your quantitative findings. Table 9.2 shows an example of a frequency distribution table based on 15 company directors and the number of cars they have. Of course, a response is not always guaranteed. If this were the case, our table would also feature non-response frequencies.

Table 9.2 not only shows the frequency distribution for cars, it also shows the percentage frequency distribution. This shows that 33.3% of directors have one car, 26.7% have two cars, 26.7% have three cars and 13.3% have four cars. A percentage frequency distribution makes a useful addition to a frequency table.

Using a small sample size such as that for Table 9.2 is straightforward to incorporate into a frequency table. However, adopting the same approach for large samples is simply not practical. To overcome this problem it is a good idea to group your observed values into classes. For instance, if undertaking a large survey on

TABLE 9.2 Frequency distribution table: number of cars among company directors

Number of cars	Frequency	Percentage frequency
1	5	33.3
2	4	26.7
3	4	26.7
4	2	13.3

TABLE 9.3 Frequency distribution showing salaries among employees

Class(£)	Frequency	Cumulative frequency	% frequency	Cumulative % frequency
< 10,000	3	3	12	12
10,000 < 20,000	11	14	44	56
20,000 < 30,000	7	21	28	84
30,000 < 40,000	3	24	12	96
40,000 < 50,000	1	25	4	100

employees' salaries, you can group the respondents into classes based on intervals of £5,000: for example, £10,000 or more, but less than £15,000; £15,000 or more, but less than £20,000; and so on. Using intervals of £5,000 is reasonable given the likely variation in salaries. However, where you are likely to have a wide range of observed values, you may wish to group them into slightly broader classes. Conversely, a narrower range would best suit a smaller number of classes.

The obvious advantage of grouping your data is that it will make your table and results look more presentable. A potential problem is failing to recognize the types of data you are using when forming classes. For example, when using continuous data such as salary, it is sometimes easy to allocate data wrongly due to poorly defined intervals between classes. Let us look at an example of a frequency distribution table showing grouped data (see Table 9.3).

As well as showing grouped data, Table 9.3 also includes a cumulative frequency and cumulative percentage frequency distribution column. A cumulative figure is obtained by simply adding the observations from the previously stated (lower) classes. For example, when establishing the cumulative frequency for the third class in Table 9.3, we simply add the two lower classes, 3 + 11 + 7 = 21. The same principles apply for the cumulative percentage frequency distribution.

So far, we have examined frequency tables in relation to *univariate data*. Frequency tables are also useful for examining *bivariate data*. A table that allows you to examine the relationship between two variables is called a *cross-tabulation*. We shall address this later in the chapter.

Diagrams used for presenting data

Diagrams or illustrations can be a useful way of presenting your data. Like tables, they help to break up your text and can make for very interesting reading. The main types of diagram are graphs and charts.

Graphs

A *graph* is a type of diagram used to present data. A graph can be used to analyze bivariate or multivariate data. Waters (1997: 107) offers the following advice when

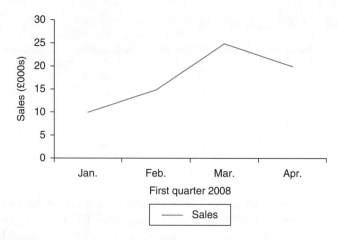

FIGURE 9.3 Sales for ABC Ltd (first quarter 2008)

producing graphs: as graphs give a very strong initial impact, the choice of scale for the axes is clearly important, with a bad choice giving a false view of the data. Although the choice of scale is largely subjective, some guidelines for good practice can be given:

- Always label the axes clearly and accurately.
- Show the scales on both axes.
- The maximum of the scale should be slightly above the maximum observation.
- Wherever possible, the scale on the axis should start at zero. If this cannot be done, the scale must be shown clearly, perhaps with a zigzag on the axis to indicate a break.
- Where appropriate, give the source of data.
- Where appropriate, give the graph a title.

Line graphs are ideal for analyzing trends over time (longitudinal data). The data should be of at least interval, ordinal or ratio status. Figure 9.3 shows a line graph. A line to illustrate the trend over the entire timeframe joins the data value for each respective time period – in this case, four months (Jan. to Apr. 2008).

The advantage of graphs is that they can clearly illustrate the relationship between two variables. A downside is that graphs tend not to be as visually appealing as charts.

Pie charts

A *pie chart* is used for summarizing categorical data. A pie chart is divided into segments. Each segment represents a particular category. The size of each category is proportional to the number of cases it represents. Typically, the number of cases is represented by a percentage. Each segment has a different colour or pattern to clearly distinguish each category.

TABLE 9.4 A summary of market share figures for seven construction companies

Companies	Market share (%)
MMP Builds	30
JP Construction	20
TML Build	15
AC Developments	11
KMC	8
Global Plex	7
Z Build	7
Others	2

FIGURE 9.4 A pie chart showing market share figures for construction companies

Pie charts are straightforward diagrams that compare a limited amount of data. By way of illustration, let us say that you are concerned with the presentation of market share figures for seven construction companies. You may begin by summarizing your data in the form of a simple table (see Table 9.4). Figure 9.4 shows the data from Table 9.4 incorporated into a pie chart.

There are two main advantages associated with pie charts. First, they are a clear way of highlighting proportional differences. Second, the use of different colours makes it easy to distinguish between categories. Conversely, sometimes it can be difficult to divide categories into segments. This is especially true with fragmented data or when there are a large number of categories.

TABLE 9.5   Numbers of departmental employees

	Agency			
	Hall Media	**BC Global**	**JLC**	**T Media**
HR	25	15	40	22
Finance	18	20	16	19
Marketing	30	15	10	20

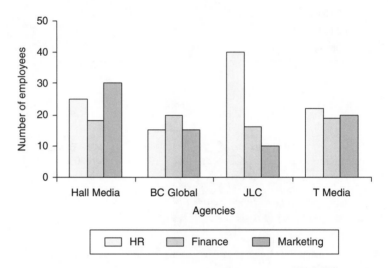

FIGURE 9.5   Numbers of employees in advertising agencies

Bar charts

A *bar chart* is similar to a pie chart in that it compares a simple set of observations. However, instead of sectors of a circle, bars are used to represent the data. A bar chart is a straightforward way of summarizing either ordinal or nominal data. It involves bivariate analysis of the main characteristics of the distribution of the data.

Essentially, there are two main types of bar chart: horizontal and vertical. Each bar is the same width, whereas the length represents the number of cases. A bar chart has a gap between each bar, while a histogram does not have any gaps because it represents continuous data. To illustrate, there are four advertising agencies located in a small town. The number of employees in each of their respective departments is highlighted in Table 9.5. Now, let us put these data into a simple bar chart (see Figure 9.5).

The main advantage of a bar chart is that it is a simplistic way of illustrating the relationship between two variables. On the other hand, a disadvantage is that a large number of cases representing small values can make the chart look cumbersome.

TABLE 9.6 Frequency table showing customer waiting times

Groups	Frequency
0–10 minutes	45
11–20 minutes	22
21–30 minutes	28
31–40 minutes	13
41–50 minutes	6

Histograms

A *histogram* is a type of bar chart that shows a frequency distribution of a set of data. It provides a clear indication of the nature of your distribution, in particular whether or not you have a *normal* or *skewed distribution*. It is an excellent way of summarizing data that are on an interval scale (either discrete or continuous). The height of each bar represents each observed frequency.

Before compiling your histogram you need to divide the range of values from your data set into groups. On the *x*-axis of your chart, each group is represented by a rectangle with a base length equal to the range of values within that particular group, and an area proportional to the total number of observations applicable to that group.

When compiling your histogram it is important that you allocate a suitable number of groups. Too few or too many will negatively impact on the presentation of your frequency distribution.

An advantage of a histogram is that it is easy to interpret the data. In addition, it is ideal where the class divisions are not the same. The main disadvantage is that it cannot provide precise individual values. By way of illustration, let us say that a bank is interested in reducing customer waiting times. It conducts research on its busiest day of the week (Saturday) in order to establish a 'typical' waiting time. Following its findings, the bank intends to take steps to reduce waiting times in order to improve levels of customer service. The results from the study are summarized in a frequency table (see Table 9.6), while the histogram of the same set of

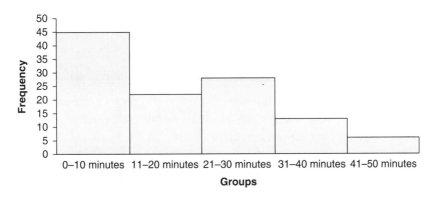

FIGURE 9.6   Histogram showing customer waiting times

data is illustrated in Figure 9.6. The y-axis is the relative frequency, while the x-axis shows the waiting times.

Describing Your Data

In the last section we looked at numerous ways of presenting and summarizing your data. These include tables, charts and graphs. The next step in your data analysis is likely to involve the use of descriptive statistics. In essence, there are two broad approaches to describing your data: measuring central tendency and measuring dispersion. We shall now examine these approaches.

Measuring central tendency

Summarizing and presenting data is fine if we want a general overview of our data. However, often we like to summarize data in a more concise way. A common way of doing this is to discuss the 'average'.

Measures of *central tendency* are used to illustrate a typical outcome in a set of data. The main ways of measuring central tendency are the *mean, median* and *mode*. First, let us look at the mean.

Mean

The mean ($\bar{x}$) is the arithmetical average of a frequency distribution. The method of calculating the arithmetic mean is:

- add all observations together; and
- divide by the total number of observations.

The mean formula for calculating single data is as follows:

$$\text{Mean } (\bar{X}) = \frac{\Sigma x}{n}$$

where:
    x = each observation
    n = the total number of observations
    Σ = the sum of

For example, if a car dealership wished to find the mean number of cars sold over the course of a week, the process would be as follows:

Number of cars sold over six working days: 12, 16, 14, 11, 9, 10.

$$(\bar{X}) = \frac{\Sigma x}{n} = \frac{12+16+14+11+9+10}{6} = 12$$

The number of cars sold over the course of the week is 12.

If we are dealing with a set of grouped data, then we need to use a different formula for calculating the mean:

$$\bar{X} = \frac{\Sigma fx}{\Sigma f}$$

where:

x = each observation
f = the frequency
Σ = the sum of

For example, Table 9.7 shows the monthly bonuses among sales staff and is grouped into classes. Using this formula, the mean monthly sales bonus is:

$$\bar{X} = \frac{\Sigma fx}{\Sigma f} = \frac{£7,800}{30} = £260$$

The answer is that the mean monthly sales bonus is £260.

One of the advantages of the mean is that it includes every score in a set of data. Also, if taking several samples from a population, the means are likely to be the same. The disadvantages are that the mean is sensitive to outliers (extreme values) and can only be used with interval or ratio data.

TABLE 9.7 Calculating the mean in a set of grouped data – sales staff monthly bonuses

Monthly bonus (£)	Frequency (f)	Mid-values (x)	(fx)
<100	7	50	350
100–199.99	4	150	600
200–299.99	6	250	1500
300–399.99	5	350	1750
400–499.99	8	450	3600
	$\Sigma f = 30$		$\Sigma fx = 7800$

Median

The median is also sometimes referred to as an average. It is the middle number in a set of numbers. The median can be found using the following formula:

$$M = \frac{n+1}{2}$$

where:

n = number of observations

For example, suppose you wanted to find the median in the following set of numbers: 42, 16, 38, 11, 9. The first step is to put them in ascending order: 9, 11, 16, 38, 42. Next, apply the formula:

$$M = \frac{n+1}{2} = \frac{5+1}{2} = 3$$

So, the median is the third number in the sequence: 16.

If our list is made up of an even number, we can simply take the mid-value between the third and fourth values. For example:

$$8, 15, 18, 27, 39, 45$$

$$\frac{18+27}{2} = 22.5$$

Our median is halfway between the third and fourth values in our set of data (18 and 27). Therefore the median is 22.5.

The median has two main advantages. First, it can be used with ordinal, interval and ratio data (it cannot be used with categorical data). Second, the median is unaffected by outliers. The disadvantages are that the median may not be a characteristic of the distribution if it does not follow a normal distribution, and it cannot be used for further statistical analysis.

Mode

The mode is the value that occurs the most often in your set of data. If, for example, we have the set of data 15, 15, 8, 9, 12, 15, 24, 2, 6, 15 the mode is 15, as it appears the most often: 4 times.

The advantage of the mode is that, unlike the mean and median, it can be used with nominal data. Moreover, it is very straightforward to determine and is unaffected by outliers. The disadvantage of the mode is that you can end up with more than one mode value. Moreover, it does not indicate the variation in a set of data and is sensitive to additional observations.

Measuring dispersion

A key limitation of measuring central tendency is that it does not give us an indication of the shape of a frequency distribution. A measure that allows us to describe the spread of values in a distribution is referred to as a measure of *dispersion*. By combining measures of central tendency and dispersion you can gain a useful description of your set of data. Typical methods used to measure dispersion include the *standard deviation, range* and *interquartile range*.

Standard deviation

The standard deviation is represented by S for sample standard deviation and σ (lower-case sigma) for population standard deviation. The standard deviation measures the spread of data around the mean value.

The steps in finding the standard deviation can be summarized as follows:

- Find the mean in your set of data (i.e. the difference between a particular value and the mean – see Table 9.8).
- Find the deviation from the mean for each value.
- Square the deviations from the mean to get rid of negative values (failure to do so will lead to an answer of zero).
- Find the sum of these values.
- Divide by the number of values in order to get an average (also known as the variance).
- Find the square root of the variance in order to find the standard deviation.

The standard deviation is expressed by the formula:

$$S = \sqrt{\frac{\Sigma(x-\bar{x})^2}{n-1}}$$

where:w
   S = the sample standard deviation
   x = an observation
   $\bar{x}$ = the mean
   n = the total number of observations
   $\sqrt{}$ = the square root
   Σ = the sum of

Please note, when calculating the standard deviation of a small sample, a better estimate is gained by dividing by $(n-1)$ rather than n.

The formula for a set of grouped data is as follows:

$$S = \sqrt{\frac{\Sigma(x-\bar{x})^2}{\Sigma f}}$$

where:
   S = the sample standard deviation
   x = the mid-point of each data class
   f = the frequency of each class
   $\sqrt{}$ = the square root
   Σ = the sum of

By way of illustration, let us say that you are researching the number of times (x) a printing press breaks down over a period of six months (see Table 9.8).

TABLE 9.8 Finding the mean and the standard deviation

x	$(x-\bar{x})$	$(x-\bar{x})^2$
10	3	9
8	1	1
9	2	4
7	0	0
6	−1	1
2	−5	25
Total 42		40

$$S=\sqrt{\frac{40}{6}}=2.58$$ The mean is 7 and the standard deviation is 2.58.

An advantage of the standard deviation is that it uses every value in the population or group of sample data. However, because all items in a data set are used it can be influenced by extreme values.

Range

The range is found by subtracting the lowest value from the highest value in a set of data. If, for example, we have the set of data 5, 6, 7, 8, 8, 12, 13, 15, the lowest value is 5, while the highest is 15. By subtracting the lowest from the highest we get: 15 − 5 = 10. So our range is 10. The main advantage of the range is that it is easy to calculate and provides a clear indication as to the broadness or narrowness of a set of data. A key disadvantage is that a range based on a small sample size is likely to exclude extreme values. Conversely, the greater the sample size the greater the likelihood that extreme values will be included. Another disadvantage is that it does not tell us anything about the values within the range.

Interquartile range

As noted earlier, one criticism of the range is that it can be greatly affected by extreme values. The interquartile range helps to overcome this problem by measuring the spread between the upper and lower quartiles of a set of data (the middle 50%). As the interquartile range only focuses on the middle 50% of a range of data, it is not as sensitive as the range, although it is less susceptible to outliers.

Finding the interquartile range requires the following steps:

- List your data in order of size, beginning with the smallest first.
- Find the position of the median.
- Find the median in the data to the left of your median (lower quartile).
- Find the median in the data to the right of your median (upper quartile).
- Find the difference between the medians for the upper and lower quartiles. This gives you the interquartile range.

The following example shows the interquartile range for a set of data. A small electrical retailer has recorded the number of returned items over a 12-month period (see Table 9.9).

TABLE 9.9 Number of returned items over 12 months

12	14	22	16	23	9	13	7	26	18	6	10

First, let us place the values in ascending order (Table 9.10).

TABLE 9.10 Number of returned items in ascending order

6	7	9	10	12	13	14	16	18	22	23	26

Next, find the median for the lower quartile (mid-value Q1) = 6, 7, 9, 10, 12, 13.

$$\text{Median} = \text{3rd + 4th observations} \div 2$$

$$= \frac{9+10}{2} = 9.5$$

Now, find the median for the upper quartile (mid-value Q3) = 14, 16, 18, 22, 23, 26.

$$\text{Median} = \text{3rd + 4th observations} \div 2$$

$$= \frac{18+22}{2} = 20$$

$$\text{Interquartile range (IR)} = Q3 - Q1$$

$$= 20 - 9.5 = 10.5$$

The interquartile range and median from our set of data can be shown as follows:

6,   7,   9,   10,   12,   13,   14,   16,   18,   22,   23,   26

Lower quartile 9.5   Median 13.5   Upper quartile 20

Now, let us presume that the company only operated for 11 months of the year, thereby giving us an odd number of 11 observations (see Table 9.11).

TABLE 9.11 Number of returned items over 11 months

6	7	9	10	12	13	14	16	18	22	23

Find the lower quartile (mid-value Q1) = 6, 7, 9, 10, 12
Median = 3rd observation = 9
Median for the upper quartile (mid-value Q3) = 14, 16, 18, 22, 23
Median = 3rd observation = 18
Interquartile range (IR) = Q3 – Q1
$$= 18 - 9 = 9$$

If we wished to measure the spread of data based on the semi-interquartile range, our answer would be half of the interquartile range. Based on the last example, half of 10.5 is 5.25.

Describing change

Measuring dispersion allows us to examine the spread of data. However, this is based on a fixed point in time. How can we examine data that change over time? For example, the percentage changes in fuel prices, house prices or interest rates? One method is to produce a simple index.

Index numbers

An *index number* shows how a quantity changes over time. Usually, the base period equals 100. Two of the most widely recognized indices are the FTSE 100, which is the list of the UK's top-performing 100 companies, and the Retail Price Index (RPI). The latter examines how people spend their income. It measures the fluctuation in the cost of a representative basket of goods and services. The RPI commenced in 1947. This therefore represents the base year. The base year can be represented by any given year, although it is typically a decade or more. This is for two reasons. First, historical data are often widely available. Second, when analyzing changes over time, we need a sufficient number of years to identify any possible trends.

It is also worth noting that the base year does not have to be 100. For example, the FTSE 100 of leading shares has a base of 1,000.

The formula for calculating an index is as follows:

$$i = \frac{c/p}{b} \times 100$$

where:

c/p = cost/price
b = base value

Let us look at an example of an index. Table 9.12 shows how the average price of a new car has changed over time. The base year (the first year when the data was collected) is 1978. Remember that 100 represents the base year.

TABLE 9.12 Average price of new cars over time

Year	Average price of new car (£)
1978	800
1979	932
1980	1,024
1981	1,098
1982	1,200

TABLE 9.13 Index of new car sale prices (1978-82)

Year	Average price of new car	C/P × 100	Index number (I)
1978	800	$\frac{800}{800}$ × 100	100.0
1979	932	$\frac{932}{800}$ × 100	116.5
1980	1,024	$\frac{1,024}{800}$ × 100	128.0
1981	1,098	$\frac{1,098}{800}$ × 100	137.25
1982	1,200	$\frac{1,200}{800}$ × 100	150.0

The next step is to apply the formula so that we can clearly compare the extent that the data has changed over time (see Table 9.13).

Weighted index numbers

A simple index such as car prices is fine if we are concerned about one observation over time. Yet, if we have a number of items, it is unlikely that we would assign equal importance to each item. In order to address this, we can allocate a weighting to each one.

Typically, a weighted price index is calculated at the end of each year, then comparisons are made over a given time period. A simple price index can be used to calculate the end year weighted price index. This is known as Paasche's Price Index and is represented by the formula:

$$\frac{\Sigma P_n Q_n}{\Sigma P_0 Q_n} \times 100$$

where:

P_0 = base year prices
P_n = the current year prices
Q_n = current year quantity

Paasche's Index can only be calculated at the end of the current year as the weights are current year quantities in a price index. To illustrate, let us say that a specialist car manufacturer buys the following products from one of its suppliers during 2004 and 2005 (see Table 9.14).

Sum of P_n × Q_n = (25 × 42) + (20 × 36) + (35 × 20) + (45 × 22) = 1050 + 720 + 700 + 990 = 3460

Sum of P_0 × Q_n = (20 × 42) + (15 × 36) + (30 × 20) + (40 × 22) = 840 + 540 + 600 + 880 = 2860

Thus, Paasche's Price Index = $\frac{3,460}{2,860}$ × 100 = 120.98.

TABLE 9.14   Car manufacturer supplier purchases (2004/05)

Parts	2004 Unit price (P_0)	2004 Quantity (Q_0)	2005 Unit price (p_n)	2005 Quantity (q_n)
Car tyres	20	30	25	42
Alarms	15	40	20	36
Bumpers	30	30	35	20
Radios	40	25	45	22

Frequency distribution

Earlier in the chapter we looked at frequency tables to gain an insight into the frequency distribution of univariate data. A frequency table can also be used to examine bivariate or multivariate data. This type of table is called a *cross-tabulation*.

Cross-tabulations

A cross-tabulation is a table that shows the joint distribution of bivariate or multivariate data. In Table 9.15, the cross-tabulation shows the nationality by gender for business school students.

The advantage of cross-tabulations is that they are simple to produce and allow for easy comparison between data. However, care should be taken with the number and types of variable. For example, too many variables will have a negative impact on the presentation of your table, and probably include several low values.

Scatter diagrams

A *scatter diagram* (sometimes referred to as a scatter plot) is essentially a graph used to assess the relationship between two variables. These are the independent variable using the *x*-axis, and the dependent variable the *y*-axis. The two variables are plotted on the graph to see whether or not a relationship exists.

TABLE 9.15   Cross-tabulation showing nationality by gender for business school students

Nationality	Male students	Female students
British	148	136
Chinese	21	14
French	22	23
American	16	28
German	10	16
Other	14	19

Figure 9.7 shows the relationship between the distance travelled by car and petrol consumption. This is a strong positive linear correlation. In other words, an increase in the value of one variable is associated with an increase in the value of the other. In Figure 9.7, an increase in distance travelled (x) is associated with an increase in petrol consumption (y).

A negative correlation happens when an increase in the value of one variable is associated with a decrease in the value of the other. For example, higher levels of unemployment might be associated with lower levels of car sales. If the points are scattered randomly throughout the graph, there is no correlation between the two variables. Another possibility is that the variables show a non-linear relationship. For example, this might be the case when examining the relationship between age and weight.

An outlier is a value from a set of data that is inconsistent with other values. It can be much larger or much smaller than other values. You should not ignore an outlier, as it can impact on the results of descriptive statistics such as the mean. An outlier can be caused by one of two reasons – an error in measurement or radical behaviour from one of the participants. Either way, you need to establish reasons for the inconsistency before progressing with your research.

Multiple bar charts

A *multiple bar chart* is a little more complex than a simple bar chart. It is a chart illustrating two or more variables in the form of bars of length proportional to the magnitudes of the variables. For example, Figure 9.8 shows the output of a drinks factory over four years.

Figure 9.8 clearly shows the changes in production output for cola, apple juice and lemonade over a period of three years. One might assume that the factory is performing well as the output for each type of drink has increased year on year.

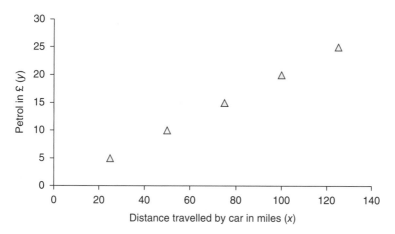

FIGURE 9.7 Scatter diagram showing a strong positive linear correlation

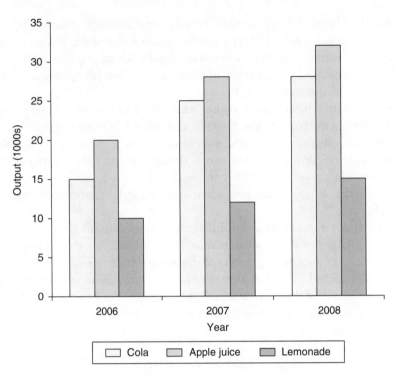

FIGURE 9.8 The output of a drinks factory over a period of three years

The advantage of a multiple bar chart is that it allows you to compare variables. Conversely, as in the case of our drinks factory example, they only describe data and do not provide an explanation of why variables are of a certain value.

Inferential Statistics

Inferential statistics are used to draw inferences about a population from a given sample. As noted earlier, inferential statistics can also be subdivided on the basis of *nonparametric* and *parametric tests*. A parametric test should only be applied if the following conditions are met: you have interval or ratio data, your sample is randomly drawn from the population, and your sample is from a population that is normally distributed. The *normal distribution* or *bell curve* is a graph that shows data scores that accumulate around the middle. The normal distribution proposes that the mean, mode and median are all equal. For example, the results of an exam would show that the majority of exam scores would centre round the middle when the frequency curve is symmetrical. When the frequency curve is skewed, the mean, mode and median all have different values.

Determining whether or not your sample is from a population that is normally distributed is important as it will influence your choice of statistical tests. One can make this assumption using something called the *Central Limit Theorem*. The Central Limit Theorem is based on the notion that the average in a set of sample data drawn from a wider population is approximately distributed as a normal distribution if certain conditions are met. The main condition is that when a random, independent sample has at least 30 observations, the distribution of all sample means of the same-sized samples closely approaches a normal distribution of the population from which the sample is drawn. Hence, for sample sizes of above 30, you can assume that the sampling distribution of means will approximate to a normal distribution.

When a parametric test cannot be used, non-parametric tests should be applied. One advantage of these tests is that they make no assumptions about the distribution of the population.

A number of parametric and non-parametric methods are associated with inferential statistics. Although by no means exhaustive, Table 9.16 shows the methods that we shall examine in this chapter. It also includes the purpose of each method (a 'P' or 'NP' alongside each method indicates parametric or non-parametric respectively) and briefly illustrates how each method might be applied.

At this stage, do not be too concerned if you are unable to recognize the conditions required in relation to each of the examples in Table 9.16. By the end of this chapter, you should be in a position to develop your own examples for all of the methods listed here.

TABLE 9.16 Examples of inferential statistics

Method	Purpose	Examples of application
Hypothesis testing	Estimation	H0 – There is no difference in the mean exam marks between male and female managers. H1 – There is a difference in the mean exam marks between male and female managers.
Confidence intervals	Estimation	Calculating a 95% confidence interval for the proportion of small firms in London that do business with Europe.
Time series analysis	Forecasting	One-month moving averages of retail sales data.
Pearson's product moment correlation coefficient (P)	Measuring association	Correlating gender with height.
Spearman's rank correlation coefficient (NP)	Measuring association	Comparing two managers' ranked assessment of ten employees.
Chi-squared test (NP)	Measuring difference	Do some manufacturers produce more faulty goods than others?
Student's t-test	Measuring difference	Comparing the sample means of ages of female finance and marketing managers (independent t-test).
Simple regression (P)	Assessing the strength of relationship between variables	Strength of relationship between advertising spend and sales.
Multiple regression (P)	Assessing the strength of relationship between variables	Strength of relationship between advertising spend and training spend on sales.

Estimation

Estimation refers to estimating a population parameter from samples. It is unlikely that you will be in the fortunate position to have access to the entire population. If you have adopted a positivist approach to your research, the likelihood is that your intention is to estimate from your sample characteristics of the population.

Two methods commonly used to estimate from samples are *hypothesis testing* and *confidence intervals*.

Hypothesis testing

Hypothesis testing is one of the main methods used in inferential statistics. It involves making a statement about some aspect of the population, then generating a sample to see if the hypothesis can or cannot be rejected. To test a hypothesis you need to formulate a null hypothesis (H0) and an alternative hypothesis (H1). The former makes the assumption that there is no change in the value being tested. For example, 'no change' could relate to 'no difference' or 'no correlation'. For each null hypothesis there is an alternative hypothesis (H1). An alternative hypothesis tends to be vaguer than a null hypothesis, as will become apparent later on. The probability of rejecting the null hypothesis when it is true is referred to as the significance level. If the significance level is $p < 0.05$ (5% level), then you reject the null hypothesis. Conversely, if the significance level is $p \geq 0.05$ then you cannot reject the null hypothesis. Be careful with your wording. We cannot say 'accept'. The convention among researchers is to use 'cannot reject' the null hypothesis.

An example of a null hypothesis might be:

H0: There is no difference between the value of bonuses among male and female employees

H1: There is a difference between the value of bonuses among male and female employees

The steps in hypothesis testing are as follows:

- State your null (H0) and alternative (H1) hypotheses.
- Choose a level of significance (typically the 0.05, or 5%, level).
- Collect your data.
- Carry out statistical tests.

Make one of the following decisions:

1. Reject the null hypothesis (H0) and accept the alternative hypothesis (H1), or
2. Fail to reject the null hypothesis (H0) and subsequently note that there is not sufficient evidence to suggest the truth of the alternative hypothesis (H1).

Type I errors and Type II errors   Once you have carried out your hypothesis you should have reached a decision about whether to reject or not reject your null hypothesis, although, due to sampling variation, your conclusion will be subject to error. A *type I error* is where the null hypothesis is true but rejected, while a *type II error* is where the alternative

TABLE 9.17 Possible outcomes of a hypothesis test

	H0 is true	H1 is true
Accept H0	No error	Type II error
Reject H0	Type I error	No error

hypothesis is true but rejected (see Table 9.17). If you set your level of significance too high (e.g. $p > 0.01$), there is a greater likelihood of you making a type II error.

Types of hypothesis test   Before carrying out a hypothesis test you need to decide which type of test to use. There are two types of test. The first of these is referred to as a 'two-tailed test', while the second is a 'one-tailed test'. Your choice is important as it will impact on how you word your alternative hypothesis. Let us look at each one in turn.

A two-tailed test is carried out to see if your hypothesis is above or below what you presume it to be. For example, you might believe that training (independent variable) has an effect on company performance (dependent variable) but you cannot predict the direction. When the alternative hypothesis (H1) is written as not equal to ($\neq$), then you are indicating your intention to carry out a two-tailed test.

A one-tailed test is used when you are making a prediction that there will be an effect in a particular direction. For example, if students are given extra classes (independent variable), their exam marks will increase (dependent variable).

If conducting a left-tailed test, H1 is written as follows:

$$H1: \mu < 200g$$

If conducting a right-tailed test, H1 is written as follows:

$$H1: \mu > 200g$$

Confidence intervals

A *confidence interval* uses a range of values that is likely to comprise an unknown population parameter. A parameter is a population characteristic such as a proportion (p) or mean (m). Confidence intervals are generally more useful than straightforward hypothesis tests as they go beyond a simple 'reject the null hypothesis' or 'do not reject the null hypothesis' by providing a range of credible values for the population parameter.

First, it is important to make a distinction between confidence interval and confidence level. For example, if you collected data on job security from finance managers, 75% might say that they felt 'insecure' in their job. Hence, you might say that 75% of finance managers are insecure. You could support this by saying that you are 95% certain (confidence level) that this will represent the true population 95% of the time.

If, for example, we take a sample of 200 employees and find a mean age of 35, can we be sure that the mean age is representative of the population? Unfortunately, our mean (or point of estimate) is unlikely to be the same as the population, although it is likely to be close to the population mean but have some error. In order to address the problem of our point estimate, we can define a range (confidence interval) within which our population mean is likely to fall. The confidence interval is expressed with a level of confidence that the interval contains the true population parameter. Typically, most researchers use a 95% confidence level. This means that 95% of the probability falls between z values of -1.96 and $+1.96$. These represent the most commonly used critical values for calculating confidence limits. A *critical value* or z-score relates to the number of standard deviations that the sample mean departs from the population mean of a normal distribution. Other examples are shown in Table 9.18.

A confidence interval is used to estimate the true mean of your entire population (π). It is represented by the formula:

$$\mu = x \pm z^* \frac{\sigma}{\sqrt{n}}$$

where:

μ = population mean
$\bar{x}$ = sample mean
$\pm$ = margin of errors
z = critical value
σ = population standard deviation
n = sample size

Let us say that you have conducted a study into the performance of manufacturing machinery among a sample of 150 companies. Your findings produce a mean length of operation before the machinery needs servicing of 180 hours, with a standard deviation of 20 hours. You now intend to determine the 95% confidence interval for the overall mean length of operation prior to servicing, among all companies that use this type of equipment.

$$\mu = 180 \pm 1.96 \times \frac{20}{\sqrt{150}}$$

$$\pm 3.19$$

$= (176.81 - 183.19)$ operational hours before servicing.

TABLE 9.18 Confidence level for each interval and respective critical value

Confidence interval (%)	Critical value
99	2.58
95	1.96
90	1.64

In the above example, we assume that the standard deviation of the population is known. In reality, it is unlikely that we would know the standard deviation of a population but not its mean. In most cases, researchers need to use the sample standard deviation (S) and mean to estimate the population mean and standard deviation.

If you have a sample size $n > 30$, a confidence interval can also be used to estimate the proportion in a population. This is represented by the formula:

$$p \pm z * \sqrt{\frac{p(1-p)}{n}}$$

where:

z = critical value
p = sample proportion
n = sample size
$\sqrt{}$ = square root

Let us say that you have conducted a study into higher education qualifications among small businesses in Cambridge. From your random sample of 100 companies you have established that 70 small firms have at least one employee who holds a higher education qualification, thus $x = 70$ and $n = 100$.

$$p = x/n = 70/100 = 0.7$$

Now let us calculate the 95% confidence interval for the proportion of small firms in Cambridge that have at least one employee who holds a higher education qualification:

$$0.7 \pm 1.96 \sqrt{\frac{0.7(1-0.7)}{100}}$$

$$0.7 \pm 1.96(0.046)$$

$$0.7 \pm 0.090$$

$$(0.61, 0.79)$$

Thus, we are 95% confident that the true proportion of small firms who have an employee with a higher education qualification is between 61% and 79%.

Forecasting

Forecasting can be defined as the estimation of a set of values at a future point in time. Forecasting plays an important role in business. For example, many organizations engage in sales forecasting to maintain better control over inventory levels, while governments forecast levels of inflation and unemployment, along with economic growth, to determine appropriate government policy. Forecasting financial data such as share prices is also important for both individual and organizational decision-making.

There are several different methods associated with forecasting. These include qualitative methods and economic models. In this section I introduce you to one of the main categories associated with forecasting – *time series analysis*. This is an introduction to the subject. For a more detailed discussion on time series analysis you will need to consult a book devoted to forecasting – see the Further Reading section.

Time series analysis

A time series is a series of data points that are typically measured over regular time intervals. Time series analysis involves using various methods to understand a time series in a 'historical' context, as well as to make forecasts or predictions. In relation to the latter, we shall now examine two of the commonly used methods of time series analysis – 'simple moving average' and 'weighted moving average'.

A *simple moving average* is used to compare possible changes in a variable over time. It is found by calculating the mean for a given time period. For example, let us say that you carried out a study into the ages at which individuals were appointed as Chief Executive Officer (CEO) for one particular company. Since the firm's inception in 1978, you have established that there have been eight CEOs. Their ages upon appointment are as follows: 53, 60, 55, 52, 49, 58, 48, 61. Our moving average depends on the number of years that we wish to use as our period. For example, using four years:

The first year is: $\dfrac{53+60+55+52}{4} = 55$

The second year is: $\dfrac{60+55+52+49}{4} = 54$

The third year is: $\dfrac{55+52+49+58}{4} = 53.5$

The fourth year is: $\dfrac{52+49+58+48}{4} = 51.75$

The advantage of the simple moving average is that it is easy to calculate and provides a reasonably accurate estimate for forecasting. However, the main drawback is that it does not account for possible trends. For example, many seasonal products experience an increase in sales over the Christmas period. Ideally, this trend needs to be taken into account when forecasting. One way to do this is to weight your data.

A *weighted moving average* is where greater significance is placed on one part of your data set than the rest. For example, in a volatile economic climate the price of petrol may fluctuate to a large degree. Hence, you are more likely to give the most recent data in your set of fuel prices more significance than earlier data, as they give a better representation of the current state of the market.

Measuring association

If you have gathered bivariate data, then an interesting test would be to find out if your two variables are associated in some way. For instance, you might be interested in researching a possible association or *correlation* between age and salary among a group of employees. Remember that correlation does not mean causation. For example, if an umbrella manufacturer finds that there is a correlation between umbrella sales and annual rainfall, this does not necessarily mean that increased rainfall causes an increase in umbrella sales. Other variables are likely to impact on sales. These might include pricing, the state of the economy, or possibly competition in the market.

Correlation coefficient

A correlation coefficient is used for bivariate analysis. It measures the extent to which two variables are linearly related. Measurement is represented between −1 and 1. A value of 1 represents a perfect positive correlation; a perfect negative linear relationship is represented by a value −1, and a correlation coefficient of 0 means that there is no relationship between the two variables. In other words, both variables are perfectly independent.

In reality, it is unlikely that you will produce findings that are perfectly correlated or perfectly independent. Typically, values usually fall somewhere between ±1 and 0.

A straightforward way to find out if there is a correlation between two variables is to plot the data. As we have seen earlier in this chapter, a scatter plot is a simple way of doing this as it clearly illustrates the correlation between two variables. However, it does not measure the strength of the relationship between two variables. In essence, there are two types of correlation coefficient – *Pearson's product moment correlation coefficient* and *Spearman's rank correlation coefficient*. These are examined below.

Pearson's product moment correlation coefficient

Pearson's product moment correlation (r) is a parametric technique that measures the strength of association between two variables or *bivariate data*. For example, you may wish to examine a possible relationship between advertising spend and number of sales, or age and height among teenagers. The data used must be of an interval or ratio type and be normally distributed.

If your answer produces a strong relationship between your x and y variables, this does not mean that x causes y. We can go on to test this possibility by carrying out regression analysis.

Pearson's product moment correlation coefficient is represented by the formula:

$$r = \frac{\Sigma xy - \frac{\Sigma x \Sigma y}{n}}{\sqrt{\left(\Sigma x^2 - \frac{(\Sigma x^2)}{n}\right)\left(\Sigma y^2 - \frac{(\Sigma y^2)}{n}\right)}}$$

where:
   n = the number of data pairs
   y = the dependent variable
   x = the independent variable
   $\sqrt{}$ = square root
   Σ = the sum of

By way of illustration, an engineering company wishes to test the association between the number of breakdowns to its machinery over a period of 12 days and the consequent time taken to carry out the repairs. The data are set out in Table 9.19.

Using the data in Table 9.19, we can now enter this into the formula. Thus:

$$= \frac{532 - 499}{\sqrt{[180 - 161][1,678 - 1,541]}}$$

$$= \frac{33}{\sqrt{(19)(137)}}$$

$$= \frac{33}{51.020}$$

$$= 0.65$$

The next step is to interpret our result. This can be made by checking the values of the correlation coefficient (r):

between 0.70 and 0.99 is a strong positive correlation;
between 0.40 and 0.69 is a medium positive correlation;
between 0 and 0.39 is a weak positive correlation;
between 0 and −0.39 is a weak negative correlation;
between −0.40 and −0.69 is a medium negative correlation; and
between −0.70 and −0.99 is a strong negative correlation.

In our above example, the result (0.65) is significant at the 5% level. This means that there is a medium positive correlation between the number of breakdowns and the time taken to repair each breakdown.

TABLE 9.19   Production output data

Day	Number of breakdowns (x)	Time taken to repair (minutes) (y)	xy	x^2	y^2
1	2	10	20	4	100
2	4	18	72	16	324
3	3	9	27	9	81
4	4	16	64	16	256
5	5	12	60	25	144
6	6	14	84	36	196
7	3	8	24	9	64
8	4	12	48	16	144
9	2	6	12	4	36
10	4	10	40	16	100
11	5	13	65	25	169
12	2	8	16	4	64
Total	44	136	532	180	1,678

Spearman's rank correlation coefficient

Spearman's rank correlation coefficient (r_s) is used to test the strength and direction of association between two ordinal variables. It is a test of association that is used for non-parametric data and can be used to aid either the proving or disproving of a hypothesis, e.g. the profit of a company increases as the size of the company increases (see Table 9.20). The formula given to Spearman's rank correlation coefficient is as follows:

$$r_s = 1 - \frac{6\Sigma d^2}{n(n^2-1)}$$

where:

d = the difference between the two rankings of one item of data
n = the number of items of data
Σ = the sum of

$$\Sigma d^2 = 0+9+1+0+0+1+0+1+1+9 = 22$$

$$r_s = 1 - \frac{6(22)}{10(100-1)}$$

$$= 1 - \frac{132}{990}$$

$$r_s = 0.87$$

As noted earlier, the closer the r_s value is to +1 or −1, the stronger the likely correlation. You should now be aware that our value for the above example of 0.87 for r_s means that there is a strong positive relationship.

TABLE 9.20 Ranked data based on company size and profit

Company	Number of employees	Rank of employees	Profit (£)	Rank profit	Difference between ranks (d)	d²
1	20	10	5,000	10	0	0
2	80	8	120,000	5	3	9
3	120	4	180,000	3	1	1
4	200	1	375,000	1	0	0
5	150	2	278,000	2	0	0
6	100	5	150,000	4	1	1
7	35	9	40,000	9	0	0
8	90	6	60,000	7	1	1
9	89	7	50,000	8	1	1
10	125	3	98,000	6	3	9

Measuring difference

Measuring the difference involves testing a hypothesis that there is a difference between an observed frequency and an expected frequency. In the last section we looked at the strength of association between variables. The data we have used to carry out these tests have been ordinal, interval or ratio data. The chi-squared test is a useful test as it can be used not only for measuring difference, but also for nominal data.

Chi-squared test

The *chi-squared test* is one of the most widely used hypothesis tests. It can be used for all types of data and is the only hypothesis test for nominal data. It is a non-parametric test used to see if there is a statistically significant difference between observed data and what would have been expected by chance. The chi-squared test can test for the null hypothesis (H0), i.e. that there is no significant difference between the expected and observed result. The formula is:

$$\chi^2 = \sum \frac{(O-E)^2}{E}$$

where:

O = observed frequencies

E = expected frequencies

The test only applies to categorical data that are counts or frequencies, not percentages. The simplest example of presenting the association between observations and categories is to use a 2×2 contingency table.

For example, five companies (A, B, C, D, E) were questioned on employee sick leave over a 12-month period (see Table 9.21). We now aim to establish if some companies have more sickness in the workplace than others. We can set out our hypotheses as follows:

H0: Each company expects the same number of employees on sick leave.

H1: Each company does not have the same number of employees on sick leave.

The level of significance to be used in this case is 5%.

The next step in our analysis involves compiling a chi-squared table (see Table 9.22).

There are a total of 90 people who have taken sick leave. If each company expects the same number, the expected number (*E*) of those who have taken sick leave is:

$$\frac{90}{15} = 18$$

The calculation from Table 9.22 shows that the value of χ^2 is 6.331.

TABLE 9.21 Employee sick leave over a 12-month period

Company	A	B	C	D	E
Number on sick leave	22	13	24	12	19

TABLE 9.22 The chi-squared table

Company	Observed (O)	Expected (E)	$O - E$	$(O - E)^2$	$\dfrac{(O - E)^2}{E}$
A	22	18	4	16	0.888
B	13	18	−5	25	1.388
C	24	18	6	36	2
D	12	18	−6	36	2
E	19	18	1	1	0.055
Total	90	90			6.331

Our actual value of 6.331 is less than the critical value of 9.49. Therefore we cannot reject the null hypothesis. In other words, each company can expect the same number of employees to go on sick leave. Any discrepancy in numbers is purely by chance.

Student's t-test

The *Student's t-test* is a parametric technique used to test the difference between sample means. The samples must be gathered from two different populations. In short, the Student's t-test establishes the probability that two populations are the same in relation to the variable that is being tested. In order to carry out a t-test, your data must be normally distributed, of interval or ratio status, and the two data sets must have similar variances. In addition, for a paired t-test (see below) each data pair must be related.

T-tests infer the likelihood of three or more distinct groups being different. An independent t-test is used to test the difference between two independent groups, e.g. male and female. Let us say that you gathered data on IQ levels among male doctors and lawyers, and compared the sample means using the t-test. A probability of 0.3 means that there is a 30% chance that you cannot distinguish between your group of doctors and lawyers based on IQ alone.

A paired sample t-test is used to establish whether or not there exists a significant difference between the mean values of matched samples. It is often used to measure a case before and after some form of manipulation or changes have taken place. For example, you might use a paired t-test to establish the significance of a difference in exam performance prior to and after a professional training programme. A paired t-test can also be used to compare samples. For instance, our exam example may involve comparing the effectiveness of the training programme in improving exam scores by sampling employees from different companies, and comparing the scores of those respondents who have taken part and those who have not taken part in the training.

Assessing the strength of relationship between variables

Typically, the final part of statistical analysis often involves assessing the strength of the relationship between variables.

Regression analysis

Although a detailed analysis and application of regression analysis is beyond the remit of this book, this section provides a brief insight into how it might be applied to your research. *Regression analysis* is a statistical technique for investigating the strength of a relationship between variables. Typically, the researcher aims to establish the causal effect of one variable on another. For example, the effect of a discount in price on consumer demand, or company size on performance. Essentially, there are two main types of regression analysis – *simple regression* and *multiple regression*.

Simple regression determines the strength of relationship between a dependent variable and one independent variable. It aims to find the extent that a dependent (y) and independent variable (x) are linearly related. A regression equation is often represented on a scatter plot by a regression line. A regression line is used to clearly illustrate the relationship between the variables under investigation. For example, in linear regression you might want to investigate the relationship between profit and advertising spend. First, let us look at the formula for linear regression, and then how this relates to our profit and advertising spend example. The formula is:

$$y = a + bx$$

where:
  x = independent variable
  y = dependent variable
  a = point where the line intersects the y-axis
  b = gradient of the line
  Profit = $a + b \times$ advertising spend

Multiple *linear regression* aims to find a linear relationship between a dependent variable (y) and several independent variables (x_i). The multiple regression correlation coefficient (r^2) is a measure of the proportion of variability explained by, or due to, the linear relationship in a sample of paired data. It is represented by a number between 0 and 1. The formula for multiple regression is:

$$y = a + b_1x_1 + b_2x_2 + b_3x_3 + b_4x_4 + b_5x_5 + b_6x_6 + \dots$$

Let us say that our example of the relationship between profit and advertising spend was to take into account other factors. For instance, profit might also be affected by staff training expenditure, price, bonuses and competition. This would be represented in the following multiple regression formula:

$$\text{Profit} = a + (b_1 \times \text{staff training expenditure}) + (b_2 \times \text{price}) + (b_3 \times \text{bonuses}) + (b_4 \times \text{number of competitors})$$

If the above equation was implemented, the regression coefficient indicates how good a predictor it is likely to be. Remember that the value produced is between −1 and +1. A figure of +1 indicates that your equation is a perfect predictor. Conversely, a value of 0 shows that the equation predicts none of the variation.

How Do I Know which Statistical Tests to Use?

Brown and Saunders (2008: 103–104) make the following suggestions before choosing a particular test:

- What is the research question I am trying to answer?
- What are the characteristics of the sample? For instance, are you using judgement sampling, snowball sampling, etc.?
- What types of data do I have?
- How many data variables are there?
- How many groups are there?
- Are the data distributed normally?
- If the data are not distributed normally, will this affect the statistic I want to use?
- Are the samples independent?

In addition, if you wish to make inferences about a population:

- Are the data representative of the population?
- Are the groups different?
- Is there a relationship between the variables?

Statistical Software Packages

If your research involves quantitative data analysis, it is unlikely that you will do the work manually. Most computers have access to some kind of spreadsheet package, such as Microsoft Excel. These certainly allow you to carry out elementary statistical analysis. Yet, they do not have the range of options typically associated with statistical packages. Fortunately, there are now several excellent software packages on the market. Many of these are user friendly and ideal for the student researcher. Two of the leading packages used in UK institutions are SPSS and Minitab. This book is not intended to provide a comprehensive guide on how to use either of these packages. The important thing is that you recognize the advantages of using such a package as opposed to undertaking manual quantitative data analysis. The advantages of using a software package are:

- it saves time;
- you avoid the need to learn how to perform calculations;
- it provides greater scope for your analysis; and
- data can be easily recorded, interpreted and presented.

Thankfully, this means that you do not need to worry about remembering different formulas! However, you still need to understand the purpose of statistical tests and the circumstances in which they can be used.

Preparing Your Data for Analysis Using SPSS

Earlier in the chapter I briefly discussed preparing your data for analysis. This section provides a brief guide as to how to enter data into SPSS. Entries are based on IBM SPSS Statistics Version 20. Before entering your data you will need to enter the codes for each question so that SPSS recognizes it. In Table 9.23 there is an extract from a data spreadsheet on household spending. It includes the following variables: case number (3 digits), age (2 digits), gender (1 = male or 2 = female), nationality (1 = British, 2 = German, 3 = French, 4 = Chinese, 5 = Other) and weekly household spending (£).

When you first open SPSS, you will be presented with a window that contains the following: Open an existing data source, Open another type of file, Run the tutorial, Type in data, Run an existing query, and Create new query using Database Wizard. We want to enter data, so select **Type in data** by placing the cursor over the circle next to Type in data, then click **OK**. This will take us to the **Data View** screen. In order to enter variables, we need **Variable View**, so click on **Variable View** in the bottom left-hand corner of the screen. We are now in the **Variable View** screen and ready to begin naming and defining the properties of the variables.

- **Name:** Here, under **Name** and to the right of box 1, type a word to identify the variable. In some surveys each question is given a number in order to preserve anonymity, e.g. 'case'. So we can call our first variable **CASE**. The name must start with a letter, should not have any

TABLE 9.23 Extract from a data spreadsheet

Case number	Age	Gender	Nationality	Weekly household spending (£)
001	42	1	1	300
002	74	2	1	280
003	19	2	2	378
004	34	1	4	500
005	28	2	3	348
006	51	1	5	484
007	26	1	1	350
008	44	2	2	388
009	60	1	3	525
010	29	2	4	650

spaces and can be up to eight characters. The second variable relates to the first question in our questionnaire (Age). A simple way to refer to this is **Q1**, so type this in the box under **CASE**. Type **Q2** to represent gender under **Q1**, and so on. Do the same for Nationality and Weekly household spending, **Q3** and **Q4** respectively.

- **Type:** The two basic types of variable that you will use are **numeric** and **string**. A numeric variable can only have numbers allocated. String variables may contain letters or numbers. If a string variable contains only numbers, numeric operations on that variable will not be allowed. To change a variable type, click on the small grey box on the right-hand side of the window. This brings up the **Variable Type** menu. If you select a numeric variable, you can then click in the width box or the decimal box to change the default values of eight characters reserved to displaying numbers with two decimal places. For whole numbers, you can drop the decimals down to zero. If you select a string variable, you can indicate the number of characters to be allowed for data entry in this string variable. For **gender** and **nationality**, select string as these are nominal data.
- **Width:** The width of the variable is simply the number of characters SPSS will allow to be entered for the variable. SPSS selects eight by default.
- **Decimals:** This is the number of decimal places SPSS will display. For whole numbers, set the number of decimals to zero. By default, SPSS inserts two decimals for each numerical value.
- **Label:** The label helps you to recognize the variable. For example, **Q1** asks about your age; you could give a label of 'Age', while for **Q2** 'Gender', **Q3** 'Nationality' and **Q4** 'Spend'. You could also use a key word for longer questions. For instance, a question on your favourite holiday destination could be called 'Holiday'.
- **Values:** Under values enter the codes and what they represent. For **Q2**, click to the right of the cell under **Values** and a window will appear called **Value labels**. In the **Value Box** enter '1' and in the **Label Box** enter 'Male' and click **Add**. Next, enter 2 in the **Value Box** and 'Female' in the **Label Box** and click **Add**, followed by **OK**. Adopt this process when coding for nationalities, entering 1 to 5 for each option.
- **Missing data:** Sometimes respondents may miss out a question because they choose to do so or it is not applicable. If it is not applicable, then you should include this as an option in your questionnaire. Any non-responses must be coded. SPSS provides a defaults measure for missing data or non-response. You can choose your own number, but make sure that the same number is used for all non-responses. Choose a number unlikely to be used and easily recognizable, e.g. 9999. In this example there are no missing data.
- **Columns:** This refers to how many columns wide you would like the variable to be presented in the **Data View**. We will leave it at the default.
- **Align:** Here you can change the presentation so that scores for the variable are left justified, right justified or centred. We will leave it at the default.
- **Measure:** Here, SPSS gives you a choice of **Scale** (this represents both ratio and interval scale), **Ordinal** or **Nominal**. We looked at these different types of variable earlier in the chapter. For **Q1** (Age) and **Q4** (Spend), select **Scale** by clicking to the right of each respective box under **Measure**, while **Q2** (gender) and **Q3** (nationality) should be **Nominal**.
- **Role:** This is a feature of newer versions of SPSS. The column here is concerned with the role your variable is going to take in the analysis. For the procedures we are going to carry out it can be left as the default role of **Input**.

FIGURE 9.9   The **Variable View** after we have named and defined the properties of the variables

Entering Your Data into SPSS

Once you have named and defined the properties of your variables, you are ready to begin entering your data. First, return to **Data View** and enter the data values for your respondents as summarized in Table 9.23. If you place your cursor over the name of a variable, SPSS will show the label you added in **Variable View** (Figure 9.9). To enter new data, click in an empty cell in the first row. Use the arrow keys to enter the values.

FIGURE 9.10   The **Data View** after we have entered the data

Entering the data can be time-consuming and tedious. However, it is important that you enter the data accurately, as incorrectly entered data will of course impact the analysis and interpretation of your findings. Figure 9.10 shows our completed **Data View**.

Producing Descriptive Statistics Using SPSS

SPSS allows you to calculate a wide range of descriptive statistics such as the mode, median and mean. In the **Data View** screen select **Analyze > Descriptive Statistics > Descriptives**. Next, the **Descriptives** dialogue box will appear. We are interested in analyzing household spend, so click on **Spend [Q4]**, then the middle arrow. **Spend [Q4]** should move to the **Variable(s):** box. Next, click on **Options**. The **Descriptive: Options** box will appear. Select **Mean, Sum, Std.deviation, Range** and, under **Display order**, **Variable List**. Click **Continue**, followed by **OK**.

SPSS now produces an output showing our selected descriptive statistics for household spending (Figure 9.11).

Producing Charts Using SPSS

As mentioned earlier in the chapter, a bar chart compares a simple set of observations. A bar chart is a straightforward way of summarizing either ordinal or nominal data. To produce a bar chart for **Nationality** the process is as follows: click on **Analyze > Descriptive Statistics > Frequencies**. The **Frequencies** box will open. Click on **Nationality [Q3]** and the **middle arrow**. **Nationality [Q3]** now moves to the **Variable(s)** box. Next, click **Charts**; the **Frequencies: Charts** box will open. Under **Chart Type** select **Bar charts** and under **Chart Values** select **Frequencies**.

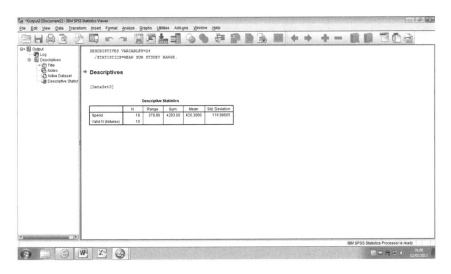

FIGURE 9.11 Descriptive statistics for household spending

Click **Continue**. Select **Display Frequency table** and click **OK**. SPSS now produces a bar chart for nationality showing frequency counts (see Figure 9.12), along with a frequency table (see Figure 9.13). Clearly, our sample $n = 10$ is very small. A much larger sample showing student nationality will make for much more interesting reading.

When you are ready to save or open your work, the steps are as follows:

Saving your work: **File > Save As** > Enter a filename in the filename box, e.g. 'household' > click **Save**.

Opening your work: **File > Open > Data** > click on 'household' > **Open**.

FIGURE 9.12   A bar chart for nationality

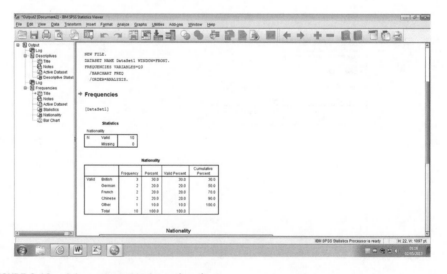

FIGURE 9.13   A frequency table for nationality

Finally, this section has provided a snapshot of how SPSS works. You will find more information on the accompanying website. In addition, recommended sources are listed at the end of the chapter.

RESEARCH IN ACTION

Using descriptive statistics and hypothesis testing

In the article below, the authors undertake a quantitative-based study to examine the growth and planning strategies within women-led small and medium-sized enterprises (SMEs). The article is useful as it illustrates how quantitative analysis might be incorporated into your own study.

Mitchelmore, S. and Rowley, J. (2013) 'Growth and planning strategies within women-led SMEs', *Management Decisions*, 51 (1): 83–96.

The authors set out the aim of the paper as exploring 'the planning strategies of female entrepreneurs who have indicated a desire to grow their businesses, the time horizons of planning strategies, and the relationship between planning horizons and number of employees and annual sales as measures of business performance'.

The paper begins by providing an introduction to the study and identifying a gap in the literature; namely, although there is a growing interest in female entrepreneurship, there is a lack of research into the influence of gender, especially in terms of growth and long-term business performance.

Following this, the authors review the key literature in the context of business performance and growth and business planning, and in female entrepreneurship. As well as having a set of objectives within the introduction, the authors also include two hypotheses that emerge from the literature review. These are as follows:

H1. There is a positive correlation between number of employees and the time horizons for business planning.

H2. There is a positive correlation between business turnover and the time horizons for business planning.

For the methodology, the authors adopted a questionnaire-based survey in order to collect data about female entrepreneurs and their businesses. A convenience sampling method was used when distributing the questionnaire. The researchers' rationale for using this sampling technique was the difficulty of identifying businesses that were owned by women.

Questionnaires were administered via email and sent as an attachment. A total of 210 questionnaires were collected. The authors state that only questionnaires where respondents wish to grow their business, and had completed all of the relevant questions on the profile of their business, were used for analysis. Subsequently, data were entered into SPSS for descriptive analysis and hypothesis testing.

The descriptive analysis begins by analyzing the respondents' profiles. This includes their age, education, years of business experience, sector and age of business. Second, a table is provided that illustrates the percentage of respondents who indicated that they used a specific strategy to promote the growth of their business. Of the various strategies listed, the most popular choice in terms of relevance to business growth strategy was 'Improving existing products or services' at 42%. Another table is used to highlight how far ahead respondents had planned for a range of activities, including: sales, cash flow, new products, entry into new markets, recruitment of human resources, expenditures and investment in infrastructure.

The next stage in the quantitative analysis examines the findings from the testing of the hypotheses. In order to measure and investigate a statistical association between the variables of planning horizons and business performances, a Spearman rho (rank) correlation was conducted. The researchers state in the main text that findings show a significant positive correlation ($r = 0.195$) between number of employees and the planning horizon for cash flow at the 5% level, and a significant positive correlation ($r = 0.171$) for the planning horizon for investment in infrastructure at the 10% level. In addition, statistical analyses are presented in two tables, one representing H1 and another representing H2. The authors conclude that H1 is upheld for two of the planning horizon variables, but not for the others, while H2 is upheld for four of the planning horizon variables, but not for the others.

Finally, a useful exercise would be to look up the original article as it provides a good example of how to present statistical data. Also, you can see how the authors make a clear link between the introduction, literature review, methodology, results and conclusion, and recommendations.

Summary and Conclusion

In this chapter we have looked at the variety of methods used to analyze quantitative data. There are two broad types of statistical analysis – descriptive and inferential. Essentially, your chosen method depends on whether or not your data has a normal distribution, the number of variables and type of data. Other key points from this chapter are as follows:

- Quantitative analysis involves the following key stages: preparing your data for analysis; summarizing and presenting your data using tables and graphs; describing your data using suitable statistical methods; and analyzing your data using inferential statistics.
- There are four main types of data: nominal, ordinal, interval and ratio.
- It is important to consider the number of variables (univariate, bivariate and multivariate), the type of data and the purpose of your research before selecting your choice of statistical method.
- There are two broad approaches to describing your data: measuring central tendency and measuring dispersion.
- A distinction is made between parametric and non-parametric techniques when measuring association and difference.
- A statistical software package such as SPSS saves time and allows for easier and more detailed analysis.
- Your project supervisor can provide invaluable advice on appropriate statistical methods.

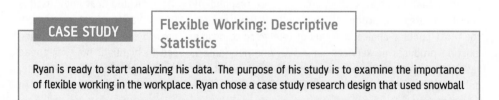

CASE STUDY	Flexible Working: Descriptive Statistics

Ryan is ready to start analyzing his data. The purpose of his study is to examine the importance of flexible working in the workplace. Ryan chose a case study research design that used snowball sampling to target personnel managers within local public sector organizations. He administered a pilot questionnaire survey via the postal system and received a total of 15 replies out of a sample size of 50. This equates to a response rate of 30%. One of the introductory questions in his questionnaire required respondents to provide the number of years that they have worked for their employer. This produced the following data: 2, 3, 10, 4, 7, 12, 9, 5, 1, 10, 12, 6, 5, 4, 3.

Case study questions

1. Find the mean, mode, median and interquartile range for the above set of data.
2. What problems might Ryan face if he was to use this type of question for his main question-naire survey?

━━━━━━━━━━━ YOU'RE THE SUPERVISOR ━━━━━━━━━━━

Abdul is a part-time student. He has decided to base his project on the sales performance of his employer, XYZ Ltd. Abdul is particularly interested in the association between the number of sales made by his company's Sales Manager over a period of ten days and the consequent time taken to achieve the number of sales. A summary of sales data is shown in Table 9.24.

TABLE 9.24   Sales data

Day	Number of sales (x)	Time taken to achieve sales (hours) (y)
1	3	2
2	3	1
3	1	2
4	6	3
5	2	2
6	3	4
7	4	5
8	2	3
9	1	2
10	4	4

Abdul has heard of Pearson's product moment correlation coefficient, but is unsure of how to carry out the test. He has come to you for advice.

Supervisor question

- Use Pearson's product moment correlation to test the association between the number of sales made and the time taken to achieve the number of sales.

1. Mathematics is not one of my strong points. How do I know which method to use when analyzing my data?

Answer: Your choice of methods depends on a number of factors. These include the number of variables, type of data, sampling method and whether you have a normal distribution. Using descriptive statistics is relatively straightforward, whereas more advanced analysis can be undertaken using a statistical software package such as SPSS. This avoids having to manually perform calculations. However, you still need to be able to understand the conditions under which a test can be carried out, understand its purpose and be able to interpret your findings.

2. Shall I analyze my data manually or use a software package?

Answer: If you are using descriptive statistics, then there is no reason why you cannot undertake manual analysis. Still, when presenting your results, there is no substitute for the likes of SPSS. A specialized package contains several options for presenting your data. Moreover, it can help to reduce the amount of time devoted to this stage of your project.

3. How should I structure my quantitative analysis within the body of my research project?

Answer: Your decision here depends on the extent of your analysis. Broadly speaking, start with descriptive, followed by inferential, statistics. If you have adopted a mixed methods approach to your research, then your decision to start with qualitative or quantitative analysis is generally up to you. This might be influenced by previous research on your chosen topic, or possibly advice from your research supervisor. Whatever you decide, the key thing to remember is that your analysis must be presented in a clear, thematic way.

References

Brown, R.B. and Saunders, M. (2008) *Dealing with Statistics: What You Need To Know*. Maidenhead: McGraw-Hill/Open University Press.
Bryman, A. (2004) *Social Research Methods* (2nd edn). Oxford: Oxford University Press.
Mitchelmore, S. and Rowley, J. (2013) 'Growth and planning strategies within women-led SMEs', *Management Decision*, 51 (1): 83–96.
Waters, D. (1997) *Quantitative Methods for Business* (4th edn). Harlow: FT/Prentice Hall.

Further Reading

Barrow, M. (2005) *Statistics for Economics, Accounting and Business Studies*. Harlow: FT/Prentice Hall.

Chase, C. (2009) *Demand-Driven Forecasting: A Structured Approach to Forecasting.*
Hoboken, NJ: John Wiley & Sons.

Field, A. (2008) *Discovering Statistics Using SPSS* (3rd edn). London: Sage.

Keller, G. and Warrack, B. (2002) *Statistics for Management and Economics.* London:
Thomson Learning.

10
Analyzing qualitative data

┌─Learning Objectives─┐

After reading this chapter, you should be able to:

- know what is meant by qualitative analysis;
- understand the process of qualitative analysis;
- appreciate how to code data;
- know the different types of qualitative analytical tools;
- know how to quantify qualitative data; and
- understand the problems associated with qualitative analysis.

Introduction

In the last chapter we examined how to analyze numerical data. We now move on to look at analysis involving non-numerical data, or qualitative data. Qualitative analysis can involve an eclectic mix of data sources, including observations, the spoken word, written text and visual data.

Another factor that distinguishes qualitative data is that there is no definitive approach to carrying out qualitative data analysis. For more inexperienced researchers, qualitative data analysis might seem like an 'easy option' compared to quantitative data. However, qualitative analysis often deals with a huge amount of raw data. The process of ploughing through vast amounts of data can be a daunting task for even the most experienced of researchers. Moreover, it can be both time-consuming and difficult when it comes to interpreting findings. Hence, the two key skills required to be an effective qualitative researcher are patience and effective organizational skills.

This chapter starts by exploring what is meant by qualitative data analysis. By now, you should be familiar with the main qualitative data collection methods – observation, interviews and focus groups. The next step is to begin to consider how to analyze the raw data generated from your collection.

Following this, we examine the process or series of steps involved in analyzing qualitative data. In essence, there is no definitive approach to conducting qualitative analysis, although many approaches proposed by various authors carry a similar series of steps. These include: transcribing your data; reading and generating categories, themes and patterns; interpreting your data; and writing your report. We shall explore each of these stages in some detail later in the chapter.

Just as the series of steps for data analysis vary, so too do the various methods by which you can analyze your data. At a broad level, these methods can be divided on the basis of qualitative and quantitative. Even though we are examining qualitative data, quantitative techniques can also be used.

Given the plethora of approaches to qualitative data analysis, one difficulty for student researchers is choosing which approach to opt for. The next section is intended as a useful guide to help you to decide which approach best suits your research. This is followed by a short section on the potential problems you may encounter when carrying out qualitative data analysis.

Like quantitative data analysis, exploring qualitative findings is now typically undertaken using an appropriate software package. Arguably, there are two leading packages on the market – NVivo and CAQDAS (Computer Assisted Qualitative Data Analysis Software). I provide a brief insight into qualitative software packages in general.

What is Qualitative Analysis?

Glaser (1992) defined qualitative analysis as 'any kind of analysis that produces findings or concepts and hypotheses, as in grounded theory, that are not arrived at by statistical methods'.

Qualitative data analysis is very much exploratory in nature. The likelihood is that you have gathered a huge amount of data, yet are perhaps a little bewildered as to what to include and what to discard from your data. At this point, it is essential to have a clear 'plan' of the steps that need to be addressed to analyze your data in an effective manner. Unfortunately, as noted earlier, there is no definitive series of steps applicable to qualitative data analysis.

In general, different authors propose different approaches. For example, Miles and Huberman (1994: 10) argue that qualitative analysis consists of essentially three activities – data reduction, data display and conclusion drawing/verification. For the purpose of this book, we shall explore many of the activities proposed by Miles and Huberman. However, these will fall under a varied set of headings. These headings are intended to make the qualitative analytical process a little more explicit and easier to understand. They form a theme throughout the majority of this chapter and are first addressed in the next section.

There are a number of different approaches to qualitative data analysis. The Honeycomb of Research Methodology (Figure 10.1) highlights some of the more common approaches to qualitative analysis used by researchers, namely: visual analysis, grounded theory, narrative analysis, discourse analysis and content analysis.

Descriptive statistics
Inferential statistics
Visual analysis
Grounded theory
Narrative analysis
Discourse analysis
Content analysis

Epistemology: Positivism,
Interpretivism, Pragmatism
Ontology: Objectivism, Subjectivism
Axiology: Value-free, Biased

Research philosophy 1

Data analysis techniques 6

Research approach 2

Research Methodology

Inductive
Deductive

Data collection 5

Research strategy 3

Research design 4

Interviews
Questionnaires
Observation
Secondary data

Quantitative
Qualitative
Combining quantitative and
qualitative strategies
(multi-strategy research)

Action research
Case study
Experimental
Longitudinal
Cross-sectional
Archival analysis
Comparative

FIGURE 10.1   The Honeycomb of Research Methodology (©2013 Jonathan Wilson)

We will examine each of these in detail later in the chapter. If we return to the Honeycomb of Research Methodology, you will notice that 'Data analysis techniques' is the sixth and final element which forms your methodology. If you have adopted qualitative data collection methods, then the likelihood is that you will use qualitative data analysis techniques when analyzing your data. Moreover, you will make reference to these techniques in your methodology chapter.

Once again, remember that the Honeycomb of Research Methodology not only shows the typical structure of a research methodology chapter by including numbered segments, but also recognizes the fact that the thought process may not necessarily be linear.

One key ingredient that is required to carry out qualitative data analysis is, of course, time. When analyzing qualitative data the likelihood is that your analysis will either be based on an interview transcript or a field note taken from observational research. Usually, this data has to be transcribed and entered into a computer. Essentially, this is the first stage in the analytical process and requires a great deal of time and patience before moving on to the next step in your analysis.

Finally, prior to carrying out your analysis, you should have a clear idea as to your research approach. In other words, have you decided to adopt an inductive or deductive approach to analyzing your qualitative findings? This is important as it determines how and when you decide on your categories. For instance, a qualitative researcher who uses inductive analysis develops categories that emerge from field notes, documents and interviews. In other words, these are not imposed prior to data

on. Early on, the researcher will develop a system for analysis. The researcher
ow rigorous guidelines described in the literature, but the ultimate decisions
e narrative reside with the researcher (Denzin and Lincoln, 1998: 47).
rsely, if adopting a deductive approach to your qualitative analysis, you
with a predetermined set of categories. The impact that an inductive or
approach has on your data analysis will be further examined later in the

Steps in Qualitative Analysis

There are numerous approaches to qualitative data analysis. As a result, some students can become confused as to which approach to adopt when carrying out their own research. Perhaps equally confusing is the fact that even though qualitative analysis is largely associated with analyzing data in a non-quantifiable way, there are those researchers who collect qualitative data and then set out to analyze it through quantification.

In order to overcome this confusion, I have proposed a series of steps that clearly take you through the qualitative data analysis process. The four analytical steps can be summarized as:

- transcribing your data;
- reading and generating categories, themes and patterns;
- interpreting your findings; and
- writing the report.

The last of these four steps is discussed in Chapter 11, so we will examine the first three here.

Transcribing Your Data

If you have undertaken unstructured or semi-structured interviews, then the first stage in qualitative analysis is the transcribing of your data (see Figure 10.2). This can be an immensely time-consuming process. If possible, it is a good idea to get someone with the necessary experience to transcribe your data for you. This will then allow you to concentrate on other areas of your research. For example, if you have adopted a mixed methods approach, by allowing someone else to transcribe your data, you can devote more time to quantitative analysis, such as inferential statistics.

One thing to be wary of if you are asking someone else to transcribe your work is to make sure that they do not alter your respondents' answers. I know one student who was pleased that someone else transcribed his work. However, to his dismay, he later found out that the person transcribing his work had changed his respondents' replies where there was evidence of grammatical errors! Remember that, when transcribing, you must transcribe the verbatim answers from your respondents.

Extract from a verbatim transcript			
Date of interview	*Name*	*Company*	*Position*
13 August 2002	Mark Wang*	Bank of East Anglia*	General Manager

1 Q: Mr Wang, could you tell me first of your involvement with the joint venture.
2 MW: I was the manager of the joint venture company. I'm manager for several companies, as
   well as our holding company operation division.
3 Q: How did the joint venture with ABC Ltd develop?
4 How did it come about?
5 MW: I think to my understanding, it was between top
6 management discussion. I think one of the top
7 management people met our chairman at that time, and
8 talked about setting up a joint venture. I think at that time
9 a lot of international insurance companies wanted to come
10 to China.
11 Q: Are there any restrictions on western insurance
12 companies?...
13 MW: Yes there are. I think up until now the market is still
14 not fully open to foreign companies. I think at that time
15 ABC Ltd want to set up a joint venture with East Anglia
16 Bank in Hong Kong maybe as preparation to enter the
17 China market.
18 Q: What do you hope to gain from the joint venture?
19 MW: Access to the Chinese market.
20 Q: How long did it take to actually develop?
21 MW: I think it took about two years for discussions. For all
22 these discussions. Top management paid great attention to this event.

*Fictitious names

FIGURE 10.2 Example of an extract from a verbatim transcript

Changing the wording may result in the clarity of the answer being lost. Once you have fully transcribed your data (most likely into a software package such as Word or NVivo), you are ready to begin to organize your data.

If you have carried out observational research, then the first stage in your qualitative analysis is likely to be markedly different from that of data arising from interviews. For a start, you do not have verbal data, but observational data. An important first stage in analyzing observational data involves reducing the data until you are familiar with them. Each phase of data analysis entails data reduction as the reams of collected data are brought into manageable chunks, and interpretation as the researcher brings meaning and insight to the words and acts of the participants in the study (Marshall and Rossman, 1995: 113).

Patton (1990: 374–375) makes a distinction between data collection methods (i.e. observations and interviews) when considering qualitative analysis. Analytical considerations when analyzing data from observations can be summarized as follows:

- *Chronology.* Describe what was observed chronologically. This allows you to tell 'the story' of your observations from beginning to end.

- *Key elements.* Present the data by critical incidents or major events – not necessarily in the order of occurrence but in the order of importance.
- *Various settings.* Describe various places, sites, settings or locations (doing case studies of each) before doing cross-setting pattern analysis.
- *People.* If individuals or groups are the primary unit of analysis, then case studies of people or groups may be the focus for case studies.
- *Processes.* The data may be organized to describe important processes, e.g. control, recruitment, decision-making, socialization, communication.
- *Issues.* The observations may be pulled together to illuminate key issues, often the equivalent of the primary evaluation questions, such as how participants changed.

Whether analyzing observational or interview data, essentially this first step is all about organizing your data into a manageable form. As noted, this usually involves entering your data into a suitable software package to facilitate analysis. However, before you begin considering analysis, you will need to become 'familiar' with your data. In effect, this means reading your data.

Reading and Generating Categories, Themes and Patterns

Once you have transcribed your data, the next stage is to read through and begin coding. Reading through your transcripts, looking over the notes you made during the data collection stage and watching video recordings are all key parts of becoming familiar with and identifying your data. This stage of your analysis is by no means a 'one-off' process. Reading and rereading will help you to identify patterns and themes in your data. Once again, this is extremely time-consuming, but it is an essential part of the qualitative analysis process.

The next step in further developing your analysis is to adopt a process of coding. Coding is simply selecting the elements of your data that you believe are both interesting and relevant to your research. Your choice in this respect should be influenced by your research questions.

Approaches to coding your data

A code can be a key word, theme or category within your transcript or notes. 'The goal of *coding* is to fracture the data and rearrange it into categories that facilitate the comparison of data within and between these categories and that aid in the development of theoretical concepts' (Strauss, 1987: 29). Coding the data allows you to identify categories and subcategories. Flick (1998: 179) defined coding as: 'the constant comparison of phenomena, cases, concepts and so on and the formulation of questions which are addressed to the text'.

There are two approaches to coding your data – *emergent coding* (inductive) and *a priori coding* (deductive). If you adopt emergent coding, then your categories will develop through examining your data. Conversely, with a priori coding your categories are determined prior to your analysis. Moreover, these categories are typically based on some existing theory. If, for example, you were interested in examining levels of trust between joint venture partners, by using an already established set of categories from a previous study, you would be following a priori coding.

One option is to combine emergent and a priori coding. The advantage of this is that it allows you to look for your specific set of codes while at the same time providing the flexibility to note any emergent or unforeseen codes.

Essentially, coding allows you to break down your raw data into something more manageable. There are three different types of coding:

- open coding;
- axial coding; and
- selective coding.

Open coding involves labelling and categorizing your data. Axial coding is based on relating categories with subcategories. Selective coding is based on identifying a core category that represents the main theme of the research, i.e. the focal category to have been generated from the data.

How you mark your codes is essentially up to you. There is no 'correct' approach. However, when carrying out qualitative analysis as part of my PhD research, I must say that I found highlighting codes using different colours to be a clear and effective way of breaking down my data. This can, of course, be done manually, although it is much easier using a software package such as Microsoft Word. Other researchers prefer to make a note of key words and phrases within the transcript. Choose whichever method you feel the most comfortable with. Figure 10.3 shows an example of a coded extract from an interview transcript, while Table 10.1 shows an example of a coding frame. A *coding frame* such as that highlighted in Table 10.1 is essential if you have decided to take a deductive approach to your qualitative analysis, as it sets out the coded concepts that you will need to look for when analyzing your data.

Table 10.1 shows the coded concepts used for a study into international joint venture performance. The first column shows the name of each coded theme, e.g. 'trust'. The second column shows an example of a sentence that illustrates trust. In this particular study, all of the themes were based on research carried out by previous researchers. This is a useful way of establishing your own coding frame, as it allows for comparative analysis with previous studies. Moreover, you are more likely to be able to argue for higher levels of validity and reliability. The third column features a code for each respective coded concept. For example, 'Satisfaction' is 'S1'. If, for example, having read through a paragraph in your transcript you identify an example of satisfaction being expressed by a respondent, you can write 'S1' next to the paragraph. This approach to coding is particularly useful if you are coding using themes as opposed to key words, as it identifies your codes in a clear and concise manner.

Having a coding system such as that highlighted in Table 10.1 also helps you to engage in data reduction. In addition, relevant quotes that apply to a given coded concept can be included in your results section. Quotations provide an interesting

Coded extract from a verbatim transcript			
Date of interview	*Name*	*Company*	*Position*
13 August 2002	Richard Wang*	Bank of East Anglia*	General Manager

```
 1   I: Are you pleased with the merger? The company seems to be performing well.
 2   R: Yes, I'm pleased.
 3   I: Were there any problems along the way?
 4   R: Well, there were certainly heated discussions on several occasions! (conflict)
 5   I: Can you elaborate?
 6   R: Let's just say that we didn't think they were serious about
 7   a potential agreement. (lack of trust). It was certainly a
 8   lengthy process that took several months to reach an
 9   agreement. A number of my colleagues were involved in the
10   process.
11   I: Did the fact that you were dealing with a company from a
12   different culture have anything to do with it?
13   R: I don't know. Perhaps.
14   I: How about the future? Does the company intend on
15   increasing its market share?
16   R: Yes. We have plans in place over the short to long term to
17   achieve this. (strategy)
18   I: Does this involve staying in the UK?
19   R: Yes. We see the UK as a key market. (commitment)
```

* Fictitious name

FIGURE 10.3   Example of a coded extract from an interview transcript

TABLE 10.1   Coding frame for qualitative research

Coded concepts (theme)	Example	Code
1. Trust	We know our foreign partner will always deliver on time and is open regarding the sharing of technological information.	T1
2. Commitment	We see this joint venture as being at least a ten-year venture.	C1
3. Cooperation	We work closely together in aiming to achieve our strategic objectives.	C2
4. Satisfaction	We are pleased with the venture in that there is regular exchanging of information.	S1
5. Performance	We have achieved our set objectives over the short term.	P1
6. Dissolution	We are considering switching from a joint venture to a WFOE in the near future.	D1

illustration of your findings. When including quotations, try not to fall into the habit of purely describing each quote from your respondents. You should adopt an analytical approach, constantly comparing and contrasting the responses from your participants. Ideally, quotations should be presented in a thematic way so as to add clarity to your analysis.

Although Table 10.1 is an example of a coding frame using themes, key words can also be used. Table 10.2 shows an example of a code and the type of unit. In

TABLE 10.2   Example of a coding frame – Chinese concept of *guanxi*

Coding unit	Example
Guanxi (word)	Examine transcripts for the word *guanxi* in relation to relationships.
Guanxi (theme)	Examine transcripts for instances where *guanxi* has been discussed as an important factor in joint venture success.

this case, the code is the Chinese concept of *guanxi* (personal connections), and the unit is a key word and theme.

Themes are often based on interpretation. However, referring to existing measures of constructs and definitions helps to support issues of reliability and validity. Also, it can help to avoid using different codes for essentially describing the same thing.

Once you have coded your data, you are ready to move on to the next step in your analysis. Coffey and Atkinson (1996) suggest the following steps after coding:

1. **Coded data needs to be retrieved.**
2. **Explore codes and categories.**
3. **Look for patterns and themes.**

Your entire set of coded data needs to be retrieved so that you can carry out more in-depth exploratory analysis by combining your codes into patterns, themes and categories. Strauss and Corbin (1990: 61) defined the latter as:

> A classification of concepts. This classification is discovered when concepts are compared one against another and appear to pertain to a similar phenomenon. Thus the concepts are grouped together under a higher-order, more abstract concept called a category.

If we go back to our example of international joint venture performance (Table 10.1), one might argue that the concepts (trust, satisfaction, cooperation, and so on), when grouped together, fall under the broad category of 'performance measures'. The process of

> [c]reating categories is both a conceptual and empirical challenge; categories must be 'grounded' conceptually and empirically. That means that they must relate to an appropriate analytic context and be rooted in relevant empirical material. Categories which seem fine 'in theory' are no good if they do not fit the data. Categories which do not fit the data are no good if they cannot relate to a wider conceptual context. (Dey, 1993: 96)

Finally, the purposes of coding procedures can be summarized as follows:

- build rather than test theory;
- provide researchers with analytic tools for handling masses of raw data;
- help analysts to consider alternative meanings of phenomena;

- be systematic and creative simultaneously; and
- identify, develop and relate the concepts that are the building blocks of theory.

   (Strauss and Corbin, 1990: 13)

Once you have completed the task of coding your data, and developing themes and categories, you are then ready to begin interpreting your findings.

Interpreting Your Findings

In this stage of your analysis, your intention should be to develop a more meaningful understanding of your findings. In the last section your main task was data reduction, coding your data, leading to the development of patterns and categories. This is all very well, but the purpose of your research is not just to illustrate your findings, but to engage in interpretation.

A major part of the interpretation of your data is looking for connections between categories that you have identified within each transcript. The types of questions that you might ask yourself concerning each category include:

- Is there a relationship between categories?
- How important are these relationships?
- Is this consistent with previous research?
- Why are there differences or similarities between categories?

Attempting to answer these questions might seem daunting at first. However, at the same time it can be an extremely interesting and rewarding challenge. By addressing questions concerning the relationships between categories, you are moving beyond simply describing or reducing your data to what I call the 'nitty gritty' of data interpretation.

Approaches to Qualitative Analysis

So far in this chapter we have looked at a very generic approach to data analysis, although I have made one clear distinction – your choice of an inductive or deductive approach to coding is likely to affect your analysis. However, this is not the only decision that is likely to impact how you go about your data analysis. In truth, there are many different approaches to qualitative data analysis available to you. Although by no means exhaustive, I have included examples of some of the more common approaches used by students. For a more comprehensive overview, it is worth consulting Myers (2009).

Grounded theory

Glaser (1992: 2) defined grounded theory as 'the systematic generating of theory from data, that itself is systematically obtained from social research'. As a method

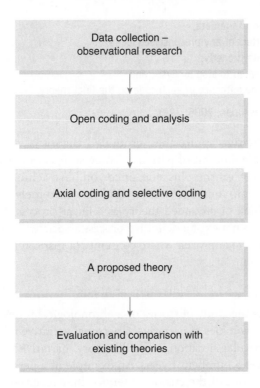

```
┌─────────────────────────────┐
│      Data collection –       │
│    observational research    │
└─────────────────────────────┘
              │
              ▼
┌─────────────────────────────┐
│    Open coding and analysis  │
└─────────────────────────────┘
              │
              ▼
┌─────────────────────────────┐
│ Axial coding and selective coding │
└─────────────────────────────┘
              │
              ▼
┌─────────────────────────────┐
│      A proposed theory       │
└─────────────────────────────┘
              │
              ▼
┌─────────────────────────────┐
│  Evaluation and comparison with │
│       existing theories      │
└─────────────────────────────┘
```

FIGURE 10.4   Stages in grounded theory

in which the theory is developed from the data, rather than theory being applied at the outset, it is very much an inductive approach.

Grounded theory was developed by two sociologists – Barney Glaser and Anselm Strauss. If you adopt a grounded theory methodology, you do not apply theory, or even start with any preconceived ideas as to what theories might be developed from your data. Figure 10.4 illustrates the stages that a researcher commonly goes through when undertaking grounded theory.

Although largely similar, Pace (2004: 337) proposed the following four stages of developing a grounded theory:

- generating categories and their properties;
- integrating categories and their properties;
- delimiting the theory; and
- writing the theory.

As you can see from Figure 10.4, we have covered many of these stages in the last section. The main difference is that the 'outcome' is a proposed theory, which is subsequently compared with existing theories.

Ideally, if undertaking grounded theory you should not have any preconceived assumptions before you collect your data. This is a difficult challenge for many researchers. It is one of several challenges that include:

- how to remain open to the data;
- how to avoid the effect of any preconceived ideas;
- how to code the data properly;
- when to start and when to stop analysis; and
- how to determine the influence of each code on the final theory.

(Adapted from Mansourian, 2006: 397)

Like most qualitative approaches, grounded theory is very time-consuming and requires a certain amount of patience. To be sure, it can take time to develop your theory. However, on the plus side, once you have achieved an outcome of a theoretical proposition, most researchers find this extremely rewarding.

Lastly, do not think of grounded theory as a linear process. This is perhaps one reason why there does not exist a definitive process associated with grounded theory. Rather, it is an inductive approach where constant comparison is the key to success.

Narrative analysis

Narrative analysis is the study of stories or a chronological series of events. Broadly speaking, there are two types of narrative: a personal narrative relating to someone's experience of a particular situation, and a 'life story' narrative that relates to someone's experience over a number of years. An example of a personal narrative might be a consumer's account of the customer service they received when dealing with a particular company, while a 'life story' narrative might relate to someone's career progression since leaving school.

Narrative analysis can be useful if you are conducting ethnographic research and are interested in the background of your respondents. Moreover, it can be useful for comparing the lives of individuals over time. Key themes that can be explored when carrying out narrative analysis include asking the participant:

- to comment on a major event;
- to discuss the most influential people in their lives;
- to discuss significant life chapters;
- to anticipate future career development;
- to discuss personal ideologies; or
- to reflect on decisions they have made.

You can illustrate your findings from narrative analysis using verbatim extracts from your interview transcripts. As noted earlier, extracts or quotations make an interesting addition to any qualitative study. The following examples illustrate how quotations can be incorporated into a study. They are based on the formation and ongoing relationship between a UK and Chinese joint venture partner. The responses come from two joint venture managers.

As a General Manager for an oil producing company remarked:

In 8–10 years it [trust] has improved very much. Still, from the Chinese side they tend not to exchange all the information they have. They tend to still hold something until you ask them. The foreign company in general is open, providing all the information for them. The Chinese are improving, still not as much as the foreign company expects.'

'I'm less trusting based on the consequences of what has happened this week! Because I thought we had agreed the prices, yet they came back and changed the terms. That makes me want to trust them less. Last year we had two channels into China, but turned one of them off because this seemed to work much better. Maybe it's not working so well now, because they are exclusive.'

(Managing Director, UK telecommunications company)

Ideally, when including narrative accounts from respondents, try to adopt an analytical approach. Comparing and contrasting different experiences is far more interesting for the reader. Also, your aim should be to interpret your findings, not just simply describe each participant's account.

Discourse analysis

Discourse analysis examines both spoken and written language. The texts that might be used by a business researcher engaged in discourse analysis include formal written records, such as news reports, company statements, academic papers, focus group discussions, transcripts of conversations, advertisements, and magazines (Elliott, 1996: 65).

Sample size is not such an important issue in discourse analysis as researchers are concerned with the way language is used, not the number of participants. A large sample size can make the task of analysis extremely time-consuming.

Elliott (1996) notes that one of the key features that differentiates discourse analysis from other methods of inquiry is that it aims to encourage diversity in participants' responses, whereas, typically, the main aim of interviews in qualitative research is to gather a consistent set of results. For example, in business research, the ways in which language is used in company minutes, promotional campaigns, mission statements and company websites can be used to identify a discourse of corporate social responsibility.

There are a number of approaches for analyzing discourse analysis. The main disadvantage is that it is extremely time-consuming. Most of your time will be devoted to transcribing and interpreting your data. For this reason, it tends not to be a favoured option among business students.

Visual analysis

Visual data analysis involves analyzing images that may come from secondary or primary findings. Images may include television advertisements, photographs, outdoor advertising or pictures from magazine articles. For example, a study into celebrity endorsement in magazine advertising may involve searching the contents of a magazine publication for a six-month period. The analysis may involve asking questions such as: How many advertisements used celebrity endorsement? What is the message from each advertisement? What is the general content of each advertisement? Ostensibly, it is less time-consuming than discourse analysis or narrative analysis, but you may find that interpreting your data on the basis of visual images is more challenging than using written data.

Quantifying Qualitative Data: Content analysis

If you decide to quantify your qualitative data, one method you are likely to adopt is undertaking frequency counts. Simply counting the number of times that a word, phrase or theme is raised by a research participant is an example of quantifying qualitative data. Another method of quantifying qualitative data is *content analysis*.

'Content analysis is a way of systematically converting text to numerical variables for quantitative data analysis' (Collis and Hussey, 2003: 250). Content analysis usually involves the following steps:

1. Identify the unit of analysis – recording unit, sentence or paragraph.
2. Choose categories that are relevant to the issues being studied. They must be reliable, so that if someone else repeated the analysis they would find the same information (increased reliability).
3. Once you have chosen your categories, read through the material and apply these codes to units of text.
4. Tabulate the material. Present the categories and list the assertions under them.

Content analysis can be used to examine patterns in your data. At a simple level, it is often viewed as word frequency counts. Certainly, this is part of the analytical process, but it is much more than this. It also involves interpreting the outcomes.

The advantage of content analysis is the ability to explore what is said (e.g. context) and not said (e.g. form) in successive stages of the interview (Merton and Kendall, 1949: 541). However, a major potential limitation is that frequency counts may include words that are used out of context, or words that have multiple meanings (e.g. an institution can refer to a university, or a private or public sector organization). A respondent's level of English may also mean that certain words and phrases are used more frequently as a result of 'limited' English language capability.

Content analysis is a method that is associated with the interpretation of both written and visual material. The analysis involves categorizing data and then comparing the frequency counts of each category. For instance, if you are studying TV advertising on one particular TV station, your analysis may involve watching the advertisements on the station for a period of five days. You decide on your categories and each advertisement is subsequently recorded in terms of those categories, e.g. type of product, brand, length of advertisement, use of celebrity endorsement, etc., and then analyzed. Alternatively, you may wish to study the reporting of

Themes	Number of adverts	Number of ads on hotel chains	Number of ads on independent hotels
Price	52	28	24
Discounts	18	7	11
Location	30	19	11
Facilities	13	8	5
Tourist sites	6	3	3
Entertainment	22	5	17
Promotions	4	1	3
Rating	18	10	8
Other locations	3	2	1
Customer service	3	3	0

intellectual property rights infringements in five business magazines. You may decide to record the number of articles on this subject in each magazine, and the content, length and writer of each article, as the basis of your analysis. Table 10.3 shows how content analysis in relation to printed material might work in practice.

There are a number of advantages associated with content analysis:

- it is relatively straightforward;
- it is an unobtrusive method of data collection;
- it can provide interesting insights into how language is used to convey meaning.

Finally, it is useful for looking at frequencies of words and their change in frequency over time. It can be used for analyzing historical trends, e.g. mention of the Internet in marketing magazines over the last ten years.

Which Qualitative Approach Should I Use to Analyze my Data?

By now, you probably realize that there is no one 'best' approach to qualitative data analysis. The approach largely depends on the nature of your research topic and your research objectives. For example, if your main purpose is to compare your findings to those of an earlier study, then this may well dictate how you analyze your raw data. In other words, you are perhaps more likely to engage in a deductive, as opposed to an inductive, approach to your analysis.

Remember that your analysis does not necessarily need to be a straightforward choice between inductive and deductive methods. When coding your data, you may wish to have a predetermined set of codes (a deductive approach), but also to develop new codes and subsequent categories as you proceed in your analysis (an inductive approach). In short, the approach that you adopt often comes down to personal preference. Nevertheless, some approaches to qualitative analysis, such as grounded theory, are more challenging than others. As we have established, grounded theory is particularly challenging because of the time involved, and it generally commands an excellent grasp of the literature.

Qualitative Analytical Software Packages

The generic approach to qualitative data analysis described in this chapter can be undertaken manually or using a software package. The latter is certainly easier and, above all, less time-consuming. Moreover, a software package is a useful tool when it comes to coding, reducing and interpreting your data. In many cases, these tasks can be easily achieved using word processing software such as Microsoft Word, although increasingly researchers engaged in qualitative analysis are turning to specialist software such as NVivo and CAQDAS.

Many institutions now teach and/or hold copies of these software packages on their computers. As software packages go, they tend not to be used as widely as SPSS. One of the reasons for this might be that in order to be able to use such programs successfully, you need to be fully aware of how to use them. There is no space here for a thorough examination of the software, but comprehensive guides are available (e.g. for NVivo, see Bazeley, 2007).

─RESEARCH IN ACTION─

Undertaking qualitative content analysis

In the academic article detailed below, an overview is provided on the methodological approach adopted by the authors when analyzing corporate social responsibility (CSR) practices in the airline industry. In short, the researchers describe their approach as 'qualitative content analysis' and describe the process involved. The article is useful as it presents an explicit overview of the analytical process employed. In addition, it may help you to develop your own ideas as to how content analysis might be carried out as part of your research project.

Cowper-Smith, A. and de Grosbois, D. (2011) 'The adoption of corporate social responsibility practices in the airline industry', *Journal of Sustainable Tourism*, 19 (1): 59–77.

The authors aim to identify initiatives related to corporate social responsibility (CSR) in the airline industry and evaluate the overall state of their adoption as reported by members of the three largest airline alliances.

The details set out here examine the methodological approach adopted by the researchers. The authors state that the data were collected from the airline's environmental or CSR reports available online. The sample included member airlines of the three major airline alliances, namely: Star Alliance, Oneworld and SkyTeam. The authors mention that the rationale for choosing these alliances is that almost all of the world's leading airlines are members of these alliances. As of January 2009, 14 airlines from 41 members across the three alliances had environmental reports publicly available online in English.

The data analysis method carried out was qualitative content analysis. The researchers explain that the CSR initiatives identified from the analysis were organized into a framework consisting of two main dimensions, namely: environmental impacts and socio-economic impacts. They then divided these further into 11 themes. The themes that come under the environmental dimension are: emissions, waste, energy, water, biodiversity, noise and other. The themes for the social and economic dimension are: employee wellbeing and engagement, diversity and social equity, community well-being and economic prosperity.

Under each theme, specific goals were identified as well as the specific initiatives which contribute to each goal. The authors explain that the themes were selected on the basis of the content of the CSR reports, along with the major principles of sustainability and CSR drawn from Global Reporting Initiative (2006) and United Nations Environmental Programme and World Tourism Organization (2005).

The researchers make clear that the CSR framework undertaken in the study is based on items reported by the 14 airlines featured in the research, and is not an exhaustive list of CSR initiatives for the airline industry. They acknowledge that a possible limitation is that there may be information on CSR initiatives from sources other than the CSR reports. However, it is notable that their research only analyzes the CSR reports.

For each goal, the number of airlines reporting the goal was recorded by the researchers as well as the number of airlines that provide a measurement of their contribution to the goal. An example of a goal and a measure is given by the authors. For instance, 13 airlines stated that they seek to reduce waste; seven of them also provided a measurement of progress towards the goal, some in terms of percentage reduction of waste over the previous year. The authors state that they identified all the specific initiatives which contribute to each goal, the numbers reporting implementation of each, as well as the numbers providing measurements for each initiative. These were subsequently recorded. An example given here is that reducing waste is an environmental goal, while an initiative used to achieve this goal is recycling onboard waste. This was mentioned by seven airlines and measured by four.

The authors recognize that

it is possible for the number of companies reporting or measuring progress toward a goal to be lower than the number of companies reporting or measuring progress toward a specific initiative that contributes to that goal. This could occur when, for example, only a few airlines measured progress toward a given goal (such as increasing diversity in the workforce), but a larger number of airlines measured a specific initiative (such as increasing the number of women in management).

The methodology concludes by mentioning that the number of airlines reporting each CSR goal and initiative, as well as the number of airlines that measure their progress towards each goal initiative, are presented in tabular format: the first table entitled 'CSR initiatives within the environmental dimension and their adoption among the airline industry leaders', and the second entitled 'CSR initiatives within the social and economic dimensions and their adoption among airline industry leaders'.

Summary and Conclusion

The main focus in this chapter has been the numerous approaches to qualitative analysis. Undertaking qualitative analysis can be both time-consuming and challenging for the novice researcher. Nevertheless, it can provide some very interesting insights into your chosen topic and can help to form the basis for future research. Here are the key points from this chapter:

- Qualitative analysis is any kind of analysis that produces findings or concepts and hypotheses, as in grounded theory, which are not arrived at by statistical methods.
- The four analytical steps can be summarized as: transcribing your data; reading and generating categories, themes and patterns; interpreting your findings; and writing the report.
- Grounded theory is a method in which the theory is developed from the data, as opposed to applying theory from the outset.
- Narrative analysis is the study of stories or a chronological series of events. There are two types of narrative: personal narrative and 'life story' narrative.
- Discourse analysis examines both spoken and written language.
- Content analysis is a way of systematically converting text to numerical variables for quantitative data analysis.

CASE STUDY **Corporate Visions of Japan's Leading Brands: A Content Analysis**

Ichiro, a final-year BSc (Hons) International Business Strategy student, has adopted an inductive approach to his research. This will involve qualitative analysis of the corporate vision statements of Japan's leading brands. An extract from his proposal is given below:

Introduction

The majority of Japanese brands are using corporate vision statements to set out their future strategic direction. However, there is a paucity of research focused on the content of such vision statements. Despite there being several studies on corporate vision and Japanese brands, there has yet to be research conducted that examines the association between the two topics. In view of this, the objective of this research project is to fill this gap in the literature by exploring the approach of Japan's leading brands to the corporate vision statement. This includes examining the content of each vision statement cited on each brand's corporate websites, and determining the extent to which the vision conforms to what can be described as an 'effective' vision statement. In addition, I will examine whether or not each vision has a 'global outlook'.

Due to the exploratory nature of my study, analysis is guided by the following research questions:

1. How easily accessible is each vision statement?
2. How many Japanese brands have what can be described as effective corporate vision statements?
3. How many vision statements have a global outlook?

Data collection

My sample consists of 30 Japanese brands taken from Interbrand's 'Japan's Best Global Brands 2013', http://www.interbrand.com/ja/knowledge/Japans-Best-Global-Brands/2013/2013-report.aspx [accessed 12th April 2013].

Each corporate website will be analyzed in order to assess the following: First, to examine the location and content of each vision statement. Second, analyze how many Japanese brands have what can be described as an 'effective' corporate vision statement. Finally, to interpret how many of the vision statements communicate what can be described as a 'global outlook.'

If the website includes a vision statement, a record of its location on the website will be subsequently made. Coding will be applied using the key elements of an effective vision statement as proposed by Collins and Porras (1996) – core purpose, core values, BHAGs (big, hairy and audacious goals) and vivid descriptions. Finally, for the purpose of this study, my definition of corporate vision is based on Parikh and Neubauer (1993: 105); namely, a corporate vision is 'an image of a desired future state of an organization'.

Data coding and analysis

Having read the vision statements, a categorizing strategy in the form of coding will be applied. The goal of coding is to fracture the data and rearrange them into categories that facilitate the comparison of data within and between these categories and that aid in the development of theoretical concepts (Strauss, 1987: 29). Identification of categories will be linked to the research questions.

There are two approaches to coding data – emergent coding (inductive) and a priori coding (deductive). By adopting emergent coding, categories will develop through examining data. Conversely, a priori coding categories are determined prior to analysis. Moreover, these categories are typically based on some existing theory. For this study, a deductive approach using a priori coding categories will be undertaken. First, this will involve the application of Collins and Porras' (1996) categories to examine the extent to which a vision conforms to an effective vision statement. Second, categories in the form of key words will be used to explore whether or not a vision adopted a 'global outlook'. Given the small sample size and relatively brief amount of textual data, I deem the creation of an a priori scheme as the preferred approach to coding categories, as opposed to a mixed methods approach.

My first research question sets out to consider the ease of access of each corporate vision. Prior to starting my analysis, I will set out to correctly classify each vision statement. This involves checking each statement to ensure that it 'fits' with my definition, and above all, that it includes a 'future' orientation. To establish if this is the case, future orientation key words such as 'to be', 'to become', 'to create', 'we will', and 'future' will be analyzed within the text of each corporate website.

My second research question examines the effectiveness of each vision statement. When analyzing my categories – core values, core purpose, BHAGs and vivid description – I will use key words associated with each category. First, a reference to core values will be operationalized by searching for key words such as 'service to', 'customer', 'creativity', 'hard work', and 'honesty'. Core purpose will be operationalized by identifying key words such as 'to experience', 'to provide', 'to give', and 'to help'.

Envisioned future, or more specifically BHAGs, will be operationalized by looking for key words such as 'number one', 'the most', and 'transform'. For my final category of 'global outlook', I will set out to address my third research question: 'How many vision statements have a global outlook?' This will be operationalized by searching for the following key words: 'global', 'world', 'Europe', and 'international' within each vision statement. Conversely, the key word 'Japan' will also be examined to determine the extent to which vision statements might be more 'domestically' focused. In other words, corporate vision centres on penetrating the Japanese market, as opposed to global brand development.

(Continued)

(Continued)

Finally, vivid descriptions will be operationalized by looking for key words such as 'years', 'time', and 'long-term'. If a vision statement is deemed to contain all four of the Collins and Porras (1996) categories, along with reference to global outlook, it will be viewed as being a 'fully effective' vision statement.

Case study questions

1. How can Ichiro present the results from his study?
2. What are your views on Ichiro's approach to his content analysis? How might he have done things differently?
3. Based on his proposal, it appears that Ichiro intends analyzing corporate vision statements in English. Given that his research focuses on the websites of leading Japanese brands and he is a Japanese student, how might he consider changing his methodology?

YOU'RE THE SUPERVISOR

Jennifer has reached the analysis stage of her research. She is fortunate enough to have carried out ten interviews with high-profile managers in her local authority. Each interview has been fully transcribed and saved on to Jennifer's computer. Even though she is making good progress with her research, Jennifer is unsure of what step to take next. During her Research Skills module she learned a variety of approaches to qualitative analysis, but is unsure which one to choose. Jennifer's raw data amount to more than 50,000 words. She is keen to start analyzing each transcript, but has arranged a meeting with you to discuss her options regarding qualitative analysis.

Supervisor question

- How would you respond to Jennifer?

COMMON QUESTIONS AND ANSWERS

1. What are the disadvantages of qualitative data analysis?

Answer: A major drawback associated with qualitative data analysis is the fact that it is a very time-consuming process. Typically, all stages of qualitative analysis require considerable attention, from transcribing your data to interpreting your findings.

2. How long will it take me to conduct my qualitative analysis?

Answer: There is no easy answer to this question as the time is dependent on a number of factors, including the research approach, the number of interviews or observations undertaken, whether or not you are transcribing your data, and any other commitments that you may have outside your research.

3. What are the steps I am likely to go through when analyzing my qualitative data?

Answer: There is no definitive approach to qualitative data analysis. I have shown you the more 'generic' steps that you may take when carrying out your analysis. In reality, the steps that you take do not follow a straightforward linear process.

References

Bazeley, P. (2007) *Qualitative Data Analysis with NVivo*. London: Sage.

Coffey, A. and Atkinson, P. (1996) *Making Sense of Qualitative Data: Complementary Research Strategies*. Thousand Oaks, CA: Sage.

Collins, J.C. and Porras, J.I. (1996) *Built to Last: Successful Habits of Visionary Companies*. London: Century.

Collis, J. and Hussey, R. (2003) *Business Research: A Practical Guide for Undergraduate and Postgraduate Students* (2nd edn). Basingstoke: Palgrave Macmillan.

Cowper-Smith, A. and de Grosbois, D. (2011) 'The adoption of corporate social responsibility practices in the airline industry', *Journal of Sustainable Tourism*, 19 (1): 59–77.

Denzin, N.K. and Lincoln, Y.S. (1998) *Strategies of Qualitative Inquiry*. Thousand Oaks, CA: Sage.

Dey, I. (1993) *Qualitative Analysis: A User-Friendly Guide for Social Scientists*. London: Routledge.

Elliott, R. (1996) 'Discourse analysis: Exploring action, function and conflict in social texts', *Marketing Intelligence & Planning*, 14 (6): 65–68.

Flick, U. (1998) *An Introduction to Qualitative Research*. London: Sage.

Glaser, B. (1992) *Basics of Grounded Theory Analysis: Emergence vs Forcing?* Mill Valley, CA: Sociology Press.

Global Reporting Initiative (2006) 'Sustainability reporting guidelines' retrieved from http://www.globalreporting.org/NR/rdonlyres/ED9E9B36-AB54-4DE1-BFF2-5F735235CA44/0/G3 GuidelinesENU.pdf

Mansourian, Y. (2006) 'Adoption of grounded theory in LIS research', *New Library World*, 107 (1228/1229): 386–402.

Marshall, C. and Rossman, G.B. (1995) *Designing Qualitative Research* (2nd edn). Thousand Oaks, CA: Sage.

Merton, R.K. and Kendall, P.L. (1949) 'The focused interview', *American Journal of Sociology*, 51: 541–557.

Miles, M.B. and Huberman, A.M. (1994) *Qualitative Data Analysis: An Expanded Sourcebook* (2nd edn). Thousand Oaks, CA: Sage.

Myers, M. (2009) *Qualitative Research in Business and Management*. London: Sage.

Pace, S. (2004) 'A grounded theory of the flow experiences of web users', *International Journal of Human Computer Studies*, 60 (3): 327–363.

Parikh, J. and Neubauer, F. (1993) 'Corporate Visioning'. In: Hussey, D.E. (ed.) *International Review of Strategic Management*, vol. 4. Wiley: Chichester.

Patton, M.Q. (1990) *Qualitative Evaluation and Research Methods* (2nd edn). Newbury Park, CA: Sage.

Strauss, A. (1987) *Qualitative Analysis for Social Scientists*. Cambridge: Cambridge University Press.

Strauss, A. and Corbin, J. (1990) *Basics of Qualitative Research: Grounded Theory Procedures and Technique*. Newbury Park, CA: Sage.

United Nations Environmental Programme & World Tourism Organization. (2005) 'Making tourism more sustainable: A guide for policy makers', retrieved from http://www.unep.fr/shared/publications/pdf/DTIx0592xPA-TourismPolicyEN.pdf

Further Reading

Bazeley, P. (2007) *Qualitative Data Analysis with NVivo*. London: Sage.

Corbin, J.M. and Lewis, J. (2008) *Basics of Qualitative Research: Techniques and Procedures for Developing Grounded Theory* (3rd edn). Thousand Oaks, CA: Sage.

Creswell, J.W. (2007) *Qualitative Inquiry and Research Design: Choosing among Five Approaches*. Thousand Oaks, CA: Sage.

Ritchie, J. and Lewis, J. (2003) *Qualitative Research Practice: A Guide for Social Science Students and Researchers*. Thousand Oaks, CA: Sage.

Silverman, D. (2010) *Qualitative Research: Issues of Theory, Method and Practice*. Thousand Oaks, CA: Sage.

11
Writing up and presenting your research

┌─ Learning Objectives ───┐

After reading this chapter, you should be able to:

- know how to go about writing your research project;
- understand the typical structure of a research project;
- be aware of how to write up your project as a theory or as an argument;
- know the criteria for evaluating research projects;
- appreciate how to present your research project; and
- know the common errors found in research projects.

└───┘

Introduction

In this chapter consideration is given to the final stage in the research process – writing and presenting your research project. However, for some of you, it may not necessarily be the final stage. You see, the approach that students adopt in relation to time management when writing up their work usually falls into one of two camps: monochronic or polychronic (Hall, 1959). If you adopt the former, then you are likely to approach your research one step at a time. In other words, writing up will only take place once you have completed each stage of your research. Conversely, a polychronic approach means that you will combine writing up with various other activities, such as searching the literature and analyzing your data. Essentially, you are writing up as you go along.

Which is the correct approach? The simple answer is that neither approach is better than the other. It is simply a matter of choice. My advice is to go with the approach that is best suited to your current way of doing things. Whichever option you choose, the important thing is that you follow the correct structure, and manage your time efficiently.

I begin this chapter by stressing the importance of working towards a clear timetable when writing up. Quite simply, having a timetable will help you to set your aims and objectives, and give you deadlines for each part of your report. I then move on to writing style. Unfortunately, adopting an inappropriate writing style is unlikely to do your work justice. Important factors need to be considered, such as the level of formality in your language, political correctness and sexism.

Next, we explore the typical structure of a research project. You may have gathered a wealth of interesting data during your research, but if your research is not set out within the structural requirements laid down by your university or college, it is likely that you will end up losing a significant number of marks.

Not adopting the right structure is not the only factor that may lead you to lose marks. Your institution will have a detailed set of marking criteria for evaluating your work. Having a clear understanding of the learning outcomes and marking criteria is vital prior to submitting the final version of your report. We therefore take a detailed look at the full set of marking criteria liable to apply to your work.

A key feature of marking criteria is likely to be presentation. Gaining marks for presentation should be relatively straightforward. However, a loss of marks due to poor presentation is sometimes all too common. Generally, there are three broad types of presentation: written, graphical and oral. Although the last of these is not always relevant to some students, we explore all three later in the chapter.

Finally, we consider the common errors found in student research projects. The purpose of highlighting these is to make sure that you avoid making similar mistakes!

Where to Start – Writing Up

Your approach to writing up is likely to be determined on whether or not you adopt a monochronic or polychronic approach to time management. Personally, I prefer to start writing as early as possible. The advantage of this is that you can develop your writing style over time. Moreover, it lessens the possibility of having to deal with a last-minute rush and the risk of not being able to submit on time. That said, there are certain disadvantages with this approach; having to make regular amendments to text due to newly discovered literature or methodological constraints can be particularly annoying.

Prior to writing up you should have organized your data into relevant chapters. Your project's structure should begin with an introductory chapter, followed by a literature review, a chapter on methodology, your results and analysis, a conclusion and any recommendations. To be honest, though, there are several variations of structure. The example I have just given is perhaps the most commonly used. This means that it contains the 'key' chapters or sections that one would expect to see within a research project. The nature of your introduction, along with other chapters, is fully explained later in this chapter.

Writing timetable

Just as you are likely to have worked towards a set *timetable* when conducting your research, ideally, you should adopt the same approach when writing up your work. Perhaps the best way to allocate time is to do it on a chapter-by-chapter

TABLE 11.1 Time allocation to writing your research project

Chapter	Time allocation (weeks)
Introduction	2
Literature review	2
Methodology	1
Results and analysis	4
Conclusion and recommendations	1
Total	10

basis. Table 11.1 provides an indication of how much time to allocate to each chapter when writing up.

Table 11.1 is purely intended as a guide. It does not account for editing your work, meeting your supervisor, printing and binding, proofreading or preparation for a possible oral presentation. Moreover, if English is not your native language, then you may find that it takes considerably longer to write up your report. If you lack confidence in your English language abilities, your institution should be able to help. Many provide excellent English language support, particularly in relation to proofreading. If you are concerned about your level of English, and this facility is available to you, make use of it.

Even if you are a native English speaker, it is always advisable to invite as many people as possible to read your work before submission. Apart from noticing grammatical and typographical errors, experts such as your supervisor can also advise on ways of improving your work.

Writing and other students

Although you are undertaking an individual piece of work, there is no harm in sharing your experience with your peers. Several benefits can be gained from working with other students. These include:

- reducing isolation;
- motivation to stick to project timelines;
- critical friends with whom to discuss specific ideas, challenges and 'knotty problems';
- sounding issues out in advance of meeting a supervisor;
- putting things in perspective if you are feeling stressed or under pressure; and
- sharing resources and search results.

(Smith et al., 2009: 21)

Writing style

Basically, your writing style refers to how you put your words together. Hopefully, by the time you reach the writing-up stage of your research project, you should have developed a competent level of academic writing. If not, it is beyond the scope of this book to teach you how to write well in English. There are many books on the market that can help you to do this. A notable example is Bailey (2006).

There are two broad types of writing style – informal and formal. While informal writing is more conversational and 'laid back', formal language adopts a more serious, impersonal and detached tone. There are varying degrees of formality. The main factors used to gauge levels of formality are sentence structure and grammar. Consider the two examples below:

1. Luke shows signs of laziness in his job.
2. Luke currently appears to be lacking in motivation in some areas of his work.

In the main, both of these examples are saying the same thing. However, the second uses a more formal style of language and is a lengthier sentence, while the first uses an informal tone and a simpler, shorter sentence structure.

How do you know which level of formality should be applied when writing up your research? Well, prior to undertaking your writing, you need to consider the following questions:

- What level of formality is expected by my university or college?
- What level of formality is expected by my supervisor?
- Who is my target audience?

In some respects, the above questions can be answered collectively. First, the level of formality expected by your institution and supervisor are likely to be the same or very similar. This is because you are undertaking an academic piece of writing. Thus, the expectation is that your level of formality is going to be more formal than informal. Second, you are writing for an academic audience. In most cases, this audience consists of your supervisor, a second marker and possibly an external examiner. Consequently, you must adopt an academic style of writing, which, once again, tends to be more formal than informal.

Long sentences or short sentences

As we have seen in the previous section, academic writing is commonly associated with long sentences. Then again, do not be afraid to vary the length of your sentences. Doing so can often improve the flow of your writing. Consider the following examples:

1. The current state of the economy is a major concern for SMEs because the consequences of a downturn in sales can be disastrous for an employee's job security.
2. The current state of the economy is a major concern for SMEs. Indeed, the consequences of a downturn in sales can be disastrous for an employee's job security.

Notice the difference in the above examples. The first is of course the more 'wordy' of the two. By splitting it into two shorter sentences, arguably the second example reads better.

Political correctness

Increasingly, political correctness is also a consideration when writing up your research. Political correctness can be defined as: 'the avoidance of expressions or actions that are perceived to exclude or insult groups of people who are socially disadvantaged or discriminated against' (Oxford English Dictionary, 2005). It is particularly important if you wish to disseminate your work.

In recent years, political correctness has had a real impact on how words and phrases are used in everyday life. Certain words and phrases that are considered discriminatory are generally replaced with those that are less offensive. Table 11.2 shows examples of politically correct and incorrect words.

Opponents of political correctness suggest that in some cases it has gone too far. Possible evidence of this is in the employment market. If you have a look at the recruitment pages of some of the national newspapers, it is interesting to note the variation in different job titles. For example, the word 'executive' has largely replaced the word 'clerk'.

TABLE 11.2 Examples of politically correct and incorrect terms

Incorrect usage	Correct usage
OAP (old-age pensioner)	Senior citizen
Unemployed	Out of work
Fat	Overweight

Some might argue that this is a form of political correctness as the term 'clerk' might seem demeaning. Others may view it as 'glamorizing' a particular job by using a word that is more contemporary and appealing to potential applicants. Whatever your point of view, political correctness is something that needs to be considered. Naturally, some words and phrases are going to be evidently more politically incorrect than others. If in doubt, ask a native English speaker and/or someone who is familiar with the current expectations on political correctness to read through your work.

Sexism

Try to avoid what might be interpreted as sexist language in your writing. In the context of your research project, sexism covers words or phrases that discriminate against a particular sex. Sometimes you may find that you do this subconsciously. Even so, it is important that you do not show bias by referring to one particular gender, particularly in relation to job description.

Notable examples of words that can be construed as sexist include gender-specific words such as 'chairman', 'fireman', 'policeman' and 'milkman'. In many cases 'person' has replaced reference to gender in many compound nouns. It is therefore better to use 'chairperson', 'fire-fighter', 'police officer' and 'milk person', respectively.

Other considerations

There are a plethora of considerations governing writing style. The following list summarizes some of the more notable ones (adapted from Levin, 2005: 104–105).

- Don't write in a polemical, opinionated and/or emotion-laden style. Your writing should be as objective as possible. Your research project is not the place to vent your anger or be abusive. Nor is it the place for you to display 'positive' congratulatory emotions.
- If your subject and approach call for you to make value judgements, save them for your 'discussion' section. In your discussion, first take your reasoning as far as you can without being judgemental. Only then should you apply your personal judgements. When you do so, make it clear what criteria you are using, and what the basis is for your judgements.
- Don't use expressions like 'I believe' and 'I think'. You do not get credit for your beliefs. Your thoughts need to be supported. For example, this can be done using illustrative case examples and/or referencing earlier work.
- Don't write in a chatty or journalistic style. Avoid using slang words and phrases that are typical in the tabloid press. For example, words such as 'quid' instead of pounds and 'footy' instead of football should be avoided.
- Don't try to write like a textbook or an authority on your subject. An academic may use expressions such as 'We consider …', 'In our judgement …', 'As so-and-so rightly says …', 'The evidence suggests …'. (Evidence on its own suggests nothing whatever, of course. The accurate expression would be: 'In the light of this evidence, I think …'.) All these expressions carry the implication that he or she is an authority on the subject and is not to be challenged. If you as a student use them, what you say and write may strike your teachers as being pretentious and inappropriate.
- Don't use long, complicated sentences when you can use short ones. Keep your writing clear and simple. It is particularly infuriating to find students using long, cumbersome sentences. It often makes it difficult for the reader to understand what it is that you are trying to say. The result will probably be a deduction in marks!
- Don't use vague expressions such as 'Many writers think …'. The reader will immediately ask: 'Who are these writers?' So give their names and cite your sources.
- Your supervisor and his or her colleagues may have very definite views about style. If you are issued with a style guide, be sure to follow it. In particular, find out if it is acceptable for you to write in the first person. Can you say 'In this research project I shall show …', 'I feel …', or 'I conclude …'? Or should you use impersonal forms (not using the word 'I' or 'me'), such as 'This essay will show …', 'The present writer feels …' or 'One would conclude …'?

In this section we have examined the importance of writing style. By now you should be aware of how to go about writing up your research so that it meets the expectations of your research supervisor. Unfortunately, the writing-up stage in your research is not just about writing. What is equally significant is the structure of your report.

There is what I would call a 'typical' structure to a research project, although in some cases this structure depends on whether or not you are writing your project as a theory or as an argument. We now look at this topic more closely.

Writing style – International students

Some international students, particularly those for whom English is not their first language, may be unfamiliar with the considerations governing writing style. As mentioned earlier, if English is not your native language, then you may find that it takes considerably longer to write up your research project. Once again, your institution should be able to help. In addition, there is no substitute for reading past research projects and journal articles to gain a better understanding of what is required and to improve your own writing. Finally, make sure to proofread your work and ask a native speaker to do the same.

Writing as an argument or as a theory

Whether you are writing as a theory or as an argument is going to impact how you structure your research. Before we explore in detail each chapter of a typical research project, it is worth making the distinction between argument and theory. Figures 11.1 and 11.2 show the structure for each one respectively. Although Figures 11.1 and 11.2 may appear markedly different, they do share several things in common. These include: an introduction, a literature review, reference to theoretical content, analysis and a conclusion.

Essentially, Figure 11.1 is an argument based on a comparative study. If you choose this option, then in the main you are comparing your working with earlier studies in the same subject area. Figure 11.2 is clearly a deductive approach as it involves the application of an existing theory.

Each of these examples is a guide to how you can structure your research project. Given that some institutions hold quite strict assessment regulations governing structure, it is worth checking these first before adopting a more flexible approach. We can now move on to examine each chapter of a 'typical' research project.

Structure of a Research Project

As noted earlier, the structure of your research project must be divided into relevant chapters (see Table 11.3). Each chapter forms an essential part of your overall project, and is primarily a way of dividing up common themes for the benefit of the reader. It does not matter which chapter you decide to write first. My advice is to start with the chapter you are most comfortable with. For many students, this is indeed the introduction.

The second column in Table 11.3 shows a percentage figure alongside each chapter. This is a percentage of the overall word count to allocate to each respective chapter. Typically, most institutions apply a word limit to research projects. The most common are either 8,000 or 10,000 words.

Table 11.3 is intended merely as a guide. For example, if you are only using secondary data, your methodology is liable to be fewer words than if you were using methodological triangulation. Also, your research project may not always follow a

FIGURE 11.1 Structure of an argument (adapted from Levin, 2005: 88)

FIGURE 11.2 Structure when testing a theory (adapted from Levin, 2005: 85–86)

TABLE 11.3   Structure of a research report

Chapter	Percentage of overall word count
Introduction	15
Literature review	25
Methodology	25
Results and analysis	25
Conclusion and recommendations	10

set structure as highlighted in Table 11.3. For example, sometimes the results and analysis might be divided into two chapters. In addition, word-based projects may only have a very brief literature review that falls within the introduction. In short, Table 11.3 is intended as a useful guide.

The remainder of this section will outline some of the necessary features that you should include in the different chapters.

Chapter 1 – Introduction

Your *introduction* should clearly set out what it is that you intend to investigate. It should provide a detailed overview of your chosen research topic, along with a clear rationale. You also need to ensure that it is well structured so that it makes for easy reading.

It is important to include a statement of the problem and outline who will benefit from your study. If, for example, you are researching the efficiency of customer service within your own company, then the obvious benefactor is likely to be your own firm. You can also argue that your findings may benefit existing work on your chosen topic, as it fills a 'gap' within the existing body of literature.

Other essential features of your introduction are your objectives and research questions. You need to emphasize these so that the reader is aware of exactly what it is that you are trying to achieve through conducting your research. Next, an overview of the layout of your study provides a 'map' of subsequent chapters. This tells the reader what to expect later on in your research project.

If you are having difficulty writing your introduction, look at some introductory sections from academic journals. These can provide an excellent guide, particularly in terms of writing style and structure.

Chapter 2 – Literature review

We examined the nature of a literature review in Chapter 3, so I will briefly summarize here. Remember that the main purpose of a literature review is to demonstrate knowledge of your chosen subject area and to acknowledge those authors who have already written on your chosen topic. You also need to analyze the literature critically and say how it relates to your own research.

The length of your literature review largely depends on two factors. First, the amount of literature written on your chosen subject and, second, your chosen research approach. For example, your review is likely to be longer if you have adopted a deductive approach and shorter if you have taken an inductive approach. The inductive route means you are moving from theory to practice, so there will be little, if any, reference to relevant theories within your literature review.

Most literature reviews tend to be organized in a thematic way. In other words, the literature is presented around developing issues. These issues are clearly divided using relevant headings and subheadings.

In order that you are familiar with contemporary work on your topic area, you should continue your literature review right up to a couple of weeks prior to submission.

Chapter 3 – Methodology

Unlike your research proposal, your methodology should be written in the past tense because, by the time you reach the writing-up stage, you will have carried out your data collection and analysis. The methodology chapter must refer to your research philosophy, approach, strategy and research design.

Other areas that also need to be discussed include: the data collection and analytical methods used (e.g. reference to descriptive and inferential statistics), sampling techniques, reliability, validity and a data analysis plan.

Chapter 4 – Results and analysis

In some cases, results and analysis are treated separately. However, in this example, we will treat them as part of the same chapter.

You need to publish your results and interpret your findings. The nature of your results and how you go about doing this mostly depends on whether you are examining qualitative or quantitative data. For instance, quantitative data may involve investigating the relationship between variables using correlation and regression analysis, while qualitative data may entail content analysis or narrative analysis. Make sure too that you do not just simply present and describe your findings. This chapter also requires a critical evaluation of your results.

You must not report your results and analyze your findings solely in the context of your own research. You also need to establish the difference between your findings and those of other researchers.

Chapter 5 – Conclusion and recommendations

Of all the chapters within a research project, this is the one that students seem to have the most problem with. In reality, writing a *conclusion* should be fairly straightforward. It is essentially a summary of your findings that sets out to discuss the extent to which you have achieved what you set out to achieve. This is the part that students often fail to fully address.

Remember to discuss your objectives and research questions, which were specified in your introductory chapter. Your conclusion is not the place to introduce new material, let alone a totally new set of objectives! By restating each objective in your conclusion you are guaranteed to address each one in turn.

The conclusion should also feature a section headed up 'Future research'. This is for the benefit of future researchers, to illustrate how your research can be taken forward. Examples of future research might focus on a different research design or propose another data collection method. In your conclusion you should also refer to any limitations that you encountered when doing your research. Examples here might include problems accessing data and financial constraints. Finally, your findings can lead you to make recommendations for managers and researchers within your chosen subject area.

Table 11.3 is a useful template of how to divide your work into relevant chapters. Each chapter also requires a clear introduction that sets out its structure. Remember that although you are fully familiar with the nature of your research, it may well be the first time that your readers have been exposed to your research topic. Therefore, it is important to 'guide' the reader. In essence, this means providing pointers throughout your work. Fully explaining why you have included a piece of information and talking through each step in a clear, concise and thematic way will certainly help to improve the readability of your work.

Preliminary features

The above structure illustrates the main chapters of your research project. Yet most projects also contain important preliminary and closing features. First, the former usually consists of a title page, acknowledgements, an abstract, lists of abbreviations, illustrations and tables, and a contents page. The main closing features include your references and appendices. Let us look at each one in turn.

Title page

Typically, a title page should consist of the title of your research project, comments to the effect that it has been submitted as a partial fulfilment of your final award, your name and student number, the name of your supervisor, the name of your university or college, and the date of submission. Different institutions may have slightly different requirements. For instance, in some cases an anonymous marking policy may be enforced, in which case you only need to include your student number. Figure 11.3 illustrates a typical layout for a title page.

Acknowledgements

Your acknowledgements give you the opportunity to thank those who helped you with your project. Acknowledgements normally come after the title page. Individuals

Inter-Partner Relationships and Performance in Canadian Strategic Alliances

This Dissertation is submitted as partial fulfilment for the award of Bachelor of Honours in Business and Management by:
David Peter Gill
Student No.: 135478
Supervisor: Dr Peter Shaw
Brampton University
© April 2009

FIGURE 11.3   Example of a title page

you may wish to thank are likely to include your project supervisor, friends, family and research participants.

Abstract

An abstract is a summary of your entire research project. The purpose of an abstract is to allow the reader to gain a fast and accurate insight into the nature of your research. Abstracts are particularly important for full-time researchers. For example, by reading the abstract, researchers can quickly determine whether or not the research is relevant to their own work, and this can save time.

Your abstract should be the last part of the project you write. In most cases, an abstract tends to be no longer than 300 words. Some students find it difficult to condense their research into a concise number of words. In truth, it will probably take you several attempts before you produce something that you are happy with. Once again, make use of your project supervisor. He or she can comment on the suitability of your abstract and provide useful suggestions. Academic articles are an extremely useful guide to writing abstracts, although different journals often insist on different ways of structuring an abstract.

Lists of abbreviations, illustrations and tables

The first of these preliminary features is relatively minor. Its inclusion is often at the discretion of the researcher. A list of abbreviations contains all those abbreviations cited in your research project. Normally, if your readership audience are specialists in your chosen topic, it is not necessary to include such a list. However, if your intended audience is unfamiliar with your subject area, including an abbreviations list can be a welcome addition. If, for example, you were reading a project on market entry methods and were unfamiliar with the subject, you would undoubtedly appreciate the inclusion of abbreviations such as EJV (equity joint venture), CJV (cooperative joint venture) and IJV (international joint venture) in such a list.

Illustrations refer to all figures and diagrams within your work. A list of illustrations typically comes after the list of abbreviations. An example of how figures might be listed is given below:

A list of tables summarizes all those tables featured in your research project. As with lists of figures and diagrams, alongside the title of each table is its respective page number. By way of example:

Contents page

A contents page provides an overview of the structure, headings, subheadings and respective page numbers of what is inside your research project. It also includes the preliminary and closing features discussed in this chapter, along with their individual page numbers.

It is essential that the headings and page numbers given in the contents page correspond with those in the body of your work. Failure to do so can be extremely annoying for the reader. Figure 11.4 shows an example of how to structure a contents page. Note the structure, main headings and subheadings.

Irrespective of the subject area, the structure of your contents page will most probably be similar to the one shown in Figure 11.4. The purpose of this illustrative example is for you to gain a useful insight into not only how a contents page should be structured, but also, and more to the point, how a research project is typically structured. In this respect, you can treat this example as perhaps a useful template for your own study.

CONTENTS

Acknowledgements
Abstract
Abbreviations
List of illustrations
List of tables

CHAPTER 1: INTRODUCTION

1.1   Background to the study
1.2   Statement of the problem
1.3   Objectives of the study
1.4   Layout of the study
1.5   Usefulness of the study

(Continued)

FIGURE 11.4   (Continued)

CHAPTER 2: LITERATURE REVIEW

2.1 Introduction
2.2 The IMP Group and inter-organizational relationships
2.3 The interaction approach
2.4 The network approach
2.5 Foreign direct investment (FDI) relationships
     2.5.1 Trust
     2.5.2 Commitment
     2.5.3 Co-operation
     2.5.4 Satisfaction

CHAPTER 3: RESEARCH METHODOLOGY

3.1 Introduction
3.2 General review of research design
3.3 Quantitative study
     3.3.1 Sampling
     3.3.2 Data collection
     3.3.3 Measurement variables and issues
3.4 Data analysis
3.5 Secondary analysis
3.6 Reliability and validity
3.7 Internal measurement issues
3.8 Data analysis plan

CHAPTER 4: RESULTS AND ANALYSIS

4.1 Introduction
     4.1.1 Nature of the industry and size of firms
4.2 Strategic objectives of the Western parent company
4.3 Achievement of strategic objectives
4.4 Means of first contact
4.5 Relationship values and performance

CHAPTER 5: CONCLUSION AND RECOMMENDATIONS

5.1 Introduction
5.2 Discussion on relationship values and performance
5.3 Contribution statements
5.4 Managerial implications
5.5 Limitations of the study
     5.5.1 Sample population
     5.5.2 Measurement issues
     5.5.3 Time factors
5.6 Future research

References
Appendices

FIGURE 11.4   Example of how to structure a contents page

Closing features

Following your concluding chapter, it is likely that you will have two additional features to your research project. The first of these is a references section. Second are the appendices.

References

The importance of referencing has been noted throughout this book. In addition, I have also noted the distinction between a bibliography and *references*. Some institutions require both a bibliography and a reference section, while others are happy for all references to go under one heading of 'References'. If in doubt, check with your institution or supervisor.

Appendices

Appendices generally contain information that is likely to be of secondary importance to readers. A question I am often asked by students is 'What goes in the appendices?' Well, information that is of less importance usually includes the following:

- an example of a questionnaire administered during the study (as a rule it is not necessary to include all completed questionnaires);
- certain 'minor' tables, e.g. a table showing GDP figures for European states; and
- theoretical models or diagrams.

If you are unsure about what to include and what not to include, once again seek advice from your supervisor. In essence, your appendices should really be kept to a minimum. In most institutions, the contents of the appendices are not included in the word count. If you are subject to a word limit, do not fall into the trap of using your appendices to 'abuse' the word limit!

Finally, your appendices must be numbered sequentially and come after your references.

What Are the Criteria for Evaluating a Research Project?

Each institution adopts its own set of marking criteria. However, in many respects the criteria for evaluating research projects is largely generic. For example, marks are usually awarded for each of the main chapters – introduction, literature review, methodology, analysis and results, and conclusion. Typically, marks are also awarded for presentation. This might include referencing, structure and the appropriate use of language. Figure 11.5 illustrates research project assessment criteria.

Area 1: Task definition and approach (25% of marks)

Objectives/rationale

- Usually found in the introduction, although context likely to be expanded in subsequent sections of the dissertation.
- Objectives are the purpose of dissertation and why it is being undertaken; there should be a clear focus.
- Rationale includes the applicability and importance of the study to business environment.
- An academic context is broader than the organizational context.

Approach/process

- Specify methodology/process (e.g. how data were collected).
- Justification for choice of approach.
- Coherence and rigour in approach.
- Appropriateness of approach to dissertation.
- Evidence of clear planning, organization and sequencing in dissertation.
- A flawed methodology will not result in a poor mark in this area if the flaws are recognized and the limitations which arise are discussed.
- Reference to research methods literature should be made where appropriate.
- For literature-based dissertations this section is likely to be shorter.

Area 2: Literature review, findings and evaluation (50% of marks)

- Summary of findings of previous work including omissions and how it relates to the dissertation.
- Scope, breadth and relevance of this work including currency of the findings.
- Development of a clear conceptual framework to underpin study including rationale.
- Bibliography lists both relevant sources used in the preparation of the dissertation and all the references included in the text.

Analysis of material

- Concern with the detail of the analysis undertaken for the dissertation, the overview and linking of different ideas are covered in *synthesis/evaluation*.
- Ability to discover, understand and analyze.
- Thorough analysis.
- How integrates with, and questions, individual issues raised by the literature.

Synthesis/evaluation

- Concerned with the linking of different strands of arguments together. It assesses the holistic approach taken in the dissertation rather than the individual components of the analysis covered by assessment.
- Ability to compare and contrast.
- Clear links with dissertation's objectives.
- Ability to synthesize and evaluate.
- Rigorous – integrates with issues raised by the literature reviewed.
- Consistency.

Conclusions/recommendations

- May not necessarily be titled 'conclusions' or 'recommendations'; another common title is 'discussion'.
- Contain overall findings of analysis.
- Conclusions and recommendations are relevant/feasible and clear.
- Take ideas forward.
- Include a critical evaluation of business application of findings.

FIGURE 11.5   Research project assessment criteria (from Saunders and Davis, 1998)

Presenting Your Research Project

Earlier in this chapter we examined the structure of your research project and style of writing. Although these are important aspects of presenting your work, presentation also relates to the presentation of data.

Presenting data

In essence, there are three methods of presenting data – tabular format, graphical format or text format. First, in Chapter 9 we examined several different types of tables. These include tables that summarize univariate, bivariate and multivariate data. When presenting your data using tables, you need to note the following considerations:

- make sure your data are suitable for a tabular format;
- clearly label your table;
- make sure that your table is legible;
- make sure that the rows and columns are of equal proportions; and
- if it is not your own work, make sure that you include your source.

Table 11.4 provides an example of how you should present a table within your research project. Note that it fulfils the previously cited considerations. The source includes the author's surname, first initial, year and page number. In this example, the table has been taken from Wong and included without any alterations. If you

TABLE 11.4 Frequency of employees attending a health and safety training programme

Department	Frequency	Percentage
Human Resources	56	33
Finance	75	43
Marketing	42	24
Total	173	100

Source: Wong, J. (1999: 24)

wanted to add your own data to the table, your reference would then become '*Source*: Adapted from Wong (1999: 24)'.

When incorporating a table into your work, make sure that it does not arrive unannounced. You need to fully explain the content and say how it relates in context to your study. Also, tables are not only an excellent way of presenting data, they can also help to break up your text. Personally, I find it somewhat laborious reading page after page of text. In many cases, tables can add variety to your work and make it more interesting for the reader.

Another method of presenting your data is to use a graphical format. This includes figures, diagrams, charts, graphs and pictures. For the latter, you will need to check with your supervisor to see if the inclusion of pictures is permitted. In some institutions this is discouraged, in others it may not be permitted at all, while in some cases the nature of the subject may dictate whether or not you can include pictures within your report. If, for example, you were conducting a study into the usage of humour in the advertising of alcoholic beverages, then pictures of actual advertising campaigns are arguably an essential part of your work.

Like tables, when including graphical work in your research, it needs to be clearly presented, labelled and referenced. Figure 11.6 provides an example of how to present

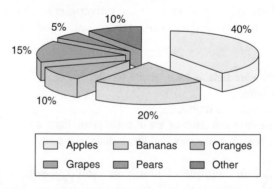

FIGURE 11.6 Daily fruit sales for ABC Grocers Ltd

Source: Adapted from Henderson (2004: 24)

data in graphical format. Notice that the source in this example is 'Adapted from', indicating that the researcher has amended the illustration in some way.

The advantage of presenting your data using a graphical format is that it can make for interesting reading. The drawback of using diagrams, pictures, charts, and so on is that they may distract from your written text. Basically, the two need to be linked together. Remember that there is no point including graphics unless they are applicable to your research.

The final method used to present data is, of course, written text. For those of you undertaking qualitative analysis, including quotations from participants is a common method of presenting data. As noted in Chapter 10, the inclusion of verbatim quotes used to provide insights and illustrate patterns in your data once again makes for interesting reading. When presenting quotations, make sure that it is done thematically and in the context of your study.

After what amounts to a probably very long journey, you will finally arrive at a point when you are ready to submit your research project. Yet, for many students, what amounts to the final hurdle is not without its potential pitfalls. The key thing when submitting your project is to ensure that you are clear on the submission requirements laid down by your institution. We explore these in the next section.

Submission requirements

When you submit your research project it is essential that you follow the rules and regulations laid down by your university or college. Although these vary by institution, they generally stipulate the following:

- Your research project must follow a clear structure as set out earlier in this chapter.
- It must be word-processed.
- It must have 1.5 or double spacing (single spacing is usually not permitted).
- A size 12 font must be used (typically Times New Roman or Arial).
- It must include a title page that includes your name, course, date, title of the project and student number.
- The research project should be bound using perfect or comb binding (the former is normally essential for postgraduate degrees).
- Two copies must be submitted (this tends to vary by institution).
- It must be submitted prior to a set deadline. A delay is likely to incur penalties such as a loss of marks.
- It must not exceed a set word limit (typically 10,000 words for an undergraduate project).
- It should include a bibliography based on the Harvard referencing system.
- It should include a student–supervisor meeting log (again, this can vary by institution).

Viva voce

In some institutions, part of the assessment criteria involves an oral examination or *viva voce*. In essence, a viva requires you to show that you fully understand your research and to demonstrate how you have contributed to your chosen subject.

The attendees at a viva depend on the rules and regulations of the institution, although they tend to be conducted in private, with the following people present: your supervisor, an internal examiner and possibly an external examiner. Certainly, the latter applies for MPhil and PhD students. However, this is unlikely to be the case for undergraduates.

Remember that a key aspect of the viva is the oral defence of your work. This is a very different proposition from writing up research. Therefore, to successfully complete a viva it is essential to prepare yourself thoroughly, well in advance.

The viva is a process that involves a number of steps. These can be summarized as:

- preparation prior to the viva;
- during the viva; and
- post-viva.

First, at the preparation stage, it is important that you are completely familiar with all aspects of your research. Ideally, prepare thoroughly for a whole range of questions that may come up during your viva. An obvious question is likely to be 'Why did you choose this particular topic?' Discuss with your supervisor the nature of the process and possible outcomes. Second, during the viva answer each question in a polite, clear manner. Do not be afraid to pause over a question. In addition, if you do not agree with the views of your examiner, do not feel that you are obliged to agree with his or her view. Say why you do not agree. The key thing here is to clearly support your answer. Finally, the outcome of a viva is not always a straightforward pass or fail. For an MPhil or PhD, the outcome is usually one of the following: a pass with no amendments, a pass with minor amendments, a pass with major amendments or a straight fail. For undergraduate students this might vary.

Typical viva questions

Even though you are likely to be asked a whole range of questions at your viva, there are what I would call 'favoured' questions among examiners. The best way of illustrating these is on a chapter-by-chapter basis. Table 11.5 shows some of the typical questions asked during a viva.

Publishing your work

Although publishing your work might be the furthest thing from your mind when writing up your research, it is certainly something worth considering. Quite frankly, I have read some excellent research projects over the years, many worthy of dissemination to a wider audience. In the main, there are three platforms from which to do this – *professional publications, conference papers* and *peer-reviewed journals*. Let us look at each one in turn.

TABLE 11.5 Typical viva questions

Chapter	Questions
Introduction	What was the motivation for your research?
	Why is your research important?
	How did your research emerge?
	What are the objectives of your research?
Literature review	Which are the three most important papers that relate to your research?
	Who are the key authors in your chosen subject?
	What has not been done before?
	How has your chosen subject developed?
Methodology	How have you addressed validity and reliability?
	What is your chosen research design?
	What are the limitations of your design?
	How did you deal with potential sources of bias?
Results and analysis	How did you present your findings?
	How did you organize your data?
	How would you summarize your key findings?
	What is the relationship between your findings and those of earlier studies?
Conclusion and recommendations	Discuss possible future research that could be connected.
	To what extent did you achieve your research objectives?
	How has your work contributed to research in your subject area?

Professional publications

Professional publications mainly relate to trade magazines and those produced by professional bodies. For example, in marketing this might be the Chartered Institute of Marketing, or for accountancy, the Association of Chartered Certified Accountants.

The nature of your writing in professional publications is likely to be far removed from your research project. For starters, your target audience will be mainly business professionals as opposed to academics. Hence, your article should make little, if any, reference to theory and theoretical application. It should also be written in a more journalistic, as opposed to an academic, style.

Conference papers

Producing a conference paper is an excellent way of both promoting your work and raising your profile as a serious researcher. Ideally, aim for conferences that closely resemble your chosen area of research. For example, in my main specialism, marketing, some of the main conferences taking place on an annual basis include: the Academy of Marketing Conference, the Industrial Marketing and Purchasing

Group Conference, and the British Academy of Management. Conferences such as these are well attended by both academics and students.

If you are interested in producing a conference paper, your project supervisor is a good starting point. They should be very familiar with the main conferences suited to your research. Moreover, your supervisor can provide you with invaluable advice in terms of producing and submitting a paper. They may also be interested in writing a joint paper.

Peer-reviewed journals

If you are an undergraduate student, in the short term it is unlikely that you will publish your work in academic journals. However, if you go on to undertake an MPhil or PhD, publishing in journals is considered 'the norm'.

Producing an article for journal publication is very different from writing a research project or thesis. Arguably the two main differences are the audience and the submission guidelines. First, your audience is going to consist of those who are interested in your topic, and who quite possibly are experts in your chosen field. This means that you have to make sure that you double your efforts in terms of referencing, structure, content and presentation. If preparing a paper for an academic journal, it is worth considering the following points (Thomas, 2004: 239):

- Do follow the journal submission guidelines to the letter. Irritating though it may be, each journal has its own house style and this must be followed. Unfortunately, no two editions seem to demand the same style of referencing!
- Do not submit rough drafts. Your paper must be a final form. Editors are likely to become uncooperative if they believe that they and their referees are being used to do work that should have been done by the author.
- Do not harass editors for a decision. Be patient. For no obvious reason, the referencing of papers always seems to take far longer than any author reasonably expects.
- Expose your paper to criticism before submitting. Present it at conferences and seminars and seek comments from friends and colleagues. Constructive criticism received before submitting your work to a journal can help you to make substantial improvements that increase the chances of publication.

Employability

Graduate employers want more than just a degree. They want so-called 'employability skills'. These include everything from communication skills, IT skills, numeracy skills, presentation skills, and leadership to research skills. You will learn a wide range of transferable skills when undertaking your research project. These can, of course, help to improve your employability in many different types of job. A job interview is often an ideal opportunity to discuss your research. This is particularly the case if the job you are applying for includes research skills as a key part of the job description.

I have known students to take their research project to an interview in order to highlight to the interviewer some of the tasks they carried out during the research process. I am not saying that this is an absolute must if going to an interview! However, it might be a useful 'selling tool' if your research is in some way relevant to the job you are applying for. For example, if your research project was based on the same company or the same industry. In short, the completion of your research project is likely to equip you with an important set of employability skills which can be conveyed to any prospective employer.

Common Errors Found in Student Research Projects

We now focus on the more common errors that I have come across in student research projects. Although by no means exhaustive, it should provide you with a basic understanding of the errors that you need to avoid at all costs! These errors can be summarized as follows:

- Lengthy/wordy title.
- Title does not fully reflect content.
- Introduction is too brief.
- Objectives/research questions are unclear.
- Does not address the importance of the research topic.
- No mention of contribution to theory and practice.
- Poorly written literature review – little or no critical analysis.
- Limited number of references – poor evidence of research.
- Methodology is lacking or is too brief.
- Methodology contains a lack of references.
- Poorly presented, with typographical and grammatical errors; Harvard referencing system not applied.
- Conclusion – objectives do not correspond with those set within the introduction and there is a limited/poor number of references.

The vast majority of errors listed here are easily avoided. All it requires is for you to edit your work several times prior to submission. Moreover, make sure that you have clearly followed your institution's rules and regulations governing submission, and considered the set marking criteria.

Writing Up and Your Project Supervisor

A common theme throughout this book has been the importance of your project supervisor. The significance of your supervisor during the final stage of your research is no exception.

Ask your supervisor to read a draft of your work prior to submission. If your institution's regulations stipulate that a supervisor may only read a maximum number of chapters, ask them to read those chapters that you are most uncomfortable with. Clearly, do not arrange to meet your supervisor a few days prior to submission. If they recommend that you make major changes to your work, it is unlikely that you will be able to complete these changes in such a short period of time.

What if you have left it too late to start writing up? The first thing is don't panic! It is important to see your supervisor as soon as possible to discuss a way forward. Don't worry about asking your supervisor for help. Although he or she is likely to question why you left it too late, they should still be supportive. Finally, the National Union of Students (NUS, 2013) in the UK has a useful guide for helping you to survive your dissertation.

─RESEARCH IN ACTION─

Writing an abstract

As highlighted earlier in the chapter, an abstract is a summary of your entire research project and is usually the last thing that is written by the researcher. In short, an abstract should provide an entire overview of the research project. Below is an abstract from an academic journal article (Wilson and Brennan, 2010). This is likely to be more structured than your own abstract, but still provides a useful example of how to give an overview of an entire piece of research in 250–300 words.

Doing business in China: Is the importance of *guanxi* diminishing?

Purpose – *Guanxi* has been well documented as being an essential part of doing business in China. Yet, as China continues with market liberalization, there are indications that its strategic importance is set to decline. From a joint venture perspective, this study seeks to examine the strategic importance of *guanxi* when doing business in China.

Methodology/Approach – First, the researchers reviewed articles on *guanxi* and established that although *guanxi* is still widely considered important, some experts are arguing that this importance is diminishing. Second, qualitative research was used to create a holistic picture of the importance attached to *guanxi* in UK–Chinese joint ventures. This involved 25 semi-structured interviews with those involved in establishing or managing such a joint venture.

Findings – Although *guanxi* remains important when doing business in China, a number of factors indicate that this importance may begin to decline. These include China's market liberalization, outward investment, '*guanxi* learning' on the part of foreign companies and online intermediaries.

Research limitations/implications – Since the paper is based on a review of existing research and 25 qualitative interviews, the findings are largely exploratory. Future research might focus on a larger sample, different industries or possibly Chinese firms engaged in outward investment.

Practical implications – The findings suggest that to simply describe *guanxi* as being 'important' is too simplistic. Hence, by identifying issues that are likely to affect the strategic importance of *guanxi* we can help both parent company managers and those engaged in Chinese business practice.

Originality/Value of paper – Both the review of existing papers and empirical findings help academics to understand a 'contemporary view' of *guanxi*, while managers that have an interest in China can gain a clear understanding of *guanxi* and its significance in modern day China.

Summary and Conclusion

This chapter has focused on the structure and appropriate writing style of your research project. Here are the key points:

- Your approach to writing up your research is likely to be based on either polychronic or monochronic time management. Both are acceptable, so it is a matter of personal preference.
- Just as you are likely to have worked towards a set timetable when conducting your research, you should ideally adopt the same approach when writing up.
- There are two broad types of writing style: formal and informal. Formal language adopts a more serious, impersonal and detached tone. Informal language is more conversational and 'laid back'.
- Each chapter forms an essential part of your overall project and is primarily a way of 'dividing up' common themes for the benefit of the reader.
- Your data can be presented in one of three ways: in a tabular, graphical or text format.
- When you submit your research project it is essential that you follow the rules and regulations laid down by your university or college.
- Do not be afraid to disseminate your work. In the main, there are three platforms from which to do this: professional publications, conference papers and peer-reviewed journals.

CASE STUDY — Submitting a Research Project

Andrea has come to see you to share her good news – she has finally completed her research project! Andrea has spent several months researching corporate social responsibility (CSR) in the oil industry and is thrilled that all of her hard work has now come to fruition. She has written up her work and saved it on to her USB stick. She has also edited her project and now feels that she is ready to have her work professionally bound.

Andrea is a French student and has never submitted such a comprehensive piece of work in English before. Understandably, before arriving in the UK, all her subjects were taught in French. However, Andrea believes that her English language abilities are of a high standard and wishes to submit her work early, approximately two weeks prior to submission. Andrea is so confident about the quality of her research that she does not believe it is necessary for anyone else to read her work prior to submission.

Case study question

- As Andrea's project supervisor, do you agree with her intention of handing in her final project two weeks early? Give reasons for your answer.

You have received the following email from a final-year Business student.

Dear ....,

Further to our meeting earlier today, I was wondering whether or not it would be possible for you to read through my completed research project prior to submission next week?

I realize that you must be very busy at the moment, but would appreciate it if you could please comment on it.

Although Dr Simpson is my project supervisor, I am sure a second opinion will also come in useful. I would understand if this were not possible, but am grateful for your consideration.

Kind regards,
Martin

Supervisor question

- How would you respond to Martin?

COMMON QUESTIONS AND ANSWERS

1. How can I check that the style of writing in my research project is appropriate?

Answer: There are three useful indicators that can help you to determine if your style of writing is appropriate. First, ask your supervisor to check a sample of your work to make sure that it is suitable. If not, your supervisor should be able to provide some useful advice on how you can improve your style of writing. Second, you can read existing research projects in order to get a 'feel' for what is required. Having said that, one problem with this approach is that any project you read is unlikely to include a final mark. Thus, you may not be able to form a judgement on the overall quality of the work. Third, your institution may refer to writing style within the project guide. Most guides include key points as to what is expected in terms of writing style.

2. What should I do if I fail my research project?

Answer: First of all, don't panic! Once you receive your project back, it will almost certainly include copious notes on the strengths and weaknesses of your work. A first step is to read through these thoroughly to make sure that you understand the comments. If not, arrange a meeting with your supervisor to discuss the comments on your mark sheet, and what steps you need to take in order to pass. In most institutions you are entitled to one re-sit attempt. Of course, before you submit a reworked copy of your project, you must ensure that you have done everything required to pass second time around. Therefore, clarifying the changes that need to be undertaken with your supervisor is absolutely paramount.

3. What makes a good research project?

Answer: There are numerous factors that determine a good research project. The main considerations include: a clear rationale, an appropriate set of research questions, a suitable structure, evidence of research, good presentation, theoretical content, and each research question needs to be fully addressed within the conclusion.

4. When should I start writing up my research project?

Answer: In many respects, this is down to the individual. My advice would be to produce a writing timetable and try to break your writing down into manageable chunks. This can either be a set number of words or sections each week. If you are finding it difficult to start, then make sure to see your supervisor to discuss the difficulties you are having.

References

Bailey, S. (2006) *Academic Writing: A Handbook for International Students*. London: Routledge.

Hall, E.T. (1959) *The Silent Language*. Garden City, NY: Doubleday.

Levin, P. (2005) *Excellent Dissertations!* Maidenhead: McGraw-Hill.

NUS (2013) 'Survive the dissertation deadlines', http://www.nus.org.uk/en/advice/your-study/dissertations/survive-the-dissertation-deadlines/, accessed 12 April 2013.

Oxford English Dictionary (2005) *Oxford Dictionary of English* (2nd revised edn). Oxford: Oxford University Press.

Saunders, M.N.K. and Davis, S.M. (1998) 'The use of assessment criteria to ensure consistency of marking', *Quality Assurance in Education*, 6 (3): 162–171.

Smith, K., Todd, M. and Waldman, J. (2009) *Doing Your Undergraduate Social Science Dissertation*. New York: Routledge.

Thomas, A.B. (2004) *Research Skills for Management Studies*. New York: Routledge.

Wilson, J. and Brennan, R. (2010) 'Doing business in China: Is the importance of *guanxi* diminishing?', *European Business Review*, 22 (6): 652–665.

Further Reading

Bryman, A. and Bell, E. (2007) *Business Research Methods* (2nd edn). Oxford: Oxford University Press.

Easterby-Smith, M., Thorpe, R., and Jackson, P. (2012) *Management Research* (4th edn). London: Sage.

Mounsey, C. (2002) *One Step Ahead: Essays and Dissertations*. Oxford: Oxford University Press.

O'Leary, Z. (2013) *The Essential Guide to Doing Your Research Project* (2nd edn). London: Sage.

Robson, C. (2006) *How to do a Research Project: A Guide for Undergraduate Students*. London: John Wiley & Sons.

Walliman, N.S.R. (2004) *Your Undergraduate Dissertation: The Essential Guide for Your Success*. London: Sage.

Glossary

Abstract A summary of an article or research project.

Academic journal A peer-reviewed periodical containing scholarly articles in a particular field of study.

Action research A methodology whereby a researcher monitors a situation in order to bring about change. The researcher is actively engaged with the phenomena being studied.

Anonymity Relates to the protection of research participants by making sure that their names are not published with the information they provide.

Applied research Research that explores real-life problems with the aim of establishing practical solutions.

Archival research A research design that focuses on secondary data that can be both historical and contemporary in nature.

Axiology Concerned with the role your own values play in the research.

Bar chart A type of graph in which the data are represented by vertical or horizontal bars. The frequencies are represented by the length of the bars.

Basic research Attempts to expand our knowledge about a particular subject. Academic researchers usually conduct basic or pure research.

Bell curve *See* 'normal distribution'.

Bibliography A comprehensive list of publications used in a particular study.

Bivariate data Refers to data involving two variables.

Brainstorming A problem-solving technique in which members of a group exchange ideas.

Business research The systematic and objective process of collecting, recording, analyzing and interpreting data for aid in solving managerial problems.

Case study A research design used to examine a single phenomenon in its natural setting.

Categorical data Data whose values cannot be measured numerically but can be classified into sets or rank order.

Causal research Concerned with how one variable may lead to changes in another.

Central Limit Theorem States that the average in a set of sample data drawn from a wider population is approximately distributed as a normal distribution if certain conditions are met.

Central tendency The 'average' value of a distribution. Typical measures of central tendency include the mean, the mode and the median.

Chi-squared test A non-parametric test used to see if there is a statistically significant difference between observed data and that, which would have been expected by chance.

Citation indices Provide an indication of the quality and expert nature of a piece of research, by showing how many times the work has been cited.

Closed question Refers to a type of question whereby respondents are required to choose their answer on the basis of a yes/no response or from a list of pre-determined categories.

Code of ethics A code that all research stakeholders are required to adhere to both during and after the research.

Coding Refers to the process of allocating codes to words, themes or sentences in order to facilitate analysis of data.

Collusion Occurs when two or more individuals work in cooperation to produce a research project that is presented as the work of one student alone.

Conclusion Usually the final chapter in a research project that summarizes the findings and makes recommendations for future research.

Confidence interval A parametric technique that uses a range of values that is likely to comprise an unknown population parameter.

Confidentiality Relates to protecting research participants by making sure that sensitive data are not disclosed to any third party.

Content analysis A quantitative form of analysis that is typically associated with qualitative data.

Continuous variable A variable that can take on any value, e.g. temperature, height and weight.

Cooked data Refers to raw data that have been organized into a more manageable form.

Correlation A measure of association between two variables.

Cross-cultural research A study involving participants from two or more countries, regions or cultural groups.

Cross-sectional design Refers to a research design that involves the collection of data from a sample at one point in time.

Cross-tabulation A table that allows you to examine the summary data for two or more different sets of variables.

Data Protection Act Passed by Parliament to control the way data is handled to give rights to people who have information stored about them.

Deductive approach Begins with and applies a well known theory.

Dependent variable A variable seen as an effect (outcome).

Descriptive research Carried out to describe existing or past phenomena.

Descriptive statistics A branch of statistics used to summarize or describe a data set.

Dichotomous variable A variable with only two possible values, e.g. male or female.

Discourse analysis A broad term that relates to a number of ways to analyze written or spoken language.

Discrete variable A variable that is measured using specific values.

Dispersion A measure that describes the spread of values in a distribution, e.g. standard deviation or interquartile range.

Dissertation A major project that usually forms the final part of an undergraduate or postgraduate degree.

Elite interviewing Conducting interviews with key decision-makers and/or those in high ranked positions, e.g. politicians, company directors or leading academics.

Epistemology Refers to the nature of knowledge, which means how we conceive our surroundings. The key question that epistemology asks is 'What is acceptable knowledge?'

Estimation Estimating a population parameter from samples.

Ethnographic research Involves participating, observing and describing how individuals from certain cultural groups behave in their natural setting.

Experimental design Posits that experiments are conducted along the lines of the natural sciences, i.e. in a laboratory or in a natural setting, in a systematic way. Experimental studies allow causal relationships to be identified.

Exploratory research Where the researcher conducts research into a research problem where there currently exists very little, if any, earlier work to refer to.

Focus group A form of qualitative research in which a group of individuals are asked their views on a particular product, service or issue.

Forecasting Refers to the estimation of a set of values at a future point in time.

Frequency A numerical value that illustrates the number of counts for an observed variable.

Frequency distribution A graph or table that shows a set of values, together with the frequency of each.

Gantt chart A type of bar chart that shows planned activities over time. The length of each block corresponds to the start and finish times.

General reports Government reports, country data reports such as those produced by the Economist Intelligence Unit (EIU), and market research reports such as those produced by Mintel.

Graph A type of diagram used to analyze bivariate or multivariate data.

Grounded theory A qualitative research method that involves generating theory from data collected in a particular study.

Histogram A histogram is a type of bar chart that shows a frequency distribution of a set of data, with the area of each bar representing frequency.

The Honeycomb of Research Methodology Shows the six main elements which come together to form research methodology, namely: (1) Research philosophy; (2) Research approach; (3) Research strategy; (4) Research design; (5) Data collection and (6) Data analysis techniques.

Hypothesis A prediction based on the relationship between variables, and through testing, may or may not support the theory.

Hypothesis testing Making a statement about some aspect of the population, and then generating a sample to see if the hypothesis can be rejected or cannot be rejected.

Independent variable Refers to a variable that is presumed as a cause or influence on a dependent variable.

Index number A number that shows how a quantity changes over time.

Inductive approach A theory-building process, starting with observations of specific instances, and seeking to establish generalization about the phenomenon under investigation.

Inferential statistics Used to draw inferences about a population from a given sample.

Interpretivism An epistemology that supports the view that the researcher must enter the social world of what is being examined.

Interquartile range Measures the spread between the upper and lower quartiles of a set of data (the middle 50%).

Interval data A set of data whereby distance between the numbers are equal across the range.

Interview Questioning a research participant or participants in order to obtain data for a research project.

Introduction Usually the first chapter within a research project. It sets out the background to the study, rationale, and includes research questions and objectives.

Journal *See* 'academic journal'.

Key word A word that is a common feature within a particular study. It can be used to help with literature searches.

Kurtosis Indicates how flat or peaked a distribution is.

Linear regression A type of regression analysis used to analyse the linear relationship between two variables.

Line graph A type of graph that uses a line to show how values change over time.

Literature review The identifying, evaluation and critical review of what has been published on your chosen topic.

Longitudinal design A study over a long period of time of a particular case or a group of cases.

Mean The arithmetical average of a frequency distribution.

Median The middle number in a set of numbers.

Method The different ways by which data can be collected and analysed.

Methodology The approach and strategy used to conduct research.

Mind map Involves writing the name of a phrase or theme of your proposed research in the centre of the page. You then branch out with each sub-theme, further sub-themes and so on.

Mixed methods research Involves the combining of qualitative and quantitative collection and analytical techniques.

Mode The value that occurs the most often in a set of data.

Multiple bar chart A chart illustrating two or more variables in the form of bars of length proportional in magnitude of the variables.

Multiple regression A statistical technique that predicts the relationship between a dependent variable and more than one independent variable.

Narrative analysis A qualitative technique that examines the way that respondents use stories to interpret real life phenomena.

Nominal data Named data that include values that can be classified into categories.

Non-parametric data Data whereby the researcher does not make any assumptions about population parameters.

Non-participant observation Where data are collected by a researcher without interacting with research participants.

Normal distribution A graph that shows data scores that accumulate around the middle.

Objectives A more specific statement relating to the defined aim of your research.

Observer as participant Where data are collected by a researcher who also interacts with research participants.

Ontology Concerned with the nature of reality. In essence, it asks how we perceive the social word.

Open question A question that allows a respondent to provide an answer to a question in their own words.

Ordinal data A type of categorical data that can be rank ordered.

Outlier A value from a set of data that is inconsistent with other values.

Parametric data Data that rely on parametric assumptions such as normality.

Pearson's product moment correlation coefficient A measure of how much two variables (X and Y) are linearly related.

Pie chart A type of chart that is divided into segments representing a portion or percentage of the total.

Plagiarism The deliberate copying of someone else's work and presenting it as one's own.

Population A clearly defined group of cases which a researcher can draw on.

Positivist approach The belief that you are independent of your research and your research can be truly objective.

Pragmatism Recognizes the importance of both the physical and social world. Pragmatist researchers focus on the 'What' and the 'How' of the research problem.

Primary data Data that are generated by the researcher for the purpose of the study, e.g. your own interviews, surveys and focus groups.

Pure research See 'basic research'.

Qualitative data Viewed as subjective and involves data collection methods such as interviews.

Quantitative data Data that are numerical in nature.

Range Found by subtracting the lowest value from the highest value in a set of data.

Ranked data Data that have been sorted into an order of preference.

Ratio data Continuous data that have a natural zero point, e.g. height, weight and age.

Raw data Data that have yet to be analyzed or processed.

References A list of sources consulted and quoted within a research project.

Regression analysis A test that allows a researcher to measure the predictive relationship between a dependent variable and one or more independent variables.

Relevance tree An alternative form of mind map; however, it tends to be more ordered.

Reliability The extent that repeat measurements made by a researcher under constant conditions will give the same result.

Research A step-by-step process that involves the collecting, recording, analyzing and interpreting of information.

Research design A framework or plan for the collection and analysis of data.

Research management program A piece of software designed to make it easier to organize and store literature in a searchable library.

Research problem Refers to a problem a researcher believes warrants investigation.

Research process The series of steps a researcher is likely to go through when undertaking a research project.

Research questions Refers to questions that a researcher intends to answer through carrying out their research.

Sample A subset of a population.

Sampling The selection of a suitable sample for research.

Sampling frame Refers to a list of the accessible population in which a researcher is able to draw a sample.

Scatter plot A type of graph used to plot two sets of data, also known as a scatter diagram.

Secondary data Data that have been produced by other people and thereby hold a different purpose to that of the researcher.

Self-plagiarism Including work in your research project that you have already submitted as part of a previous piece of assessment.

Skewed distribution A frequency distribution which is not a normal distribution.

SMART Specific, measurable, achievable, relevant, and timed.

Social responsibility Relates to the public's expectations of companies to act in a manner that is socially responsible.

Spearman's rank correlation coefficient Used to test the strength and direction of association between two ordinal variables.

SPSS Statistical Package for the Social Sciences.

Standard deviation Measures the spread of data around the mean value.

Statistics A branch of mathematics that is applied to quantitative data in order to draw conclusions and make predictions.

Student's t-test The t-test is a statistical method used to test the significance of the difference between two sample means.

Supervisor An academic assigned to a student in order to guide and support them with their research project.

Survey A method used to collect responses from research participants, e.g. email, fax and postal.

SurveyMonkey A tool that allows users to create their own web-based surveys.

Theory A set of principles on which an activity is based.

Time series analysis A series of data points that are typically measured over regular time intervals.

Timetable A plan of times showing intended start and completion dates of stages in a research project.

Triangulation The use of multiple data collection methods and/or sources of data by the researcher during one particular study.

Type I error Where the null hypothesis is true but rejected.

Type II error Where the alternative hypothesis is true but rejected.

Univariate data Data involving a single variable.

Validity The extent to which a measure accurately reflects the concept that it is proposed to measure.

Variable A characteristic that can be measured.

Variance A measure of the dispersion of a set of values.

Viva voce An oral examination that requires a student to defend their research project.

Web-based survey An online method for collecting data.

Weighted moving average A forecasting method that uses different weights so that more recent values are more heavily weighted than values further in the past.

Work-based project A piece of assessed work based on an individual's employer.

X variable *See* 'independent variable'.

Y variable *See* 'dependent variable'.

Index

Page references to Figures or Tables will be in *italics*

knowledge, *23*, 70
  chosen topic, 3, 30, 63, 76, 118
  development of, 4, 8
  and experience, 30, 43, *200*
  increasing, 2, 3
  literature review, 62–3
  as object, 19
  of philosophy, 8–9, 116
  subject, 3, 13, 23–4, 26, 309
  see also epistemology (nature of knowledge)
knowledge management (KM), 82, 83
kurtosis, 333

language
  foreign language sources, secondary data, 199,
    206–7
  research skills, 22–4
Levin, P., 306, *308*
Lewin, C., 7
Lewin, K., 120
Likert, R./Likert scale, 170, 235
Lincoln, Y.S., 14, 282
line graphs, 240, 333
linear regression, 333
literal replication, multiple case designs, 122
literature review, 61–88
  abstracts, 74–5, 329
  academic journals, 71–3, 329
  benefits, 63
  bibliographies, 69, 75, 329
  case study, 84–5
  chapter numbers, 86
  citation indices, 76, 330
  comparison of academic and newspaper
    articles, *72*
  conclusion, 78, 330
  conducting of search, 65–6
  critical review, 62, 76–7
  defined, 25, 62, 333
  drafting, commencing, 69–70
  evaluation, 68
  good quality, 81, 84–5
  Harvard Referencing System, 67, 69, 79–81
  introduction, example, 77–8
  key elements, 62–3
  key words, 64–5, 333
  length, 85
  main body, 78
  nature of, 61, 62–3
  obtaining literature, 67–8
  as ongoing process, 81
  parameters, defining, 64
  planning of search, 67
  poor quality, 82
  presenting, 78–9
  process, 64–70
  reading existing reviews, 81

literature review *cont.*
  reasons for conducting, 63
  recording the literature, 68–9
  relevant sources, finding, 67
  research management software, use, 69, 336
  research project, structure, 309–10
  research questions and objectives, 64
  and secondary data analysis, 191–2
  sources of literature, 61–2, 70–6, 86
  structure, 77–84
  systematic, conducting, 82–4
  writing, 85–6
London Olympics 2012 logo, 4–5
London Organising Committee of the Olympic
  and Paralympic Games (LOCOG), 5
longitudinal studies, 51, 333
  cross-cultural research, 178
  research design, 124–5, 128
  secondary data collection, 195–6

Malhotra, N.K., *221*
Mansourian, Y., 290
Market Research Society (MRS), 22
marketing
  and ethics, 93–4
  focus groups, 158
  professional publications, 321
  research design, 129
  research topic, 40, 43–4
  see also Chartered Institute of Marketing (CIM)
marketing managers, 94
Marks & Spencer, 41
Marshall, C., 283
Mascarenhas, O.A.J., 94
Masters degrees, 6
Matlay, H., 125
maturation, validity, 135
Maxwell, J.A., 219
Maxymuk, J., 179
Mays, N., 136
McClelland, S.B., 164, 170
McCluskey, L., 57
McDonald's, 143–4
mean, 234, 244–5, *248*, 333
median, 245–6, 333
Merton, R.K., 292
methodological triangulation, 136, 181, 307
methodology *see* research methodology
methods, research *see* research methods
Microsoft Excel, 173, 267
Microsoft Word, 23, 67, 173
  qualitative data analysis, 283, 285, 294
Miles, M.B., 280
Milgram, S., 96
Millward, L., 219
mind maps, 46–7, 334
Minitab, 267

Mintel, 70
misconduct, 90
missing data, 237
Mitchelmore, S., 273
mixed-methods research, 17, 334
mode, 246, 334
monochronic approach to time management, 301, 302
Morgan, D.L., 20
Morgan, R.M., 79
mortality, validity, 135
Moser, C.A., 129
moving regression, 266
MPhil degrees, 70, 320
multiple bar charts, 253–4, 334
multiple case designs, 121, 122, 128, 129
multiple regression, 334
multiple-choice questions, *169*, 170
multi-stage sampling, 218
multi-strategy research, 16, 17–19, 20
  and ICT, 30–1
multivariate data, 236, 239, 317
Myers, M.D., 102, 288

Nachmias, D., 132
narrative analysis, 290–1, 296, 334
Näslund, D., 16
National Union of Students (NUS), UK, 324
Nelson, K., 90
Neubauer, F., 297
Neuhaus, C., 74
newspapers, 71, *72*
NHS (National Health Service) Trusts, as clusters, 216
Nikandrou, I., 128–9
nominal data, 235, 334
nomothetic case studies, 123–4
non-parametric data, 334
non-participant observation, 175, 334
non-probability sampling, 210, 218–20
non-verbal communication, 154
Norfolk County Council, *20*, 21
normal distribution, 234, 243, 254, 334
null hypothesis (H0), 53, 256
NVivo (software package), 173, 280, 283, 294

objectives, research
  versus aims, 52
  definitions, 52, 334
  developing, 52–4
  importance, 54
  literature review, 64
  research proposal, 137, 139–40
  and research questions, 55
  researchable, formulation of, 54
objectivism, 11
objectivity, 102

observational research
  disguised observation, 174
  non-participant observation, 175, 334
  observer influence, 131–2
  participant observation, 175, 334
  primary data collection, 150, 174–6
  qualitative data analysis, 283
  recording of data, 175–6
  undisguised observation, 174
O'Dell, W.F., 225
O'Leary, Z., 64, 81, 97
online branding, 143–4
ontology (nature of reality), 11, 19, *19*, 334
open coding, 285
open questions, 168–9, 334
ordinal data, 235, 246, 334
organizational management, 24
organizations
  and business research, 20–1, 31–2
  fieldwork, conducting within own organization, 176
  organizational participants, 101
outliers, 335
Oxford English Dictionary, 75, 305

Paasche's Price Index, 251
Pace, S., 289
parallel studies, multi-strategy research, 18
parameters, defining, 64, 222
parametric data/tests, 234, 254, 255, 335
Parikh, J., 297
participant observation, 175, 334
participants, research *see* research participants
part-time students, 44
Patton, M.Q., 13, 219, 283–4
Pearson's product moment correlation coefficient, 261–2, 275, 335
peer-reviewed journals *see* academic journals
personal conduct, 102
personal interviews, 153–5
Peterson, P.G., 225
PhD degrees, 70, 320
philosophy, research *see* research philosophy
pie charts, 240–1, 335
pilot studies, questionnaires, 168
plagiarism, 99–100, 335
  see also self-plagiarism
political correctness, 305
Polonsky, M.J., 104
polychronic approach to time management, 301, 302
Pope, C., 136
populations, sampling, 210–12, 213, 214, 228, 335
Porras, J.I., 297, 298
Porter, M., 55
positivism/positivist approach, 9–10, 19, 335
  post-positivists, 10